Mallika Sengupta is a poet who fought against gender politics, professed not to worship women as deities but treat them as humans. She explored Sita in her poems and prose as well as the first woman on earth who spoke for non-proliferation of weapons.

Kabir Bouthan (The Bard and his sister-in-law) is Mallika's last work written from her hospital bed as a cancer patient. A post structural novel about Tagore, the first Nobel laureate from Asia and his elder brother's beautiful wife Kadambari who committed suicide, it is a unique story quintessentially rooted in Indian-Bengali ethos. *Kabir Bouthan* is a mosaic of history and hysteria, elan and illusions, pathos and power. Lopamudra Banerjee, now based in the US, has brilliantly captured the nuances of Bengali culture in her profoundly smart translation.

Subodh Sarkar
Noted author, poet, Sahitya Akademi awardee, Fulbright Fellow, Faculty of English, University of Iowa, Reader in English Literature, City College, Kolkata

'Kobir Bouthan' by author and poet Mallika Sengupta is a research-based creative narrative on the women and also men of Tagore's family. Each chapter is an insight into Jorasanko Thakurbari, the illustrious Tagore household in which the women displayed their emotions, views, conflicts and bonhomie. Lopamudra Banerjee, whose skill in the field of translation is unquestioned, plays with words without entering into a word-to-word translation method. Her lucid prose, the way she has retained the appeal of the original Bengali expressions in English, the ambience she creates with her diction speak volumes of her deep involvement with the art. The readers will definitely find that nothing has been lost in her translation. Rather they are sure to get the flavor of the original book intact, in her transcreation. Kudos to the translator!

Dr. Ketaki Datta, India
Translator, poet, novelist, reviewer

The Bard and his Sister-in-Law
('Kabir Bouthan')

Mallika Sengupta

Translated by
Lopamudra Banerjee

BLACK EAGLE BOOKS
Dublin, USA | Bhubaneswar, India

Black Eagle Books
USA address:
7464 Wisdom Lane
Dublin, OH 43016

India address:
E/312, Trident Galaxy, Kalinga Nagar,
Bhubaneswar-751003, Odisha, India

E-mail: info@blackeaglebooks.org
Website: www.blackeaglebooks.org

First International Edition Published by
Black Eagle Books, 2023

**THE BARD AND HIS SISTER-IN-LAW
('KABIR BOUTHAN')**
by **Mallika Sengupta**

Translated by **Lopamudra Banerjee**

Original Copyright © **Mallika Sengupta**
Translation Copyright © **Lopamudra Banerjee**

All rights reserved. No part of this publication may be reproduced, stored in a retrieval system, or transmitted, in any form or by any means, electronic, mechanical, photocopying, recording or otherwise without the prior permission of the publisher.

Cover & Interior Design: Ezy's Publication

ISBN- 978-1-64560-424-2 (Paperback)
Library of Congress Control Number: 2023943134

Printed in the United States of America

Foreword

Esteemed author and translator Lopamudra Banerjee's translation of *Kabir Bouthan* (*The Bard and his Sister-in-Law*) fills a much-needed void that addresses the lack of reliable documentation about the lives of the women of the Tagore household. Though Chitra Deb had exhaustively researched and recorded the lives of the women of the elite Jorasanko Thakurbari in her critical biography, author and poet Mallika Sengupta's *Kabir Bouthan* stands apart on many levels. The first significant often understated or overlooked fact is that despite the use of the singular in the title, 'sister-in law,' the young Rabindranath Tagore who was slowly blossoming into a phenomenal creative writer, had in fact two sisters-in-law vying for his complete attention.

Young Rabi was irresistibly handsome and extremely talented. Young women, including white British teenagers were attracted to him instantaneously. Yet as time evolved, Rabindranath increasingly expressed a passionate and intense love for his younger sister-in-law Kadambari, just two years older to him. This aroused the wrath of his elder sister-in-law Gynadanandini. Also, the presence of the talented Jyotirindranath, the elder brother of Rabindranath, married to Kadambari, the cynosure of all eyes, complicated familial tensions further.

All credit is due to the author Mallika Sengupta, a sociologist by training, a feminist poet of great renown, who brilliantly fictionalized details from available documents on the Tagore family in order to construct the fictional narrative. Mallika Sengupta emerges as an outstanding creative historian, who has seamlessly woven facts and emotional history stated in a free-flowing narrative, where fiction and factual details are blended with remarkable skill. Lopamudra Banerjee's empathetic and informed reading of the original text and her translation cum transcreation is a seamless and successful endeavour in recreating the nuances of the Bengali narrative. Banerjee's meticulous attention to the cadence and word play of the original and the transference of the same into the English version is an admirable feat that will surely win the hearts and minds of global readers as well as researchers immersed in Tagore studies.

Dr. Sanjukta Dasgupta

President, Executive Committee,
Intercultural Poetry and Performance Library, Kolkata
Visiting Professor, Jagiellonian University, Krakow, Poland (2018)
Honorary Visiting Professor, Dept. of English,
Sister Nivedita University
Professor, Dept of English (Retd)
Former Dean, Faculty of Arts
Calcutta University
Kolkata 700073

Translator's Note

Writing my own poetry and prose along with translating classic works of poetry and prose has always been perceived by me as both sides of a single coin, where the nuances, the various shades and layers of a poem or a story need to emerge from the depths of an inner consciousness. In 2015, when I had first emerged in the translation scene with my humble effort to translate Bengal's Nobel laureate Rabindranath Tagore's novella 'Nastanirh' into 'The Broken Home' (in English), I had depended mostly on my literary consciousness and unflinching passion to explore the complex world of the female protagonists. Thereafter, I have also translated into English Tagore's famous feminist dance-dramas 'Chitrangada' and 'Chandalika' as 'Tales of Transformation' (Virasat Art Publication, 2019), and in this work, my objective has been to illustrate the feminine subjectivity of the two powerful female protagonists of Tagore in these two dance dramas. My previous solo book of translation has been 'Bakul Katha: Tale of the Emancipated Woman' (Avenel Press, 2021), originally penned by Bengal's doyenne of literature Ashapurna Devi, which is the final part of her famed Subarnalata trilogy, a world of three generations of women who find the meaning and essence of their freedom and emancipation in their own unique ways. Translating these works of literature, I have attempted to use my feminist consciousness, projecting the female protagonists of Bengal, while looking for the meaning and resonance of their self-identities.

The vernacular Bengali literature of my own ethnic lineage that I largely grew up on was a fertile ground of unforgettable stories, exploration of language, cadence, lyrical and metaphorical truths of myriad human experiences. As a sensitive reader exposed to this rich literary world, I was not only intrigued by these classic masterpieces, but day after day, I kept feeling that as a translator, I could act as a cultural bridge, connecting the diverse trajectories of the poetic and fictional worlds of the vernacular authors par excellence and the global readers who want to taste those intriguing poems, stories, narratives.

'The Bard and His Sister-in-Law' is my English translation of a historical Bengali novel/biographical nonfiction originally titled 'Kobir Bouthan', a much-acclaimed literary work by feminist author/poet Mallika Sengupta, award-winning poet, author and academician of Kolkata, India. The book focuses on the multifaceted history of the illustrious Jorasanko Thakurbari, Kolkata, the birthplace of Nobel laureate Rabindranath Tagore (mentioned in the book as 'Rabi') and how the interpersonal relationships between men and women inside that mansion become historically significant in terms of gender and culture studies of the pre-independence era in India and also in terms of the development of Tagore's poetic persona. Through this important translation work, which is a deeply layered narrative, I have tried to unfold the subtle nuances of the socio-political history of Bengal in those times, while retaining the original flavor of the characters and the daily rigmarole of their lives through this period piece set in the backdrop of the Renaissance in India, and particularly, in Bengal.

My translation of this classic work will, I believe, enhance the emotional and creative landscape of this beautiful original book, as I hope to convey the fluidity between languages, continents, and cultures. This is my humble gift to the global readers interested to know the diverse cultural history of the illustrious Thakurbari, the rich legacy of Bengal, the dramatic and inspiring transformation of women during the Renaissance period in India with special emphasis on Bengal.

Lopamudra Banerjee
Author, poet, translator,
Texas, USA,
April 2023

Chapter 1

Gyanada Nandini

One fine day in the Bengali year 1866, a horse carriage stopped in front of the main entrance of the illustrious Jorasanko Thakurbari of Kolkata. As the door of the carriage opened, one could see two dainty legs adorned with fancy shoes and socks stepping on the ground. The pleats of her finely embroidered rust-coloured sari fell over her legs, drooping like a sweet surrender. She stood firmly on the ground of her in-law's ancestral home, the sixteen-year-old vein of lightning, and started walking towards the inner quarters of the home. That day, with the bold, unabashed emergence of *Mejo Bou* Gyanada Nandini, the young bride of Jorasanko in broad daylight, right in front of its bevy of servants and attendants, the inner quarters of the mansion had shaken to the core, like a sudden earthquake.

The old servants of the household, who hadn't witnessed such a scene ever before, wailed in despair, as if they had experienced a bad omen. Manada *dashi*, the maid servant peeped stealthily from the quiet nooks inside the house, absorbing the scene and ran quickly to inform her *Karta Ma*, the mistress of the house about this incredible phenomenon. The male stewards and agents of the estate stood with glum faces. Their dear *Mejo Babu* had just been back from Bombay after a long, long time, and he had entered his home together with his young bride, which they knew, was the most unusual event that had happened in this household, especially when Debendranath, the master of the house was absent. They had their mouths sealed, but they had no doubts that the aftermath of such a phenomenon would be tremendous.

The second son of Debendranath, the master of Jorasanko *Thakur bari*, Satyendranath was a meritorious scholar of those days. He was the first Indian man to crack the Indian Civil Services examination and become an I.C.S. officer. Not only was he gifted academically, but he also was instrumental in various thoughts and acts regarding women's liberation. When he was married to Gyanada, she was a child bride of seven, according to the *'gouri daan'* rituals of the old times. She had just been initiated into the Bengali alphabet in her maternal home then. Satyendra's fight to attain the emancipation of women had started during those days, along with his naïve child bride dressed up in a sari, with her head covered in a veil, her nose adorned with a *nolak* (nose ring). From a very young age, Satyendra's firm and unwavering protest was against the imprisonment of women within the four walls of their home, even in the nineteenth century. He would often insist his mother Sarada Debi to step outside the peripheries of their home and see the outside world. Sarada, with orthodoxy deeply rooted in her blood, would admonish him.

"Will the women of our house roam around with you in the open field of Maidan now, like the *memsahibs* (English women)?" She would blurt out.

"So what, if they end up going there?" Satyendra's young mind was inquisitive to know.

"If they ever do, it will only taint the sanctity of the household. Don't you know, even the men of our house do not venture inside the inner quarters at their own will, unless night falls and it is time for them to sleep? Has anyone ever heard that the women of such a household as ours roam around in the open, along with the men? They will be ridiculed, if that ever happens!"

Many years have passed after this conversation, or rather, argument between mother and son. Meanwhile, the mother has been more rigid in her orthodoxy, and the son has been more liberal, progressive. And his young, docile bride, the *Mejo Bou* had witnessed many a storm in her life along with her invincible ICS husband, having lived in Bombay with him for two years. She had now morphed into a bright, emancipated lady. When she stepped inside the inner quarters, her mother-in-law Sarada Debi's sombre face became darker, seeing her emerge as the anglicized shadow of those *memsahibs* she had heard about. She participated in the welcoming rituals of her son and daughter-in-law with her austere face, surrounded by fourteen or fifteen girls and women of all ages, all belonging to the Thakurbari clan. With curious, gaping eyes, they witnessed the bride who had sailed in a ship all the way from the shores of Bombay to Calcutta. There were ripples in Gyanada's mind too, looking at the awkward gestures of these girls and women, their attires and their demeanours. She strongly felt that the souls, the 'persona' of these girls and brides were buried under the heavy burden of their saris and ornaments. She looked intently at a young teenage girl, her heavy Banarasi sari entangled with her legs. She noticed a bride's fair, beautiful body covered in the shameless jingling sound of her gold ornaments. She also noticed that with all this grandeur of their attires and ornaments, their voluptuous femininity came out like gushing fountains of youth. It was really impossible for them to come out in the open in these attires, to subject themselves to male gaze.

Right then, she guessed perfectly well why it was forbidden for the men of the household to step inside the inner quarters during the daytime. Saradasundari Debi, her mother-in-law had reclined her body over a pillow, seated on a large bedstead in her room, her soft muslin sari, the colour of sandalwood, looked much like her second skin. Looking at her face, Gyanada remembered all her bittersweet memories with her mother-in-law. The fact that she couldn't be tamed by her mother-in-law the way she wanted had made young Gyanada suffer her harsh words many times. But she had memories of her mother-in-law tending to her as a child, trying hard to enhance her beauty and health. The memories of the child Gyanada sitting on the bedstead, watching the maids of the house applying *maida* (flour) and milk cream on the faces of the brides reappeared in her consciousness. She remembered her thin, dusky childhood form which her mother-in-law disliked. She had made it her mission to groom Gyanada, beautifying the child bride, making her a befitting bride of the Thakurbari in all aspects.

The memories of a day flashed in front of Gyanada's eyes, when the brides of other households came to pay a visit to the Thakurbari. Her mother-in-law had regretted, noticing the healthy, robust appearances of the brides. The young brides of the Thakurbari looked dull and unappealing, like wooden stakes with their lanky features, she remarked. She had sworn to make Gyanada healthier, fuller. She started feeding rice to her daughter-in-law, preparing the morsels herself. The veiled child bride felt embarrassed, unable to either gulp or throw away the rice. While the mistress of the house approached her daughter-in-law's mouth with morsels of rice in her nimble fingers, the child bride would wait for the moment her mother-in-law would go away and she would throw up the food in the big corridor of the house.

However, Gyanada felt that her mother-in-law had been totally averse to the idea of her son Satyendra going away to England to take his ICS examination. After Satyendra, her second son left for the foreign land, she took some jewellery belonging to her *Mejo Bou* and gave them to her daughters as their marriage gifts, seething in an unknown rage. Of course, Gyanada did have no regrets for those jewellery taken from her. But the moment *Babamoshai*, her father-in-law came to know of this, he became very angry on his wife and sent a diamond neck-piece for Gyanada.

Forever accustomed to living inside the inner quarters of the house, Sarada would actually find it difficult, rather impossible to accept any changes within the structure of her home. As Gyanada grew up in the later years, her defiance of the norms of that inner sanctum, her free will, her introduction of modern ways of living inside the home enraged Sarada. Gyanada had understood quite well that her decision to sail in a ship to reach the shores of Bombay, to live with her husband in the alien land for two long years would never be tolerated by her mother-in-law. She also knew it would be more difficult to live with her mother-in-law under the same roof from now on.

It had been an uphill task for her to grant permission to go and live in Bombay, for that matter. Ever since her husband went away to the city, he was keen to take his wife there, to get her introduced to the free, empowered women of the outside world. It was an era when it wasn't customary for the women to tag along with their husbands when they ventured to distant places for work or travel. But Satyen, made of a different clay, had been reluctant to live far away since the beginning, while his wife remained within the four walls of the Thakurbari. His letters written to his wife during those days bore testimony to this fact. Once, he wrote to her: "You know, all the incredible progress and state of bliss that we see in the human society here, all its beauty and praiseworthy attributes…at the core of it all, lies the goodness, the bounty of women. I strongly want you to be an unforgettable example for all women in our own society, but remember, it all depends upon your own will."

Gyanada, a teenager during those days, would read those letters of her husband and silently prepare herself for her journey towards light. However, it all remained a distant dream as *Babamoshai*, her father-in-law did not grant her permission after all. Dejected and bruised by his thwarted dream, Satyen settled down in Bombay, his workplace, while his wife started preparing herself in a different way. The girls and women of the house had started taking Bengali lessons from Hemendranath, a brother-in-law of Gyanada, and she joined his little academy along with her sisters-in-law Neepamayee, Sukumari, Swarnakumari and Barnakumari. This would cause the ire of her mother-in-law who would open stop talking to her, or punish her by ostracizing her from all the other women of the family. This again, would provoke the anger of Maharshi Debendranath, her father-in-law, and hence, when Satyendra appealed to him to send Gyanada to him for the second time, he gave his permission without further delay. This permission proved to be a historic one, opening the doorway to the greater universe for all Bengali women.

However, due to the aftermath of this event, Gyanada also had to bear the brunt of her mother-in-law's fury, take in all her pent-up bitterness. Gyanada was a wise soul; she had instinctively understood the psyche of her mother-in-law, shackled by the limitations of patriarchal values, and so, she was not angry. She stooped to offer her *pranaam* to her mother-in-law, knowing very well that she would get a good scolding.

Sarada, seated on the large bedstead, was annoyed as she looked intently at Gyanada's attire and her bold gait.

"What's this new way of draping a sari?" She asked.

"Ma, this is the way women wear their saris in Bombay. If you drape it in this way, you can come out and meet people from outside." Gyanada replied.

"And what have you worn in your body? A jacket like those *mem-sahibs*?"

Gyanada felt embarrassed at this question. But Satyen talked on her behalf. "Why Ma, don't you like it? You know, all high-class, sophisticated women in the west drape their saris in this exact way these days. Now our own girls and women will imbibe this style."

"Stop! It is enough that you are dressing up your wife as a clown, don't pull my good-natured girls and brides into this. They will follow exactly what they have followed for all these years; I won't allow the sanctity of this household to be spoilt!" Sarada blurted.

As the heated discussion between mother and son continued, the women of the household kept listening to it and watching their *Mejo Bou*'s attire and get-up with full attention. Her sophisticated frilled jacket, her soft chemise that peeked from her waist where the jacket ended, mesmerised them. They were in awe of her rust-coloured silk sari, the border of which was adorned with fine Parsi embroidery work in black and gold. They were in awe of her style of draping the sari with intricate pleats in the waist area, the *aanchal* attached to her left shoulder with a dainty brooch, in awe of her socks and imported shoes. But some of those women who were traditional to the core, silently took the side of Sarada.

Sarada looked at her son and remarked: "I don't know what you are up to, such ominous acts you indulged in…making your wife sit in an automobile, making her board a ship, uprooting her from her home, her husband's land and leaving her in an alien land! Can you imagine the humiliation, the criticism we have to face? I alone have to bear the brunt of it all!"

Suddenly, a woman came running all the way from the open courtyard to the big corridor and gave a big, celebratory hug to Gyanada. She was the ubiquitous saleswoman of the Thakurbari.

"*Mejo Bouthan*! Do you know you created history today? All Bengali women will hail you in pride a hundred years from now!" She screamed in excitement.

"Oh, Malini, when did you arrive?" Gyanada said to the bookseller woman, startled by the sudden call.

Seething in anger, Sarada threw her hand-fan at the saleswoman. "Stop your drama and get out of here! History! What an explainer of history we have here! Go away at once!" She screamed.

Satyen came up to his mother and hugged her tight. "Why are you so angry, Ma? It is indeed history, what Gyanada did today. If you would ever step outside of this house, you would see the gait, the personality of Marathi women, and understand how superior they are, compared to our own Bengali women. If only you would see them once, you would realize the concoction of softness and sternness in their persona, which ought to be the ideal for every Bengali woman."

He noticed a sari-clad young girl seated silently, next to his mother, and shook her braid in jest. It was his younger sister Barnakumari. "Barna, tell me the truth, don't you want to dress up like your *Mejo Bouthan* (sister-in-law)?

Barnakumari kept mum, and the other girls surrounding her hesitated to speak too, in fear of Sarada. However, after some time, their initial phase of shock and surprise subsided, and they started talking to Gyanada. Their *Mejo Bouthan* had always been the nucleus of their attraction in the household because of her individual personality, and besides, she was social and amiable too, who knew how to tempt them towards new attractions.

The bookseller woman held Gyanada's hand and stood silent, with a glum face.

Only two years back, there was quite an uproar in the Thakurbari centered on their *Mejo Bou*'s decision to journey to Bombay. The members of the house were brimming with questions, anxieties, curiosity. What she would wear while on her way, they all had questioned. After a lot of speculation, they ordered an incredible 'oriental dress' from a French tailor, custom-made for her. The attire was so complex that Gyanada herself couldn't manage wearing it, nor could the other women in the family help her with it. Finally, her husband Satyen helped her in the mission.

At that moment, Gyanada had realized that in order to attain the liberation of women, it was essential to liberate the attire of women from its shackles of custom. From that time, the idea of draping saris in a fashionable way kept haunting her mind. She had observed the simple, convenient way of draping saris imbibed by the Parsee women in Bombay, and from that, she envisioned the image of the sari-clad Bengali women.

Gyanada had become the emblem of emancipation, an endless source of knowledge to the women of the Thakurbari, trapped within the four walls. They were oscillating between two extremes: their fear of *Karta Ma* Sarada Devi's admonishment and their irresistible attraction towards Gyanada. While chatting with Gyanada, they took her to her new bedroom, and Malini, the bookseller woman accompanied them. She would check what new books Gyanada brought along.

Sarada looked at them and said: "Look, Satyen, your *Babamoshai* (father) had already made my life miserable by changing his religion and becoming a Brahmo, now don't make me suffer again by thrusting your theories of women's liberation."

The people of Thakurbari were originally Vaishnavas, worshipping the idols of Lakshmi-Janardan as their family deity. For generations, the sons and their wives had observed all the pujas and rituals with austerity. Since long, Sarada had learnt all the customs and the puja rituals from her grandmother-in-law Alaka Shundari and her mother-in-law Digambari. But her heart and soul were in tatters when her husband Debendranath had initiated himself into

Brahmo religion, rejecting all forms of idol worship. Stuck between her husband's newly embraced religion and her years of allegiance to Hinduism and its numerous customs, she continued being bruised, battered in her heart. As for Satyen, he understood the psyche of his mother when she spoke thus, but he had already taken an oath to himself to free his mother of all her shackles of obsolete rituals.

"Ma, why don't you understand, unless you change yourself, the civilization becomes stagnant; either in religion, or in society. Alas, a country which keeps its women imprisoned within the four walls is forever seeped in darkness. And listen, if it is the question of enhancing the dress sense of our women, didn't *Babamoshai* himself experiment with the attire of my sisters? Didn't he keep changing their attires from Peshowaj to Indian gowns? Remember, even you have made your daughters wear those dresses designed by our Muslim tailors!"

"It was because I had been forced to! Otherwise, how would our daughters sit to study in front of the *Pandit Moshai*, their tutor with just a sari draped over their bare bodies? Hence that arrangement to cover their bodies!" Sarada replied.

"It's the same, Ma, with your *Mejo Bou*! How would she get out of home and mix with others in our society without covering her body with a proper attire? The way women in our household drape saris over their bare bodies is unfit for being exposed to the civilized world. She has to mix with so many people from the genteel, aristocratic society, courtesy my job, Ma!" Satyen said, with full enthusiasm.

"I don't understand why a woman of a respected family need to mix so much with outsiders!" Sarada replied with an austere face. "Look at us, we never stepped out of our home…if ever we got permission to have a bath in the Ganges, we had to remain inside the palanquins, closed from all sides. Don't you remember going with me for the bath, as a child? You've seen with your own eyes how our bearers would plunge the entire palanquin with us in the Ganges for a number of times, and that was the only way we could take the holy bath! And now, you made the bride of our house journey in a car, walk all the way to the inner quarters in front of the servants, uncovered, unabashed? Alas, why am I even alive to witness such sacrilege?"

"Goodness, Ma! What is the need to maintain the Islamic purdah system in our house? How long will our girls and brides remain imprisoned in our princely prison?"

Sarada seemed extremely annoyed. "Go away, don't bug me now! Go to your room, freshen up and have something to eat. I thought you would exchange some good words with your mother after your long journey, but instead, you are keen on arguing with her."

"Manada…Go and check if food is served in their room." She called for the maid servant.

"Yes, the food is being sent, *Karta Ma*." Manada, the maid answered. As Satyen stepped inside his room, Sarada asked again, looking at the semblance of his long, handsome physique: "Did you arrange for the food the way I told you to?"

"Yes Ma, we have sent sweets made of coconut, *Annanda naru* (dessert), luchi (puffed bread), eggplant fritters in silver trays, wrapped in laced covers. Also, there is watermelon drink with ice in silver glasses for them."

Sarada took a betel leaf from a Capricorn-faced tray made of silver, put it in her mouth, and with an anxious face, reclined on the pillow again. Manada, the maid started massaging her feet, as usual.

When Satyen reached his room, he noticed the lavish arrangements of the morning meal, the silver tray stuffed with food, beverages, all adorning the wooden stool beside the *palanka* (bed). He noticed the women surrounding Gyanada in the verandah, seated on a sprawling mat. Let them chit-chat to their heart's content for a while, he thought to himself, while having his food. Memories of his excruciating struggles to let his wife out of this very corridor, verandah, this very home flashed in front of his eyes. His eyes had opened up the first time he had been to London for his ICS examination. He was in complete awe of the open, liberated western society, and its free, enlightened women. The free spirit of those outgoing, emancipated women made him think of the western society as an ideal one. Their uninhibited mixing with the men in society didn't seem to disrupt the domestic rhythm one bit, rather those elegant, educated women seemed to complement the men as their most deserving partners. Why on earth wouldn't our own Bengali women be like them? He wondered. Those days, he often thought how he could bring Gyanada to London with him. Of course, when she would be there, observing the free spirit, the unhindered lives of these women, she would be inspired to change herself too.

And while he was fascinated by the appeal of those Englishwomen, he didn't forget his beautiful thirteen-year-old bride for a single moment. As a matter-of-fact, his grandfather Dwarakanath was fascinated by English ladies too, while he was in London. He had enjoyed his days immensely with his sweet tete-a-tetes with Queen Victoria, his exploits with the *memsahibs* inside luxurious boat-rides in the heart of Thames. He had liberated himself by seeking those light pleasures. After some years, when he was led astray by his Anglicized companions, his wife Digambari had almost renounced his company, fearing that she would lose her religion. In spite of his unlimited wealth, his social status and his accomplishments, he couldn't mould his wife to accept his ways of livings. Prince Dwarakanath indeed had a princely disposition. His lavish parties with meat and drinks, his ball dance with *memsahibs* in his Belgachhia villa had invited enough scandal during those days. Rupchand Pakshi moshai, a poet of those times had composed a sarcastic rhyme on his exploits.

"Only the Thakur company knows what there is in that red drink,

What do we know of its attributes, but only the people of the Thakur ilk."

Digambari Devi, his grandmother, however, fascinated Satyen more than his free-spirited grandfather. She had the ethereal looks of Goddess Jagaddhatri, but her spitfire personality was something which Satyen knew as her essence. One of those nights, when her husband Dwarakanath would indulge in partying and merrymaking in his villa, she went out of the house in her closed palanquin with her troop, to witness the scene with her own eyes. During those days, it was quite a daring act for a conservative woman who remained confined within the inner quarters. When they both were young, she had shared a beautiful, hearty relationship with her husband. When Dwarakanath worshipped the family deities of Lakshmi-Janardan, his beautiful, teenager bride Digambari would be his accomplice, the beauty of her fair face, of her pristine devotion being amplified by the incense and Indian frankincense. Dwarakanath, the devotee of sheer beauty had been enamoured by her charm during those early days. Being orthodox Brahmins, their kitchen was devoid of meat, fish, and even onion and garlic. But then, as Dwarakanath's businesses ventures became incredibly successful, his mixing with the *sahibs* and *memsahibs* grew exponentially. While the advent of neo-liberalization and his involvement with it, with his irresistible attraction towards the *Babu* culture which had spread its wings then, his dependence on his orthodox Hinduism gradually dwindled. Also, the Brahmin Pundits back then had declared that he was rendered unworthy of worshipping the Hindu deities. He had been impure, they said, mixing indiscriminately with the Englishmen. Then, what his own wife Digambari did to him had been history.

Just before going to London, one day, Satyen called his teenage wife Gyanada and narrated the story of his grandmother to her.

"You can't even imagine what a daring woman my grandmother was, Genu," he said, to provoke a fire within her.

"For quite a while, she had been listening to the stories of *Dadamoshai*'s (grandfather) adventures in his Belgachhia villa, that he was drinking alcohol along with the English men and ladies, that he was having meat dishes cooked by a Muslim chef. *Than didi*, my grandmother discarded those stories initially, but after repeatedly listening to them, she decided to go and check for herself, what really happened inside the villa. Just think, what a daring act for a young woman during those days!"

"Oh my, my heart palpitates, just hearing about this act of hers! Did *Than didi* go there alone, all by herself?" The young Gyanada asked, trembling.

"Not alone...she took my mother and a couple of women from the inner quarters along with her. Three palanquins of the Thakurbari, with yellow borders and red satin covering stopped in front of the Belgachhia villa. My mother, a timid young girl back then, was petrified, she said to me later. Her hands and feet had frozen in fear."

"What happened then? What did they see?" Gyanada asked, curious.

"When she came out of the closed palanquin, she witnessed something which she had never experienced in her life. The entire villa, at night, was transformed into a beautiful phenomenon of light. It was quite a spectacle when my grandmother entered inside the giant hall with her battalion of women, crossing the majestic garden embellished with the fountain, the nude feminine figurines, the mammoth pillars and the stunning architecture of the huge mansion. Amid the tinkling sound of the cups and glass vessels, amid the shimmering splendour of the fancy chandeliers and the grandeur of the imported furniture, the dancing men and women stopped, stood transfixed. With her own eyes, *Than didi*, our grandmother saw the Muslim chefs serving fish and meat dishes in the tables, the white men dancing with white women, embracing them tightly. Her eyes were transfixed on her husband Dwarakanath, who had a glass of wine in one hand, while with the other hand, he was dancing to the tunes of an English song with a *memsahib*, holding her waist with his other hand. For some seconds, she stood statue-like, witnessing this unthinkable scene, and then, was overwhelmed by a seething anger. *Dadamoshai* trembled for a moment, perhaps he had gauged the rage and the fire brimming inside his wife from under her veil. As he approached her in an attempt to pacify her, she glared at him with her contempt-filled eyes, piercing him with her glances, and left the hall haughtily."

"That means *Than didi* was the boldest woman of this house, wasn't she? I want to be like her," Gyanada said. "The moment I find you have been led astray, I will distance myself from you. Beware!"

"Will you be as stone-hearted as her, really?" Satyen laughed and asked her. "Do you know what she did after that? When *Dadamoshai* lost his right to perform the daily puja rituals, she asked herself, would she lose her religion if she remained close to him in her conjugal life? After conscious deliberation and after discussing in detail with the Brahmins, she decided to tend to all her husband's needs, and then take a bath to sanctify herself. It was her conscious decision to quit co-sleeping with her husband in his bed at night."

"What are you saying? What gave her the courage to perform such an act in an orthodox family like yours?" Gyanada asked, surprised.

"You do not have half as much courage as her, Genu," Satyen said affectionately, pulling her head to his inviting chest. "Gradually, she stopped *Dadamoshai* from entering the inner quarters and made arrangements to shift his bed in the living room. A separate kitchen was also made for him in due time, severing their ties permanently."

The twelve-year-old Genu was all the more astonished. "But is it good to sever ties with your own husband? Isn't the husband supposed to be the religion of every woman?" She asked.

"Listen Genu, it is extremely difficult to judge what is just in the name of religion and what is not. Do you know, our

Didi thakurani (Grandmother) would start her puja rituals as early as four in the morning, and have only vegetarian food which she cooked herself? A Brahmin cook used to help her in arranging her meals and also organizing the ingredients for the puja. During every *Ekadashi*, she would survive only on fruits, and even fast during some *Ekadashi* seasons. Since her husband couldn't gel his life with her own *satwik* life, she had deliberately abstained herself from the pleasures of her husband's company. Her allegiance to her religion was greater for her than her allegiance to her husband.

"But wasn't she a married woman? Why did she observe the *Ekadashi* fast then?" Gyanada was shocked in astonishment.

"I have heard about Grandma's unconditioned faith in her fasting, for the welfare of her husband. Why an immensely devoted wife like her turned so cruel and hardhearted, is the subject of much thought."

Satyen's eyes had almost closed in sleep due to fatigue, while reminiscing these old stories. The tender touch of Gyanada's fingers woke him up from his slumber. The other girls had left already. Gyanada was decked up in a soft *tant* sari, blue in colour, and the aroma of the *bakul* flowers in her hair tied up in a bun was welcoming the migrant Satyen with the all richness of his Bengali homeland. In the privacy of her own room, Gyanada didn't care about wearing the jacket she wore when she stepped outside, but she couldn't wear the sari over her bare body too; it would be too rustic for her tastes. Hence, she chose to wear a very light satin chemise and to wrap the sari around it as gracefully as she could. The fragrant aatar she wore to complete her dress-up made her even more charming. Was it the same young girl whom Satyen had taken to Mumbai along with him, crossing the *laxmanrekha* of the four walls of this palace, he wondered in awe.

"Do you remember, Genu, what you did on the first day of our dinner party in Mumbai?" Satyen asked, embracing her passionately.

"Ah, don't forget, I was just a young, adolescent Bengali bride then, who had recently stepped outside the threshold of the Thakurbari. How was I even supposed to know the manners of the *Gora Sahibs*? It was unthinkable to sit together with the firangis, to eat or drink with them! You know, I had decided beforehand that I would set up the table with all food and drinks with great care for them, but I wouldn't sit for a meal with him, not on the same table. Remember, that *Gora Sahib*…as soon as he took my hand in his hand and tried dragging me to the dinner table, I thought what an insolent man he was, freed my hand with all my might and ran, ran far away."

"Ha ha ha!" Satyen laughed out loud. "You know how I had to plead and beg to open the bolted doors that day! Well, I do not blame you for your behaviour that day, the uninitiated young girl that you were…But I feel proud of you to have witnessed your gradual transformation, the way you have moulded yourself to absorb the manners and etiquettes and become the worthy wife of the first Indian civilian!"

Within the young girl of those yesteryears, Satyen felt the aura of a new woman, ushering like the golden rays of the sun in her body, mind and spirit. With a tremendous surge of his passion, he took her in his warm embrace and started kissing her.

"Ah, what are you doing? Have you become a child?

Can't you see the open doors and windows…anybody can barge in at any moment!" Gyanada uttered, shamefully.

"Do you remember what I said to you back then?" Satyen asked his wife.

"Well, you have told me so many things…how do I know what you are referring to right now?" Gyanada replied, in mock anger.

"Remember the letter I wrote to you from England where I had mentioned: 'Until you have turned into a truly mature, educated woman, progressive in your thoughts in all aspects, we won't consummate our marriage."

Gyanada remembered those early days after their marriage, how she had searched for the meaning of her husband's words, strolling in the long terrace of the Thakurbari during the lone moonlit nights. A strange, unknown fear had grasped her young mind when she was gradually realizing that her husband was not accepting her fully, was distancing himself from her. Those early days when her husband wrote to her: "Our marriage has been thrust on us by our parents, it has not happened in the presence of our free will." Has the time of their sacred union come now?

Gyanada blushed like a new bride. "Why do you tell this now?" She asked.

"But the time is ripe, right now, dear!" Satyen uttered, his voice trembling in unbridled emotions. "In our sacred nuptial room, I am the old seeker of love, this *palanka*, the cherished bed of our long-awaited union. You are no longer a shackled housewife. O free-spirited woman, I beg to be one with you today, wouldn't you grant my plea?"

In such an unprecedented moment, Gyanada couldn't decide what to do, and fell over her husband's bosom. "Now, now, no more drama!" She said.

In an intense surge of passion, Satyen took her in his arms, lifted her blushing face with his hand and kissed her in the lips. In that long-awaited moment of their union, their bodies were crushing each other with fierce passion and longing. Satyen threw away his clothes on the floor, and Gyanada's sari too was laid out on the dirty ground. His impatient fingers started playing with her body, finding a home in her tender breasts, covered with her chemise. Even a piece of thread between the two bodies seemed like a barrier to them.

"*Bou* (bride), you know, this chemise won't be a much desirable thing for married women. You'll need to think about this issue a bit." Satyen uttered boldly at this point.

Amused at her husband's mischievous thoughts, Gyanada made a fist at him in mock anger.

"What are you doing, *Bou*? Would you start beating your husband as the first step towards your freedom? You know, the orthodox Hindus might have kept their women within the four walls of their homes, fearing this!" Satyen said, smiling.

"See what I do to you now!" Gyanada said. As she came closer to her husband, supporting her body with her knees, she placed her tender lips on top of his masculine lips, closing his lips with her own.

At this moment, her husband realized that the free woman had sought freedom in her love. After their prolonged kiss, when she had released her lips, this proclamation of freedom had been made.

Chapter 2

Sarada Sundari and her family

The inner quarters and the main living area of the Thakurbari were always segregated as two separate buildings. One had to cross an iron gate to enter the two buildings. The original ancestral abode of Dwarakanath Tagore was one single house with two distinct sections— the 'baithak khana bari', the outhouse which was meant for the visitors and guests and the 'basat bari', the domestic quarter for the family. A few days back, some differences occurred between the two brothers Deben and Girin, resulting in the two separate buildings. Now Deben and his wife Sarada lived in the 'basat bari' which was upstairs, with a strict demarcation between the outhouse and the inner quarters. The outhouse was exclusively meant for the males, the masters of the household, and the servants.

The women of the household were strictly confined to the inner quarters. The courtyard of the inner quarters was a storehouse of paddy, crops and lentils which would be used yearlong. But the ghee (clarified butter), salt, oil, the masalas for cooking were in the outhouse, in full control of the masters who gave them to the Brahmin cooks every day according to the needs and measurements of the day. Every day, the dozens of Brahmin cooks started cooking the daily meals since dawn in the mammoth kitchen. In both sides of the kitchen, mountainous piles of cooked rice were spread over clean white cloths. The cooks prepared the *dal* (lentils), vegetables and fish curry to go with the cooked rice, poured them into stone utensils and served them in both the outhouse and the inner quarters, meticulously counting the members of the household. The staple dinner at night used to be *luchi* (puffed bread) with vegetable curry.

However, Debendranath wasn't always happy with the taste of such daily meals. After a long stay outside Kolkata, when he returned home for restrengthening his bond with dear ones and home-cooked food, he was naturally discontent with the food prepared by the Brahmin cooks. He ordered Sarada Sundari, his wife to teach cooking to the brides of the household, so that they develop an affinity towards cooking. When *Kartamoshai* Debendranath was at home those days, Sarada sat in the kitchen with her plump body, monitoring the activities of cooking. Once, at the order of Debendranath, the brides had started their cooking experiments inside the inner quarters with full zest and vigour. There was a distinct, marked difference in their style of cooking, compared to the large-scale meals prepared by the Brahmin cooks. Their meticulously prepared dishes paved way for a unique *gharana* (school) of cooking which became a trademark of the illustrious Thakurbari.

It was a daily ritual for the brides and the unmarried girls of the household to bathe early in the morning and get dressed in specially made *'patta vastra'*, and then, assemble in the prayer room. After the prayer was over, they had to go back to their own rooms, leave their silk clothes worn during the prayer, change into the traditional Bengali tant saris and assemble at the open courtyard close to the kitchen pantry, a haven for their womanly chit-chat. It was a familiar scene those days, *Karta Ma*, their mistress ordering from the stool where she sat, and the brides and girls of the house preparing the vegetables for cooking. Since the times when they were Vaishnava's, they wouldn't utter phrases like 'cutting vegetables', which might carry a hint of cruelty in the utterance. Hence it was referred to as 'preparing the vegetables.' The fruits, vegetables, succulent mango bars, *bori* (dried lentil dumplings), *naru,* the flavourful coconut and jaggery laddoos and *sandesh,* the delightful Bengali dessert were managed by the women solely, and in such August company, the unmarried and married girls joined the brides of the household in delightful exuberance. Soudamini, Sarat Kumari, Barna Kumari, Sarada Sundari's girls joined in and learnt the culinary skills under their mother's supervision.

Sarat Kumari had been married very recently, and staying with her husband in the Thakurbari, her parental home. She had earned quite a good reputation as a cook these days.

'Ma, I've learnt a new recipe, Mulligatawny soup with eggs. I'm thinking of making this soup for Babamoshai (father) today." She said to her mother in an indulgent, childish voice.

"My child," Sarada said, "See if you can make your father happy, feeding him some delicacies for a couple of days....by the way, where did you learn this recipe from?" She was curious.

"You know *Mejo Kakima* (aunt) of the mansion next

to us, she has learnt it from somewhere and sent it to us as a handwritten recipe. Really, Ma, our house feels so empty since they moved away, isn't it?"

"So true..." Sarada sighed. "I feel so sad when I think of them. We literally grew up in the same house together with such happiness and mirth...In fact, she was my sole companion in my in-laws' house when I came here as a child bride. *Kortamoshai*, your father was the one who disrupted it all with his loose, unruly ways, trying to drive away our divine Lakshmi-Janardan from the house! They took away our cherished family idols and moved away to the other mansion."

Looking into the history of the Thakurbari, the strife and the estrangement between the two brothers' families began when a wall was built to segregate the large, original home of Dwarakanath's children. They became separated as house no. 5 and house no. 6. The huge garden was divided into two, the bank of the family pond was also divided. It should be pointed out here that the Brahmo religion started rearing its head in the Thakur family during the lifetime of Dwarakanath. In fact, when Raja Rammohan Roy had gone to England, the *Brahmo Samaj* and its activities were patronized by none other than Dwarakanath himself. During those days, he also received incredible honour and respect from the Sahibs of London and started losing interest in his livelihood in Kolkata. He had decided to settle down in England only. During such a significant time of his transition, Deben, his son took the responsibility of the *Brahmo Samaj*. In the Bengali year 1250, during the winter month of *Poush*, Deben was initiated into the Brahmo religion along with some of his close friends. But then, the two brothers were different in their outlooks.

Girin, unlike his brother Deben, was not as involved with the Brahmo religion and its way of life. Their home was a traditional Hindu one, with all orthodox Hindu rituals followed to the core.

The first crisis emerged with the news of Dwarakanath's death arriving all the way from London. Deben, already a Brahmo by then, performed his father's funeral rites according to the Brahmo rituals, without the use of *Shalgram Shila* in the ideal Hindu way. His acts invited fury and mayhem, as many of his relatives, and the so-called gatekeepers of Hinduism ostracized him socially. Girindranath, his brother, on the other hand, performed his father's sraddha rituals according to the Hindu faith, despite being initiated into Brahmo religion. His wife Jogmaya could never allow her husband to perform such an act of blasphemy, and Girindra, naturally didn't have the courage to act against his fierce wife's wishes.

While supervising the act of cutting vegetables in the kitchen, Sarada showed a bit of temper. "But I tell you, it's not good for a woman to be as fierce as Jogmaya. It's true that I myself was panicking at the thought of driving away the family Gods, but does that mean she would have to move away to a different home?" She said, with visible angst.

"But Ma, did you become a Brahmo by heart, just like our *Babamoshai* (father)?" Her elder daughter Soudamini was curious.

Sarada looked a bit embarrassed at this sudden question asked. "Are you referring to your sister Sukumari's marriage? Listen, it was done absolutely at your father's stubborn wish, he was adamant about a *Bemmo* (Brahmo) marriage. There were no traditional Hindu rituals, no sacred fire, no *shalgram shila* as marriage witness. How we lost the poor girl in the hands of cruel fate after that! Wasn't it inevitable?"

"But we all were dismayed due to her untimely loss, weren't we? Why do you blame her Brahmo marriage for that, Ma?'

'And there were all other Hindu rituals performed during her marriage day, just the sacred fire ritual was absent. Suku lost her life during childbirth, it's not uncommon, after all. Don't take it to your heart, Ma.' Neepamayee, one of the brides referred to as *'Shejo Bou'* spoke now.

"You won't understand my agony, dear...I am under immense pressure from both sides." Sarada was irritated. "On one hand, the truth is that your father is such a highly educated man, he cannot say anything unjust. But again thirty-five years of my life in this house have been spent, learning and internalizing the puja rituals from my mother-in-law, my grandma-in-law since a very tender age; I can't throw all that away for him, can I? Ah, such a pain it is!"

Sarada looked at Neepamayee with slanted eyes now and revealed an explosive event. "*Shejo Bou,* have you forgotten the tremendous scuffle that happened during your own marriage? Good Lord, I haven't seen such a marriage in my life! Don't you remember how the orthodox Hindus hired goons to attack my son on your marriage night? Finally, the police had to be called so that the marriage could happen. Wasn't it only because of the stubbornness of *Korta Moshai,* your father-in-law and *Beyai Moshai,* your father that your marriage rituals were complete, in spite of all odds? Or I must say, because of the strength of my daily puja, however much it might annoy our *Korta Moshai*?

Debendranath Tagore had married off his sons Hemendra and Birendra with the two daughters of his very dear friend Haradeb Chattopadhyay, Neepamayee and Prafullamayee respectively. Haradeb, a *kulin* Brahmin of those times had decided to marry off his daughter to a Pirali Brahmin family with Brahmo marriage rituals, which attracted the ire of his kith and kin. They wreaked havoc, trying to stop the marriage with all their might, from the fear of getting ostracized by the people of their own community. Haradeb's elder son started living separately with his wife and children, pressurized by their folks. But that didn't deter his father who stuck to his decision steadfastly; he had already vowed to his gem of a friend Debendra, and now he couldn't break his promise because of the illogical demands of his relatives. His opponents, on the other hand, conspired together to jeopardize the marriage, and to that effect, they had already selected a *kulin* groom for Neepamayee, an elderly man. It was decided that on the marriage night, as many as hundred goons would attack the groom Hemendra, hijack the bride Neepamayee from the marriage venue and marry her off with this elderly man. But Debendranath had gauged the onslaught ahead of time and called the police to intervene, hence the marriage took place without further ramifications.

The Brahmo marriage took place beautifully with the rituals of *Saptapadi,* as in a traditional Hindu marriage. The welcoming rituals for the bride and *Brahmopasana,* the puja rituals according to the Brahmo traditions were performed uninterrupted, and thereafter, the bride and the groom entered the *bashor ghor* for their first nuptial night. Hemendra, the somber young gentleman, dressed up as the new groom was quite a sight with his irresistibly handsome features. He looked like the king of the gods, *Debraj* Indra, dressed in exquisite ornaments. Prafullamayee, his new sister-in-law, however, assumed that her elder sister's husband was a reincarnation of Lord Shiva. But the young girls among her relatives countered her with their own logic.

"You know that our Lord Shiva is a renouncer of all worldly objects, then why would he wear a diamond neck-piece, a pearl necklace, or a ruby ring? This *Jamai Babu* from the *Thakurbari* is nobody else but Lord Indra in disguise. He was mesmerised by our Didi's beauty, and came to marry her."

Hemen had contrived a strategy for the marriage night beforehand, lest he would have to confront the loud, unavoidable feminine banter. As an antidote to the light, frivolous environment inhabited by the womenfolk, he started discussing about the education of women. In the Thakurbari, many women could not only read Bengali, but also studied Sanskrit and English, he declared, astonishing the scarcely educated Brahmo women present there.

"You will also have to learn Bengali, English, Sanskrit, the literature and languages." He also addressed his new bride Neepamayee, the coy, docile bride who listened to him quietly.

Neepamayee remained silent that night. How could she talk to her new husband in front of everybody? But she felt strongly that her husband was a unique human, different from the other grooms she had seen in her family.

Hemen again said to Nepamayee in front of the women present for the *Bashor*, the night following the marriage ceremony: "If there is enough music in your voice, I will give you music lessons, of course with due permission of *Babamoshai*."

The women in the room shivered in astonishment and shock. Has the boy gone crazy? How can a married woman, a domesticated bride sing? How blasphemous would that be? What would be the difference between a courtesan and her, then?

But Hemen had been true to his words eventually. He had started a home-school in the inner quarters of the Jorasanko Thakurbari with his wife Neepamayee and the other girls and young women of the household. Soudamini, Sarat Kumari, Gyanada Nandini, Swarna Kumari, Barna Kumari were among his regular students there, and under his tutelage, they were progressing in their studies remarkably.

He had even made the impossible task of the music training of his wife possible. *Babamoshai*, his father was a bit reluctant at first, but gave in later. The in-house music tutor Bishnu Chakraborty was hired for Neepamayee's music lessons, in the face of harsh criticism by the family members. Hemendranath had undertaken a truly courageous task, since the times when Aurangzeb had snatched away the gift of music from the voices of domesticated women in India. After ages and eons, Hemen seemed to bring back that very gift of music in Neepamayee's voice.

The birth of babies and marriages were among the common phenomena inside the Thakurbari. Swarna Kumari, the beloved daughter of Debendranath was married with much pomp and grandeur to an extremely pleasant, good-looking gentleman Janakinath, a social-reformer from Krishnanagar, whom Debendranath himself had chosen for his daughter. For this alliance with the Thakur family, Janakinath's father disowned him, depriving him of his father's property. The hard truth that nobody wanted to marry off their children to the Thakur family propelled Debendranath to seek decent, well-established grooms for his daughters, marry off his daughters to them and bring them to live in the Thakurbari permanently. Janakinath, on his part, was tempted by the allure of light of the illustrious Thakurbari and the charm of his learned, beautiful bride Swarnakumari, married at the tender age of thirteen. Compared to her, the other brides of the household had been married even earlier. Just before her wedding day, Swarna had hugged her mother Sarada in a fervent plea: she wanted to listen to the story of her mother's wedding.

Sarada replied, trying to recollect the almost forgotten story: "I was just a small village girl of Jessore in Bangladesh. There was an uncle of mine who had gathered from his visit to Kolkata that the process of bride-hunting was going on for the *Korta*. That was it, I was married off in haste."

"What are you saying? That means no woman from our household went to see you before arranging the wedding?" Swarna said, astonished. All along, she knew it was the customary ritual of the Thakurbari to see the potential bride for the first time with their old maid Putul, and if they liked the girl as their bride, they would go again with the women of the household, according to their convenience.

"But my uncle feared that the groom would be married off elsewhere, you know!" Sarada replied to her daughter Swarna. "Just when he entered our house, he noticed me, all of six years, playing with my toy utensils in the courtyard. He pulled me away from my game forcefully, dressed me up and packed me off to Kolkata. My mother had gone to bathe in the nearby river at that time. I started wailing for my mother, helpless and vulnerable.

"I'll go once my mother comes back." I said, repeatedly. But my uncle wouldn't listen to any of my pleas, and I didn't even get the chance to say 'goodbye' to my mother, for one last time. I had heard upon returning from the river, she had cried for me inconsolably, lying below the canopy of trees at the courtyard, and died from the shock of my sudden disappearance. This was the story of so many girls of our age. You girls are so privileged, having born in the Thakurbari, having such a God-like father as *Babamoshai*! Having born here, you are so blessed to be educated, to inhale the outside air and cherish it!"

There was a strange dichotomy inside Sarada's heart when she spoke. "Just because *Karta* is such a God-like human, I can't help but love his religion, though I must love my own religion too! Don't the girls and womenfolk of this house understand this?" She thought to herself.

Barnakumari, Swarna's sister was a tender girl of twelve. "Ma, didn't you send me to our *Mejo Kaki* (aunt) with puja offerings for Lakshmi-Janardan, our family deities? Did that make *Babamoshai* angry?" She asked her mother in her characteristic innocence.

The words of the uninitiated child agitated Sarada. "Ah, what is the need to know all this, Barna? Just follow my order, that's all. Go away from here now, I say."

Sarada couldn't really forget the pain and anguish of the family deities leaving her home. She kept on sending puja offerings to her Lakshmi-Janardan secretly, while participating in the *Brahmo Upasana* rituals performed by her husband. Even Girin would participate in the

Hindu puja rituals, in spite of being a *Brahmo*. *Kartamoshai* Debendranath, on his part, hadn't thought about rejecting the puja rituals at first; but during the Durga puja days, he avoided being at home and went out of town for sudden travel. Sarada too couldn't partake in the Durga puja festivities, stricken with grief and anguish. When the others partook in the revelry, she imprisoned herself in the silent corners of her room, voluntarily. Jogomaya would come to her, pleading to her to join in the festivities in the *Thakur dalan*, their giant hall downstairs, but she wouldn't relent.

Once, when *Kortamoshai* had gone away to the west, the fateful days of the Sepoy mutiny had started. Day after day, there was no news of him, and Sarada had almost given up eating, bathing, living a normal life due to her anxieties about her husband. When he was busy with his newfound Brahmo spirituality, Sarada was tormenting herself, anxious, grief-stricken. But even those days seemed better than the moment when he announced the annihilation of the puja rituals. Didn't that single act propel Girin and Jogomaya to move away to a separate home, along with their Lakshmi-Janardan idols?

"This compels me to pray to my Hindu Gods while physically sitting at the altar of our *Karta*'s Bhahmo *Upasana*. Isn't it the same practice that Jodha Bai did, worshipping her Lord Shiva while sitting inside Akbar's harem?" Sarada said.

Sarada's love for her husband didn't diminish one bit though, due to their differences. Still now, she waited eagerly for her *Karta* to summon her at night, whenever he was at home. He usually called her at night, when their sons fell fast asleep. After her night bath, she wore a bright coloured, soft *taant* sari, sprayed *aatar*, the exotic oriental scent on her earlobes, her neck. Sometimes, she wore a garland made of the bud of *bel* flowers in her hair, and thus, dressing herself up was complete. She never wore extravagant jewellery, never wore vermillion in her head or *alta* (red paint) in her feet as lavishly as the other women and brides in the household. Her husband, a frequent sojourner of the mountains, was fond of her simple, minimalist dressing, whenever he came back home, or to her.

Once, when Debendra had decided to spend his days in the bosom of the river Ganga, to sever his materialistic ties, Sarada had cried, begged to him so that he allows her to accompany him. Due to her repeated pleas, Debendra had rented the 'pinis', a vessel in the bosom of the river. With her three sons who were babies then, Sarada stepped outside the inner quarters of her home for the first time, and followed her husband to the 'pinis'. That was her first view of the holy river Ganga. Her husband didn't renounce her, owing to his Brahmo spirituality and vision. Rather, the children born in her womb every year bore testimonies of their love for each other. Not all of her children survived, nor could she tend to each of them equally. She satisfied herself by tending to her husband's needs, and by gaining his love and affection abundantly.

In twenty-three years, starting from 1840, Sarada had given birth to nine sons and six daughters, but only ten of them had survived. Just after two years of her eldest, Dwijendra, Satyen was born, and two years after, Hemen came along, followed by Biren, who came after one year and ten months. Two years after that, her daughter Soudamini and son Jyotirindra came in quick succession. Her second daughter Sukumari died at the tender age of fourteen. She had a son Punyendra after Sukumari, but he died as a child of six, drowned in an accident. Then came her three daughters, Saratkumari, Swarnakumari and Barnakumari. Even after her younger sons Somendra and Rabindranath, another son, Budhendra was born, but he too died as a child. All these children she bore were tended to by the servants and maids of the house.

It was customary of rich households in those days that the infants were sent to the midwives after birth, and also nursed by them, nurtured with their breast milk. After birth, each individual infant was assigned a midwife as the wet nurse, and another maid to raise him/her, thus there was no significant bond that developed between the biological mother and child. The same happened between Sarada and her children. Untill her sister-in-law Jogomaya lived in the same house, the children found great solace in her company; she was the one who tended to their childish demands. The children missed their *Mejo Kaki*'s presence during the time that they grew up. However, Rabindranath, Somendra and Barnakumari were entirely deprived of their share of love from *Mejo Kaki*, born much later. They never felt the absence of a mother figure, as the poor children never knew how the tender form of motherly affection was.

In the meanwhile, an assembly of women congregated in Sarada's kitchen for the act of cutting vegetables, and Swarnakumari, the newly married daughter of Sarada joined the women too. The newly married girls of the Thakurbari usually stayed on at their parents' home after marriage, but Swarna was an exception. The Thakur's were different in all respects; on one hand, they were Pirali brahmins by race, and on the other hand, they were Brahmo by spiritual leanings. Hence, the ones who married their daughters had to leave their father's homes and live with their new wives in the Thakurbari. Swarna's husband Janakinath, a free-spirited young man, was also disowned by his own father, but Janaki had set two conditions prior to marrying Swarna. First, he wouldn't convert himself to a Brahmo, and second, he wouldn't live in his in-laws' house. Debendranath had accepted both his conditions with deep regard. Swarna lived in a separate house with her husband and often visited her parents' home in Jorasanko.

Swarna, the fashionable young woman was dressed today in a pistachio-coloured Crepe silk sari with Parsi embroidered borders, accompanied by a beautiful laced jacket. Inspired by her fellow warrior, her sister-in-law Gyanadanandini, she had worn her sari in the *Bombay*-style, with a brooch adorning the short *aanchal*, which made it difficult for her to cover her head with the aanchal. Hence, she wore an embroidered cap to cover her head, which was her own style statement.

Swarna picked up a stool, sat on it and started chatting with the women folk in the house, all of whom looked at her inquisitively.

Gyanada too had come downstairs to meet her, the moment she knew of Swarna's arrival. They were the best of friends. Swarna looked at her sister-in-law Gyanada lovingly and asked: "*Mejo Bouthan*, have you heard about all those gossip columns being written about the way we dress up these days?"

"Yes, *Notun Thakurpo* (brother-in-law) was telling me that day, some youngsters in college were naming us as the '*Bou-bibis* of Thakurbari', and what not!"

"And still you will indulge in stepping outside

for fresh air? I can't tolerate such ill reputation of our Thakurbari anymore." Sarada said, annoyed.

"But why, Ma? Didn't you see, so many Brahmo girls and women are coming to learn this new way of draping saris after seeing the advertisement posted by *Mejo Bouthan*? They had even contemplated wearing gowns outside. Some of them had even gone so far as to drape the *aanchal* of their saris over those gowns, wouldn't that look weird? I would rather love this Bombay-style of draping our saris, which is our own Indian way of wearing them."

Amid this conversation, a little girl of eight came running towards Sarada and started crying, hugging her tightly.

"Who is this girl?" The women of the house questioned, astonished by this sudden incident.

Sarada tried to release herself from the girl's embrace. "Who are you? What made you cling to me suddenly, where did you come from? Don't you know I don't like all this! Move away, I say!" She said, indignantly.

The girl lifted her innocent face and said: "They are coming to take me away, please save me, *Karta Ma*! I want to live with you!"

"Manada, who is this girl? I assume she is the daughter of some of our relatives of the extended family, isn't she? Can you take her away?" She asked her old maid.

Manada pulled away the girl from Sarada, and slapped her in her cheek. "Who are you, shameless girl?"

"I am Rupa, I sit behind you all, close to the kitchen area, didn't you see me?" The girl managed to say, amid her muffled cries.

Sarada noticed her sweet, tender face and questioned: "Where do you live? Who is your mother?"

"You are my mother! Why are you driving me away? I won't go with them...they don't love me one bit!" The girl replied, crying still.

Just then, a young woman with her face covered in veil appeared, and started pulling the little girl. "Wait, who are you?" Sarada asked. "Is this girl your daughter?"

The young woman folded her hands in a gesture of *pranaam* and said: "I beg your pardon, *Karta Ma*. We belong to your extended family, sheltered in that part of your house where your relatives stay. This girl is the daughter of my husband's first wife, who is no more. Such a fearless girl, she doesn't listen to anything I say. I keep beating her black and blue, but the beatings didn't teach her a lesson yet, I see!"

"I warn you, don't ever beat her again!" Sarada ordered the woman. "Just because she is your rival, your co-wife's daughter, you don't have the right to raise your hands on her... I will never tolerate this as long as you are in my house!"

"Manada!" She called her maid again. "Keep a close watch on our relatives' area. Such a huge herd of people feeding on our money, and violating the rules of our house! Do you think I would tolerate this? From today, not a soul will dare to raise his/her hand on any girl child of the house."

Rupa released her little hands from the hands of her stepmother, trying to run towards Sarada. The clever little soul had realized that she would have a new lease of life, if she would be sheltered by Sarada. This was an enchanting world of free will, laughter and endless chats, a world defined by the sunshine and fresh air of the outside world. She would never venture inside the dark, quarrelsome world which she inhabited till now, if she got the chance to live here, amid these ladies.

But she had to go back. Just before the girl left, Sarada's heart was overwhelmed with tenderness to see her moist, pitiful eyes. "Come to see me every morning, Rupa, to convey your *pranaam* to me... don't forget!" Sarada said.

This one word changed the girl's life. She understood she would not have to be beaten up and oppressed ever again.

Meanwhile, Malini, the book-seller girl joined in the women's assembly and added more life and vigour to it. It was her job to sell books among the women of the aristocratic households. When she arrived, the souls of these women confined to the inner quarters of the mansion of Thakurbari danced in joy; her presence was like the welcoming ray of sun protruding their dark, lack-lustre lives. Not only did Malini bring along a treasure-trove of books, the endless world of gossip and chatter which she carried with her attracted the women folk as they surrounded her, like bees clinging to flowers. Her stock of gossip included a delectable range, from the colourful stories of the *Babu-bibis* to the newly featured story of 'Bamabodhini' magazine.

"Come, Malini, come and join us. Long time didn't see you...Why don't you come to us for some chat from time to time?" Sarada came to her and held her hand.

"Do I have the leisure to chat, *Bouthan*? I have so much travelling to do, within such short span of time. You know, I can even tell you the secret stories of the books which might come out soon... but those being secrets, I can't divulge them to all." Malini replied in good humour.

"Your words sound so mysterious, dear Malini...It seems you are an inhabitant of a magical world, far beyond our mundane everyday world, and when I speak to you, it seems I have already entered that world! You know what, I summon you to listen to these enticing words that you speak, they appeal to me a lot more than the books that you carry with you!" Gyanada said this time.

"*Mejo Bouthan*, tell me, do you want to visit that magical world? If you want, I can take you there for a memorable sojourn!" Malini laughed and added: "Besides, to speak the truth, you are in no way an ordinary woman. Your stories travel beyond the boundaries of this mansion and are in everyone's lips these days...Wherever I travel, folks keep enquiring about you! Also, your appearance in the party at the Honorable Governor's House has been the talk of the town too. Most of the folks present there mistook you for the Begum of Bhopal. In fact, she was the only lady of aristocratic lineage who ventured outside all by herself till now. Hence..."

Sarada couldn't help expressing her anger at Malini's words. "Don't fuel the fire of her arrogance, Malini! You know what, our relatives and members of our extended family present at that party saw our own *Bouma* amid the *gora sahibs* and *memsahibs* and ran away from the scene, in their tremendous sense of shame! Prasanna Thakur, one of our respected relatives was seething in anger, he expressed his feelings to our *Karta Moshai*." She said, indignantly.

Swarnakumari appeared on the scene to defend Gyanada. "Whatever you might remark, Ma, my heart was filled with pride upon seeing *Mejo Bouthan* that day...In fact, it was me who had dressed her up for the occasion. I dressed her head parting with the sparkling 'sinthi', and her whole body with gold ornaments. With that sky-coloured Benarasi sari, with the glittering ornaments adorning her body, with her beautiful gait, she really looked like a queen. Since *Mej da* had other urgent work and couldn't join the party, a *memsahib* escorted her there on his behalf. Can you realize how grand it was? She was the only Bengali lady among hundreds of British ladies. *Mej da* was so proud of her!"

Emboldened by Swarna's statement, Malini opened the pages of a magazine and pointed towards a news story: "Look what Somprakash's Winter issue has featured… 'Last Thursday, at a lavish party at the Governor General's mansion, Babu Satyendranath's wife was present, wearing our national costume. Never before this day had a Hindu woman stepped inside the residence of a royal representative."

"Even if she went there, wouldn't it look good if she went with her husband?" Sarada said.

'So, the invincible wall of inhibitions is breaking, gradually!' Gyanada thought to herself. All hell had broken loose in the words of *Karta Ma*, her mother-in-law, when she returned to the Jorasanko mansion, her husband's ancestral home in a horse carriage. The same woman was now protesting about her husband not joining her at the party in softer words, as if she was bound to comply to Gyanada's escapades in the outside world. She knew she had to wipe away the web of dark prejudices from all Bengali women's minds in this way, bit by bit. This was just the beginning.

Meanwhile, Malini had started opening the treasure trove of books she brought along with her, and Gyanada started browsing them, one by one. There were new novels, books of poems and also fantasy stories. Alongside glossy books and magazines like *Manbhanjan, Rati Bilaap, Kokil Doot* and *Bastraharan,* there were the classics like Arabian Nights, *Geet Govindam,* the classic Persian novels, *Laila Majnu,* mythological tales like *Basabdutta.*

Swarna picked up another classic book and was astonished to see its contents. "Ah, this is the Bengali translation of Robinson Crusoe! Malini, how exciting this new book filled with illustrations is! And I must say, the illustrations look beautiful!"

"Let me see, let me see!" Barna, the younger sister of Swarna, a curious child came along, snatching the book from her. The images and illustrations of the book were the primary attractions to her.

The girls and women of the Thakurbari had created quite a sizeable library in the house, accumulating most of the books brought by Malini, the book-seller girl. The girls were initiated into reading novels from this very home library. The boys of the house got to know of these books after a long time, since it was customary for them to stay at the servants' quarters till a significant part of their childhood. Unless and until they became the pets of their aunts or *Bouthans* (sisters-in-law), stepping inside the inner quarters was forbidden. As per the customs, the boys could step inside the inner quarters only after they got married, when separate rooms were assigned for their new brides. Satyen, after his marriage to Gyanada, became a regular reader of this library. Satya and his younger brother Rabi would browse these books for women whenever they could enter the inner quarters by sheer manipulation. They were keen to read the forbidden books secretly, surreptitiously. Sarada was not an avid reader by any means, but she called for her sons to read out the epic Ramayana or the Slokas of Chanakya to her. This worked in their favour and their entry to the exclusively feminine arena of books was well established.

The six-year-old Rabi committed an exceptionally bold act, propelled by his insatiable greed for books. Their distant aunt was reading Dinabandhu Mitra's book 'Jamaibarik'. When Rabi insisted on reading that book, the elders forbade him to do so, and locked the book in an almirah. *Mashima*, the aunt who was reading the book, tied the key to that almirah in a key string and then, tied the key string to her sari's *aanchal*, hanging the *aanchal* over her shoulders. One day, Mashima was playing cards with the other ladies, placing the key on her lap. The child Rabi, dying to read the book, started to contrive a plan of stealing the book from the almirah. He stole the key and also got caught in the act.

The immensely smart child Rabi arranged for a container of betel leaves and dried tobacco leaves for *Mashima* in an attempt to please her. Just as the lady bent down to spit some betel juice from her mouth, the key fell from her lap, and little Rabi didn't have any problem in stealing it. *Mashima*, on her part, was totally unaware of Rabi's act. He unlocked the almirah with the key and took away the book to read secretly, while nobody was able to catch the book thief. Later, when Rabi himself confessed the crime, everybody shouted at him, but he received no real punishment for it.

...Sarada called out the girls, fighting with each other over the books that Malini brought along. "Girls, will you only keep snatching the books from one another, or read out some of them for me too? Swarna, come here my dear, read out a few pages from the Slokas of Chanakya, please!"

But Malini intervened at that very moment. "Come on, *Karta Ma*, you have listened to Chanakya Slokas for thousand times now, today let me read out a new story for you today.

It is 'Sita's Exile in the Forest' by Ishwarchandra Vidyasagar. The tragic tale of Sita will move you to tears, I promise! Or else, if you like, I can read out a comic tale which has recently been published in the 'Bamabodhini' magazine.

Swarna could not help expressing her indignation at the mention of 'Bamabodhini'. "Ah, you've brought that useless magazine again? Didn't I tell you not to bring those cheap articles and columns filled with advices for wives, written by petty-minded husbands? How regressive those words seem, reiterated for a thousand years now, killing our senses! Reading those, it seems the only objective to educate women is to prepare them as good mothers, good wives and ideal housewives! I have no taste for those write-ups!"

"Swarna didi, you know, people are going crazy, as they are following the lifestyle of the neo-liberated women folk of this new era; they are the ones who are tempting the writers to compose such articles. They are afraid of the newfound freedom that women have attained by virtue of their education, and now if they start venturing outside, invading the man's world, they will really be invincible then. They won't do their housework or raise their children then, nor would they revere their husbands or tend to their mothers-in-law. Didn't you read Bankim Babu's writing? Didn't he create Debi Chowdhurani as Woman Power in the beginning, but later make her stoop at the feet of her husband? Even Swami Vivekananda wrote: "In the western culture, women are primarily wives, and our own Indian women are primarily mothers." He also wrote: "It is the duty of mothers to raise healthy, brave and valourous, patriotic children, with truly Aryan attributes."

Swarna protested. "How terrible! As if all onus is upon the women folk! If that is the only truth, and women are only occupied with housework, when will they pursue literature or art? And how will they work for the betterment of the country, in that case?"

Malini added: "Look at all these magazines, 'Antahpur', 'Bharatmahila' and others…they seem to lose sleep over the household responsibilities of women. On one hand, they want to see them as progressive, educated humans, but on the other hand, they don't want to rid them of the shackles of domesticity. And look at those conservatives, how they are trembling at the mention of education for women! Writers like Pyarichand Mitra have already publicized that in ancient India, women were put on a pedestal of honour. If that is true, can you tell me why it is so dark in our inner quarters?"

"But Malini, since you seem to be so knowledgeable, are all the *memsahibs* in England free and happy?"

"At least they are happier and far more liberated than our own women folk, *Karta Ma*, but even they have their own woes, their own shackles of anguish and oppression. You know, one English woman Mary Wollstonecraft has created quite a furor in the community there for her writings on women's liberation. She has fearlessly stated that women must love their husbands and be their true companions, but they must never bow down to their oppressive machinery reprimanding them. Her husband, needless to say, has forsaken her for writing these, and the society around her has teased her relentlessly, but she remained steadfast in her dissent. Only recently, she has created a few followers among women who seem to adore her philosophy and opinions. *Karta Ma*, we think western ladies epitomize freedom and emancipation, but even they have questioned their own freedom! Where do we stand, in that case?"

"I don't understand half of your words, Malini! How

do you know what an English woman is writing in her own country while sitting here, thousands of miles away?" Sarada replied, amazed.

"Didn't I tell you that I have a magic spell with me? Tell me what you want to know about this world! I am unbound, time cannot chain me, and years cannot make me age. If you want to know about the classic epic writer, poet Kalidas, I might have been the flower-girl of his garden. In fact, my ability to predict future is so strong that I can foresee what your son Rabi will write in the future. Do you want to hear that, or about the secret stories of the *memsahibs*? Or do you want to know about the city of Kolkata two hundred years from now? Or else the tale of Vikram-Betal or 'Bamabodhini'?" Malini replied, with a tinge of mystery in her voice.

"Stop joking, Malini! Tell me, honestly, are these magazines like 'Bamabodhini' only teaching the curriculum of slavery to their women subscribers? But again, if the women folk forsake their housework absolutely, who will do them? To think of it, most of the English ladies are excellent housewives, competent in housework to the core. Isn't that something to imbibe too?" Gyanada said.

In Gyanada's dictionary, the art of housework was very significant, and she had transformed herself into an exponent of that art with years of constant practice. Her attention was equally distributed into all aspects of her household, her family. Her sense of dressing was impeccable; at the same time, she was the one who successfully balanced both the choicest attributes of Indian and Western culture to a delicious effect. She was phenomenal for keeping herself as well as her room prim and proper at all times.

Swarnakumari, on the other hand, was not a great

fan of household chores, and didn't care about maintaining perfection in housework like her sister-in-law Gyanada. She was of the opinion that housework was just a wastage of time, and she was destined for far more important things. She protested, in reply to Gyanada's words.

"Why *Mejo Bouthan*, why do we need to dedicate our lives to domestic work only because we are born as women? You know, I had received this book by Mary Wollstonecraft titled 'A Vindication of the Rights of Women' from Mrs. Smith, I read it and it opened new horizons for me. What a fiery writer, and what robust, seething, scorching words! I have heard that even she had to bear the brunt of the conservative English society for her writing. People opposed her dissent, boycotted her meetings and assemblies, her husband divorced her, yet she remained relentless in her stance, her opinions."

Gyanada joined in now. "Well, I also have heard about Mary and her works while living in London. The ordinary, middle-class English women were scared to hear her name and the men reacted in anger while anybody mentioned her. *Thakurjhi* (sister-in-law), you know, we are fortunate than her, our men are on our side, in fact they are the ones who are patronizing our quest of women's freedom. Mary, on the other hand, had to fight for her rights, even while living in the west. She had been ostracized by her society for ignoring her domestic jobs and writing, so I don't think 'Bamabodhini' has committed a grave sin, imploring on educated women not to ignore their domestic duties."

Malini intervened now. "Swarna didi! You know, there has been a small ripple in our community too. Only a couple of years back, a letter by Bama Sundari was published in 'Somprakash', regarding the dependence of women. It had clearly stated, let the women folk decide what they want to do."

This fueled fire inside Swarnakumari. She said: "Why does one need an educated woman to do the domestic chores that a maid or a servant can easily do? Why would all hell break lose if I chose to defy housework? Why would Bamabodhini advise me on my domestic duties, and why would I even listen?"

Malini was entertained immensely as the debate was in full swing. "But Swarna didi, listen," she said. "This is a new write-up which I want to share with you. There is this wonderfully entertaining conversation featured in 'Bamabodhini', a dual of words between the traditional and the neo-liberal woman, listen to it, please!"

****

The 'Bamabodhini' episode dragged on till noontime, and meanwhile, some of the ladies left. It appeared dull, boring to them. In the open space beneath the courtyard, the maids sat with a huge pile of fishes, working to cut them into pieces, removing their scales. Their job was done; now, the Brahmin cooks would prepare the lunch in the kitchen. Before that, the members of the household had enjoyed their breakfast with coconut *narus* (laddoos), yogurt with flattened rice, bananas and *batasha*, the sugary, sweet confection. The breakfast items were sent at the apartments of the male members in exquisitely made stone utensils. The children, who were the fussy eaters, were usually reprimanded, and even slapped by their maids when they refused to eat. This was never a department of their mothers, who had other things to care about. Each of these children were gifted with a set of dishes, bowls and glasses carved in white stone, products of Jaipur. Also, a silver bowl would be gifted to each of them for drinking milk. The maids would bring food for the children in those utensils, but the room for drinking milk was a different one. After some years, when those white stone utensils broke, they were replaced by black stone ones made in Munger. The servants and maids, Brahmin cooks and the clerks of the estate ate their meals in bell-metal and brass utensils. Those were the days when glass utensils weren't in vogue.

Malini enjoyed having her share of the delicious breakfast with all other ladies of the Jorasanko household. Content with her book-selling spree, she promised to visit Swarna Kumari's house the following week, just before leaving. Needless to say, the ladies would gather in her house on that day and chat incessantly, relaxing on Swarna's lavish *palanka* bed. Her bedroom, with the grand *palanka* happened to be a mecca of fun and festivities for her sisters, sisters-in-law, her nieces, and other women of Jorasanko. Their evenings were made vibrant and memorable with playing cards, reciting poems, reading from classics, endless chat along with scrumptious snacks. Malini, with her attractive repertoire of books, would add so much to the charm of such chat sessions. Just after one such session, the ladies brimmed with the excitement and possibility of another round of tete-a-tete with her.

The erudite males, the *Karta's* of the household, of course, never thought of giving any importance to such tete-a-tete between Malini, the bookseller woman and the Jorasanko women, which rejuvenated them time and again. Little did they know of their world of simple, mundane joys and sorrows. So, unbeknownst to them, Malini visited the ladies, igniting the light and fire of controversy and revolution in their souls.

Chapter 3

Enter Kadambari

'Only that day,

I remember the heroine of the play—

Holding a mirror to her face,

Her lips reddened with betel juice,

Her brain hatching conspiracies, with such grace!'

The boys of Jorasanko were enthused to perform a stage play titled 'Nabanatok' (The New Drama) in their family stage, under the able guidance and mentorship of their Jyoti dada. The boys were enacting female roles. Dwijendralal, the poet had composed a comical rhyme after watching the performance of Amritalal as the feminine Chandralekha, and needless to say, that had amused the performers of the play to such an extent that their laughter continued, unabated. The learned pundit Ramnarayan Tarkaratna had written this play with the goal to educate people about the miseries of the ritual of multiple marriages among Kulin Hindu Brahmins. The boys were beaming with excitement, given the opportunity to act. They were propelled by both Jyotirindra and Ganendra, representing both the mansions of Jorasanko. Jyoti didn't have the courage to include the women and girls of the household in such an endeavour, though they were extremely keen to participate. It was quite a daring act to involve the boys of the aristocratic gentry in the drama project, especially because the Bengali society was still confused about the difference between the 'jatra' sessions meant for the lowly, uneducated crowd and sophisticated theatre, meant for the discerning, educated audience. Jyoti and Ganendra were anxious about *Babamoshai*'s response towards this initiative, their labour of love.

Contrary to their fears, Debendranath was quite happy to hear the news and wrote a letter to his nephew Ganen with the following words: "It's heartening to know that your drama club has opened its door...Your hearts are brimming with joy, dancing to the ecstatic music of the orchestra in unison...there is a great sense of fulfilment and joy in savouring your poetic, artistic gifts and talents. You know, there has been a great lack of pure, unadulterated entertainment in our nation, and your endeavour will be a welcoming gesture to fill that void. But at the same time, let me also warn you with my affection and love, let not this gesture of entertainment turn into a vice."

Jyotirindranath was a great connoisseur of literature and arts, and had been trained formally in a recognized art school. He pursued his passions for writing poetry and plays with utmost sincerity. The handsome Jyoti performed the role of a beautiful 'nati' (dancer girl) in the play and mesmerised the audience with his flawless histrionics. They literally rolled on the floor laughing, witnessing his feminine demeanour and body language.

Neelkamal, a son-in-law of the Jorasanko Thakurbari

enacted the role of a 'nat' (male dancer), and another son-in-law of the Thakurbari clan, Jadunath, the husband of Sarat Kumari enacted the role of Chittatosh. His father-in-law Debendranath had a hard time coping with his daily tantrums. Quite often, this irresponsible fellow Jadunath would bring over his worthless friends and indulge in his drinking binges, avoiding his daily duties. In the initial days of their marriage, his wife Sarat Kumari didn't realize the importance of her husband as a fully grown human. Hence, she used to call him by his name 'Jadu' and was often reprimanded by her mother Sarada Debi.

In the play they performed on stage, the character Gabesh had two wives. The elder wife was played by Soudamini's husband Sarada Prasad, and Amritalal, son of the clerk of the estate of Jorasanko played the role of the younger wife. The audience was amused beyond words to witness their performance on stage. The comic rhyme of Dwijendra bore testimony to their ecstasy.

When such a play was being staged, it was unthinkable that this Amritalal's sister Kadambari would graduate as the auspicious Goddess Lakshmi of the Tagore household, coming from the humble home of one of their employees. There was no question of marrying off Jyoti at that time. He was immersed in his music, poetry and drama during those days, encouraged by his elder brother Satyen and his sister-in-law Gyanada.

One fine day, when they were all rehearsing their new drama in the sprawling verandah of the Thakurbari along with puffed rice and scrumptious fritters, Jyoti came along, panting, with a newspaper in his hand. "Look, the magazine 'Somprakash' has written this review of our play: 'Last Saturday, we went to see the new play, hosted by the drama club of Jorasanko, and we must admit, we were moved by the performances of the actors. The process of acting that we witnessed was unique, and if it is carried out with elan everywhere, it will turn into the purest means of entertainment for us. The props and the settings, the whole atmosphere of the play was executed beautifully, especially the ambiance of the sunset and dusk was created very aesthetically. The seating arrangements and the reception of the live audience, however, was tremendously lacking; with the door opening for just one time, all the audience members rushed in at once, and vied with each other to secure the front seats. This resulted in an ugly chaos, friction and terrible disruption. Finally, in terms of casting, the person enacting Sabitri seemed an extremely awkward choice, looking neither a woman, nor a eunuch...However, these little shortcomings notwithstanding, in our overall analysis, both the script and acting seemed superior."

'Somprakash' was a very significant publication; hence everybody was elated to receive a favorable review in such a venue. There was also a good review of the play in the nationally renowned papers. With such widespread appreciation, the crew members staged the play for as many as nine times in Jorasanko. But in springtime, during the Bengali month of *Falgun*, Satyendra went back to Ahmedabad, his workplace and took Jyoti along with him. In Jyoti's absence, the others felt demotivated and the production of 'Nabanatok', their play, stopped temporarily.

For the first time in his life, Jyoti had stepped outside the confines of the Thakurbari and its stifling aristocracy and explored yet another universe, a delightful one, in his sister-in-law Gyanada's domestic kingdom. When Satyen went out for work, it was the time of their blissful leisure, and they both used it with their keen interest in exploring new books and music, in their animated discussions on Shakespeare's plays. Jyoti was so enthused after reading Shakespeare's 'Cymbeline' that he even started translating it into Bengali. But after proceeding a bit, it occurred to him that it would be a better idea to write a Bengali adaption of the play, rather than just translating it mechanically.

"What would be the name of this play, *Mejo Bouthan*?" Jyoti asked Gyanada one day, reading out some parts from his adaptation.

"Why, you can name it Sushila, after the name of the heroine! I don't think the name of her father would be a good title, considering the audience of our country." Gyanada replied.

Jyoti mulled over the matter. 'Sushila' was not bad as a title, after all, but he thought if there were better options. In the original play by Shakespeare, Imogen, the daughter of King Cymbeline had married Posthumous, a man belonging to a lower caste. Cloten, the man whom her father had chosen for Imogen, left no stone unturned to estrange the lovers, in a desperate bid to win her heart. The union of Imogen and Posthumous was attained in the end, after a whole lot of strife, conspiracies and crisis situations, when King Cymbeline realized his mistakes. But then, if Imogen was the central protagonist throughout these developments, why did Shakespeare name the play after her father?

"Whatever be it, you can't name the play after the girl's father! Rather name it after the hero of the play, can you? You are so finicky about everything, *Natun Thakurpo*!" Gyanada said.

"Tell me, how does 'The Saga of Sushila-Birsingha' sound as the name of the play?" Jyoti asked suddenly.

"Yes, that sounds like an apt name, a combination of valour and grace! It will attract the interests of the audience, I'm sure." Gyanada was enthused.

The play was published in book form while Jyoti was still in Ahmedabad, in the month of March. He could feel the subtle touch of his dear *Mejo Bouthan* in every page, every layer of 'The Saga of Sushila-Birsingha'; the young playwright became fertile with thoughts and imagination galore, spurred on by Gyanada. Of course, Satyen's indulgence went a long way too, in shaping the minds of both of these avid drama lovers. In the midst of his work responsibilities in Ahmedabad, Satyen kept close contact with Ganendra in Jorasanko, writing letters to him frequently. Among his hundreds of other responsibilities, he willingly took upon himself the task of publishing this book of Jyoti, being the most progressive among the Jorasanko men. He was the unmistakable champion for all great causes, be it the education and empowerment of women, or the nurturing of his brother's talent.

When Jyoti had arrived in Ahmedabad, Satyen took great care not to hinder his brother's artistic and intellectual development in any way. He made Jyoti take sitar lessons so that his mind was filled with the untainted pleasure of music. He also hired a French tutor for both Gyanada and Jyoti for a few days. During their stay in Ahmedabad, they had started mixing with a couple of Parsi and Marathi families. Once, they went together to attend a party at Satyen's old friend Atmaram Pandurang's house in Bombay. There was a lavish party at his house, for the occasion of his daughter Anna Tarkhare's birthday. Gyanada wanted Jyoti to attend the party, to see how he would react in front of the multicultural, cosmopolitan crowd. It was a mixed crowd of *sahibs* and *memsahibs*, along with quite a number of aristocratic Indian families. With awe and admiration, they looked at the Marathi and Parsi girls, at their bright, confident faces, feeling in their hearts the stark contrast of these girls with the shy, timid Bengali girls who never stepped outside their inner quarters. Anna, the birthday girl mesmerized everyone with her unique beauty and intelligence. The quick-witted, smart Anna was still in the threshold of her girlhood, though she looked like a young woman in the way she dressed, and carried herself. There was no dearth of young suitors swarming around her, craving her attention, but she took a strange fancy for the newcomer Jyoti.

Anna came up to Jyoti, extending her hands towards him for a formal handshake. "My name is Anna. Are you Mr. Tagore Junior?" She asked, unhesitatingly.

Jyoti's soft, young heart, however, was more inclined towards the shy, reticent Bengali girls.

"Did you get any drink for yourself?" Jyoti asked this time, looking intently at the glass which Anna held in her hand.

"Why, don't you know? It's red wine! And why are your hands empty? Come on, have a drink!" Anna replied, with a mysterious sidelong look.

It should be mentioned here that drinking was never a taboo among the Tagore clan, but the sons of Debendranath were connoisseurs of pure, divine living. They loved to get intoxicated with reading the gems of poetry, not with drinking alcohol. Gyanada was watching Jyoti from afar, and could sense his hesitation quite well. She approached him now and said, gripping her hand: "It's truly strange that you aren't helping yourself with a drink, *Notun*. We are in a party, after all! Anna is right, let's go get some drinks." She pulled him by his hands, taking him to the cellar.

Anna followed them and asked Jyoti: "Would you like to have some scotch, or wine?"

Jyoti looked at his sister-in-law with questioning eyes and said: "You tell me what I would get, *Mejo Bouthan*."

"Scotch." Gyanada replied instantly.

But Anna had a different opinion. "Since you're drinking for the first time like me, have some red wine, Mr. Tagore Junior." She was rather frank and forthright.

Just then, Satyen's friend Mr. McGregor came to help himself with a drink. He glanced intently at Gyanada, enthralled by her youthful presence. "Oh look, how beautiful you are looking tonight!" He remarked.

Gyanada blushed to hear this. "Mr. McGregor, please don't make me feel embarrassed. There are so many beauties around!" She replied.

"But you are the most uniquely beautiful among them all, Mrs. Tagore! Your dress, your body, your words, everything about you is so beautiful! The epitome of true Indian beauty you are…Come on, let's dance! Please be my partner!" McGregor pleaded with Gyanada, holding her hand.

Jyoti's expressions changed rapidly, from amazement to annoyance, witnessing the scene. Why would a random stranger, a *sahib* dare to hold the hands of the bride of the aristocratic Thakurbari, and drag her by the hands? He looked around and saw Satyen, his *Mejdada* from afar, rather amused at the scene. Then, he took the step which he thought was right at the moment. He went to McGregor and forcefully severed the *sahib*'s hand from Gyanada's.

"Don't disturb her, leave her alone." He remarked, not trying in the least to hide his anger.

McGregor, on his part, wasn't ready for this sudden, random attack, as he didn't know Jyoti. "How dare you?" He asked, countering him with equal force. "Look, lady!" He looked at Gyanada and said: "If you don't like me, please tell me directly. But control your bodyguard first."

Satyen, watching the scene from a distance, got the inkling that things were going a bit too far now. He came up and hugged his younger brother Jyoti, trying to pacify his anger. "Mac, why are you so tensed? Listen, my younger brother is a bit possessive about his *Bouthan*, his dear sister-in-law. Please don't mind." He appealed to McGregor.

He pulled away the aggrieved, excited Jyoti from the scene and had a talk with him privately. "What hell will break loose if Mac wants to dance with Gyanada? Don't you know this kind of dance between males and females is part of Western culture? I know Gyanada is still a bit shaky about it, but she will learn to be easy with it soon. You too have to learn all this. In fact, we come to these parties to learn about these things. Why are you behaving like a frog in a well?"

Jyoti moved away to a corner, with an anguished mind. 'Why would we have to imitate everything about Western culture? Would *Mejdada* force his wife to dance with the *sahib*, even if she is unwilling?"

Pandurang, the master of the house started chatting and joking with McGregor, Anna and Gyanada in order to lighten the environment, seated with them in a sofa at the corner of the hall. Soon, Mrs. Pandurang joined them. She was dressed in a Kashmiri silk studded with stones, and wore a traditional pearl necklace. Gyanada was mesmerized by her presence, as always. Such a beautiful amalgamation of wealth and refined tastes, she thought to herself.

Gyanada had the pleasure of being hosted by this this aristocratic family when she had first landed in Bombay. Staying with the women of this Marathi family, she was deeply attracted to their sense of dressing, their make-up, the way they draped their saris. This was her first school where she learnt her first lessons of modernism. Pandurang's wife was an educated, fashionable woman, adept at mixing with *sahibs* and *memsahibs*, females and males equally. Their three daughters, Anna, Durga and Manik were being raised in Western culture and manners. Their family played a pioneering role in social reforms in the city of Bombay. In fact, the bold, feisty social reformer Pandita Ramabai was a regular visitor in their house.

Gyanada was always inspired by their gracious presence. But now, while chatting with them, her mind was filled with anxiety for Jyoti. Why did the boy turn hot-headed in the party? She knew her husband Satyen would scold her for this, once they went back home.

Thus, outside the extended family of Jorasanko, the seventeen-year-old Gyanada, the eighteen-year-old Jyotirindranath created their own pristine world with their common thread of art and culture, Satyendranath being their mentor. After pursuing the studies of English literature during her stay in Ahmedabad, Gyanada became keenly interested to study the gems of Sanskrit poetry. Even Jyoti, her brother-in-law didn't have much exposure in Sanskrit language and literature, despite studying English and Bengali in the Thakurbari. Inspired by Gyanada's keen interest in Sanskrit, he started studying classic Sanskrit poems and plays. In the evenings, when Satyen returned from work, the three of them started their literary soiree. Jyoti and Satyen took turns in reciting passages from Kalidas' classic 'Abhigyan Shakuntalam'. Jyoti's keenness to translate the play into English became stronger every day.

Meanwhile, Satyen was stricken with pain due to acute arthritis. One fine day, he said: "The pain is getting worse every day. I am thinking of taking leave from work and going to Calcutta for treatment."

Gyanada sounded anxious. "Wouldn't it be painful for you to be inside the steamer for fifteen days in such a condition?" She asked.

"Listen, there's some good news. There's no need to travel in a steamer now. The Bombay-Calcutta railways have started operating since October 11th, 1867. We can reach Calcutta in just five days now." Satyen replied.

As the Indian railways started operating, there was renewed enthusiasm and energy among people. Gyanada and Jyoti were extremely excited about the possibility of a unique experience. Spurred on by their keen interests, Satyen booked three rail tickets within a couple of days. He returned to their Jorasanko home along with Gyanada and Jyoti. However, upon reaching their ancestral home, there seemed to be no end to their frustration. Had the people of Jorasanko changed, or had Gyanada become so free-spirited while staying away from Calcutta for such a long time that she found adjusting with these people a tremendously difficult task? The various commands, injunctions of the house seemed to shackle her into subservience, impeding her free movements. She was having frequent conflicts with

Sarada Sundari, her mother-in-law. As a result, Satyen's treatment was not proceeding favorably, and moreover, he was not having adequate rest.

After a few days, Satyen sought the permission of his father Debendranath and moved away to another property, their beautiful villa in the outskirts of the city with his wife. This arrangement, he was sure, would heal him quickly, and his treatment would be carried out in an unperturbed way. Jyoti accompanied them both. Their literary meetings that had stopped abruptly after leaving Ahmedabad, grew wings again in this idyllic setting.

Meanwhile, in the Thakurbari, the cultivation of art and culture continued with full gusto. Neepamayee was pursuing her studies and vocal training, and also receiving training in instruments like *tabla* and cymbal under the tutelage of her master Benimadhab Babu. Hemen, on his part, was teaching her Milton's epic poem 'Paradise Lost' regularly, right after completing another classic, Kalidas' 'Abhigyan Shakuntalam.' Hemen's beloved wife Neepamayee was also trying her hands at painting, being trained by renowned artists from India and abroad.

The *memsahibs* came to the inner quarters of the Thakurbari, to teach English to the women and girls of the household and also to groom them. Maharshi Debendranath had sent his dear daughter Saudamini to the prestigious Bethune school, but after that, no girl of the Thakurbari was sent to school for formal studies. They were initiated into Homeschooling, and their studies were continuing much satisfactorily. Saburan Bibi was Gyanada's mentor in English, and she had learnt the language under her mentor's able guidance and tutelage. Sarat Kumari, her sister, on the other hand, was more interested in enhancing her beauty and culinary skills. Every day, she used a concoction of *maida* (flour) and *malai* (condensed milk) and applied it on her body with great care just before having a bath. Also, to enhance the beauty of her skin tone, she massaged her skin with Italian olive oil, mixed with imported alcohol which she got from her husband. Once, when her husband's friends asked the beauty secret of the women of Thakurbari, he replied: "milk and liquor" with a tinge of mystery in his voice. The women of the household were also adept at other necessary feminine skills, including sewing, nursing the sick, raising children, among others.

However, Swarna Kumari, the sister of Saudamini and Sarat Kumari was the only one who remained absent from this institution of good housewives. Just as before her marriage, she kept herself busy in her literary pursuits, shutting herself in her room. Reading Bankim Chandra's novels with intense passion, she dreamt of the day when she would be the first woman novelist of Bengal and create a literary cannon for herself. Malini, the bookseller girl came to her from time to time and stoked the fire within her.

Meanwhile, yet another marriage had been commenced within the premises of the Thakurbari. When Prafullamayee, Neepamayee's younger sister had come to meet her elder sister after her marriage, Sarat Kumari and Swarna Kumari adored her and started to plan their brother Biren's marriage with her. When they made the little girl dress up in sari and jewelry and brought her in front of Biren, the shy, timid boy fled from the scene. Deben Thakur was made aware of the proposal, and he readily agreed to it, and so, another girl of his friend Haradev entered the huge mansion of the Thakurbari, decked up as a new bride. Her groom Birendra, however, had signs of craziness. Maharshi, his father thought marriage would be a remedy to his son's abnormal behavior.

Immediately after Biren's marriage, Thakurbari was getting ready for his younger brother Jyotirindranath's marriage. Satyen and his wife Gyanada, however, were opposed to the idea, and Satyen had even shared his thoughts with Debendranath. "*Babamoshai*, why are you thinking of Jyoti's marriage so early? He is barely nineteen now, and such a young talent! I have plans to send him to England for further studies, so that he comes back as a refined gentleman." He pleaded to his father.

Debendranath, on his part, was extremely keen to marry off his son Jyoti. How long would he roam around from one part of India to the other, along with his *Mejdada* and *Mejo Bouthan*? He wanted Jyoti to be more responsible now, and marriage was the perfect way to make that happen. Talks about Jyoti's marriage with one of the daughters of Shyam Ganguly, an employee of Jorasanko Thakurbari, were floating in the air. The eight-year-old girl was a beauty, though illiterate till then. Such a match among known people was a blessing, or so Debendranath thought, hence there was no reason for delaying the marriage.

As for Gyanada, she didn't endorse the idea of such early marriage of Jyoti at all. This was the age to groom him, to nurture his talents. She dreamt that Jyoti would compose dramas, poems, articles one after the other, and she would be his muse, his inspiration in all his creations, while her husband Satyen would be his patron, his benefactor. In fact, hadn't they planned such a life while living in Ahmedabad? And if the marriage of Jyoti was such a necessity, wouldn't it be with an educated, fashionable girl of an elite family, well-versed in English, an England-returned, accomplished girl? She had such a girl in mind for her beloved Jyoti. It was the darling daughter of Suryakumar Goodiv Chakraborty, who had just returned from her stay in England. The girl was perfect in all respects—educated, accomplished, with a dusky complexion, but a pretty face. The girl had come to Calcutta then, and Gyanada invited her to the Jorasanko Thakurbari, so that the other women could see how beautiful she was. But to her dismay, Debendranath was the one who strongly opposed this match. Satyen's wife Gyanada had been more free-spirited than necessary, ever since she received her education and was living outside the Thakurbari. Debendranath was a bit annoyed and irritated to see her whereabouts these days. Ignoring Gyanada's proposal, he ordered to finalize Jyoti's marriage with none other than Shyam Ganguly's daughter.

Satyen had written to Gyanada from Ahmedabad: "If I were in *Notun*'s (Jyoti) place, I would have never agreed to this marriage alliance. How is this girl even considered as a bride of *Notun*, I fail to understand."

He also added: "I would suggest, if *Notun* has decided to go to England, it would be better if he goes without marrying. As for me, I am fortunate to have a gem of a wife, someone on whom I take a lot of pride...But if poor Jyoti goes to England for four-five years, marrying an unknown, stranger girl, would it be a good idea? Would he be able to accept an alien woman, almost uneducated, after he gets exposed to the Western culture? I know ours is a different story, but many of my friends and peers have suffered the same fate, after marrying."

As for Maharshi Debendranath, he didn't give much importance to Satyen's anxiety about his brother's life. Wasn't Satyen's wife herself a village girl from Jessore,

Bangladesh? Most of the brides of the Thakur clan had been brought in from remote villages of Bengal, but with the passage of time, with proper grooming and education, they became role models for all Bengali women. As for Shyam Ganguly's daughter, Debendranath had found her quite pleasant and bearing auspicious marks on her persona. He wrote to his son Satyen:

"We are fortunate to have found a good girl in all respects for Jyoti. You know how difficult it is to have people as guests for our weddings, because of the fact that we are *Pirali* Brahmins, and even the other *Pirali* Brahmins fear us because of our Brahmo identity and rituals. The future is in your hands, my son…in your generation, this narrow-minded vision of people will be a thing of the past."

Frustrated with his father's decision, Satyen wrote again to his dear wife:

"See how the Thakurbari is getting ready for *Notun*'s marriage. Remember how keen you were to be a part of his marriage ceremony? Now your wish is going to be granted. I am only concerned since I know Shyam Babu's daughter can never be a good match for Jyoti in any respect. I wonder how Jyoti himself had at all agreed to this marriage alliance… it seems strange to me."

The marriage took place anyway, after some days. Satyen and his wife's opposition to the alliance didn't alter the course of Jyoti's fate. On 23rd *Ashadh*, the third month of the Bengali calendar, the little girl Kadambari stepped inside the illustrious mansion of the Thakurbari, decked up in a vermilion-red *cheli*, adorned with heavy jewels. With her exquisite gold necklace and gold bangles, with heirloom *jorowa* ornaments in her hands and traditional earrings in her ears, with an anklet and toe-ring, and a key string tucked to her waist, and with a gold ornament in her head parting, she looked enticing, a demure, young bride. Most of the ornaments she wore were provided by Debendranath as her dowry, as was customary of the Thakurbari. Gyanada was anxious and apprehensive of the age gap between the bride and groom, since Jyoti was nineteen and Kadambari was barely nine years. She feared that her beloved brother-in-law wouldn't like an uneducated village dame. But contrary to her fears, Jyoti, the romantic soul, was enamoured by the little girl. He would groom her according to his whims and desire, he thought on the first nuptial night. If *Mejo Bouthan* had transformed herself from a village belle from Jessore to an epitome of aristocracy and grandeur, this girl could do it too. Also, when Rabi, the youngest brother-in-law of Kadambari, only two years younger to her saw her for the first time, she appeared in his eyes as a princess of the fairytales of his dreams. The little boy's heart and soul trembled with an unknown ecstasy as she saw her.

Debendranath's sons Satyen and Hemen were averse to this marriage alliance from the very beginning, and so, he entrusted his nephew Ganendra with the responsibility of the marriage ceremony, being in the Himalayas himself. Ganemdra got himself busy for days, getting new clothes for the young ones, and fancy shoes from stores, getting gifts and tokens of thankfulness for the matchmaker, the *kulin* Brahmins, the professors et al. And yes, this time there were a few esteemed Brahmin guests in the marriage. Debendranath, upon knowing this, insisted that this news gets published in the very popular 'Tatwabodhini' magazine.

But amid all this enthusiasm of festivities and fun, a pall of gloom shrouded the Thakurbari, which had been forming since quite some time now. Biren's madness has reached its peak, and the members of the household were scared, lest things went out of control. For quite some time, Debendranath had given him the responsibility of maintaining the accounts of the family, but as the days went by, he started showing signs of carelessness in the task. Gradually, when he started to avoid eating, her wife Prafullamayee took him to Bolpur, far away from the Jorasanko mansion, in the hope of his recovery. The other brides of the Tagore family—Neepamayee, Braja Sundari, and even Kadambari went along with them. Unfortunately, there was no sign of improvement of his health and behavior, even in Bolpur. Feeding him became a persistent problem. Often, he would survive only on a spoonful of rice and pointed gourd, resisting anything more. When they came back to Calcutta, a white doctor came to treat him. However, his disease remained the same.

This was the time when little Rabi's tryst with poetry had started, within the Thakurbari premises. Whenever he could, he would memorize the poems of his school syllabus and recite them to his mother, desperately craving for her attention. When he went inside the inner quarters where the women resided, weaving an excuse to meet his mother, he would meet his sister-in-law *Notun Bouthan*, a teenager close to him in age. A clandestine friendship was forged between the two, as they looked at each other's eyes furtively. Rabi's heart trembled with an unknown thrill and the secret pages of his diary filled up with numerous verses. His eyes scanned the glass almirah of *Notun Bouthan*'s room, the collection of her toys mesmerized Rabi. How he craved to chat with the mysterious young bride! But Barna didi, her elder sister was always with her, scolding her whenever he approached *Notun Bouthan* for a talk. Rabi envied the blessed fate of the girls. These days, they went to their tutor, *Guru Moshai* to study together, but when Rabi, Som and Satya were sent to the suffocating jail, their school, following their lessons, Barna and *Notun Bouthan* were privileged enough to go back to the paradise of their private dens. Whom would Rabi convey this sense of pain and anguish to?

Neepamayee, Hemen's wife took on the responsibility of grooming *Notun Bouthan*. She was rechristened as Kadambari after her marriage, wiping off her maiden name Matangini and her maiden identity completely. Neepamayee bought two books for her, 'Barna Porichoy' and 'Dharapat', both foundational texts, and started teaching her regularly. She was quite a diligent and meritorious student; it was discovered soon. Apart from studies, her training in housekeeping and cooking was also going on fine.

After a few days, Kadambari came close to Rabi, Som and Satya during their sacred thread ceremony. The boys were really coming of age now. Although the Thakurbari followed the Brahmo faith, all the rituals were maintained to the core. The boys' heads were shaved off, they wore gold *Beerbouli* earrings in their ears, and held the sacred *bilwa danda* in their hands, following the Brahminical tradition, while their initiation into the holy Gayatri mantra happened. While they begged for alms from their mother, their *Babamoshai* and other elders of the family, the alms collected were offered to Acharya Annanda Chandra Vedantabageesh, their revered pundit performing the sacred thread ceremony. And when the boys tasted the *habishyanno*, boiled rice with ghee after a whole day-long fast, cooked by none other than Kadambari, Rabi felt he was tasting the divine elixir from heaven. Never having the privilege of tasting food cooked by a woman in the inner quarters of Thakurbari till now, this opportunity overwhelmed Rabi. Fascinated by the incredible taste and flavour of the food, the boy's heart and soul was filled with gratitude for Kadambari, his *Notun Bouthan*. Kadambari, by now, had transformed into a mature, intelligent bride of the Thakurbari. With her natural housekeeping, culinary skills and her intelligence, she won the hearts of not only the boys including Rabi, but also the women of the household. From the evening of the boys' sacred thread ceremony, she was entrusted with the responsibility of cooking the *habishyi* (sacred rice) for the young, celibate *brahmachari* boys initiated into Brahminism for three days, as was the ritual.

Rupa, the girl who came to Sarada, craving for her affection, had now become her pet. She came to Sarada every afternoon, massaged her hands and feet, plucked her grey hairs and talked with Sarada endlessly. The girl was quite a chatterbox. Sarada loved the attention she received from the girl. When Rupa's nimble hands massaged her body, her eyes closed in slumber.

One day, she called Rupa and said: "Rupa, would you remain uneducated all your life? Wait, let me send you to the *Baithak Khana* hall for studying with the other girls. You'll take lessons from *Master Moshai*, the family tutor along with Barna didi, Rabi dada and *Notun Bouthan*. You are going to love it."

Rupa wanted to dance in glee, hearing her *Karta Ma*'s words. She touched her feet and replied: "You know, I don't like calling you '*Karta Ma*'. Why can't I call you Ma, like Barna didi does? Would you be angry with me if I call you Ma?"

Sarada felt strange to think how this orphan girl had entangled her with a nameless bond of love. Rupa had earned a place in her heart which her own biological children had never attained, simply because they never had the chance to be as intimate to her as Rupa was. Since she followed the tradition of aristocracy maintained by the Thakurbari and never nursed her own children with her milk, the physical bond between her children and herself had never been strong. But this young girl massaged her body every day and she felt as if she was her own blood, her daughter. At the same time, her gestures and her body language didn't have the bearings of sophistication like the other girls of the family. When she spoke, her unpolished rural accent reminded Sarada that she was different. Sarada decided she would change this. She wanted to see what Rupa becomes, once the glorious light of education and aristocracy of the Thakurbari enters Rupa's being.

"Listen, I am naming you Rupkumari from today. This new name of yours will rhyme well with Sukumari, Sarat Kumari, Swarna Kumari, Barna Kumari, my other girls, what do you say? Tell everyone your new name from today, even if *Master Moshai* asks, tell him you are Rup Kumari."

"But everybody knows I am Rupa. What if they still call me that?" The girl was visibly happy, but impatient and anxious.

"Let them do that…After all, Rupa can be your nick name!" Sarada tried to explain sensibly. This foster daughter of hers was quite a gem. Yes, 'foster daughter' was what Swarna and Barna, her own daughters called Rupa already.

"But remember, you must curb your wild ways and be more tamed from now on. If you want to remain my foster daughter, you have to learn to be polite, educated and well-groomed, just like my own daughters. You have to learn housework, cooking, and other skills…. you cannot waste your time in tomfoolery, the way you have done till now."

Though Sarada had a soft corner for Rupa, she knew the girl was an untamed horse. She would take all of Sarada's love and affection, but taming her wouldn't be easy. Raised at 'Kutum Mahal', the other side of the Thakurbari infested with lowly, uneducated folks, she never learnt to imbibe the good rituals and manners of a domestic life.

Sarada pulled the girl's hair tied in a braid, and said: "You have to be a good girl, have you understood?"

"What do the good girls do, Ma?" Rupa asked her. Sarada couldn't figure out if there was sheer innocence in the question, or a childish mischief. With all her determination, she promised to herself to tame this untamed horse, to be true to her name Sarada Sundari.

She replied: "Well, good girls are like my Swarna and Barna. They obey all words of their mother, do their household chores slowly and diligently. They take care of others, nurturing them, tending to them, yet never neglecting their studies. Haven't you heard the proverb: 'Goddess Lakshmi in beauty, and Goddess Saraswati in virtues and talent?' Haven't you heard another one: 'A home is blessed with happiness with a woman's virtues?'"

Rupa was a bit older now, and since Sarada indulged her more than ever, it sparked her courage and forthrightness. "Why would we girls always have to be tame, Ma? Why would we only slog and suffer, suffocated inside the four walls? Don't we also wish to spread our wings and fly away like birds in the sky? Have you ever thought, when men can always have wings and fly away wherever they want to, why are we women always wingless, powerless?"

Sarada was scandalized to hear this. Her own daughters would never speak like this, she thought.

"Wait, I will teach you a lesson or two about life...just wait!" She said to Rupa.

From the next day onwards, Rupa's initiation into studies and her grooming sessions started. She would be transformed—from Rupa to Rup Kumari, from a caterpillar to a butterfly with the passage of time.

As for Barna Kumari, she couldn't accept this 'foster daughter' of her mother Sarada, and the indulgence she was enjoying, sitting so close to her mother every single noon. She was also a regular presence at their home school at the *Baithak Khana* hall, studying along with them.

Barna whispered in Rabi's ears: "See how shamelessly this girl is accompanying us everywhere, such an unsolicited presence she is!"

Rabi, on his part, was totally unfazed by such happenings. His only concern was going to school every day, right after the private lessons with the family tutor ended. Barna didi was so lucky, wasn't she, retreating to the girls' den and its comforts after studies? The inquisitive soul that he was, Rabi had tried to follow Barna didi and *Notun Bouthan* till the inner quarters one day. He was tempted to chat for a while with Kadambari, his *Notun Bouthan*. But his cruel elder sister Barna didi drove him away, and he had to return to the servants' quarters where he was raised along with the other boys, dejected and sad. Rabi had decided then, that he would never side with Barna didi regarding the new entrant Rupa. Instead, he would try to befriend the girl, as she was his mother's pet. Why wasn't his luck as glorious as that of Rupa? He thought to himself.

Rabi tried defending Rupa. "She is just here to study with us, why are you behaving like this? She came here because Ma sent her…And remember, if you can take lessons from the tutor, anybody else can." She replied to Barna didi.

As for Rupa, she had understood early on that she would have to keeping fighting to claim her rightful place. She was living among these rich, pampered kids and it was difficult to complete with them. When Barna Kumari pushed Rupa, she pushed her in turn. They both made faces at each other, and Rabi giggled, witnessing the amusing exchanges between the two girls.

Kadambari joined the league of the boys when *Master Moshai*, their tutor came for their lessons. Their lesson for the day was 'Meghnad Badh Kavya,' the epic poem by Michael Madhusudhan Dutta. Undoubtedly an extremely tough poem, and it became all the more unintelligible to the students with the very difficult rendition of *Master Moshai*.

Rabi passed a sheet of paper to Kadambari. He wrote there: "What did you understand?"

The reply came almost instantly. "I understand that you are the demon Raavana and I am the captive Sita in the Ashoke forest, waiting for Raamchandra to release me from there."

'Why did *Notun Bouthan* imagine me as Raavana?' Rabi thought, bruised and insulted. 'Didn't she see any capability in me, which could make her think of me as Raam?'

Saddened and pained, Rabi tried to concentrate on *Master Moshai*'s teaching, avoiding Kadambari with all his might. But the silent smile of the mysterious young woman intervened with his iron determination to concentrate on his lesson.

Chapter 4

The Loner Woman (*Virahini*)

There were a few new rooms constructed in the third floor of Thakurbari. Gyanada had decorated her room and her private chamber in one of those living spaces. She placed an area rug on the floor, beautifully embroidered with flowers. In the corner of the room, she kept a small tool, over which there was a brass water-pot filled with a bunch of red roses. On one of the walls, a portrait of hers, created by Jyotirindranath hung with its majestic beauty. She sat unmindfully, immersed in thoughts, looking at her own portrait wistfully. In her hands, there was a bunch of letters addressed to her by the artist Jyotirindranath, for whom she was the muse.

The maid Bini *dashi* entered the room with a silver tray full of cut fruits. "Eat these, *Bouthan*. You need to be healthy and strong during this time." She ordered.

Gyanada was feeling lazy and sleepy. "Take these away, Bini. I can't eat fruits all day. Go and bring some tamarind pickle for me instead. Ask *Shej didi* for it, silently, so that nobody else knows."

Bini flashed an all-knowing smile. "I know, women crave for sour food, like pickles during this time of their lives. I also felt the same...*Bouthan*, chew some fruits, I say, it will nourish the little one in your womb. Let me run and grab you some pickle in the meanwhile. Ah, it would have been really good if you could stay with your parents now, but that is not customary in *Karta*'s house."

Just as Bini left, Jyotirindra stepped inside suddenly, like the Nor'wester wind. With a notebook in his hand, he sounded rather excited.

"*Bouthan*, would you care to listen to my latest composition? I wrote it just a while back."

Gyanada looked at his beloved brother-in-law's face with a bright, expectant face. "Ah well, did you find the time to come to me after all this while, *Notun Thakurpo*? I was thinking you forgot your old *Bouthan*, after having your new bride." What are you saying, *Bouthan*? You will never be old enough for me, but I'll have to give some time to Kadambari, since I married her, isn't it? After all, the poor girl has entered this mansion, leaving everything behind, and I am the one she depends on the most." Jyoti was visibly emotional as he spoke, holding the hands of Gyanada, as if pleading to her.

Gyanada stared at Jyoti for a while. He seemed to blush with the ardour of passion characteristic of a newly married young man, looking fiery and gorgeous. Her heart was overwhelmed with envy for a moment or two. Who was this Kadambari, coming out of nowhere, who was seated at the throne of her dear Jyoti's heart? But she reprimanded herself silently within seconds. Why was she thinking so ill of the new bride? After all, she couldn't bind her brother-in-law always with the *aanchal* of her sari, he needed freedom, a life of his own.

Often these days, in Gyanada's room, in her antique *palanka* bed, Jyoti and his sister Swarna Kumari would carry on their tete-a-tete sessions, with Kadambari, the reticent teenager girl sitting quietly in one corner of the bed. She stared at Gyanada, awestruck by her refined sense of dressing, her love for literature and arts. Gyanada, however, was visibly unresponsive to the presence of the new bride in her room. Kadambari felt awkward, thinking of herself as a misfit in such august company of illuminated souls. She made a silent promise to herself to learn all the good things of life that her husband had a liking for. She had to make herself worthy of his love.

At night, lying in the bed with her husband, Kadambari asked him one day: "You love your *Mejo Bouthan* a lot, don't you?"

Jyoti embraced his bride and replied: "Yes, it is true that I love her and admire her. But I love you much more than her, a hundred times more."

"She seems such a learned lady! I am an uneducated girl, I'm not worthy enough. I wish I could speak as eloquently as you both do!" Kadambari said, burying her face in her husband's chest.

Jyoti had the same desire, after all. He knew he would have to mould his bride according to his heart's desire. He kissed her ardently and said: "You know, you are like soft clay at this moment. But I will groom you to my heart's content and turn you to a doll of my desire. Wait for a few years, then everyone will look up to you in awe and admiration."

Gyanada sat in her room for hours and read her husband Satyen's letters intently. With deep interest and awe, she realized how the mundane everyday words were imbued with beauty and meaning in those beautifully written letters. She realized how her familiar husband was rediscovered by her in new avatars every time, with each new letter he wrote to her. Almost every day, a letter from him came to her like a whiff of fresh air.

"How are you now, Genu? By now, you might have understood how your remaining days would be like, far away from me! Who else is staying with you at night? Does Swarna and her husband Janaki sleep in the third floor? Also, do you have to eat alone in your room? Are the arrangements as per your expectations? Do let me know in details in your letter. Give my affection to *Notun* and tell him to write to me from time to time.

Sree Satyendranath Tagore

P.S. Sending you Neelkamal and Charu's photo for your album, as promised.

Sree S."

"Dear Genu,

You know, I met a blind Brahmo man at Allahabad, an intelligent, conscientious soul. He sang a few songs (Brahma sangeet) for me and they were quite perfect, if not in terms of the use of *raagas*, but in terms of their melody. He even seems to know the Upanishad, the religious Brahma texts by hearing them from others, and you will be amazed to know, he has memorized many slokas from those texts. I remember how much you dread the idea of blindness, but meeting this man, I got to know how much an individual can accomplish even without his eyes.

Anyway, I departed Allahabad on the morning of 26th and reached Jabalpur in the evening. Thank God I procured a novel from Charu to read on the way, and it helped ward off my boredom so effortlessly. Right now, I am immersed in the novel 'Oswald Cray' penned by Mrs. Henry Wood. It's an enjoyable read, commenting on the merits and shortcomings of the British society. The descriptions are quite engrossing in certain sections. I'm sure you will love reading it once you manage to get hold of the book from somewhere."

In reply, Gyanada wanted to know of Satyen's health. Wasn't so much of travelling tiresome and strenuous for him? She enquired. How was the pain in his foot? Did it get any better? Did he get a companion worthy of talking while travelling?

Satyen replied:

"I have reached Bombay within a week, staying in a hotel for now. It's much better than 'Adelphi' in all respects. By God's grace, I have found accommodation in a bungalow, not far from this hotel. Govind, my colleague and friend is putting up at another bungalow nearby...you know, he always advises me to send you to England, but that is impossible now, isn't it? We'll see what we can do later, what do you say, Genu? You know, today I enquired about my holidays. You'll be glad to know I am getting three months leave from 15th March. Tomorrow, I'll ask for the rest of the amount of my salary. For now, Ahmednagar will be my workplace. But honestly, I am still looking for the position of the Assistant Judge...I heard there is an opening in Pune."

Gyanada wrote to her husband:

"What food do you eat there, and how does the food taste? Can you please let me know about that? Did you get to eat adequately during travelling, or was that a pain? I detest this separation which you and me are suffering! I am so tired of it! God knows how much longer I'll have to stay without you…"

Satyen replied to his wife:

"Dear Genu,

No, I didn't have any problem regarding food while travelling. Yesterday when I reached Daspur just before the evening, I had a good supper with soup, meat and peach, and also other fruits. There were other food items with me, all packed nice enough, and I didn't have to open any of them. The heat of the sun was also not painful, in fact it was quite tolerable, and the best thing was that I got to travel all by myself, with a rather voluminous book as my sole companion. How long could a man live with a book alone? Anyway, I spent my time somehow, sitting, lying down and thinking in equal measures. Yesterday evening, when the moon rose, filling the sky with her feminine beauty, I remembered you, and then I gradually fell asleep when the sky became darker.

Who would have thought that this time, you and I would have to remain separated for a year? But that's what happened to us. Perhaps, some God had been angry with me, and cursed me like *Yaksha*, with the doomed spell lasting for an entire year. What to do now? You will have to wait this one year with patience, and thinking of it as an important duty ordained by God. Don't hesitate to ask for anything you feel would be necessary, and Janaki will bring it for you. If perchance you don't get it and it causes you pain or discomfort, do write to me and I will try my utmost to find a way to alleviate your pain. If you fall sick, you must let somebody know—if you hide your pain or sickness, it will result in unwanted harm. I have full faith on Rajendra Babu, he will take full care of you, I strongly believe. Whenever you feel like seeing him, just call for him."

Gyanada was delighted to know Satyen's travel stories through these letters, his lucid description of the places and the people he met in his journey amused her immensely. In one of his letters, Satyen described a black *sahib* he met during a dinner party.

"You know, I met this black man, and felt he was quite like a 'firangi' in his attitude and manners. He didn't seem to like anything of this country. Nor did he seem to have any taste for Indian cuisine. Roasted beef and beer seemed to be the staple diet of this obedient slave of Queen Victoria. Living away from his father, he expressed his fascination for the climate of England; the dirt and smoke, the mist and cloud of London seemed immensely pleasurable to him. On the other hand, he detested the climate, the heat and the scorching sunlight of our country. We were so irritated and annoyed to hear his words! On our part, we went on criticizing England and its people to our heart's content, and spoke unabashedly about all the evil customs of the English society. He sounded somewhat embarrassed, listening to our discussion!"

During her stay with her husband, Gyanada had met Mrs. Oliphant and became a good friend of hers. In a letter to her husband, she enquired about the lady, and Satyen replied, after meeting his wife's friend:

"You will be glad to know that I had my 'tiffin' with the Oliphants today. Mrs. Oliphant was asking about you a lot—whether you had learnt horse riding, whether you liked living in Calcutta. You know what I replied to Mrs. O? I told her: 'If you had taught her horse riding while in Ahmedabad, she would have learnt it well by now... but it is impossible to do it now, in Calcutta.' And I also told her that you would have loved Calcutta more if you could have the freedom to live there according to your heart's desire. I explained to her the way we live with all the members of our family together, within the structure of joint families. Perhaps you had told Mrs. Oliphant about Soudamini, hence she was asking if you get to meet her often in Calcutta."

Gyanada felt stifled, anguished amid the august gathering of the Jorasanko mansion. She knew that during her pregnancy, she shouldn't be worrying about everyday affairs, but from time to time, she was overwhelmed with unexplained anxiety. Was her position in the household threatened with the arrival of Kadambari, the new bride? Why was Jyoti, her dear brother-in-law giving that uneducated little girl so much importance? Even little Rabi too was seen to roam around *'Notun Bou'*, following the girl everywhere she went. Perhaps he was attracted to her new attires, the glittering appeal of her jewellery might have caught the boy's fancy. How would this girl be a befitting companion to the bright, intellectual soul that Jyoti was? Jyoti's mind and soul had been elevated to a lofty level, by virtue of his cultivation of the arts, his refined grooming; how would she ever reach that level? Gyanada felt amused to think that, even as she felt a tinge of pity for Kadambari.

She had started to feel claustrophobic within the confines of the mansion, with the other brides and the girls. However, she was learning new skills these days, like taking

English lessons, sewing clothes for the soon-to-arrive little guest. Her days passed in a slow, leisurely pace, reading Bengali and English novels, and also her husband's letters.

Jyoti had taken his wife Kadambari to Bolpur for a change of climate. In a letter to her husband, Gyanada requested him to arrange for a house where she could stay for a while, outside of Jorasanko. This request perplexed Satyen's mind. How could he offer freedom to his wife from the confines of the four walls of the Thakurbari? In such a delicate state of her health, he couldn't send her off to live alone in another house.

"Dearest Gyanada,

I know you are passing your days with utmost difficulty, and I am anxious for your health and wellbeing. Yesterday, a letter from you arrived along with a picture of *Babamoshai*, and I felt somewhat relieved to receive it. I can understand your ardent wish to live near the river Ganges...but is it possible for you to arrange for a house near Jorasanko? It is important that someone from our family stays with you at all times now, and also, the Doctors can attend you whenever necessary. As you know, you'll have to be very cautious in your current state."

In another letter, Satyen wrote to Gyanada:

"I couldn't decide what to do regarding your wish to stay in a separate house, Genu...I believe *Babamoshai* will be coming home in a few days, and I really don't know what his opinion will be in this matter! Moreover, you cannot stay in a shabby alley among lowly, indecent people. You know how difficult it is to get a decent house these days in a sober, polished Bengali neighbourhood.

What do you say, Genu? And what about *Notun Bou*

Kadambari's photo I had requested you to send? It didn't arrive me yet."

Satyen, on his part, was keen to see the new bride, *Notun Bou*'s photograph, and he wrote about it in every letter. Gyanada, as usual, would forget about it every time. It was not difficult to call photographers and request them take pictures these days; they came to the inner apartments of the Thakurbari every now and then to do the same. But this girl, Kadambari had become her arch rival ever since she made her entry in the mansion, snatching away her childhood friend Jyoti from her. She felt lonely, dejected. She didn't wish to comply with her husband's wish and send him Kadambari's photo.

Meanwhile, Satyen gave her news of his buying a new Tonga, getting a pet dog in his new Bungalow. He wrote to his wife:

"You know, I forgot to let you know, I have got a cow recently, and yesterday, she has borne an adorable calf. I've heard she produces milk and is worth Rs. 50. Can you suggest a name for her? Didn't you have a cow named Lakshmi in your maiden home whom you loved dearly? Then let this cow be named Lakshmi too, what do you say? I haven't received your letter for two days now, and hence I'm worried. How is your health, is it any better now?"

Satyen was a bit overwhelmed financially, having to maintain his expenses in two establishments. Though Gyanada was staying with his extended family in Jorasanko, he had to pay the tuition fees for her English lessons with a Memsahib teacher, for her books and other items. Deben Thakur had some reservations in offering pocket money to Satyen since he was already working and he believed, was also earning a handsome salary. But then, Satyen knew how important that pocket money was for Gyanada herself. Satyen, in a letter to his father, appealed to him not to discontinue giving him the pocket money. It was his right as a son to receive that amount from his father, irrespective of his work status. He wrote to Gyanada again:

"I have to let you know it's uncertain whether I can send you some money next month, as you know the kind of expenses that I had to bear recently. Probably in August, I can send you Rs. 200 or 300. You might get some amount from Jadu and also meanwhile, if *Babamoshai* sanctions your monthly allowance of Rs. 100, I have requested Janaki to give you that amount.

I am also hoping I would get promoted to the position of the Assistant Judge. There is a possibility that I might get it soon. I assume it would be published in the Gazette which is forthcoming.

Sending you all my love and affection and showering my kisses on you."

Gyanada was somewhat envious of her husband Satyen's free, uninhibited lifestyle in his new dwelling. He was leading a beautiful life with his friends and peers at work, partying and merrymaking with them, making his sojourns to new, exciting places. She should have accompanied him to all these places, but now, the pregnant Gyanada was stuck to this wretched, old-fashioned Jorasanko mansion. Satyen had found a new job as an assistant judge at Ahmednagar, with a monthly salary of Rs. 650. Every evening, he had to attend formal meetings at the residence of some or the other *sahib*. He had been introduced to so many *memsahibs* that within such a short span of time that he couldn't remember any of their faces. He wrote:

"There are too many *bibis* that I have met here…it's as difficult to recognize each of them in just one meeting as it is to differentiate one sheep from the other among a herd of sheep. It is easier to remember the ugliest, or the most beautiful among them, though. And you know, the pressure of work is not a big nuisance here, so there's some leisure to read as well."

Gyanada received Satyen's letter every day.

"*Amchi* Genumoni,

It is truly irritating and annoying to stay alone for such a long time. I finish my breakfast after 10 am and then leave for office around noon. After working for 2-3 hours there, I return home to have some tea and then, in the evening, I take a walk, strolling around the city for some time. Yesterday, I tested my walking a bit, to check how far I could go. You know, I wasn't feeling too tired even after walking for a mile. I think I will have to increase my walking miles gradually. Nights are always peaceful here, and I am sleeping well almost every day…and moreover, there's no need of mosquito nests here, as there are no mosquitos around. How much longer do you think it will take for you to come here?

…You and me are living apart for such a long time! It feels like numerous days, months, ages…"

Some days later, in another letter, he expressed his indignation and frustration.

"I don't like anything much these days…Almost always, I feel irritated with myself, irritated with the people here. I don't feel like mixing with anybody. There are regular places to meet with the British people—Gymkhana, Band Stand, but even when I go to these places now, I do not go there by my own will. I cannot seem to stand the artificial, pretentious behavior of the *Bibis* any longer. As the days are passing, my belief in the inherent differences between us and the British is getting solidified, and I know this difference will never obliterate. If there is any gesture of uniting, that is only verbal, and superficial. You can say that I didn't think in this way while living in England. But my thoughts have transformed now."

One late night in the Bengali month of *Ashwin*, Gyanada went into labour, and Sarada called the *dai* (midwife) for the delivery. The old midwife demanded extra money for being called at such an untimely hour, and later agreed to, when she was given eight rupees for the night. The delivery room was a makeshift one, prepared at one corner of the courtyard. After the delivery, the *dai* severed the baby's umbilical cord from the mother's and came out with the newborn in her arms. 'It is a baby boy,' she announced. Hearing the news, the ladies of the house welcomed their new male member by blowing conch shells and by ululating. Upon seeing her new grandson's face, Sarada happily gave away a new *dhonekhali* sari of hers and plenty of sweets to the *dai*, before she left.

Early next morning, a wet nurse and a *dhaima* (caregiver) were summoned to the Thakurbari. The birth of babies in the Thakurbari was almost a daily phenomenon, so they had their fixed *dudh ma* (wet nurse) and *dhaima*, who worked in shifts and tended to the newborns. But this time, something seemed wrong since the start. The newborn, while suckling on the breasts of the *dudh ma*, cried and shrieked continuously.

Gyanada became restless as the baby's wails and cries continued. 'Why is he crying so much? Is he feeling pain in his stomach, or is he feeling some other kind of pain?' She questioned. She tried to comfort her newborn son by taking him away from the *dhaima* and placing him in her own lap, but he continued crying and shrieking. The British doctor came to examine the newborn and prescribed some medicines. However, the baby looked fainter and feebler after the medicines were given.

After two days of constant crying, the newborn baby boy took shelter in death's cold arms, and not a soul was able to understand why he couldn't survive. Gyanada, dumbfounded in shock, sat with the tiny, lifeless body of her firstborn the whole night. The tears in her eyes had dried up, she had turned into stone with the sudden onslaught of the tragedy.

She received her husband's letter a few days later. He had written:

"Dearest Gyanada,

On 11th October, Janaki in his letter had informed me about the birth of our first child, our son. But today I received your letter written on the 13th, when you wrote about his tragic death. Nobody is to blame for this mishap, neither the doctors treating you, nor you. We have to accept the eternal truth that birth and death, both are in the hands of destiny, we cannot control any of it. We can only try to follow certain rules of living, and that is our essential duty. Now once you regain a bit of your strength…in a month or two, you can try to come here and stay with me. Please keep informing me about your health from time to time, and once I know that you are doing well, I can arrange for your journey."

The distraught Gyanada was taken away from the

Jorasanko mansion during this time. For some days, a farmhouse in Peneti had become her new accommodation. Jyoti, Sarada Prasad, Hemendra, Soudamini, her brothers-in-law and sisters-in-law lived with her as her companions in that new abode. The river Ganges flowed very close to the new house, and they wondered if that would provide some solace to the bruised heart of Gyanada. She shed tears for the first time after losing her firstborn in this very house.

Jyoti, Gyanada's favorite brother-in-law proved himself as her true companion amid these trying times. He had even left his wife Kadambari in Jorasanko, so that he could give his *Mejo Bouthan* constant company. They would sit together on the banks of the Ganges and pass their time, looking at the serene beauty of the river.

Meanwhile, in the garden of Konnagar, situated on the other side of the Ganges, Gunendra and his family had settled in. Gunendra belonged to the extended family of Jorasanko, and even after the original mansion was partitioned into two separate houses, Guno and Jyoti's friendship remained unperturbed. Both of them were first-year students at the Art School of Bowbazar. During the evenings, when the boats ferried the passengers from one side of the Ganges to the other, they sent signals to each other by firing their guns. It was their characteristic way of communicating with each other.

Gunendra had a fancy for everything artsy and beautiful. With a natural flair for the arts, he would collect precious artefacts from all over the world. He had decorated his wife's mirror, placing a flower vase in front of the mirror with a bunch of crystal tulips in it. Every time his wife's reflection fell over the mirror, the tulips smiled with all their glory along with her smiling face.

The garden of Konnagar was also filled with bounty of the other members of the Thakurbari clan. People from all stations filled the space there. Once, a barber brought along a baby squirrel, and also a nest of the *Babui* bird. The 'bahurupi' (polymorphic) dancers came to dance and perform with their troupes.

The women of the house supervised the cooking in a small room outside the verandah. And beneath the jackfruit tree, the men, including Gunendra, Jyoti, Jadunath assembled, seated on a bedstead. In their assembly, the men entertained themselves in various creative ways. Sometimes, they would listen to fun-filled songs performed by young local singers. One such song sung by a local performer had very interesting lyrics, commenting on the ways of a *sahib* named Blackwar who rode a horse and traveled till the neighbourhood of the milkmen to get milk for himself. Jyoti and Gunen couldn't control their laughter upon listening the song.

One day, Jyoti and Gyanada were seated on the banks of the river Ganges, and Joyti was reading out to his sister-in-law his translation of 'Shakuntala', the Sanskrit play by Kalidas. Gyanada's heart was filling up with joy again after a long time, listening to the incredibly beautiful flow of language, rhythm and cadence of Jyoti's composition. Just then, Hemen, Jadunath and Sarada Prasad joined in.

As Jyoti paused his reading after a while, Jadunath asked him: "Brother, your poetry is mesmerizing! But who is the muse, the inspiration behind this creation of yours?"

As for Gyanada, she knew the answer only too well. Every pore of her being was connected to this composition of Jyoti; it was her exquisite presence that refined Jyoti's pen, but that was not for the world to know and talk about.

Sarada Prasad commented: "Why are you bugging the poor fellow? Don't you know that the contours of Shakuntala in his heart is carved in the image of his new bride, Kadambari?"

With a red, flustered face, Jyoti told them that he wanted to discontinue reading his translation to such mindless folks. He was visibly embarrassed. Hemendra, Jyoti's elder brother was a serious fellow. He left the scene immediately, noticing his embarrassed younger brother. But Jadunath kept on dancing and frolicking, teasing Jyoti with the name of Kadambari. Gyanada was annoyed beyond words. She felt as if Kadambari was the showstopper this time too, even being physically absent in this trip.

Gyanada had been the queen bee for all these days, wherever she went. Erudite gentlemen from her own land and also from foreign lands surrounded her, awed and amazed by the beauty of her persona. Mr. McGregor seemed to have a special fascination for her, choosing her among the other beautiful ladies at the dinner parties in Ahmedabad and Bombay, appreciating her beauty in exquisite words. He never chose any other dance partner in those parties, when Gyanada was around. Even Satyen, her own husband was so proud of her always. And Jyoti, her brother-in-law treated her as an asset. But now, at the bank of the Ganges, she suddenly felt as if she was not the nucleus of attraction any more. It was somebody else. Her near and dear ones had come here to comfort her, give her some solace after the loss of her child. Jyoti had come to give her solace too, and he hadn't brought along his new bride Kadambari. But she knew Jyoti had left his soul in Jorasanko, in the *aanchal* of his wife Kadambari's sari.

Gyanada wanted to move away, far away from these

petty conversations. The discussions sounded annoying and meaningless to her; she broke away from the gathering and walked a few steps forward to absorb the boundless beauty of the river banks.

In the magical twilight hour, Jyoti looked at the mysterious, beautiful woman walking slowly towards the river, drenching her feet in the water. For a few fleeting moments, he wondered who the woman was, her dear *Mejo Bouthan* or the Shakuntala of his play. It felt as if she would lose the ring from her finger in the water, just like Shakuntala.

Some time later, Jyoti followed her and came close to the river. He placed his hand gently on Gyanada's back and said: "*Mejo Bouthan*, let's go home and play some music. You'll be catching cold here."

Gyanada held Jyoti's hand and replied: "*Notun*, let's get back to Jorasanko...I don't like staying here any longer."

Jyoti was relieved to hear this. After all, it was in Jorasanko that his new bride was, he felt a strong pull towards home.

A few days after they came back to Jorasanko, Gyanada boarded a steamer and went away to Bombay to live with her husband in his workplace. Janakinath and Sarada Prasad, her two brothers-in-law accompanied her in the journey.

......Gyanada received each and every news of Jorasanko while living in the far western India. Jyoti had composed a satirical play titled 'Kinchit Jolojog' and published it anonymously. She was amazed to know that he had presented the emancipation of Brahmo women in a demeaning, satirical way, which had raked up enough controversy in the magazines and journals of Calcutta.

Satyen, her husband was visibly dismayed at the news, while reading out a review of the play published in the magazine 'Dharma Tatwa.' The reviewer in the magazine had clearly stated that in the play, the playwright had openly cursed the preachers of Bharatashram, Brahma Mandir etc. The reviewer also wrote in details how the playwright presented the Brahmikas (Brahmo women) in a derogatory light. "This only reflects the lowly, perverse mindset of the author/playwright. We are shocked and surprised to know that the author is nobody else but the son of most revered chief Acharya of the Calcutta Brahmo Samaj."

Gyanada seemed very annoyed to know of it all. "I can't even imagine how our dear *Notun Thakurpo* can even think of composing such a terribly misogynist play! I can't seem to think how he has satirized the act of men and women sitting together in the assembly for praying! How low has he stooped after marrying that lowly girl, Shyam Ganguly's daughter! What a shame!"

Satyen said: "And see how Bankim Chandra is adding fuel to the fire, writing a positive review in the 'Bangadarshan' journal. Even Radhakanta Deb has called Jyoti and staged the play in his 'natmandir.' You know, the satire titled 'Eke-I Ki Bole Shobhyota' by Madhusudan Dutta and 'Kinchit Jalajog' was staged together in the same hall this Saturday."

"Why at all did Jyoti join the league of the conservative chauvinists?" Gyanada was amazed. "You know, I think *Notun Bou* Kadambari is brainwashing him with all this nonsense. This is why I insisted on Jyoti marrying an educated girl. I don't understand why *Babamoshai* objected to it, now let him face the consequences of his blunder... Jyoti has used the power of his pen against his own father."

"But let me tell you, our Jyoti was a bit strange from the very beginning." Satyen replied. "Genu, don't do remember, when we went together to the Maidan area in our horse carriage, Jyoti always expressed his discomfort? Remember, he didn't allow you to lift the curtain of our carriage? When we convinced him finally about lifting the curtain, he demanded a fully closed carriage for the girls. You know, if he would see you roaming freely like this in an open carriage, he would probably wish to die of shame! As for his own wife, he would probably stifle her within the four walls, like the old days of our foremothers!"

"Then call him here, to stay with us. Once he is in our company, the fog in his mind will clear up on its own. Can't he see how courageously we, the women are treading our paths? Then why would someone as talented as Jyoti lag so far behind?"

"Well, you can't call him alone, I believe...not any more. You'll have to call him together with *Notun Bou*. Would you like that?" Satyen asked. He knew how strongly Gyanada disliked Kadambari, hence this comment.

Alas, who would save the moon from the *Rahu*, the wicked planet, about to eclipse it fiercely? Who would save her dear brother-in-law from the unenlightened soul of Kadambari? The lunar eclipse was there to stay now. Gyanada became silent, immersed in profound agony.

Chapter 5

Swarnakumari's stay in Bombay

Swarnakumari was fifteen now. Gifted with the ravishingly beautiful features characteristic of her Thakurbari clan, she also had a fiery spirit that shone through her presence. She had accompanied her Jyoti dada to a couple of poetry meets in the city and her presence had created quite a stir within the circle of the young poetry afficionados. Young poets crowded the poetry meets to have a glimpse of the slender, fair-skinned beauty who happened to be an accomplished poet already.

One day, Swarna came to a poetry meet at an aristocratic house in Sovabazar, decked up in an exquisite patola silk sari, in a three-tiered pearl necklace. However, the small, dainty hat she wore and the pearl ornament she wore in her forehead were the real showstoppers. Rumours and stories started spreading around; Swarna herself chanced upon some whispered talks.

"Look at her! Are we supposed to ogle at her dress and ornaments, or listen to her poetry? You know, she is the mother of a daughter, and also a poetess!"

Another voice replied: "Don't tell me to believe that all those poems are really penned by such a flamboyant, fashion-conscious woman. I bet her elder brothers write those poems in her name. Can you think of women and literature in the same breath? What else should we have to witness in this *Kali yug* (modern age)?

"If that is the case, her writings might have been published due to her beauty and attractive looks…Imagine the editors getting smitten by physical charm!"

"*Arrey*, don't you know, these editors are just waiting to get some prasad offerings from the illustrious Thakurbari! Vidyasagar Babu has introduced female education to the world, and Deben Thakur, inspired by him, wants to raise his daughter as an esteemed author! If women like Taru Dutta, Jane Austen can do it, then why not the daughters of the Thakurbari?"

Swarna felt like crying out loud in despair, listening to such cheap, derogatory words about herself. Didn't they value her continued dedication towards literature one bit? When the others praised her effusively, she was shocked to hear the negative remarks of these handful of critics.

She gripped her Jyoti dada's hand in the midst of the meet and said: "Let's go back home. It doesn't seem the people are liking me enough here."

Jyoti was surprised at his sister's reaction. "Why leave so soon, dear? See, everybody is praising your poetry so much! Who stuffed your brain with negative thoughts?" He asked.

At that very moment, the crowd came forward to support Jyoti's words. The ones who were criticizing Swarna some moments back, came up to her and said: "Why, if you go away, this meeting will be dark and meaningless! The people of England are blessed to have their own George Eliot, and we are blessed to have you... In fact, the other women who write articles and columns in the 'Bama Bodhini' magazine are no writers at all!"

Swarna couldn't stand such shameless hypocrisy of these people. She protested: "Please do not comment so harshly. Those women are trying to work amid many obstacles, and many of them write well. And I am a beginner in the writing world, just like them..."

"Don't compare yourself with them..." One of them said, belittling all those women writers.

Jyoti expressed his irritation at these disturbing voices. The organizers of the program took strict action and some of them were taken away from the meet. The poetry reading started after this brief fiasco.

...................There were two festivals in the Thakurbari—the naming ceremony of Swarnakumari and Janakinath's baby daughter and the marriage of Barnakumari, Swarna's sister. Everyone was in a festive spirit. It was a tradition set by Deben Thakur to observe the naming ceremony and 'annaprashan' (rice-eating) ceremony within six months to a year of a baby's birth. The rice-eating ceremony was named 'annaprasan' by the employees of his office, not by Deben Thakur, who didn't follow the names of the Hindu rituals.

The naming ceremony of Swarna's daughter was observed with much pomp and grandeur at the farmhouse of Peneti. In fact, after Rabi's birth, the naming ceremonies were observed in a grand way, following the Brahmo rituals. During the day of the ceremony, the name of the baby girl 'Hiranmayee' was carved in a low wooden stool.

An intricate *alpana* pattern was drawn, surrounding it, and the children of the house lit candles and placed them around the wooden stool, following Debendranath's instructions. It created a divine ambience, and Swarna, overwhelmed with the scene, felt as if *Babamoshai*'s blessings were being showered on her daughter's name.

Janakinath felt sad, though, thinking of the absence of his estranged parents. 'It is such an honour to be blessed with a bride like Swarna,' he thought, 'but my father never realized it. Wouldn't he come to see his granddaughter too?'

Deben Thakur had sent a heavy gold necklace to his wife Sarada as a token of his blessings for his dear granddaughter. There were also the exquisite white stone utensils from Jaipur, a family heirloom which was their prized possession. The maternal uncles and aunts blessed the child with gold ornaments in abundance, and also with soft silk for sewing the baby's clothes. Hiranmayee was a beautiful, delightful baby, playing in everyone's lap in turns.

As the guests left after the ceremony, Swarna and her husband Janakinath sat at the banks of the river, enjoying the mellowed rays of the sun. Hiranmayee was seated in her mother's lap.

"You cannot imagine how happy I feel today, Swarna!" The proud father Janaki said. "But it's just the absence of my father which I feel strongly, even amid such joy."

"But will you love only your daughter from now on? Will your affection for me cease to exist?" Swarna complained, like a pampered child.

"Swarna, I've left my mother, my motherland for you! Now, if you ask me to leave my daughter too, I won't be able to do that. Don't take any more test of my love, my dear!" Janaki replied, in good humour.

"Ah, I know all about your love…Weren't you telling me you would send me to Bombay to live with *Mejo Dada* and *Mejo Bouthan*? Don't you like to live with me anymore?"

"But…Swarna, it's only for a couple of years, the days will pass in the blink of an eye! And imagine the comfort you will cherish in your brother's company… I am the one who will suffer alone! But when you will come back after two years, with your refined, aristocratic new avatar, my heart will be brimming with so much joy! It gives me so much pleasure to think of that day…"

"Well, you conspired with *Mejo Bouthan* about all this, didn't you? But how will your dreams be materialized? Wouldn't I have to look after our daughter? How would I have the time to groom myself the way you are dreaming?"

"Please leave that to *Mejo Bouthan*, Swarna! I am sure, once she herself has taken your responsibility, she will arrange for everything flawlessly!" Janaki assured his wife.

"And you admire *Mejo Bouthan* so much, you have this irresistible desire that I became an exact replica of her! But once I am at my own writing table, I am a different, unique persona. Don't you notice that?" Swarna asked, her heart heavy with emotions.

Janaki pulled his wife and baby daughter closer to him and said, laughing: "You are merely a child, Swarna. You are still a pampered doll of your *Babamoshai* and elder brothers, haven't matured a bit still…But let me tell you, this childish heart of yours is what attracts me the most!"

"Then why are you sending me so far away? I hate to stay away from you!" Swarna complained.

"You know, you are just a raw, uncut diamond, fresh from the mine, but once you will be groomed by *Mejo Dada* and *Bouthan* in Bombay, enhance your education and learn to carry yourself like an aristocratic lady, you will be transformed into a priceless Kohinoor!"

"And will that Kohinoor be the glory of your crown only? That's not done, mister! Just wait, I'll call for a *swayambar* party and choose the new love of my life in that party." Swarna giggled as she said.

"And let me be the watchman of that *swayambar* party of yours!" Janaki laughed out loud. The baby Hiranmayee resting in her mother's lap, got scared to hear that roaring laughter and started to cry. When they were unable to pacify her even after repeated attempts, the new parents summoned the *dai*, the elderly caregiver and handed her the crying infant. Janaki and Swarna sat close to each other by the river banks for a while and looked at the boats sailing at a distance. With wistful eyes, they watched the dusk arrive, and the oil lamps fueled by castor oil lighting up inside the boats.

Soon after the naming ceremony of Hiranmayee, the wedding ceremony of Barnakumari happened in November, and quite naturally, became the talk of the town instantly. This time, Deben Thakur was fortunate to have a brilliant student of the Calcutta Medical College as the groom of his beloved daughter Barna. Satish Chandra, the groom belonged to a respectable Brahmin family, with his ancestral home in Goswami-Durgapur. Married to a girl from the *Pirali* clan, this boy was severed from his family too, and took shelter in the loving cocoon of the

Thakurbari. After their marriage, his father-in-law started taking care of his expenses in the medical college. Maharshi Debendranath was also determined to send him to England for his coveted medical degree, once the time would come. Arrangements were made for a spacious room with ample light and air, in which Barna and Satish, the new couple would live from now.

During those days, in the Bengali year 1870, tap water technology was used for the first time in Debendranath's bathroom. Those were the days when such technology was in its nascent stage, and the clean, filtered water of the Hoogly river was brought via Palta to the Jorasanko home with the help of a water pipe. The children and the elders were unanimously amazed and ecstatic to witness the gushing water from the tap, that too, in the third floor of the mansion.

Rabi was merely a child then, and he ardently wished to bathe in the incessant water showers that emerged from the tap in his *Babamoshai*'s bathroom. But he couldn't possibly do it when *Babamoshai* was around. Hence, he started hatching a plan along with his nephew Satya how to do it secretly, avoiding the hawk's eyes of their servants.

One day, just after their wrestling session was over, the two boys, Rabi and Satya entered the bathroom surreptitiously, opened the tap and surrendered their little mud-smeared bodies under the gushing showers. What an incredible pleasure they felt, surrendering their bodies to the water! But just then, their old servant Shyama appeared in the bathroom and took the little convicts to Sarada's court for a hearing.

Sarada looked at the boys intently, from head to toe, and asked: "What made you go to *Babamoshai*'s bathroom, boys?"

The boys replied somehow, on the verge of crying: "Well, our bodies were dirty, filled with mud while practicing wrestling…" They knew Sarada hated the idea of the boys wrestling.

"What is the need of doing it then?" Sarada asked. "It's a nasty game, and your body gets so dirty while practicing it! Look at you, Rabi, your skin is dusky anyway, why turn yourself into an ugly ghost by smearing your skin with so much mud?"

"What do I do, mother? Hem Dada and Gana Dada are the ones who take me there…Do I myself like this game of wrestling at all, applying oil and mud all over my body?" Rabi mustered enough courage to reply.

Sarada called her old maid Manada *dashi* and ordered: "Manada, go and bring the concoction of *maida* (flour) and milk cream and massage the boys' bodies vigorously with it in front of me. And I need you to do it regularly, without fail. This youngest boy of mine is dark-complexioned, let me see if this massaging helps his skin."

This was undoubtedly a new punishment for little Rabi, but he couldn't escape it by any means. The massaging went on, day after day in front of his mother, a beauty regime for the boys to restore their complexion.

There was a new development in the Thakurbari again, during this time. One day, Prafullamayee, Biren's wife came up to her mother-in-law Sarada, with tears in her eyes. "Ma, please help me, I can't tolerate the madness of your son anymore. See how he has beat me up, tortured me! He has broken everything in his room, and I couldn't stop him."

Perplexed, Sarada summoned the maids of the house.

"Call Hemen right now. See if he is around." She ordered them. "Why didn't you tell me earlier that Biren's madness has worsened thus, *Bou*? You could have avoided being beaten up then!" She asked her daughter-in-law.

Sarada felt tender affection and pity for this quiet, anguished young girl. Biren's madness was worsening every single day after his marriage, all efforts to restore his mental health went in vain. Prafullamayee, however, was blessed with a beautiful baby boy, in the midst of all her agony. Debendranath named his new grandson Balendranath. The infant Balendra or Bolu, as he was called, giggled and laughed, seeing the mad outbursts of his father.

There was utter chaos in the family as they all struggled to manage Biren. Hemen called for the British doctor to check for his younger brother.

Biren, upon seeing the doctor, shook his hands vehemently and asked: "Where is my *Kola-Bou* (Banana bride)? Where is she?"

Hemen reprimanded him, and said: "What madness is this, Biren? Your wife Prafullamayee is right here, see! Who on earth is this *Kola-Bou*?"

Just a few days before his wedding, Biren had demanded to his elder sisters that he would marry a *Kola-Bou*, a banana plant veiled and dressed up as a fictitious bride, which he had seen during the weddings in his house. Perhaps, the recollections of that image haunted him still. When Prafullamayee entered the house as a new bride, he removed her veil and looked intently at her beautiful face. Within seconds, he pushed her violently to a corner and remarked: "You are not my *Kola-Bou*...Go away!"

Prafullamayee cried out loud, at this heartless rejection. Her elder sister Neepamayee, also her sister-in-law, moved her away from the scene. She was ecstatic when the marriage alliance between her dear sister and brother-in-law was finalized, and more ecstatic when the marriage happened. But these days, the agony of her younger sister moved her to tears, it was difficult to accept her suffering silently, helplessly.

Biren was sent to a lunatic asylum without further delay. He was certified as a clinically lunatic patient. His was the first clinical instance of madness for any of the sons of the Thakur family, though madness ran in the family in a subtle way. A pall of gloom overshadowed the Jorasanko mansion with Biren's incident.

As much Biren's incident shook the members of the Thakurbari, tragedy struck yet again with the sudden death of Ganendra at the young age of twenty-eight, due to cholera. Ganendra was a tall, fair, enterprising young man who had the unique power to unite all the members of the two separate mansions of Jorasanko, even as the family was divided due to their difference of religious ideologies. The new dramas staged at Jorasanko were all due to his dedication and passion for creative productions. He had also been the main organizer of the *Chaitra Mela*, the annual fair during the Bengali year end. After the untimely demise of this beloved nephew of Debendranath, the old fissures between the two mansions seemed huge and demonic, ready to swallow the people of the two families. On one side of the wall, Sarada shed tears for her dear Ganendra, while on the other side, Jogomaya, Biren's aunt shed tears for him. Debendranath's perpetual absence from Jorasanko made Sarada even more miserable; she felt she couldn't bear the burden of this mammoth family alone, not anymore. The two sisters-in-law were separated after the family feud a long time back, and she had no companion to share her agony.

Maharshi Debendranath didn't like the idea of staying in Calcutta any longer. There was a time when he journeyed far away to the mountains just to avoid the Durga Pujas, and as time went by, he lived in the mountains almost the entire year. Following his father Dwarakanath's death, a huge burden of debt was on his shoulders. One of the debt collectors had also sent an arrest warrant in his name. However, he was able to ward off the danger by cutting off many of his family expenses and since then, living frugally had been the essence of his existence.

Sarada remembered a very interesting incident that happened during those days. Debendranath had received an invitation of a musical soiree, a *jalsa* from the Sovabazar Rajbari in Calcutta, which he had the obligation to attend. All the rich, aristocratic men waited with eager enthusiasm, keen to see what attire Dwarakanath's son would wear for the occasion, whether he would wear any ornaments at all. The soiree started with much grandeur, the Babus dazzled the show with their sparkling diamonds and other pricey jewels, their exquisite attires with intricate *zari* works, but when Deben entered the scene, they stared at him in awe and wonder. He was dressed in a milk-white *achkan* (long, loose shirt), wore a white *pagri*(turban) in his head, devoid of any gold or silver jewellery. But when he reclined on the pillow and extended his legs forward, they noticed his white satin shoes, with two large pearls embedded in them. The king of Shovabazar, Deben Thakur's friend, gestured with his hand and called the young attendees of the soiree.

"See, this is called a true aristocrat. Such exquisite pearls, which adorn our necks and our heads, are adorning his feet!"

Debendra roamed around the mighty Himalayas, exploring the mountains with a couple of his favorite disciples. Sarada, confined within the mansion, remained worried and anxious about her husband's wellbeing. One day, she summoned Rabi, her youngest son to her chamber in the inner quarters, and needless the say, the boy seemed overjoyed to have the opportunity to meet his mother. He waited for a moment like this, to free himself temporarily from the claustrophobic environment of the servants' quarters where he lived along with the other boys. His mother wouldn't call him often, and the boys were forbidden to visit her inside her chamber if she didn't call them. Hence Rabi fervently waited for a call from his distant mother, which was a rare, occasional happening.

As soon as Rabi entered her chamber, Sarada ordered him: "You know, Rabi, *Karta Moshai* has been living in the mountains for a long time now, I haven't heard from him in quite a while. Please write a letter to him on my behalf, child!"

Rabi's heart leaped in unexplained ecstasy. His mother didn't call his elder brothers for this important task. The fact that she had chosen himself for it filled his heart and being with a sense of pride. He ran fast and came back with a paper and pen, and asked his mother, sitting close to her bedstead: "What do I have to write, Ma?"

Sarada had called Rabi after some conscious deliberation, and there was a backstory behind it. A few days back, a well-wisher of Sarada let her know that Russia was invading India, and that a war was just around the corner. Neither Sarada, nor her well-wisher relative knew where exactly the war was about to happen. She also asked her sons Hemen and Jyoti, and neither of them were able to tell anything. But due to Debendranath's prolonged absence from home, Sarada continued to worry for him. Her anxiety grew manifold when during those days, the newspaper 'Somprakash' carried a news article where the writer mentioned: "Babu Debendranath Thakur has decided to renounce his family life and live permanently in a *dharamshala* (inn) in the foothills of the Himalayas." Jyoti, after reading out the news article, advised his mother not to pay heed to rumours, but Sarada wanted to write a letter to her husband just to ward off her doubts and anxiety. Since Jyoti and Hemen chose not to give importance to her thoughts, she decided to call Rabi. But then, neither Rabi, nor his mother knew how the tone of the letter should be like. Just then, Mahananda Munshi, an officer of the estate came to his rescue, and helped Rabi draft a letter addressed to his father. The contents of the letter were read out to Sarada, and upon her approval, were sent by post.

Maharshi Debendranath's reply came within a few days. He wrote that he was doing well and there was nothing to worry about. He would drive away the Russians, he wrote in jest. Sarada's worries diminished after receiving this letter from her husband. As for the boy Rabindranath, he became so excited to write a letter for the first time to his father and to actually receive a reply, that he started visiting Mahananda Munshi's office every now and then, with the hope of writing a letter to his father. He pretended to draft the letters every time to meet Rabi's demands, but those letters never reached the Himalayas. Rabi wrote a nonsense rhyme in his notebook, depicting Mahananda as a character in the poem.

Hemen, Rabi's elder brother had craved for a horse which he could ride, hence he got one, which was tied to a stable near the outhouse. The horse stirred the romantic, multihued dreams of the *'pakshiraj'* horse of fairy tales in the young hearts of the Jorasanko mansion. Such multihued dreams were being woven silently in the chamber of Jyoti and his young wife Kadambari.

Kadambari, the pampered wife demanded to her husband: "Can't you take me to the Maidan to get some fresh air? Please, I want to go out with you!"

Jyoti sensed danger in his wife's words. "Listen, if I go out with you to get fresh air, Ma will get to know and she will be furious! All hell will break loose, don't you know that? Otherwise, I too wish to ride my brother's horse and take you along on the horse's back, far, far away! Wait, princess, I'll take you one day, I promise!"

Kadambari pouted her lips and complained: "But *Mejo Bouthan* is such a frequent traveler, going to faraway lands in a steamer so often! And you praise her so effusively! Why fear going out with your own wife, then?"

"I admit, she boards the steamer and travels frequently, but she hasn't gone out in the city of Calcutta to get fresh air yet. Let her do that and set an example for you first, then you will…"

Kadambari felt hurt at her husband's words. "Why would she be the first one to do everything? Why can't I do it for a change? You know, you are the one who lacks courage, but I don't!"

…. Just then, Rupkumari entered the chamber like a whiff of tempest. She was standing by the window and eavesdropped on the conversation between the young husband and wife. "Jyoti Dada, I will accompany you too! I want to ride the horseback and go out with *Notun Bouthan* to get fresh air." She uttered excitedly.

"See, the mad girl has arrived again!" Joyti was a bit annoyed. "Why do you follow us like this, tell me? You know, *Notun Bou*, this girl stands before me and demands to go out with me every time I plan to go somewhere."

"It proves that she is courageous and I am the docile one, always suppressing my desires. My heart is as restless as this girl's heart. We both resist living in our cages."

"I see now, what a nuisance this horse of *Shej Dada* (Hemen) is! It has triggered in you both the desire to fly away, riding on the mythical *pakshiraaj*, the winged horse... Come, let me read out to you my new play, 'Sarojini'."

Kadambari started listening to her husband's new play, 'Sarojini', immersing herself in the melody and cadence of its words, that created a universe of joy within her. This distracted her from her desire to fly away, but then, Rupa had vanished from the scene, and they didn't know where she went. After a while, Jyoti came outside, listening to a sudden uproar that had been created in the outhouse. Rupkumari had vanished from the house, riding Hemen's horse, he learnt.

Kadambari came to the verandah of her mother-in-law Sarada's chamber. There was some hue and cry there.

Manada *dashi*, the old maid started shouting excitedly. "I told you not to indulge and pamper that girl so much, didn't I, *Karta Ma*? Look at the audacity of the shrew! Just wait till she turns you insane, completely, insane!"

Sarada tried to keep herself calm, in spite of the

chaos around. "Ah, quiet, Manada, don't rake up a storm! I'm worrying for the girl; she might die once the notorious horse throws her away! Did anyone rush to save her? Go and find out!" She said.

"Ma, your son has gone to enquire about the matter, he must do something about it, don't worry." Kadambari assured Sarada.

Sarada's fears diminished a bit. "Jyoti went there? See if he can save her!" She said, and started chanting the family deity's name silently.

Soudamini, Sarada's eldest daughter came up and said: "Enough is enough, Ma! Either you make her tamed, or stop yourself from spoiling her further. Look how disobedient she has become these days; she will not let you stay in peace!"

"Drive her away, right now, *Karta Ma*, I tell you! Look at us servants, we toil day and night to get some morsels of rice, and you chose this girl from nowhere as your foster daughter, so that she can wreak havoc over our heads!" Manada sounded furious.

Kadambari couldn't take Manada's words anymore, and rebuked her strongly. "Ah Manada, don't you have any sense? She is a child, after all…whatever she has done today is an impulsive act. That doesn't mean you will throw such harsh words on Ma's face!"

Emboldened by Kadambari's words, Sarada regained her power and confidence to speak up. "Manada, you are crossing your limits, I say! Go away and never utter such ominous words! Go away and don't appear in front of me before the girl comes back to me, safe and sound. Remember!"

After an hour or so, a group of watchmen and palanquin bearers of the Jorasanko mansion could trace Rupkumari along with the notorious horse of Hemen, which was quite a conquest in itself. Rupa was drained, exhausted by the exploits of the day. She had chosen to ride on the horseback, driven by a sudden impulse, but didn't know anything about the art of riding. Just as the horse started to race, she sensed her danger, but then, the horse was unstoppable. She didn't know of any way to tame the horse. Meanwhile, Jyoti had sent his army of men in all corners to search for Rupa and the horse. She shouted helplessly for humans to come up and rescue her. They came, surely, but to ogle at her and derive sick pleasure to witness the scene. They threw away some crude comments at Rupa too, she could hear them well enough.

"Come, see the wild game of the ripe woman's body on the horseback!" Some said.

Some others said: "Is the Goddess arriving on a horseback this year? Well, we see the human Goddess here, and that too, with gold ornaments all over her body!"

"But this cannot be a girl from a respectable family... no decent girl will come out alone in the open streets. She must be a whore, out in the open to attract potential *Babus* (customers). This must be one of her tactics to lure the *Babus*."

Rupa cried out in deep agony. She couldn't get the horse to stop, however hard she tried, and now, she had to listen to these filthy talks of men. She didn't have the slightest idea that the world outside could be so dirty, and that men could be so sick and vulgar. Alas! Was she dying to have a glimpse of the world outside to experience such garbage? Her eyes brimmed with tears as she was overwhelmed with shock and fear.

Finally, the horse was made to stop with the cumulative effort of the onlookers and the battalion sent by the Jorasanko mansion. Just as the horse stopped, some wicked men tried to touch Rupa's body. An ugly-looking man of a tall, lanky frame started to pull Rupa by her hand, and the daring girl gave the man a tight slap on his cheek. The watchmen of the Thakurbari gaped at the men and at Rupa. It all happened within a few seconds, before they could grasp what was happening.

The shameless men started vying with each other in their attempt to embrace Rupa. "Look at this dame, she is quite a delightful thing! She even dares to raise her hands at us! Let's see who can save you from us now!" They pounced on her.

Just before things could turn worse, Jyotirindranath arrived at the scene in his palanquin, along with the bearers. The onlookers ran away after seeing him, but threw abusive words at him while they left. The very next day, there was news featuring Jyoti Thakur and this incident, published in two newspapers.

Chapter 6

Sarada's Death

Jyoti was feeling tremendously upset about the untimely, tragic demise of the brilliant poet Michael Madhusudan Dutta. He died, helpless and bankrupt, in a charity hospital, left with no funds for his treatment. The son of a wealthy father, Madhu had thought of making a name for himself in world literature, and started writing verses in English. For the same reason, he felt the urgency of converting to Christianity, shedding off traces of the Hindu religion from his existence. This outrageous act of Madhu created quite an uproar in his traditional family, his society, and his father Rajnarayan Dutta disowned him.

Poor Madhu left the cocooning warmth of his mother's love, his peers at Presidency college, his homeland in Bengal, and went far away in search of his own destiny. His Goddess of destiny, however, was not kind to him. While Saraswati, the Goddess of knowledge and art blessed him abundantly and his notebooks were always filled with poetry and plays, Lakshmi, the Goddess of wealth never blessed him enough. Very soon, he realized his mistake, and also decided that he would have to choose writing only in his native Bengali language, to earn a name for himself. There was a very tough competition in the field of English literature, and nobody there would allow a 'native' like him to outshine the English writers. But there was still scope to grow and flourish in Bengali literature. In fact, the Bengali writers Pyarichand Mitra and Tekchand Thakur wrote in a pedestrian language, only fit for the uneducated readers. No timeless classic could be created by such writers. Madhu had a void to fill in there, and thus, he was determined to embellish his poor, neglected mother tongue Bengali and dress her up as the 'shuyorani', the cherished queen. He had documented his last wish for the Bengali language in one of his verses.

"Mother, do remember your humble servant, I beg at your feet.

If ever, a disaster happens, while fulfilling my heart's desire, / Let not your lotus heart be devoid of its nectar 'madhu'…"

Once, in the Thakurbari, a satire of Madhu was staged along with Jyoti's play 'Kinchit Jolojog.' Madhu used to frequent the Thakurbari even before this happened.

Jyoti, while lamenting his death, said to his wife Kadambari: "*Notun Bou*, you have never seen him, so you can't imagine how talented he was. Such a pity that an unfathomable talent like him perished away, for want of money and proper nourishment. And imagine, all his father's wealth and assets are worthless now, in need of the heir!"

"But how will his foreigner wife live alone, with her small children, how will they sustain their lives? There is not a single soul to take care of them in Calcutta!" Kadambari asked, agonized.

Henrietta, Madhu's widowed wife was in grave danger, with her pure French beauty, her utter helplessness. There was no dearth of womanizers roaming around her to have fun, but nobody who could really help her. She was in a truly pitiful state.

"But isn't there any way you can stand beside her, support her?" Kadambari asked, like an innocent young girl.

"But won't you feel afraid to send me to that beautiful, attractive widow? What if I fall in love with her?" Jyoti said in jest, touching the chin of his wife, and shaking it a bit.

"Oh, then I'll have to swallow poison and end my life!" Kadambari said, lowering her face.

The child bride had uttered an outrageously shocking statement; Jyoti was stunned to hear such an utterance from her. "*Notun Bou*, never utter such words again, even in jest! It will make me very angry if you do." He said to her.

Kadambari buried her little head in her husband's chest in an unknown fear. To Jyoti, it seemed she was a gentle clove tree, attached to the body of a giant tree.

Just as the couple were immersed in loving each other, Gyanada witnessed their intimate union, while entering their room. It stuck her heart like a thorn.

"What's the matter, *Notun Bou*? The sun has been up long back, and you are still in bed, chatting with your husband? Is this your sense of courtesy? The women of the house have started working already, and look at you, still glued to the bed for your husband's love? Won't you let Jyoti work?"

Startled at this reprimanding gesture, Kadambari

sat up on the bed, shy and wary of her sister-in-law's intimidating presence. Jyoti, however, greeted Gyanada with a mouthful of smile. "Come in, *Bouthan*! Guess whose face did I see when I woke up today? Yours, of course! I was feeling sad, depressed all this while, but I will feel better, now that you're here."

"But what were you talking about?" Gyanada interfered a bit, wondering about the topic of conversation between her dear brother-in-law and this very young bride.

"See, *Bouthan*, she is threatening me with suicide if I ever go to other women, now you tell me, should she speak like this?" Jyoti asked his sister-in-law.

Kadambari was astonished to hear such words from her husband. "What a lie! And I had asked you to go, but you were talking about something else, so…"

Gyanada felt irritated. "I see, there's so much fire inside such a little girl! You know how much *Thakurpo* loves you, but still you are threatening him?" She came closer to Jyoti and added, with an air of mystery: "Won't you allow your husband to mix with me too, *Notun Bou*?"

Jyoti said hurriedly: "What are you saying, *Mejo Bouthan*? You are my inspiration since long, while Kadambari has just entered my life!"

Kadambari's heart was bruised at her husband's words. She turned to Gyanada and said: "I don't have the audacity to forbid him to mix with you, *Mejdi*! And why should I forbid him at all, for that matter? With whom my husband will mingle, and how, is entirely his discretion. It is my good fortune that I have found a place in his holy feet!"

"Good Lord, this girl has started to talk now! Jyoti, I tell you, I cannot mingle with you anymore while bypassing her. Please invite her to our literary meetings from now on!"

There was a tinge of sarcasm in Gyanada's voice. She knew for sure that once Kadambari came to their literary assembly to assert her rights as the wife of Jyoti, her shortcomings will be apparent, and Jyoti will also realize his mistake. In his quest to become a celebrated author, he should have listened to Gyanada; he should have married an educated woman. Can this young girl be her husband's muse, his inspiration only by virtue of her beauty?

Jyoti looked at his tender, young wife and said: "Remember, don't stoop yourself to anyone's feet, not even your husband's. *Notun Bou*, never forget that your place is in my heart, always."

Gyanada asked: "And where is my place then, *Thakurpo*?"

"*Mejo Bouthan*, can't you feel your place? I've made you the crown on top of my head!" Jyoti replied. When he looked at Gyanada's face, he felt a tinge of sorrow, that might have its roots in his intimacy with his wife Kadambari. But why should that sorrow be nestled in Gyanada's heart? Was she apprehensive that Kadambari would be a hindrance in the tender, affectionate relationship between him and Gyanada? If yes, then it was important to nip it in the bud.

Jyoti said to Gyanada: "Now that you are staying in Jorasanko with us, *Mejo Bouthan, Notun Bou* will grow from a caterpillar to a butterfly, such will be the magic of your company."

Gyanada didn't seem elated to hear these words. She replied: "But *Babamoshai* has given that responsibility to

Neepamayee, and the results are already showing. *Notun Bou* is getting quite vocal of late! You know *Babamoshai* didn't trust me with this responsibility, so why pull me into it? Instead, do read out your new composition to me; I came to you today morning to listen to your poetry on Shakuntala."

Jyoti and her sister-in-law became immersed in reading poetry, and unbeknownst to them, there was someone else, along with Kadambari, who drank the elixir of poetry. It was Rupa or Rupkumari, who was the silent onlooker standing outside the window of their room.

The news that Rupa not only followed Jyoti to the literary assembly of men, but also chatted with them reached Sarada very soon. One day, Barnakumari came to her and complained: "Ma, your foster daughter is becoming incorrigible day after day. You know, she is willingly destroying the honour of all us women of the household!"

"Why? What did she do now?" Sarada asked, bewildered. It had been such a pain for her to give shelter to the girl; she could neither accept her ways, nor abandon her. She was extremely disobedient, yet Sarada felt her soul was pure, like an opaque lake. And yes, she didn't even realize why her acts were always so forbidden.

"Why Ma, don't you know how far she has gone? It is you who pampered her to the hilt...But on the other hand, you gave us so little freedom! Don't you see her age?" Barna said, annoyed.

Sarada felt hurt at these allegations. Was it her failure that she couldn't raise this girl properly? All her own children were jewels in their own ways, but Rupa wasn't her biological offspring. Was that the only reason why she couldn't tame the girl? But she still asked: "Why, even Swarna and *Mejo Bouma* (Gyanada) join in those literary assemblies. What's the harm if Rupa joins in too?"

At this, Saudamini chimed in to counter her mother. "Ma, why do you even compare her to Swarna and *Mejo Bouthan* (Gyanada)? Does Rupa really understand or appreciate literature? The truth is, literature holds no attraction for her, she is rather lured by the young boys there. You can't even imagine how Rupa mingles with them and chats with them openly. I have seen her from the distance of the curtain, she gets really close to that young British boy Harry, chirping like a bird with him, laughing and frolicking with him!"

Manada *Dashi*, the maid was dressing a betel leaf for her *Karta ma*, leaving it in a silver vessel. She couldn't stay calm, hearing such an entertaining discussion. She knew Sarada would reprimand her for her words, but still she went on.

"What a shameless scene of lascivious behavior! Looks like she came from the quarter of prostitutes!"

"Shut up, Manada, I say! Don't interfere with everything we say or discuss. Give me a betel leaf." The *Karta Ma* scolded her maid.

Amid this spirited discussion, Rupa arrived from nowhere and suddenly sat down near Sarada's feet. Everyone in the room was stunned into silence.

Sarada caught the girl's hair in her fist and asked: "Wouldn't you let me live in peace, you shameless girl? Why does everyone complain about you every day? Why can't you be polished and obedient like the other girls in the house? Just wait, I'll marry you off to the first man I see tomorrow morning!"

Rupa, amused at this hypothesis, laughed out loud. "Ma, in that case, you will have to marry me off to a girl! How would you even see men's faces without venturing outside?" She said, rather frivolously.

"What a girl, oh good Lord!" Saudamini said, "We are getting into so much trouble for you, and look at you, so careless and irresponsible! Now, now, don't laugh…We'll have to look for a groom for Rupa right away, she is already thirteen or fourteen."

"But I won't marry!" Rupa retorted, like a pampered child.

Sarada replied in a stern voice: "Then I'll have to forcefully marry you off! I won't be able to die in peace without sending you away!"

"Is it? Then I will run away, I will surely run away!" Rupkumari pronounced, determined.

A few days later, a sudden accident happened in the Jorasanko mansion. Sarada Sundari had been to the Peneti farm house for a vacation. One day, the heavy cover of an iron chest fell over one of her hands during her stay in that house. She was brought back to Jorasanko immediately after the accident. Sarada, the Goddess Lakshmi of the household became bedridden, fraught with tremendous pain. Initially, the attempts to cure her pain with Arnica and a number of ointments failed. Then, two renowned physicians, Dr. Nilmadhab Haldar and Dr. Patridge, professor of surgery at Medical College, Calcutta were appointed for her treatment, but both failed. Doctors came and went away in quick succession, unable to cure her malady. After further examination, it was found out that a small piece of iron had been stuck inside her flesh.

A surgery was done, following the diagnosis, but the pain didn't subside even after that.

In such a grave crisis, Deben Thakur was absent from the household. He was living in the mountains of Dalhousie, along with his youngest son, Rabi. The members of the house sent him a telegram notifying him of Sarada's condition, when the pain didn't seem to diminish even after two months. He received the telegram, and started sending his advice in a series of letters and telegrams.

Finally, a board of five renowned British doctors was formed at the Medical College to cure Sarada's ailment, each of them charging thirty-two rupees as their fees. All of them unanimously declared that a transplant was necessary, getting rid of the flesh at the site of the pain through another surgery. Nobody in this country had ever heard about such a procedure earlier. Only the British doctors could think of such weird ideas, the members of the house remarked. But then, if the transplant was the only option, who would volunteer to donate a piece of flesh from his body to Sarada? Someone who had a blood relation with her, someone from the family, her own kith and kin? Otherwise, Sarada would prefer to die without any treatment whatsoever.

In the absence of their *Babamoshai* Debendranath Thakur, Hemendranath aka Hemen, one of Sarada's younger sons came forward to donate a piece of his own flesh to save his mother's life. However, even after the transplant, the pain didn't subside as expected. Debendranath was still absent from the house. Stricken with the disease for a long time, Sarada wished to see her husband badly. Would she be able to see him again in this life? She wondered. Hemen, at her earnest request, sent a letter to his father, urging him to come back to Jorasanko.

At that time, Maharshi Debendranath had just got back to the plain lands after a long stay in the mountains of Dalhousie, and had desired to stay in Amritsar for a while, before returning to Calcutta.

At the start of the winter season, Sarada's pain worsened. During that time, Hemendra rented a boat at the river Ganges for his mother to experience a 'change', as suggested by the doctors. Sarada felt the change very welcoming, like a whiff of fresh air after being cooped up inside the house for long. The boat seemed her very own, and she started her old ritual of worshipping her Lakshmi and Janardan at one corner of the boat, with two earthen water-jars in both the idol's names. Manada *dashi*, the maid was instructed to bring fresh flowers for her. After her daily bath, she offered those flowers along with the holy Ganga water to those two earthen water-jars.

One day, her son Hemen came up to her and said: "Ma, *Babamoshai* is returning soon, he wrote in his latest telegram."

Sarada heaved a sigh of relief and lifted her one hand to her head in a gesture of prayer. The God of the household had indeed listened to her prayers. She wouldn't be able to die in peace without meeting her husband for one last time.

Dwarikanath Gupta, the house physician came to the boat every day to check on Sarada's health. Her daughters and daughters-in-law came to see her too, and some of them stayed with her after visiting her. Whenever Prafullamayee came to visit her, she felt saddened, looking at the young girl's dismayed face. Sarada felt helpless, unable to do anything for the girl, widowed at such a young age, along with her baby boy. If she herself couldn't get over the shock of her son Biren's death, how could this beautiful young girl cope with the trauma?

Debendranath Thakur came back to Jorasanko within a month's time. On his way back, he had been to Shantiniketan, staying there for a while with his son, Rabi. It was his unique way to blend the pleasures of discovering nature along with surveying his *zamindari* estate.

Sarada came back to her dear mansion of Jorasanko after her husband's return. Their reunion at the third floor of the mansion, in her own chamber, filled her eyes with tears of gratitude.

Debendranath touched her head affectionately and said to her: "Now, now, I'm here, Sarada! I will stay with you from now on."

Sarada hugged her husband's arm and shed tears of happiness. "If you wouldn't have come this time, I wouldn't be able to see you again. I might not live much long."

Deben consoled her. "Who said so? You're not fifty yet, where are you planning to go so soon? I will get you treated with the best doctors, now that I'm here. Let me see that you get cured completely."

With the presence of her husband, Sarada felt a new spurt of life. Her health had improved considerably. Her pain was still persistent, but her strength to tolerate that pain increased manifold. Sometimes, she also joined in the assembly of women during the preparation of breakfast in the morning, or when the women were together during their hair braiding sessions in the evenings.

Ever since Rabi came back with his father from his

Himalaya trip, he seemed big and mature. The elders started looking at him with regard, his mother summoned him to her chamber to listen to his stories of the mountains. Quite magically, the closed doors of the inner quarters had opened to him, welcoming him with open arms. Even his *Notun Bouthan*, Kadambari wanted to listen to his mountain stories. It seemed as if Rabi was the open page of an enchanting travelogue.

Sarada called Rabi to her chamber one day and asked: "Rabi, did your *Babamoshai* eat properly all these days, while you both were roaming around the mountains?"

Rabi felt a bit hurt that his mother didn't enquire about his own eating and nutrition, but only about his father's. But wasn't his mother like this all her life? In spite of this apparent indifference of his mother towards him, wasn't his heart brimming with joy that she called him to listen to his tales?

Rabi replied, enthusiastically: "You know, Ma, every morning, we used to fill our stomachs with *roti* and milk, just before going out for our expeditions in the mountains, riding on the horseback. What spectacular beauty it is, Ma! I can't explain it, one has to see it for once. When I grow older, I will take you there, Ma!"

Sarada sighed. "Alas, my son! Would I live till that long?" The words escaped from her lips in silent agony.

Rabi hugged his mother in desperation. "Where will you go, Ma? I won't let you go anywhere…You'll see, I will be a grown-up man very, very soon."

"But you know, 'I'm very ill these days. Perhaps I can't stay with you all for long." Sarada touched her son's head in a gesture of blessing and said: "Rabi, live with your

Babamoshai always, the way you did, it will do you good... you will grow up as big as a mountain!"

Rabi hugged his mother's frail body tighter and said: "No, Ma, you will live, you will live. All my childhood, I wasn't allowed to come close to you. Now that you have called me for once, you can't leave me. I will board a palanquin one day soon with you, and take you to the faraway land of *Tepantar*."

Sarada laughed at Rabi's childish imagination. "Where will you take me all alone, Rabi? What if dacoits come and plunder everything we have?"

"Let the dacoits come, let there be a battle, I will win over them, and drive them away!" Rabi took a stick from his mother's room and posed it as a sword. Swirling the imaginary sword in swift, rhythmic motion, he said: "Look, Ma, I am the *Birpurush*, the brave, valiant boy! I am all out to fight with the notorious dacoits!"

At this, Sarada replied in jest: "Do not go, *khoka*, my boy! I am feeling so scared! Why would you risk your life, fighting with so many dangerous souls?"

For a long time, Rabi continued to swirl his imaginary sword like a real fighter in a battlefield. Sarada enjoyed being a witness of this wondrous game of her son, which let her forget about the pain in her body for a while.

After a long tryst with the dacoits in his mind, Rabi felt tired, exhausted. He wiped away the sweat in his face and appeared in front of his mother again. "See, the battle has ended now. I have won, Ma! You need not be afraid anymore."

Sarada lifted her body with a bit of effort. After a long

time, she took her son Rabi in her arms and kissed him. "Thank God, my *Khoka* was there in the battlefield! Else, who knows what a disaster would have happened!" She said.

For quite a few days after this, the little traveler Rabi was loved and pampered by his mother and the women of the inner quarters, as he narrated his mountain tales to all the women there. He enjoyed limitless freedom inside the house now. The reprimanding servants changed their attitude towards him, and his bond with his school loosened. The adolescent Rabindranath started to enter the soiree of music, literature and the arts along with his elder brothers and sisters. At the new poetry association of Jyoti and Kadambari, upcoming poets and their works were discussed and appreciated. Kadambari had become quite a fan of Biharilal's verses, memorizing his 'Sarada Mangal Kavya' quite often, while Rabi roamed around his playmate Kadambari in the hope of drinking the elixir of those verses. This turned into an exciting game for both of them. Kadambari wanted to teach Rabi all that she learnt from her husband Jyoti. She became her husband Jyoti's favorite disciple, while Rabi became her disciple and her shadow, following her in everything she did.

There was a fresh surge of literature and art in the Thakurbari now. Dwijen had composed a poem titled 'Swapna Prayan' (The Death of a Dream), and it was appreciated by all. When Satyen and Gyanada came to the Jorasanko mansion these days, renowned authors and poets of the city congregated in their room for their literary meets. Jyoti was already an established poet and playwright. Along with him, Swarnakumari, the author spread the splendour of her writing like the soft moonlight in a dark sky. The intoxication and light of the presence of both his siblings overwhelmed Rabi, he gradually lost himself in the divine manna of poetry.

Jyoti and Dwijen both decided to host an assembly of erudite scholars at the Thakurbari premises during the coming spring. They got involved in the preparations of that august assembly. In fact, the country was in the threshold of a dramatic change of the Renaissance, and who else but the Thakurbari would take a pioneer's role in it?

After Sarada's health improved a bit, Debendranath Thakur himself came to a meeting of the Brahmo Samaj one winter evening in the Bengali month of *Poush*. He came along with his own kin, his sons Jyoti and Dwijen and his sons-in-law, and looked very relieved. The assembly seemed full, as they all joined in for Brahma Sangeet, the ritual of songs. In the mellifluous voices of Jyoti and Dwijen, there seemed to be a new surge of energy among their Brahmo group. Deben, however, prayed for his wife Sarada's health for the whole time of the *Upasana* (prayer). Sarada's illness had made him disoriented and sad, even when he had returned home.

Within a few days, Debendranath went to Shilaidaha to look after his zamindari estate, and also to soothe his restless spirit. Once he went away, Sarada decided to go back to the bosom of the river Ganges once again, to inhale the fresh air and the invigorating environs of Ma Ganga. But she started feeling sick all over again, due to the absence of her husband. This time, the women of the household tried black magic and voodooism to cure her ailment. One day, a lady ayurvedic doctor, who really was a quack, suggested applying a paste of burnt tamarind around the site of wound. Within no time, it made the wound turn septic.

Sarada was sure that she wouldn't live any longer now. It would be good to return home at Jorasanko for her last few days.

Sarada was sleeping close to Rabi in the boys' room at night for some days, according to Rabi's wish, but she was sent back to her own chamber in the third floor, and it was there that her ailment got worse. Gradually, she lost the power to lift her body from the bed. A special air-filled pillow was ordered for her from the Wilson hotel to prevent her bed sore. A man was fetched every day from the hotel to puff up the pillow with air.

Debendranath was dismayed to get the news of Sarada's illness yet again. Wouldn't they be able to retain her in this life anymore? With his wife's absence, it would be difficult for him to have any bond with the house whatsoever.

In the Jorasanko mansion, there were ominous rounds of cries. Would *Karta Moshai* be able to see his wife upon returning from Shilaidaha? They were skeptical about the possibility. But Sarada, even as her nerves stopped responding, said in her feeble voice: "Don't worry. I won't die without touching his feet for one last time."

Sarada's prediction about her last day on earth was true. As Debendranath returned to Jorasanko, he went straightaway to his wife's chamber in the third floor. Sarada, in spite of her terrible pain, touched her husband's feet with her frail hands and said: "I beg your leave now. I will see you in my next birth."

She breathed her last after taking her husband's blessings, in the full presence of her family—her sons and daughters, daughters-in-law, grandchildren, and a bevy of servants and maids. A Brahmo woman who came to pay her last respects to Sarada said, standing beside her dead body, "Look how fortunate she is, she went away with her vermillion and *shankha* (conch shells) intact, with the blessings of a married woman!"

Silent with agony, Debendranath went away to the terrace to spend some time in solitude. He came down just before Sarada's body was taken away to the crematorium. Sprinkling the holy sandalwood powder and flowers on his wife's body, he said to himself: "It was me who had brought her to this house when she was a six-year-old child, today it is me again who is bidding her goodbye."

Satyen came to Jorasanko with Gyanada after seven days of his mother's demise. He couldn't see his mother's body for the last time. Her last rites were performed according to the Brahmo rituals, in the presence of her living sons and daughters, daughters-in-law, her entire family. Along with her death, the women of Jorasanko felt the end of an era in the inner quarters of the Thakurbari.

Among the men of Jorasanko, there was the beginning of a new era. A month after Sarada's death, her sons started their assemblies with erudite scholars at home yet again, after their period of mourning ended. With Satyen's presence, the arrangement of such assemblies was always delightful. In one such meeting, Dwijen recited his poem 'Swapna Prayan' (Death of a Dream) and Jyoti read out a particular act of his new play in the august company of authors, editors and scholars including Rev. Krishna Mohan Bandyopadhyay, Babu Rajendralal Mitra, Babu Rajnarayan Basu, Babu Pyaricharan Sarkar et al. But then, a disaster happened when Pyarimohan Kabiratna, the renowned poet read out a poem of his dedicated to England's queen, where there was a reference to using foreign goods. An unwanted argument ensued, owing to the difference of opinions among the members of the assembly, which was quite natural, considering the huge number of people present there. Finally, when Satyen announced that a musical session would take place, the chaos subsided. The young boys of the Thakurbari had rehearsed a lot for this musical session. What was a better way to stop the unwelcome argument than music?

Rabi was delighted to be present at this beautiful assembly. He was in absolute awe of the authors whose works he had read before, whom he had heard about since long. Seeing them in person was an incredible experience! His happiness knew no bounds when those very esteemed personalities encouraged him to perform.

As an unwritten rule, the women of the house weren't invited to the meeting. However, two women appeared on the scene, with their faces covered in black shawls, surprising everybody present. The men couldn't ask about their identities out of sheer courtesy, but curiosity was killing them every moment.

"Are they really women?" Somebody asked.

Someone else whispered: "I'm sure Muslim girls can't come out in the open like this. Are they females or eunuchs?"

Jyoti was rather intrigued to find out the real identity of the girls. For a while, he wondered if his sister Swarna was one of the girls, who accompanied a friend of hers to the assembly to play a prank. She wanted to attend it badly, but Jyoti couldn't allow her as some conservative men rejected the idea. It was a first assembly of its kind inside the mansion; hence Jyoti didn't want any controversy to mar the pleasures of the event. The girls could join in the next time. But again, curiosity was killing him. Who were the girls?

The girls, on their part, were immersed in their own world of chit-chat and laughter, covered under their veils. Jyoti sent Rabi to interact with them and find out who they were.

Rabi appeared in front of them and said just as his Jyoti dada had instructed him. "Excuse me, if you can please introduce yourselves first and then take part in our discussions, we will truly appreciate it."

The girls, however, ignored Rabi's plea and gestured for him to get lost. But Rabi was persistent in his appeal, given the responsibility. He kept on asking their names. Finally, one of the girls replied, irritated by his constant questioning: "Go and tell your Jyoti dada, we are *Sakhi Samiti*."

Rabi asked, curious and astonished: "Both of you have the same name? *Sakhi Samiti*?"

"It is our joint name. Understood, you dimwit? Go and tell your Jyoti dada and save us. The people here are already ogling at us!" The girl said.

The voice of the girl sounded familiar to Rabi's ears. He replied, in sudden excitement: "Ah, I got you, you are Swarna Didi!"

Swarna hurriedly closed Rabi's mouth with her hand. "Shhhh! Silent!"

But Rabi was also adamant. "Who is it with you? Tell me, Swarna didi, otherwise I'll shout and tell everyone about your exploits!" He enquired.

"Rabi dada, I am Rupa. Please, please keep it a secret and be mum. We are playing hide-and-seek with the scholars of this assembly."

It was Rabi's turn to burst out in peals of laughter now, watching the girls frolicking and laughing under their veils. It seemed he was a secret partner in their hide-and-seek game.

When asked if Rabi found out the girls' identities, he replied, quite diplomatically: "Listen, it's a secret, which I can tell only Jyoti dada, not anyone else."

At the end of the festivities and the grand feast, the guests returned home with a question in their minds. The identity of the two girls remained shrouded in mystery.

And when the assembly ended finally, Debendranath was witnessing the marvel of an exquisite sunset in the peak of a mountain, far, far away from Jorasanko.

Chapter 7

Hecate Thakrun

In the year 1876, Queen Victoria was titled 'Bharat Samragnee' (queen of the Indian subcontinent) and the announcement was made with a lot of pomp and grandeur. During the same time, there was a sea of changes in the Jorasanko Thakurbari, following Sarada's death. Sarada's elder daughter Saudamini took the responsibility of the entire family on her shoulders and on the other hand, Kadambari started feeding and taking care of the motherless Rabi and gradually, he became very close to his sister-in-law. Rabi, on his part, started to get the very first essence of a woman's tender love through Kadambari's sincere effort to tend to him.

With his *Mejo Bouthan* Gyanada living in Bombay now, Jyoti, too, was fully dependent on his wife Kadambari, giving her his full attention that she had always deserved. The clash between these two strong-willed women being non-existent now, Kadambari was now the new shining star inside the inner quarters of the Thakurbari. Kadambari's chamber in the third floor of the mansion, her terrace and the garden she nurtured with her tender care became her husband Jyoti's den where he carried on his music and poetry, his literary meetings et al. Rabi was eternally a guest in that personal chamber of Kadambari. With the joint effort of Jyoti and Kadambari, the purdah which was a signature of the inner quarters, became a thing of the past. Rabi was completely deprived of the essential beauty, the flavour of joy and pain which was the backbone of his own house for the first ten years of his life. But now he started enjoying the beauty; he started drinking from that wellspring of joy and love to his heart's content.

When his *Notun Bouthan*'s favorite doll got married in a homely ceremony, Rabi was invited as the esteemed guest. The treat was simple and unassuming, 'chochchori' made with prawn and 'panta bhat', a specially prepared stale rice dish with hot chilies. To Rabi, it seemed out of this world!

The very next day after her doll's wedding ceremony, Rabi made a grim face as he went to Kadambari's room and discovered that her familiar pair of slippers was missing. 'She had surely gone to an invitation without letting me know!' He thought to himself. Just as Kadambari had entered home, he hid her doll's ornaments and started quarrelling with her.

"Am I your watchman? Who will look after your room when you're gone?" He said, without any pretext.

Kadambari laughed and replied: "You don't have to look after my room, Rabi, you better look after your own hands!"

Rabi's childhood memories with Kadambari were replete with fun, amid the mundane activities in the terrace. Sometimes, there were crushed lentils made in the shape of doughs, left to dry in the terrace in the sunlight, sometimes *amshatto* or dried mangoes were there in the terrace, tempting him with their fragrance. In the quiet of the winter afternoons, his *Notun Bouthan* Kadambari sat lazily, indulgently on a mat, with her long tresses untied, guarding those food items from the birds. Her accomplice was her brother-in-law Rabi.

One fine day, Jyoti brought along a piano and it was established in the terrace with quite a huge celebration. Jyoti played the piano and Rabi, his younger brother added his own lyrics to all Jyoti's compositions. Jyotirindra was the one who indulged his young sibling Rabindranath in all his creative pursuits. After all, Rabi was twelve years younger than him, and he had seen the first sparks of brilliance in Rabi.

But Kadambari, on her part, didn't agree much with her husband, when it came to acknowledging her brother-in-law's brilliance. She loved to tease Rabi at the slightest pretext. Often she would remark in jest, "Well, I don't see much specialty or uniqueness in you, Rabi! Neither in your appearance, nor in your talent!"

Rabi felt hurt, and replied: "I know you can't acknowledge my talents yet, *Bouthan*, but is my appearance such an eyesore to you?"

Kadambari intended to play along with him further. She teased him again: "No, *Thakurpo* (brother-in-law), I can see your nose is much blunt, compared to your elder brothers and sisters."

"Ah! Even if my nose is a bit blunt, do I really look bad?" Rabi instigated his sister-in-law further, so that he could listen to some more words about his own appearance from her.

Kadambari's eyes danced in a strange gesture. "Well, you do have a dark skin, Rabi. Your mother tried so many home-made remedies to lighten your skin, but to no avail, really." She teased him.

"But I am a man, after all, and men don't have to be fair at all!" Rabi protested. "Didn't you read about tall, dark, handsome men in English literature? Aren't those heroes celebrated in a grand way in all those English stories and novels?"

Kadambari was elated to get the opportunity to counter Rabi now. "My, my, now someone is obsessed with the idea of becoming a hero! But how will you be a hero, tell me? By writing verses? Can you write verses like our revered poet Bihari Lal?"

Kadambari's obsession with Bihari Lal annoyed Rabi to no ends. He silently promised to himself he would write better than the poet some day soon! One day, soon enough, he would have to prove his literary abilities to his *Bouthan*. Since Kadambari threw that challenge to Rabi that day, Rabi's blue notebook filled up with a plethora of verses.

After a whole day of writing poetry and playing the piano, in the evening, they used to spread over a mat and a takia (pillow) in the terrace, waiting for a literary gathering there. Kadambari sprinkled water on the garland of bel flower kept in a silver vessel, arranged for iced water in a saucer, and also betel leaves in a box. After taking her daily bath, Kadambari would dress up in Nayansukh or Begum Bahar cotton saris in soothing colours, tying her hair in a bun, wrapped with a garland of bel flowers. When she would come and sit on the mat, all decked up, Rabi felt as if Goddess Saraswati, the Goddess of wisdom herself had arrived from the heavens, filling the terrace and the evening air with her beautiful essence, mingling with the aroma of French perfume.

Jyoti, on the other hand, came along in a white dhoti or pajama, wearing a light 'urni' or scarf covering the upper part of his body. The fragrance of *attar* that he wore permeated the air around. Rabi, on his part, came prepared with a few songs of his own, but Kadambari never paid much attention to his songs. She waited eagerly for her husband Jyoti to sing instead. Having Jyoti, the very handsome and talented, accomplished man from the Thakurbari as her husband, she thought of herself as a princess of the fairy tales of yore. If Jyoti would have ignored her presence, not paid her enough attention, Kadambari had contemplated of suicide. She was especially frightened when her sister-in-law Gyanada had belittled her before her marriage to Jyoti, labelling her as unworthy and undeserving of Jyoti. But Jyoti's tender love and care made her blossom like a beautiful, fragrant flower. She felt like the happiest woman in the world, immersed in the marvels of housekeeping along with her studies and her passion for poetry. She had this rare ability to make an ordinary dish taste extraordinary by her sheer culinary talent. The terrace garden, on the other hand, flourished incredibly, as she tended to it with all her love and attention. The palm trees lined up in one corner of the terrace, the *chameli, gandharaj, karabi, dolon champa* flowers blossoming in the flower pots transformed the terrace quite dramatically.

Some women in the extended family of Jorasanko still belittled and ignored her as the daughter of a humble employee of the estate, but she didn't care much now. Her days were filled with the love and attention of her loving husband and her brother-in-law, accompanying them everywhere like Lakshman in the epic Ramayana.

Sometimes, Jyoti would have to go to Shilaidaha to

take care of the zamindari estate, and at other times, he would be stuck at one of the rehearsals of his upcoming plays, unable to come back home and be with her. During those times, Kadambari felt lonely, dejected, and Rabi tried hard to entertain her lonely *Bouthan*.

Ever since the purdah had been lifted from the inner quarters of the Thakurbari, eminent poets like Akshay Chowdhury started accompanying Jyoti in their tete-a-tete at the terrace. Such an august gathering, such free, uninhibited mixing between men and women was inconceivable only a few days back. Akshay, on his part, had this irresistible urge to impress the young and beautiful Kadambari, and turned to singing songs. However, he had no talent in it, and also, there was not an iota of melody in his voice. He found a fat, hardbound book in front of him and tried using it as his table while singing. As soon as his song started, Jyoti and Kadambari looked into each other's eyes meaningfully.

Jyoti said: "Akshay, leave your singing for another day, read one of your poems today. It's been so long since Kadambari hasn't listened to your poetry!"

Akshay seemed overjoyed. "Really, *Bouthan*? If you are interested, I am very keen to read out my new series of poems for the monsoon that I composed very recently. Unless I don't read them to you, the metaphors of those poems aren't coming alive somehow." He expressed with newfound emotions.

Apart from reading from his own creations, Akshay Chandra would recite from 'Irish Melodies', the famous poetry collection in his robust voice. Rabi had been a great admirer of Akshay's renditions from 'Irish Melodies'. He had discovered the essence of a new world of verses and their gracious beauty in the patronage of Akshay Chandra, a world which he had never found in his dry textbooks. Rabi would sometimes translate those verses in Bengali and read them out to Jyoti and Akshay in turns. The pages of his notebook titled 'Malati Punthi' were thus, filled with his passionate verses. But though his elder brother indulged his literary interests, the young, juvenile poet didn't get as much attention and importance from his sister-in-law Kadambari.

One day, Rabi and Kadambari started an argument centered on Kadambari's fascination for caged birds. Rabi had noticed that the girls and brides of rich, wealthy families had this queer habit of taming birds inside cages and hanging those cages in the verandah. Rabi couldn't tolerate the shrill cry of the cuckoos inside their cages. Kadambari, on her part, got for herself the Chinese version of the Indian 'Shyama' bird and started taming her.

Rabi started quarreling with her on that pretext. "Don't you feel sorry for the caged bird, its agony of being trapped? Why have you tied it inside the cage? Set it free, I say!"

Kadambari didn't reply; she ignored Rabi and continued feeding the bird with grains. Every morning, a man came to her room to supply the bird with grasshoppers and other insects, its daily diet. She became busy conversing with this man, which enraged Rabi further.

"Why aren't you replying me? You know, Jyoti dada replies to all my queries!" Rabi said.

"What reply? Would I have to be answerable to you for everything I do? I'm afraid I don't have that much time; can't you see how busy I am with work?" Kadambari replied, not hiding her anger.

Rabi was also filled with silent anger, deep within, but he refused to be defeated by his *Bouthan*'s verbal accusations. He replied, enraged: "What kind of work are you doing? All you are doing is tormenting this helpless soul by putting it in a cage!"

"So you're saying that it's a sin to tame birds as pets! But can't you see how I am taking care of it with all my love?" Kadambari said, in a compromising tone.

But Rabi was determined to win over his *Bouthan* today in this verbal dual. "Why, not only birds, but you have also trapped two squirrels in a cage, to tame them and make them your pets! Don't you know how sinful it is to incarcerate wild animals?" He charged her.

Kadambari frowned upon her brother-in-law, hearing these accusations and said: "You don't have to act as the stern *guru moshai*...I will take care of my right and wrong deeds."

This didn't seem like a reply, it was rather a decision, which Kadambari let him know, by virtue of being just a bit older than Rabi. But Rabi's heart didn't agree with this... why wouldn't she understand if it is truly a wrong deed on her part? Telling this to Jyoti dada would also not help, Rabi thought; of late he himself had kept a wild deer as his pet. He assumed that Jyoti dada would take his wife's side only, and avoid any further argument. He went quiet for some time, and then, did an outrageous act silently. One day, he secretly opened the cages and set all the wild animals free. After this, Jyoti had to appear on the scene and intervene to stop the tremendous fight that had ensued between Rabi and Kadambari, his *Bouthan*.

Jyoti was now an accomplished playwright; his new

play titled 'Sarojini' or 'The Onslaught at Chittore' had been quite rage among the readers, just after its release. The play was also staged at the Great National Theatre, with Nati Binodini, the eminent stage actress in the lead role. Rabi himself had composed a song which was featured in the play. Jyotirindranath had entrusted Rabi with this responsibility out of sheer affection for his younger brother, and Rabi, delighted with this incredible opportunity, harnessed all his creative prowess and composed the song.

Kadambari, however, had reservations about Rabi composing this song, as she believed this play was the best creation of her husband till date. She thought Jyoti had done an injudicious job in giving this opportunity to young Rabi, completely ignoring how significant the play was in his career. She strongly believed that Jyoti himself should have written and composed such an important song.

However, when the play was performed on stage, that particular song mesmerized the audience. Rabi had written this song in the context of a very crucial scene in the play, where there were countless funeral pyres burning. The Rajput girls and brides dressed in gorgeous red attires, in flower ornaments sang the song in unison and surrendered their bodies in the burning pyres. The poet Rabi crafted these lines in the song:

'Burn, burn, keep burning, the pyre

We widows will surrender to the fire

Let the fire burn strong, quenching our anguish.

See how our hearts burn, let the Gods be witness to this.

Remember, you'll have to suffer, bear the brunt of it all,

Burn, burn, keep burning, the pyre.'

The stage was truly set on fire. The women sang in

unison and jumped into the fire; kerosene was sprinkled to fuel the fire. The actresses made it all real and palpable, their bodies scalding, their hairs burning in the fire. They remained unperturbed still and participated in it on an impulse, as it also indicated the love and passion they had for their motherland.

Binodini *dashi*, the actress playing the part of Sarojini in the play mesmerized the audience with her histrionics. The playwright himself looked at her with deep awe and admiration. His heartbeat accelerated, his heart palpitated, seeing her perform on stage so effortlessly.

"*Bouthan*, it doesn't seem so bad, after all, what do you say?" Rabi asked Kadambari with a frown.

"Not bad!" Kadambari smiled and patted Rabi on the back. "You deserve a gift after this!"

Rabi became restless to know what his prize would be, which amused Kadambari to no ends. He kept roaming around her, but she wrapped her desire in a cloak of mystery and never disclosed anything. In the meanwhile, Jyoti took along Rabi to one of his trips to Shilaidaha. Rabi's composition in the play 'Sarojini' had mesmerized Jyoti, and he had decided to take him wherever he went, as an ideal companion. Rabi received the honour of being his peer not only in poetry writing and composing music, but also in horse riding and bird hunting skills. Kadambari, on her part, wrote letters to both her husband Jyoti and Rabi. And Rabi wrote long letters in reply, almost religiously.

The town of Shilaidaha provided a sense of freedom from all shackles to Rabi, he felt like he had just experienced a bout of rain showers after prolonged summer heat. Even Jyoti bared open his heart here, indulging in his characteristic craziness, which continued even after they went back to Calcutta. Upon his return, he started thinking of a political group named 'Sanjeevani Sabha'.

Surendranath Bandyopadhyay, a great leader of Bengal then, had made quite a name for himself among the youth of Calcutta by propagating the story of Guiseppe Mazzini, the exemplary Italian leader and his quest to attain the freedom of his nation. The fire and zeal of freedom that he had lit in the hearts of countless young souls in Italy, the secret society that he formed in support of his freedom movement against Austria had inspired quite a number of young enthusiasts to follow the same ideals and maintain other secret societies, and 'Sanjeevani Sabha' was one such group. Its objective was the welfare of people and the cultivation of nationalism.

Jyoti and Rabi both became the members of the group. Since it was a discreet group, they usually met at a secret place, which was a haunted house in the Thanthania area. During the day of the initiation, the president of the group, Rajnarayan Basu came, dressed in a sacred red attire, a *patta bastra*. The meeting started with holy chanting from the Vedas and then, a book with the contents of the Vedas was placed on a table, wrapped in a piece of red cloth. Two dead human skulls were placed on both ends of the table and their eyes were lit up with candles. The dead skulls, according to the group, represented the dead spirit of India, hence the two brothers took a vow to rejuvenate the dead spirit of their country, to illuminate the senses of the nation and her people.

It was decided then that the members would donate one-tenth of their earnings to the group. It was also decided that the money would be invested in manufacturing home-made or 'swadeshi' matches, machines making 'swadeshi' clothes et al. After the first matchbox was made, the excitement among the members was incredible. Jyoti was the first one to discover the news in 'Samachar Chandrika': "An auspicious sign—Today we saw a new matchbox which is shaped pretty much like the small boxes of safety matches of the European company Bryant and Mere. The box has been created beautifully by using the quintessential Devdaru wood, with the masala to ignite the matches on both sides of the box. Moreover, the matches have been made of bamboo instead of Devdaru wood, they were ignited as soon as they were rubbed against one side of the box. However, when there is cold wind blowing, the bamboo woods get cold and lose their power of ignition, and we noticed the same with these matches."

Jyoti called Rabi and conveyed the news to him excitedly. "Look, Rabi, 'Samachar Chandrika' has such effusive praise for our swadeshi matches!"

But Rabi felt hesitant. "It's very expensive, though...It will be difficult to continue making these kinds of matches. You know the cost of manufacturing one such matchbox? It is equal to the fuel cost of an entire village for a year!"

Jyoti tried to diminish his younger brother's anxiety. "Isn't it great that we could at least create swadeshi matches with our own resources? We can always collect the money required to make it, as needed. Let it be launched in the market first."

But Rabi's anticipation about it all was very true. Making swadeshi matches was an expensive affair, and soon they were overwhelmed with debt, and tremendous financial crisis. The machine for manufacturing swadeshi clothes, which was installed with a lot of money, made a few 'gamchhas' (Indian bathing towels) and then stopped working as the burden of debt was too heavy to make it run. But this didn't dampen the spirits of the swadeshi enthusiasts. Babu Annanda Chandra Chattopadhyay of Pathuriaghata created the first swadeshi printing machine, and Babu Girish Chandra Chattopadhyay installed the first home-made machine manufacturing cotton. Satyaprasad, one of their brightest members, was sent to Coopers Hill Engineering College for the study and cultivation of the sciences. Rabi, on his part, was encouraged to study the finer industrial skills in London.

During the same time, it struck upon Jyotirindranath to design swadeshi clothes for the Indians which would have a universal appeal. After a lot of thought and conscious deliberation, he invented his own signature style of dressing. One day, he dressed himself in a pajama and tucked a piece of cloth over it like a loin cloth, and also wore a head gear which looked like the cusp of an English hat and an Indian 'pagri'. In the broad daylight, Jyoti Thakur passed by the streets in such unconventional attire, in his unflinching zeal to serve the people of his nation. People gathered in the streets, tempted to watch the strange phenomenon.

Besotted with admiration for his elder brother, Rabi said to his *Notun Bouthan*, "What a great man your husband is! We've surely seen many bravehearts who would give up their lives for our nation, but how many of us have seen someone wearing such an unconventional fusion attire and roam around the streets of Calcutta in a vehicle? I'm sure it's a rare sight!"

Kadambari, on her part, was besotted by her husband's charm and charisma. "So true, Rabi *thakurpo* (brother-in-law), I feel so much pride in my heart for such a daring and gallant husband. You know, this is why nobody else can win my heart!"

"Why would anybody else win your heart? What is the need, after all? In fact, you are the one who makes men fall heads over heels in love with your charm!" Rabi glanced at Kadambari and remarked.

The very next day, Jyoti did something phenomenal that made heads turn. In the morning, Rabi and Akshay Babu gathered at the drawing room in the third floor. They competed with each other, reading out their poems, and Kadambari went on supplying *luchi* (fried bread) and potato curry to the enthused poets.

Suddenly, it struck Jyoti that the verses and songs of these two poets would fly in the firmament with no acknowledgement, hence it was crucial to have some permanent arrangement for both of them. He stopped them and declared: "Listen, I have a new idea for you both."

Kadambari replied in jest: "Well, your brain is stuffed with ideas all the time, dear! There's nothing new in it."

"No dear, I promise it's a new idea, you'll be amazed if you listen." Jyoti replied. Akshay and Rabi relied a lot on Jyotirindra; they listened, excited.

"The idea is about bringing out a new literary journal from our own Thakurbari. We will be instrumental in bringing out this journal which will startle everyone. No need to fly around like nomads from now on, all your verses and prose will be contained within the pages of this journal."

Rabi replied with a lot of excitement in his voice: "Ah,

Jyoti dada, this idea of yours is like a trump card, I say! But will you be able to convince *Babamoshai*?"

"Let's first go to *Bordada*'s (elder brother) room in the second floor. Once the king bird is convinced enough, *Babamoshai* won't object, I believe." Jyoti said.

The four of them flocked together at Dwijendranath's room in the second floor, who was busier with the cultivation of wisdom, rather than the cultivation of arts and literature. He supported their enthusiasm and suggested: "The idea seems very good…But why do we need a new journal after all, Jyoti? What if we revive our old one, *Tatwabodhini* instead?"

Jyoti seemed a bit hesitant. "Borda, *Tatwabodhini* has quite a heavy, erudite smell to it. We want a literary journal which will be flavourful, yet experimental in its essence. We want the journal to reach out to the mass readers, with the objective to enhance their literary tastes."

"But the readers will read a good journal anyway, don't worry about that at all." Dwijen wanted to assure his brother.

But Akshay was not convinced enough. "But *Bordada*, can't you see, the tastes of our Bengali readers these days have deteriorated so much! They are still attracted by the cheap, pedestrian stuff!"

Jyoti literally snatched his words and added: "So you see, we have this big responsibility to educate the readers lacking literary tastes! As we all know, a nation cannot progress unless its people have refined literary tastes. Since *Tatwabodhini* is not really reaching the mass readers, we really have to start afresh with this new journal."

"What would be the name of our new literary journal?" Dwijen asked, curious.

"You decide the name, *Bordada*!" Rabi said.

"How about *'Suprabhat'* (The New Dawn)?"

Everyone became quiet at this announcement. Jyoti was not quite fond of the name, as it seemed from his reply. "If you ask me, even this name has a tinge of arrogance to it. It seems we are claiming that we are finally bringing in the new dawn in Bengali literature with this publication."

"Okay…How about *'Bharati'* then?" Dwijen asked, after giving it some thought.

Jyoti seemed to like the name 'Bharati'. It had a home-grown or swadeshi feel to it, and on the other hand, 'Bharati' also meant wisdom and learning.

Dwijen explained the meaning further. "The Indian Goddess of wisdom, Goddess Saraswati is synonymous with Bharati, in the same way as Britannia, the Goddess of Britain, or Athenia, the Goddess of Athens."

The name 'Bharati' was unanimously agreed upon. Five hundred copies of its inaugural issue were sold as soon as they were published, and then it gained more momentum as the Thakurbari became the ubiquitous venue of grand literary assemblies. Every Sunday, Rabi and Jyoti visited Akshay Chandra's residence, where Akshay's wife Sarat Kumari had recently stepped in from Lahore. She joined them in their enthusiasm for literature. Some days, they also went to Bihari Lal's residence for a tete-a-tete. Except Sundays, all other days, they gathered at Swarna and Janaki's home in Rambagan in the evenings. Their home had literally become the office of 'Bharati'. Sometimes, Prafullamayee joined along with Kadambari, to ward off her depression with the elixir of music and poetry. Swarna would never let them go away without having dinner at her home, so the siesta became prolonged as the nights stretched on.

One day, Rabi was reading out 'Macbeth', the play penned by Shakespeare to Kadambari, seated on their terrace at the third floor. He had it in his mind to translate the play into Bengali and publish it in *'Bharati'*. Kadambari seemed too excited after listening to the vivid descriptions of the three witches of 'Macbeth'.

"Imagine how free the three witches are…They live at their own will, and chew on the heads of men at their own will!" She remarked.

"*Bouthan*, you're envying the witches?" Rabi laughed as he said. "Aren't you already chewing on my head already? And poor Akshay Babu's head is vanished long time back!"

"Are you calling me a 'witch', Rabi? It's not fair, let me tell you!" Kadambari said with a tinge of resentment. "Sarat Kumari is now at Akshay Babu's house, don't badmouth her like me, I warn you, Rabi."

"Hey Goddess, the one who chews on my head every day, I am naming you Hecate *Thakrun* from today. You are Hecate, the third witch of Macbeth, and you are the Greek Goddess Hecate with three heads. Which spell of yours has turned me into a timid sheep, can you tell me?" Rabi said.

"Go away, I say, why do you think I would ever care to turn you into a sheep? You are still so young, but you are a precocious kid!" Kadambari replied.

Rabi's tender heart of sixteen years was filled with

unspoken anguish, listening to his sister-in-law's words. He knew that in the Sanskrit scriptures, sixteen-year-old boys were considered adults. Even now, sixteen-year-old boys became fathers of children after their marriage. Just a few days back, his nephew Satyen, close to his own age, was married off.

Rabi failed to understand why his *Bouthan* joked so cruelly about him. She was supposed to give him a gift as promised, which she didn't give till now. Moreover, Rabi noticed that she wasn't giving him half of the attention that she was showering on Jyoti dada, her husband. But the young poet's heart craved for that little bit of praise and attention from her. He felt angry on himself for that. They started reading and reciting poetry when Jyoti and Akshay came together at the terrace on the third floor.

Eventually, at the end of the literary soiree in the evening, everyone returned to their dens. Even Jyoti and Kadambari retired to their own bedroom, but Rabi loitered alone in the terrace for a long time, impatient, restless, with haywire thoughts that crowded his mind. In the moonlit night, he gazed at the shadow of the palm trees lined together, which appeared as exquisite artistic pieces. He loitered there till the wee hours of the night, witnessing the paraphernalia outside.

One day while Rabi was roaming around in the terrace quite late at night, his eyes were stuck at the window of his Jyoti dada's bedroom and he stood there, transfixed. The curtain of the window had blown in the wind, and the moonlight had revealed a private, intimate scene in the quiet of the room. That night, Rabi had witnessed a magical scene of union between a man and woman. His head reeled; he experienced a strange, unspoken sense of excitement for some fleeting moments. Witnessing the scene for those few moments, he felt he had crossed the boundaries of his dreamy, innocent adolescent years and reached adulthood in a sudden jolt. Young Rabi felt like he had just committed the crime of seeing the forbidden apple. He felt the beautiful moonlit woman dancing in his mind, deep within him. He envisioned her time and again for the whole night, unable to sleep, and then, fever struck him in the wee hours of the night.

In the meanwhile, there had been a few developments in the lives of the kith and kin of Thakurbari. Satyen had been posted as a District Judge in the town of Shikarpur, and there, a son had been born to him and Gyanada. They named him Kabindra. In Swarnakumari's house, her youngest daughter Urmila had just been born.

Satyen and Gyanada had come to Jorasanko with their children with the objective to make arrangements for their upcoming London trip. Satyen wished to take Rabi along with him, for it was his ardent wish that Rabi would study in London to became a barrister. Once Satyen and Gyanada arrived, there was a new tide of excitement in their literary soiree every evening at the terrace on the third floor. Every evening, Satyen and Gyanada joined Rabi, Jyoti and Kadambari in their meeting. Swarnakumari was a regular presence there, and also Bihari Lal, Kadambari's most favorite poet came occasionally and recited his own poetry. It was truly an august gathering of poetic and artistic souls that filled the terrace with creative energy. Rabi, of course, was a bit distanced from Kadambari, his *Notun Bouthan* since a few days.

One day, they all had gathered to listen to Bihari Lal's poetry. Satyen and Gyanada seemed most enthused to listen to the acclaimed poet, his gracious verses. After a long period of deprivation outside Bengal, finally they had the opportunity to listen to a poet reciting his poems in his own voice. However, during the poetry session, Gyanada noticed that the poet Bihari Lal was craving for the attention of a special person, as if all his verses were being read out only for that person. She was none other than Kadambari. And she on her part was listening, mesmerized, awed by his poetic brilliance. She seemed so effortless amid the presence of such outsiders, Gyanada thought, surprised. During her absence, the women of the Thakurbari seemed to have changed a lot. The purdah system which was a customary phenomenon inside the mansion, seemed obsolete now. Kadambari too has turned into a queen bee in the literary assembly, shedding off her veil. But wasn't Gyanada supposed to be happy to witness this change? Why was she hesitant to accept it then? She was the pioneer of such a revolution inside the mansion, after all. She remembered the fierce opposition, the glum faces of *Babamoshai* and her mother-in-law, the wails of the servants and maids, the taunts of the strangers in the streets. She had carved her own path, her own niche with her own grit and determination, and now, Shyam Ganguly's daughter was seated in the same altar she had created with such toil and accumulating all the praise! How significant had this young woman been, with Bihari Lal praising her ardently, Akshay looking at her with awestruck eyes? Rabi, her younger brother-in-law seemed to be under the spell of Kadambari, his *Notun Bouthan*. As for Jyoti, he seemed to have cut off his own head, dedicating it at her holy feet.

Gyanada felt claustrophobic amid such surroundings. Have they all gone crazy? They seemed enthralled by the spell of Kadambari, in spite of Gyanada's towering presence.

She went to her sister-in-law Swarnakumari and requested her: "*Thakurjhi*, let's leave from here and chat somewhere in private."

Swarna didn't like to leave the august company, not so soon. She was supposed to read out her poetry to Bihari Lal in a few minutes. "Wait, *Mejo Bouthan*, let us listen to some brilliant poets for now; we can chat to our heart's content at night!" She replied.

Bihari Lal looked at Gyanada and joked: "What, *Mejo Bouthan*, is my poetry so terribly bad that you want to leave right now, without listening to them?"

"Well, you are blessed with many admirers anyway, our presence wouldn't matter much." Gyanada said, with a hint of sarcasm in her voice.

"Please sit, *Mejo Bouthan*," Jyoti insisted. "The party will be totally drab without your presence."

Gyanada replied in a sombre face: "You all carry on… let me go inside and arrange for some refreshments to be sent at the terrace."

Just then, Kadambari awoke, as if from her trance-like state, and said: "You don't have to worry about that, *Mejdi*, I've already told the maids, they will come with the food just now!"

Right then, two maids came along with trays filled with abundance of food. Akshay Babu couldn't suppress his excitement at the sight of the grand feast. "Look, look at those plates filled with fish cutlets, mutton chops!" He exclaimed.

"Ah, no, Mister! No mutton chops, but today we have a different menu." Kadambari grinned and replied.

Akshay made a sad face and said: "Oh my, Kadambari *Bouthan*! You know, the main attraction while coming here every day is you, and then the special mutton chops handmade by you! And we don't get to taste them today?"

Everybody laughed, and extended their hands to pick up the smokey, succulent sheekh kababs, and Gyanada wondered if her younger sister-in-law was usurping her position in the kitchen too. Perhaps, she was gradually losing her importance in Jorasanko, and Kadambari had utilized her absence quite skillfully, to solidify her prominence in the mansion.

Kadambari, on the other hand, noticed that Gyanada was looking at her with her sharp, fierce gaze. Deep within, she felt quite amused. One day, this same *Mejo Bou* had neglected and downgraded her, she thought. Let her see the new Kadambari, loved and admired by such accomplished poets. They surrounded her, sang melodious songs to her, all they wanted was to make her happy. The young bride whom *Mejo Bou* had discarded like broken glass is now the precious necklace that her dear brother-in-law Jyoti wears with pride.

The bitter wind of cold war between Gyanada and Kadambari blew strongly and continuously, unbeknownst to the members of Jorasanko.

"Wait, *Notun Bou*, wait..." Gyanada said to herself. "Do you think you have attained the same height and authority as me, simply because you have learnt to read some verses?"

There was a deep, dark foreboding of doom that kept growing stronger, right beneath the unadulterated wind of literature.

Chapter 8

'Bharati' v/s Catchpenny Books: The war

One day, when Malini, the bookseller woman stepped inside the Thakurbari courtyard, some young girls and women of the household noticed her and pulled her towards the marble verandah, the main venue for their congregation. Indulgently, they requested her to sing 'dhop', 'kheur', 'jhumurgaan', regional folk songs with ethnic, rustic feel to rejuvenate their spirits. Malini's mouth was filled with the juice of betel leaves, she spat it all out and rinsed her face with water. Then she seated herself comfortably on the mat and sang a 'jhumur' song, The song, in its essence, was a popularized parody version of a traditional *Vaishnava Padavali* rendition, written and composed by Bhavani or Bhavarani.

This composer named Bhavani or Bhavarani, the woman who was the founder of a group of jhumur singers, was quite popular in the city of Calcutta. The women of the inner quarters of the Jorasanko mansion who were still devoid of the touch of modern education, seemed to be ardent admirers of Bhavani's songs. The song and dance sequences of the jhumur singers and performers were a staple of every wedding ceremony in those times. In the rural areas, the jhumur singers and dancers used to dance on top of carts driven by cows during the wedding seasons.

Malini's song brought in a wave of emotions, stirring the quiet, uneventful inner quarters of the Thakurbari.

"Sing another song, please!" Rupa pleaded, and clung to Malini's neck indulgently.

Malini replied, "Then listen to a 'kheur' song after 'jhumur', Rupa, my queen! It is about the sweet, seductive conversation of love between a man and woman."

"Listen to it…" Malini hummed a tune and the song begun. "Oh my fatal bee, come, plunder the honey from me."

"What did the man reply?" The women of the household asked unanimously.

Malini flashed a smile and hummed the tune of the song yet again. "You know what the man replied? 'How can all the other bees suck your honey when I am there?' He said.

The young girls and women rolled on the floor, laughing their hearts out. Most of these women, uneducated, with old school thoughts took a particular liking for these kinds of rustic songs with erotic lyrics. Even Saudamini, Neepamayee and Saratkumari found the humour in these songs appealing enough. As for Rupkumari, she sauntered around the verandah gleefully, brimming with gaiety, and also ran around the high pillars adjacent to the verandah, trying to sing the songs along with Malini, sticking to her like glue.

In Gyanada's urban ears, of course, these popular rustic songs sounded quite vulgar, cheap, devoid of any sophistication and polish whatsoever. While cutting betel nuts in the fancy silver nut cracker, she commented, annoyed, with a frowned face:

"What are you singing, Malini? This has no proper rhythm, nor does it have any aesthetic sense!"

Swarna, on her part was tremendously annoyed as well, listening to these cheap, girly 'kheur' songs and the language used in them. Weren't these the times when the intellectuals of the city were hell bent in rescuing the Goddess of language and the arts from the shackles of vulgar, rustic influence? She thought, while reading the new issue of *Bangadarshan,* the literary journal.

She lifted her face from the journal and said: "What is going on, Malini? Look at you; you are blessed to know the contents of so many good books of literature...You have even taught alphabets and letters to so many illiterate women, and now you are humming such cheap songs?"

"They are not only cheap, but extremely uncouth and vulgar rhymes in the form of these songs! Don't ever utter these here, Malini!" Gyanada interfered.

"Rupa!" She called out loud. "Come away from there, I say! And never sing such songs ever! No woman in our house has ever sung such kind of songs."

Malini felt hurt at such comments, and started to pack up her belongings quickly, in a desperate bid to go away. "I won't sing these songs if you do not want me to, but tell me, Swarna didi, can you belittle those village women who compose and sing these folk songs? You think they are sub-human...Is that right on your part? You know, even this mat in which you all are sitting is a product of the same village where these songs have originated!"

Swarna argued: "But what about that rustic, impure culture that they are part of, can it be placed in the untainted ground of literature? The Bengali language we have been gifted with today is the hard work and perseverance of Vidyasagar, Michael Madhusudan Dutta and writers of their ilk, they have modified it with so much polish and sophistication for years! If they would not have persevered, Bengali literature wouldn't have progressed beyond the primitive 'Hutum Pyanchar Noksha' and 'Alaler Ghorer Dulal.'"

Neepamayee, who was listening to this conversation intently, commented: "What is this segregation of music as polished and uncouth, Swarna *Thakurjhi*? If you ask me, any song that has a pleasing tune appeals to me. I really don't feel any discrimination between the sitar and the ektara, both instruments are equally beautiful to me, as long as the music is soothing enough to the ears."

"What a strange thing to say, *Shejo*!" Gyanada couldn't hide her expression of shock. Look at you, you are such an accomplished singer, trained in classical music, how could someone as discerning as you speak such words? Isn't there such thing as 'quality of music?' How can you say sitar and ektara are the same?"

Neepamayee was cutting pointed gourds, removing their veins in a *boti*, a sharp cutting instrument with a long-curved blade, her fingers drenched in the juice of the vegetables. She wiped her fingers with the border of her sari and replied: "I don't really mind listening to these rustic songs, in fact I like 'dhop', 'kheur', 'keertan' songs; I believe they carry the language of the human soul, the essence of rustic lives."

Saratkumari was rubbing *maida* (flour) and cream in her skin, a regular beauty regimen for the women in the household. She remarked: "Even I like these songs, *Mejo Bouthan*, when Malini sings them, I can visualize the easy, unadulterated life of the countryside."

Malini kept on her glum face still and remarked: "You know, *Mejo Bou*, it is because of your sense of pride and ego that there is so much segregation between the educated and the uneducated in our city."

"Let there be such segregation, you cannot uplift the tasteless rustic culture by any means, no matter how much you love to clap to the rhythm of those cheap 'kheur' songs! And you know, such songs are spoiling the refined environment of our home. Go and listen to them in your own rooms if you please!" Gyanada left no stone unturned to express her displeasure.

Neepamayee was visibly irritated to listen to Gyanada's words, her bossiness in all aspects of their lives annoyed her. "*Mejdi*, we know that you are polished, beautiful and sophisticated. But since you dress up prim and proper all the time and attend the elite parties in the Governor's house, do you have the authority to negate all that we say or think? Aren't we entitled to any opinion whatsoever inside the house, since we don't step outside regularly, like you do? Remember, we have the same rights inside the house as you do!" She said.

"Our opinions will never match, *Shejo bou*," Gayanada replied, "but I can't simply swallow my objection to something as tasteless as this!" The diamond flower ring in Gyanada's nose swelled along with her nose, in her pent-up rage.

Malini, the bookseller woman shook her silver anklets in anger and replied: "Look, *Mejo Bouthan*, those rustic women are mocking your education, emancipation of women, your cultivation of literature, music and the arts, and the clothes you wear, and you, on the other hand, are desperate to discard their tradition and heritage—their rhymes, 'kheur' songs, the use of their loud language in their songs. In such a grave crisis of our nation, both of you need to come together and fight against the British…but no, you are happily fighting among yourselves. Does it seem good to you, Swarna didi?"

Malini was right, at least partially. In those times, there was a strong tug of war, a class struggle between the educated, higher class and the lower class, the uncouth and uneducated mass. With the massive infiltration of the village folks in the city, came the rustic theatre form, 'jatra' and other folk cultures, including 'kathakata', 'panchali', and the 'dhop' and 'kheur' songs. Earlier, these rustic performers were called to entertain the opulent, wealthy zamindars, both inside the inner quarters and the outhouses. But of late, the brand of their spicy, sleazy Bengali language was being replaced by the more polished, high-class Bengali language, more influenced by Sanskrit. Both were strong opponents, and lacked the patience to tolerate each other.

Malini wanted Swarna to be her ally in the argument, but Swarna didn't reply to her. Gyanada said again: "Don't you know about that composer named Karadas who composed a song, mocking and ridiculing us? Trust me, the words are so cheap and filthy, and all those lower-class, uncouth folks are dancing to its tune! And you call it 'culture', Malini? What a shame!"

"Which songs are you talking about, *Mejo Bouthan*?" Malini asked in pseudo-curiosity, though she very well knew that recently Karadas, the composer had composed a sarcastic song, mocking the behavior of higher-class, enlightened women. The song had been immensely popular. Malini started humming the song, as if attempting to tease Gyanada with its lyrics.

"In the rotten *kali yug* in the city of Kolkata, the urban dame rides a carriage

A stick in her hand, a hat in her head, she has really come of age.

She doesn't adhere to the Hindu rituals of 'shasthi', 'makal', 'sejuti', she is anything but feminine.

She doesn't even look at herself in the mirror, she isn't the traditional damsel genuine.

She asks for photographs, rides on a horse, wearing a gown.

She has abandoned her bathing rituals in the Ganges,

In the bathroom, her 'khansama' (cook) wipes her wet body with a towel."

"Beware, beware, never sing that song ever again, Malini!" Swarna appeared extremely annoyed. "The cook wipes his mistress' wet body? What a shame! How scandalous! It seems they are trying to belittle, demean the women of higher-class families willfully. Besides, the inconsistencies in the rhyming and the tune, both are atrocious!"

"I understand, Didi," Malini replied. "You know, I think the rustic poet and composer hasn't ever witnessed the behavior, the daily lives of higher-class, urban women.

He might have heard about them from someone, and the rest is a product of his imagination. He just wanted to have pure fun, and hence the lyrics. You know, in most of the compositions penned by men, women are hidden beneath the veil of imagination, and this image is one of them. The poet might be completely unaware that the 'khansama' or cook works in a Muslim household, so he might have unknowingly entrusted him with the responsibility of drying the body of the Hindu or Brahma housewife."

"Don't try to argue on their behalf, Malini!" Gyanada replied, visibly annoyed. "Bring out what you have in your collection of books, instead! And if you have found out about a new woman author, tell us about her."

"But you all have dampened my spirits so much today, *Mejo Bouthan*!" Malini replied, visibly anguished. "You seem so interested in women's writings, then let me share a fact with you…long before you, the educated women of privileged families have flourished, these so-called cheap, downtrodden women have composed their own brand of rhymes, sang their own *'dhop, jhumur, kheur'* songs, participated in *kobir loraai*, the dual between poets, their passion and love for cadence matching their male counterparts. Have you ever heard of the famous dual between Haru Thakur and Jagyeshwari in verses? You cannot imagine the massive crowd that the event attracted. Why, even some twenty years back, the renowned singer Jaganmohini had come to this Thakurbari of Jorasanko to perform her exemplary *'dhop keertan'* songs. There was no such discrimination and disrespect towards these singers in your grandmother's or your mother's times."

Swarna too felt a bit hurt. She knew she was the pioneer among women authors of her times, but she received no recognition from Malini, the bookseller woman. She asked Malini: "You mentioned so many women composers just now, can you memorize the lines from any of their creations?"

"Of course, I can!" Malini replied promptly. "Listen to the washerwoman Rami's lyrics, then…Perhaps she is the first woman poet of Bengal."

Malini recited a few of her rhymes:

"What do I say, my love, I'm not able to utter,

In my attempt to cry and tell you, I end up in loud laughter.

What courage do these worthless men possess,

In their insolence, they stop worshipping the Goddess.

I won't live on in this country where judgement has died,

I'll move to the land where demons have been denied."

"You can sense how fierce the lines are, how bold and unapologetic! Just notice how she doesn't cow down to the overpowering patriarchy and carves her own voice with her statements!" Malini said, after her recitation.

The fact that these women belonging to underprivileged, marginalized communities kept on challenging and refuting the unquestioned dominance of patriarchy, while also mocking them with their insolence was quite a revelation, especially when the so-called educated, emancipated women of privileged families didn't have the courage to do so. And the truth was, they didn't acknowledge those women for their exemplary acts of bravery.

Hence Swarna remarked: "Well, they may have all the bravery in the world, but they are devoid of poetic excellence!"

Malini, dressed up in a green *dhanekhali* sari with a purple border which she tied around her in a tribal fashion, became the representative of Rami, Jaggeshwari, Jaganmohini and the other marginalized woman. It was as if she spoke with a deep anguish in her heart, on their behalf. "I don't like to stay around anymore today, Didi. I beg your leave."

Rupkumari, the foster child of the Thakurbari, had been immersed in a newfound essence of insolence in the meanwhile; unbeknownst to all, her quest to seek that essence grew manifold. She left the courtyard of the inner quarters and started following Malini, lured by her tempting words, her attire, her unique choice of jewelry, all of which signified a different world of femininity to Rupa. The insolence in her behaviour seemed to testify to the fear that the 'Babus' of the elite society had, the fear of educated, privileged women getting influenced by the free, uninhibited language and social conduct of the marginalized women.

So now, the British men and the Bengali Hindu 'Babus' joined hands to drive away, to ostracize their rustic, marginalized women singers of *'jhumur'*, *'dhop'*, *'keertan'* et al. The renowned journal 'Somparkash' expressed their utter displeasure towards such singers in their editorial: "While listening to the descriptions of Sri Krishna's *Rasleela* in elaborate details in these songs, it is quite impossible for an uneducated young girl to keep her passions in check; and the ones who allow the women of their homes to visit the site of such immoral storytelling must be cautious at once about the outcome of such visitations."

As if the men of the households had all the right of the world to show their passions with wild abandon, as if they had all the right to visit the inner quarters of the *Baijis*, the nautch women, to listen to erotic songs and compose sensuous renditions of Krishnaleela, but the moment women would indulge in such pursuits, all hell would break loose. As if the men were born to be the gatekeepers, scrutinizing each and every act of the women, who were nothing but dolls they played with.

Rupa felt agitated, annoyed to witness such discrepancies between men and women. "Why would you boss over us so much? Are we lesser than you in any way?" She questioned, unapologetically.

Malini laughed and replied to Rupa: "You know what, there's an old saying: 'When they fail to get a place in the court, they return home and beat up their women.' All these men are the same, identical in their meanness. Look at those worthless Babus; spurned away by their British masters, they go back home and start bossing over their wives and bullying them!"

Malini's words were not untrue, after all. The elite men of the Bengali Hindu society had oppressed the women of the household, denying them education and enlightenment of any sort, and thus, they provoked the ire of the Englishmen. The more they mocked and ridiculed the Bengali men as regressive and parochial, the more the Bengali men became adamant about changing their stance regarding women. All they wanted was to allow women to be educated, in a desperate bid to prove their transformed, liberal attitude. However, though they allowed for women's education, they were still unprepared to allow women their full sense of freedom. They became anxious, rather petrified of the possibility of their own women starting their own feminine revolution at home, inspired by the acts of the lowly, underprivileged women. Hence, it was part of the inherent politics of the Babus to stop the free, indiscriminate mixing between the rustic singer women and their own wives. In fact, highly educated, elite women like Gyanada and Swarna had learnt to save themselves from the influence of such lowly popular culture.

Swarnakumari started enquiring about Rupa. "Where did she go?" She asked, perplexed. "Did she go after that book-seller woman Malini? What a mess I'm handling, just imagine...Ma has entrusted the responsibility of this good-for-nothing young girl on my shoulders!"

She tied the *anchal* (border) of her sari in her characteristic style and went up to Manada, the maid. "Manada, there are plenty of vegetables for cooking, go and send them to the kitchen for cooking."

"It's all your fault, you haven't been able to raise her properly!" Gyanada expressed her displeasure quite openly. "She didn't seem to imbibe an iota of education or culture from this household."

Soudamini looked enviously at the gorgeous Gyanada, dressed in a soft *taant* sari, with a flower tucked in her hair. "Hmm, look, the *Fulbibi* has started to teach her lessons all over again." She thought to herself.

Manada, the maid, while gathering the vegetables in the basket and cleaning them up, remarked: "Well, have you ever heard of the root of a plant getting attached to a different plant? No matter how much you train her, she won't learn, I say!"

"That's not always true, Manada!" Swarna spoke

up now. "Remember, your *Dada moshai* (grandfather) had been adopted by our *Boro Dadamoshai* (great grandfather). But then, our grandfather Dwarakanath was the child of the Thakur clan only, albeit from a different branch of the clan. As for Rupa, she needs to be raised under strict discipline and admonished from time to time."

Soudamini replied with a glum face: "You know, it's extremely difficult to reprimand her. Earlier she used to bury her face in our mother's sari and now, after her death, she takes refuge in *Notun Bou* Kadambari's room in the slightest pretext. *Notun Bou*, not having children of her own, is extremely protective of her."

"Yes, that's what we all say. *Notun Bou* is such a good woman, but she couldn't conceive any child in so many years after her marriage." Just after Manada's remark, Sarat Kumari joined in. "I feel rather bad for Kadambari. Such a gentle, pleasing girl with so much beauty and grace, but God made her a barren woman…"

Gyanada stopped her chore of cutting betel nuts and remarked: "Well, you all seem to feel so bad for her, but all I'm thinking is of *Notun Thakurpo's* fate. He's been married to her for eight years; I don't think he'll ever see the face of his offspring. He is only trying to fill up the void in his life with music, literature and his business endeavours."

Swarnakumari was dressing up her sister-in-law Gyanada's hair with a silver ornament. She lifted her face and remarked: "What would the poor woman do, tell me? Though she is barren, her heart is full of affection for our children. You know how busy I am with my writing, with so little time to take care of my children. But *Notun Bouthan* takes such good care of my little Urmila in spite of her multiple chores at home. She protects Rupa with all her might, and also has been raising Rabi, almost single-handedly."

The maids brought along an assortment of fruits for breakfast in multiple exquisite dishes. Neepamayee was the silent listener of this conversation for all this while, but now she picked up a couple of grapes from one of the dishes and opened her mouth. "I personally do not like such intimacy between Rabi and *Notun Bou*, if you ask me. There was no such thing between brother-in-law and sister-in-law in our home in all these years, you seem to have started it all, *Mejdi*. *Notun Bou* is pampering Rabi in the same way that you have pampered Jyoti all these days. You know, such display of affection in abundant measures becomes an eyesore for many."

"But then, that's just pure affection between brother-in-law and sister-in-law, and I don't think that's such a bad thing. Don't you know, these unadulterated bonds within the family enriches the mind with human qualities? The exchange of poetry and literature extends the boundaries of our mind and soul." Gyanada replied. "Also, what about your music, which you learnt at home with so much care and diligence? Why don't you share it with the world outside?" She couldn't help ask Neepamayee.

But Neepamayee, on her part, was annoyed at this intrusion, violating her privacy. "Why do you care about that, *Mejdi*? I love, and rather cherish my own private corner in my own room. I've learnt music for my own sake, not to invite outsiders and share my gifts with them. Though the purdah system has become defunct now, I believe it is good for us brides of this household to maintain some decorum, some sense of privacy. Neither can I manage to sit around a crowd of men in a literary gathering, being the queen bee, nor can I go and dance at parties with *memsahibs* like you do. It is all beyond me." She replied.

The women of the house were hell bent on attacking each other with their caustic words. Soudamini spelled danger of a cold war and instructed the maid to look for Rupa. "Go and find her without any further delay. Bring her back from wherever she is, I want to see the extent of her courage today!"

Swarna's mind was gradually slipping away from the world of these women and the inner quarters of the mansion. Just when her breakfast was done, she wanted to flee away to the third floor, taking along Gyanada, her trusted accomplice and confidante. Right there, the august assembly of 'Bharati' waited for them eagerly.

For the time being, Jyoti's chamber in the third floor was set up as the office of their in-house journal Bharati. In the room, one could see Rabi, Jyoti, Akshay and Kadambari performing the editorial work rather enthusiastically. A yellow box had been bought recently from the funds of the Thakurbari, in order to reserve all the submissions, and Kadambari was entrusted to take its full responsibility.

There was quite a huge stir of activities inside the Bharati office, along with coffee and scrumptious fritters. Both Rabi and Akshay were busy selecting and compiling the writings for the journal, and Kadambari was busy accumulating those selected works in the coveted yellow-coloured tin box. She looked so uniquely different than all other women of Jorasanko, like a beautiful winged fairy flying above the ground in the midst of all her worldly chores.

Jyoti, on the other hand, was busy taking care of

the accounts. Both Jyoti and Dwijen had contributed fifty rupees to take care of the smooth running and maintenance of the journal. In addition, there were donations from some subscribers of 'Bharati' as well. There were also some applications from potential subscribers, which created a lot of enthusiasm among the members of 'Bharati'. It seemed that the idea of putting up the advertisement for subscribers in the Hindu Patriot worked quite well. The advertisement had the following contents:

"This is to notify you all that from the Bengali month of Shravan, a monthly journal of critical studies in literature, sciences, philosophy will be published. Many of the renowned authors of our times will contribute to this journal. With a considerably big volume, the journal is priced at three rupees (monthly subscription fees). For countries outside India, there is a postal fee of six anas (yearly). The journal will be published on the 15th of every month. Those who are interested to be our regular subscribers can write a letter to Mr. Prasanna Kumar Biswas at Dwarakanath Tagore Lane, House No. 6, Jorasanko.

Yours sincerely,

Dwarakanath Tagore (Editor)

When the first issue of 'Bharati' came out, it was sent to the contributing writers, subscribers and eminent personalities all over Calcutta and Howrah. Also, eighty-four copies were sent to the suburbs of Calcutta by post, on the very first day of its appearance.

'Bharati' was also special because most of its contributing authors were from the Jorasanko household. The main writers were Rabi, Jyoti and Akshay. The inaugural issue carried Rabi's poetry and short story together, and

Akshay, on his part, was trying his hand at literary essays, apart from his verses. Dwijen, on his part, wrote somber, critical essays from time to time, while on the other hand, he wrote humorous pieces as the main columnist of the 'humour' section.

It was an august gathering in Jyoti's chamber, with Swarna and Gyanada, along with Rabi and his accomplices. Rabi complained to Swarna, "Look, *Naw Didi*, we have so many poetry submissions from women poets! You know, whenever these women are able to write in fourteen meters and rhyme their verses, we praise them, but when it comes to us men, we are judged so critically!"

Swarna argued with her brother: "That's not true, Rabi! Even the prose and poetry by women are judged with harsh criticism. But tell me, didn't you seem to like any of the poetry submissions of the women you received?"

"Well, I don't think Rabi is at all interested in the quality of writing of these women poets! He is only interested in writing poetry about women!" Kadambari joked, smiling naughtily. The women would only be his muse and his inspiration, not write poetry themselves, she meant to say.

Rabi smiled and replied: "True, '*Notun Bouthan*', aren't you yourself the muse of this humble poet's fragile heart? Dressed in a saffron-coloured long attire over his white pajamas, Rabi walked up to Kadambari and started roaming and dancing around her with hand gestures like a young *baul* singer. "I have made you the north star of my life…my beloved *Bouthan*." He hummed in a melodious, mesmerizing tune.

"Oh my, Rabi, you are raining poetry these days!"

Gyanada exclaimed, in surprise. Was it just the indulgence of Kadambari that has transformed him in such a way, or was it because he was no more that young, adolescent boy she had known? He was talking in a very adult language, which was totally unfamiliar to her.

Akshay too joined in the conversation. "*Mejo Bouthan*, you don't know, she is not only Rabi's muse, she is our three-headed witch Hecate. Jyoti, Rabi and myself are always competing with each other for her inspiration."

"And you know, the great poet Bihari Lal too seems to have joined our league recently!" Rabi added with an impish grin.

"Wait, wait Akshay Babu, let your wife Sarat Kumari come back from Lahore, then you'll see...all your power will be rendered meaningless in her presence." Swarna said.

Gyanada wondered how Jyoti was listening to all this effusive praise about his wife with a pleasing face. She couldn't help asking him: 'Notun, isn't your soul burning in envy to know that your wife has stolen all these young poets' hearts?'

Even before Jyoti could reply to her, Kadambari defended herself. "But what about my husband who has stolen the hearts of so many actresses during his never-ending rehearsals? Does *Mejdi* even know about that? Of late, he is absent from home for many days and nights."

It was totally true. Recently Jyoti would be stuck at his drama rehearsals, unable to return home from time to time. It was also true that the diva of theatre, *Nati* Bindoni, for whom all other men were crazy in love, was mesmerized, awestruck by Jyoti's handsome features and his sheer talent.

However, Jyoti still felt an irresistible attraction towards his young wife Kadambari, to whom he was married for eight long years.

Jyoti could sense the subdued tinge of agony in Kadambari's voice as she replied to Gyanada. "Well, even when I am outside, busy with work, my heart is kept safe in your vault, my dear wife...but still you doubt me?"

"But I am a simple woman, I don't know the histrionics of attracting men like those women do, and I'm not as beautiful as them either." Kadambari replied to her husband in a hushed voice.

"What are you talking about, *Notun Bou*?" Gyanada admonished her. "Do you want to stop Jyoti from going outside? Look at him, how famous he is already, how busy with his creations! Even if a couple of actresses and dancers get attracted to him, what harm will that cause you? Don't get disheartened by that. Look at the admirers of your own, even they are awestruck by your beauty!"

There was an obvious hint of dissatisfaction and annoyance in Gyanada's voice. Jyoti's chamber was witness to a cold war between the two stunningly beautiful, emancipated, educated women of Jorasanko. There was the dark foreboding of a storm in the soft yellow Chanderi sari attached to Gyanada's body, and the open tresses of Kadambari seemed the metaphor of a *kalbaishakhi* (Nor'wester storm).

Jyoti now got the hint that his dear *Mejo Bouthan* was dissatisfied with his beloved wife still. She was still not seeing all this praise about Kadambari in a favorable light. He was in a fix, as both these women who were his near and dear ones were in a cold war with each other, at loggerheads since the beginning of their relationship.

Jyoti said in on lighter note: "*Mejo Bouthan*, I'm still the mesmerized deer, awed by your presence since forever. If my wife is the Hecate from Macbeth, you, then, are the 'Barjini' (Discarded one)."

"So did the discarded *Bouthan* cast a spell on her deer like the heroine Shakuntala in the epic Mahabharata?" Kadambari asked her husband with a sarcastic tone.

Swarna, on the other hand, was becoming impatient to hear such superficial talks. "Are you people going to indulge in such useless gossip, or read out the writing submissions for 'Bharati'? Give me the new pieces that have arrived, let me read them!" She insisted.

Rabi gave her a poem from one of the folders of the submission and said: "See, *Naw Didi*, this composition is by a woman belonging to the Akrur Dutta family. Read it, it's quite well-written."

Swarnakumari took the piece of paper with the poetry submission from Rabi. The handwritten name of the poetess gleamed like a pearl, scribbled on top of the poem: Girindra Mohan Dasi, it read.

Just when Swarna had started reading the poem, a maid came running to the room and summoned Kadambari in confidence. She whispered some words in Kadambari's ears, and then, Kadambari rushed with the maid. Gyanada followed them both, curious to know what had happened to prompt such action. Downstairs, in the women's inner quarters, there was a quite a pandemonium, Rupa was nowhere to be found. There was mixed news regarding her disappearance, some said she was seen to run away with Malini, the bookseller women, while a watchman of Jorasanko reported that he spotted her with a white *sahib*, both riding a horse and leaving the Thakurbari premises.

A young maid who was only a child was massaging olive oil on Soudamini's body, while Soudamini reclined on her bed, resting her body on a soft pillow. Her body was absorbed in the soothing act of the massage, yet her voice reflected her anger on Kadambari: "Enough now! Drive your foster child away at once! Don't let her in once she returns. We have tolerated all her tantrums till now, but she has crossed all her limits." She ordered.

With a sombre face, Kadambari replied to her sister-in-law: "Well, she was the foster child of Ma, our mother-in-law who really doted on her in her lifetime, now if you want to drive her away for your own peace of mind, what I can say, *Thakurjhi*?"

Gyanada, who came downstairs too, gauged the grimness of the situation for a while, and took the side of Soudamini. "She is speaking the truth, *Notun Bou*, we can't really keep this girl any more. She is becoming a bad example for all the other girls in the household. I know that Ma had pampered her and kept her as her foster daughter out of sheer affection, but now that she has been such a spoilt girl who has been led astray so many times, it's impossible for us to foster her anymore."

Kadambari argued: "Well, if she has done wrong, all of you can mend her ways, can't you? Tell me, who among you has really tried to do that, honestly? I know she has a simple, pure persona. It's just that she sometimes tries to have fun while crossing these societal boundaries, and that's when she commits some wrong actions, but rest assured, she doesn't know that she is doing anything sinful.

Don't be so cruel in judging her, I say, otherwise Ma will feel tormented even in heaven!"

Gyanada admonished Kadambari. "Why are you supporting her shameless acts of aberration in the name of our mother-in-law? Would any other girl in our family ever dare to commit such an act like Rupa? If she had been your own daughter, would you still indulge in such a shameless act on her part?"

Kadambari's eyes stung with indescribable pain. *Mejo Bouthan*, her elder sister-in-law was trying to hurt her without any rhyme or reason, but she remained mum, sealing her lips in agony.

Soudamini hurled her wrath at Kadambari in more fierce words now. "It's me who has to look after the family, *Notun Bou*, and you are only adding more fuel to the fire of unrest and lack of peace by sheltering her. I already have to listen to others' sarcastic words about your own ways, and on top of that, you are fostering that rebellious, shameless girl!"

"What did you see in my own ways, that you're speaking of, *Boro Thakurjhi*?" Kadambari asked her sister-in-law, obviously hurt by the allegations.

"What would you gain by hearing that, dear? You are hardly there among the women in their quarter downstairs, how would you know at all?" Soudamini replied. "Look at us, we are toiling all day, with stains of oil and turmeric in our saris, and you, on the other hand, are relishing your days, dressing up like a queen since the morning and exploring literary pleasures. If that is what you like, don't come to interfere in our family matters, I say."

"But what particular domestic chore didn't I do, tell

me, *Thakurjhi*? Why are you so hell bent in accusing me?" Kadambari was in tears now. "Tell me, then, who is more of an eyesore to you, Rupa, or myself!" Looking at Soudamini and her gestures, Kadambari thought to herself, 'And look at you, you are just a lazy woman, sitting on the bed for the whole day and ordering the maid to do all your duties!'

"God help you...Why would you be an eyesore, of all people, *Notun Bou*? But we all have to adhere to some rules if we are to survive within a family, isn't it? Any exception to it gives rise to controversies, and gives the opportunity for people to talk about you." Soudamini replied.

"But what rules didn't I adhere to, may I know?" Kadambari asked again. It seemed to her that all of these women were unanimously taking a stance against her. Wasn't there anybody in the family who could support her, empathize with her feelings?

Saratkkumari, another sister-in-law of Kadambari was applying 'rooptan' all over her, a special beauty remedy made of natural ingredients, and as it was drying up, she was busy rubbing off the *maida* and milk cream from her face and body. She spoke up now. "Leave her alone, I say! The poor woman is deprived of children of her own...if she finds pleasure in literature, gardening, or in raising Rupa and Urmila, let her do that, please."

"No, I want to know today, I beg of you all!" Kadambari implored, sitting beside her sister-in-law Saratkumari. "Please share all your grievances against me, whatever comes to your mind right now."

Gyanada, on her part, felt a bit guilty now. She felt like she had accused Kadambari a bit more than was needed, really. She tried to console Kadambari a bit. "Look, *Notun*

Bou, you are always alienated, distanced from these women, and mix openly with the outsiders of Jorasanko, especially the men who come to visit us at the literary soirees. The women aren't seeing all this in a favorable light, as usual. In fact, I myself have been the first one to break the purdah system, and also mix with men freely, uninhibitedly. But then, I also make it sure that I mix equally with the women of this household."

"But it's totally wrong to think that I don't mix with them, *Mejdi*. On the contrary, it's they themselves who keep me at a distance, and don't ask me why. For this sole reason, I've cocooned myself in the warmth of my own chamber in the third floor, the *'tetola-r ghor'*, my own paradise."

Manada *dasi*, the old maid interfered at this point. "*Bouthan*, why don't you perform a prayer ritual of Shasthi Thakrun, the Goddess of fertility? You have been infertile since so long, if you give the puja, it will remove the bad omen. Once you are blessed with a little one in your arms, your craziness for this girl Rupa will go away."

Kadambari broke into tears now, weeping profusely like a child. All these women had cruelly, nakedly exposed her pain, her anguish—they were deriving a sick pleasure at her expense. Was a woman's life so useless, after all, if she couldn't have a child? Why would the women of this mansion ostracize her simply because she couldn't bear a child?

Swarna, who was always empathetic towards Kadambari, felt rather bad to see her crying. She came up to Kadambari and patted her in the back. "Don't cry, please. You just aren't blessed with a child yet, but are fortunate in other ways, aren't you?"

At this, Neepamayee replied: "Oh yes, we never had

the good fortune to ride on a horseback with our husbands and roam around the Maidan area for fresh air! Nor did we ever have the privilege of listening to poetry or music, surrounded by our admirers! Crying befits us, not you, *Notun Bou!*"

Swarna felt annoyed at these words, mocking Kadambari. "Ah, why such sarcastic words about our *Bouthan*? It might be that someone else could accomplish something you couldn't do yourself, isn't it? Remember, when *Sejdada* brought in an Ustad for your formal training in music, many folks had frowned upon that idea, but did that stop you? Moreover, you are very rigid about your own daughters, you don't let them mix with others, training them in music, academics etc. Have we ever objected to that? In fact, our *Babamoshai* has given us all enough independence to build our respective lives. Why would anyone of us object to that?"

Saratkumari came up to Kadambari and gave her a hug. "True, why are you all making the beloved wife of our *Notun Dada* cry?"

Gyanada, on her part, found this crying of Kadambari fake and attention-seeking. 'She is out to win the game by showing her tears…' Gyanada thought, though she didn't reveal those thoughts to Kadambari. She said instead: "*Notun Bou*, you can stay alone and enjoy your own private life, only don't indulge Rupa much, and you'll see, nobody will say anything about you."

At this, Kadambari stopped crying, as a new surge of rebellion within her was fueled all over again. "I'll tolerate whatever happens to me, *Mejdi*, but I'll not let that helpless, innocent girl be a victim of your collective fire of anger." She said.

Kadambari's defiant words served as ghee to the latent fire, letting it smoulder all over again. The women surrounding her—Gyanada, Neepamayee, Soudamini's faces seethed in anger. Soudamini opened the knot with which the string of keys was tied to the *aanchal* of her sari, and threw away the string of keys in the floor.

"Very well, then please take the responsibility of this home from now onwards, *Notun Bou*, and please free me from the useless task of looking after the family!" Her voice was brimming with angst. The silver keys with intricate design fell on the floor with an intense sound, much like the sound of incessant fights of these women.

After a few moments of impenetrable silence, Gyanada opened her mouth again. "Let us write to *Babamoshai*, then, let him decide the course of action taken for Rupa's future. Either he will care take of her, or else we will follow whatever he instructs for her welfare." She announced.

"But what about the keys? Who will take the responsibility of the family, may I ask?" Soudamini asked, curious.

Gyanada, with her intelligence and presence of mind, was efficient at taking decisions during moments of crisis. She quickly picked up the keys from the floor and tied them back to the *aanchal* of Soudamini's sari. "Don't be so hot-headed at these small things within the family, *Boro Thakurjhi*. These keys perfectly suit you, and your sari only." She assured her elder sister-in-law.

Kadambari, on the other hand, felt further anguished, alienated. It was as if every entity in this house was against her, and all the seething unrest was only due to her presence. All she wanted was to save the innocent, guiltless girl. Suppressing all her tears about to burst forth, she retreated to her solitary corner in the third floor, her own private cocoon.

But Swarna went running towards her sister-in-law with her baby daughter Urmila in her arms. The child was an angel, two-and-a-half years of age. *"Notun Bouthan,* Urmila, my child is your daughter from today! Take her in your arms, she will stay with you from now onwards..." She implored.

With the lilting tune of laughter of Urmila, the cherubic baby girl, the verandah lit up with a numinous light. Kadambari lifted the tiny body of the child in her arms, and filled her mouth with moist, sweet kisses. Her eyes brimmed with unexplained tears of joy.

Chapter 9

Deepnirvan

Swarnakumari happened to be one of those rarest women, privileged and fortunate enough to be blessed with her husband who had strewn her path with roses when she aspired to rise and shine as an author. He was extremely strict and took utmost care to ensure that neither her children, nor her domestic chores would create any impediment to her path of writing. For some years, Janakinath and his wife Swarna had built their love nest with their three children, Jyotsnanath, Hiranmayee and Sarala at Baithak Khana Road in the Sealdah area of Calcutta. The children were promptly entrusted to the care of the maids, and in this regard, Swarna was a bit more indifferent than her own mother, Sarada Sundari.

The maids attended the children of Swarna with meticulous care, washing their faces and hands, dressing them up in freshly cleaned clothes and taking them for a walk at the Sealdah station in the evenings, accompanied by watchmen to take extra care of the children. The watchmen let the children sit in one of the coaches of the train, not ready to depart yet, and indulged in flirting and chatting with the young maids. Those evenings and the tempting opportunities they offered were much sought after by both the maids and the watchmen. One evening, however, while the children were seated in a coach, the train started to move. Puzzled and scared, Sarala started to scream.

"Why is the train moving at all? Where is it going?" She asked, perplexed.

The maid too screamed in fear, and the watchman, on his part, decided to exhibit his bravery, waving his hands in sync with the moving coach of the train. Nobody knew if the train stopped at this gesture of his part or not, but it was a huge relief for all. Swarna or Janakinath never knew about this 'adventure' in which his children took part. But one significant development happened after the birth of these children. Janakinath's father, the grandfather of the children couldn't sustain his anger on his son, and came to see them, to give them his blessings, his tender love and care. The children too would be eagerly waiting to see their grandfather, to receive his tender, affectionate touch.

After a few years of staying in the Sealdah area, Swarna and Janakinath moved to Shimle para, another neighbourhood in North Calcutta, close to the illustrious Minerva theatre. One day, four-year-old Sarala was playing in the terrace of that house, she met with an accident, tumbling off the stairs of the terrace. The maids discovered her, bleeding and in severe pain after the fall, as her two front teeth came off, scattered on the floor. In her desperation to prove herself innocent, the maid started admonishing Sarala severely. The poor girl, already in too much pain, couldn't even cry due to the harsh scolding.

Her elder sister Hiranmayee teased her: "You'll forever be a gap-toothed, ugly girl!"

Moreover, the maids added their bit to the teasing words. "Sarala didi will never get married...the groom will return home without marrying her, seeing her toothless face!"

After this chaos subsided a bit, Janakinath, the child's father came downstairs and applied medicine on the little girl's wound. However, Swarnakumari remainded steadfast in her penance, glued to her writing room amid the mayhem. She held the firm belief that her children needed no pampering on the parents' part, and only then they would become independent souls. She abhorred the typical Bengali mothers who sacrificed all other pursuits of their lives in order to tend to their children. In this regard, Swarna and her dear *Thakurjhi* (sister-in-law) Gyanada held quiet opposing views. When Swarna went to visit Gyanada and her husband in Bombay, this subject gave rise to a lot of argument between both the sisters-in-law. In Swarna's opinion, motherhood was but a mere biological act for women, and if they attached too much importance to it, they would end up jeopardizing their studies and their process of learning. Gyanada, on the other hand, didn't believe that motherhood was ever an impediment to the true emancipation of women. She stated that since as a mother, she had brought her own children to the world voluntarily, she would not leave them behind in her process of personal and educational growth, but rather take them along in her onward journey.

Presently, Swarna was living with her children in her parental home in Jorasanko, while her husband Janakinath had gone to London for studying law, to become a barrister. Swarna was living in the third floor in her bedroom, her own secluded paradise, very next to the bed chamber of her dear

Jyoti Dada. She would remain in that very private paradise for the whole day, reading, writing, and also helping in the editing of 'Bharati', their home-based literary journal. Saraswati, the Goddess of learning was present inside this private periphery with all her incredible glory.

The children were far removed from her, under the watchful care of the maids in the inner quarters of the third floor. Sometimes, they didn't get to see their mother even for once during the whole day. The children—Sarala, Hiranmayee and Jyotsnanath would spend their time amid the huge expanse of the Jorasanko mansion, in the presence of their family members—the cousin brothers and sisters, the servants and maids, 'master pundit', their home tutor et al. The other children were still able to enjoy the company of their parents from time to time, though they were entrusted to the maids' care. Swarna's children, however, were totally raised by the servants and maids of the house.

The three children were taken care of by three different maids, and each of the maids tried to arrange for good meals for the child they were tending to. They looked after the daily needs of the child, bathing them, cleaning their bodies, maintaining health and hygiene. But then, since the maids had difference in their nature, the way each maid looked after the individual child was obviously different. Mangala *dashi*, the maid looking after Sarala was a rustic milkmaid from outside Bengal; and her skin was as dark as was her mood. If Sarala ever dared to commit any mistake or disobey her words in any way, she beat the child severely, turning her pale white skin red. Poor Sarala felt bruised and her anguish would be directed towards her mother during those days. Jadu *Dai*, the old maid of her previous home in Sealdah came to visit Sarala sometimes, holding a paper packet full of snacks for the child. She had a very affectionate nature, filling the child with kisses and love whenever she came. But then, the cousins of Sarala in the house laughed and teased her whenever this maid came, and Sarala felt very shy due to their behaviour.

The children on their part, were being raised in a strict, reprimanding environment. Satish Pundit, their tutor beat them up almost all days during his classes at the *paathshala* (school). Since he was their home tutor too, based at the Jorasanko mansion, there was a possibility of getting spanked by him even outside their school, and the children had to deal with that. Every morning, they had to drink milk and visit him in the study room close to the outhouse. He scrutinized whether the children had brushed their teeth properly; the failure to do so resulted in terrible spanking by the teacher, who was quite a terror to them.

The two sisters, Sarala and Hiranmayee had started going to school. Every day after school, they also took lessons in Sanskrit from Shashi Pundit, their Sanskrit tutor, followed by music lessons from another tutor named Bheem Babu. Swarnakumari was extremely proud of the talents of her elder daughter Hiranmayee. But when Bheem Babu, the accomplished musician from the school of Sourindramohan Thakur praised Sarala's voice, Swarna looked intently at her younger daughter, giving her the attention she deserved for the very first time.

Suprabha, Saratkumari's daughter, on the other hand, was a mischievous soul, with an incredible presence of mind. Though education was not her forte, she became the leader among the young girls in no time. When Sarala became impatient about the prolonged hours of her music class, she suggested a simple way for rescuing her cousin sister.

"If you don't feel like practicing music for so long, why do you have to do it?" She asked one day.

"How can I do that? There's no way I can do without practicing." Sarala replied, nervous, perplexed.

"Well, there is a way..." The fearless Suprabha announced. "We can adjust the clock every day around the time of your music class!"

"God! No, I can't do that!" Sarala shivered at the thought of the proposal.

"That's alright...let me do it for you, in that case!" She promptly climbed on a chair, reached the hands of the clock to make it twenty minutes faster, and then left the scene surreptitiously.

When Swarna entered the room, she sensed something wrong. Although she knew that Sarala, the tiny girl couldn't reach the clock, she had seen Suprabha, her niece hovering around Sarala in the room. She could now understand everything that had transpired, but then, she couldn't admonish her niece Suprabha openly in front of others. That didn't seem proper to her. Moreover, Swarna knew that Sarala was the partner in this crime, in fact, she was the original culprit. She was determined to give a tight slap in her daughter's cheek to teach her a lesson, but there were others in the room, and in her judgment, it was improper to beat her daughter amid their presence. She waited till everybody else went away, and then punished her daughter with a slap on her cheek. But this slap from her own mother was hundred times lighter than the heavy spanking Sarala would receive from Mangala, her attending maid. Moreover, the fact that her mother was sensitive and empathetic enough to understand that beating her up in front of others would violate her self-respect lit up her innocent soul with awe and wonder at her mother's magnanimity. Swarna, on her part, had much difficulty understanding how Sarala felt happy even after receiving the punishment. However, after this incident, she reduced the duration of Sarala's music lesson by half an hour.

Hemendra and Neepamayee's children, on the other hand, spent their days in the Jorasanko Thakurbari under the strict disciplinarian regime set by their parents. They were strictly ordered not to mix with the other children in the house; their lives revolved around a tight routine of studies and music observed within the confines of their own quarters. In case of the slightest aberration from that routine, they got severe spanking from Hemen, their father.

Swarna's youngest daughter Urmila, still a baby, was the most unaffected by such strict rules and orders. Kadambari, Swarna's sister-in-law was the one who took care of her all day and night, and was totally immersed in raising the child. Baby Urmila absorbed all the love and affection of the childless woman's heart. Only when she was enrolled in a school, she got the opportunity to mix with her elder sisters Hiranmayee and Sarala during the time they went to school together in their palanquin.

Janakinath was staying in London presently, and Swarna, his wife was determined to utilize the whole duration of her husband's stay abroad in reading and writing, in serving Goddess Saraswati, the Goddess of wisdom and learning. She was out to dispel the prevalent myth of those times that women were illiterate beings. She had just finished writing her first novel titled 'Deepnirvan'. Presently, she was inspired to write in the genre of historical fiction along the lines of Todd's 'Annalogues and Antiquities of Rajasthan,' which was a staple favourite among the children of the Thakurbari. She was also immensely inspired by the novel 'Kapal Kundala' penned by Bankim Chandra Chattopadhyay, one of the eminent authors and novelists of those days, and wanted to pen a historical fictional tale like him.

Swarna had seen the awe and wonder in the eyes of her dear Jyoti dada when reading the valourous tales of Rajput heroes. Like Jyoti, Swarna too had taken the mission to uphold the rich Hindu culture and heritage cornered by the pressure of the colonial rule and Muslim invasion. She was determined to carry out her mission through her pursuit of writing her stories. Some years back, Rabi had composed a poem titled 'The Defeat of Prithviraj' during his stay in Shantiniketan, documenting the war between Prithviraj and Mohammad Ghori. This significant episode in Rajput history and Prithviraj's defeat in the hands of Mohammad Ghori inspired Swarna immensely, so much so that she derived the elements of her patriotic novel from this historical event. It documented the defeat and deterioration of the Aryan rulers of India, and Prithviraj was obviously the emblem of the extinct valour of the Aryans. The women characters were also painted as reflections of the imaginary Aryan women, generating pride and honour among the readers. Jyoti had the strong belief that this novel would help to initiate the feelings of nationalism and 'swadeshi' sentiments in the minds of his countrymen, all of whom were originally Aryans. Hence, both he and his wife Kadambari were eager to get the book published. The preparation for the publication was going on strong.

Apart from her writing and publishing endeavours, these days Swarna was busy spending her time with her

Notun Bouthan Kadambari and Jyoti Dada, in their private soiree of 'Bharati'. From time to time, she also went downstairs to join in the women's gathering, to chat with them for a while.

One day, Bishu *Tantini*, the lady who sold saris for women, came to visit the Jorasanko women at the open courtyard of the mansion. Seeing her huge bundle of saris, the young girls and women of the house flocked around her. Swarna too came downstairs, hand-in-hand with Kadambari.

Kadambari picked up a Bishnupuri silk sari, the colour of clouds, and toyed with it indulgently. "Bishu is saying an exorbitant price for this one!" She remarked.

"But *Bouthan*, this sari has a class of its own...it can be used by two-three generations of women and still remain intact. And wouldn't the one wearing it look like a real queen?" Bishu argued.

Rupkumari, the rebellious one present in the scene, found a lot of humour in the mention of 'two-three generations.'

"Why are you talking about 'generations', does it apply to us women too?" She burst out in her characteristic giggles.

Saudamini, who was cutting betel nuts, lifted her face from her meticulous chore and searched for an extinct sari, a special one.

"Our mother used to wear a *Paynapal* sari with peacock blue colour, with subtle, intricate designs throughout its body, can't you bring a sari like that now?" She asked the sari seller woman.

Swarna was ecstatic to see a traditional cotton 'Ganpere sari' woven with thick threads at the mill, especially because she noticed two lines of an exquisite poem woven throughout the border of the sari, making it a classic creation. She read the lines of the poem:

"At the banks of the river Yamuna, Radha Binodini, the consort of Krishna cries,

She pines for her 'Banka Rayshyam', in his absence, her anguish never subsides."

"My, my, I've never seen such a wonderful sari ever!" Swarna couldn't keep her eyes off the sari.

But Kadambari reminded her sister-in-law: "Why, *Thakurjhi*? When Vidyasagar *Moshai* had initiated the education of women and the remarriage of widows, the weavers of Bengal created a custom-made dhoti for him, in which these lines, "Long live Vidyasagar, may he be immortal!" were embedded, to pay their homage to the noble man. Don't you remember?"

Bishu Tantini, the weaver and sari seller woman had quite a huge and impressive repertoire of *gamchhas* (Indian towels). She was adept at creating rhymes instantly, and in her characteristic style, she said:

"Do you know, dear *Didimonis* (sisters) and *Boumonis* (brides of the house) of mine? The adage goes like this: 'Look at those plain men, devoid of talent they are all/ They wear *gamchhas*, and wrap around their grandfathers' shawls…"

"But what does this rhyme mean at all?" Rupa asked the sari seller woman. She was still a foster child enjoying her shelter in Jorasanko, courtesy Debendranath Thakur and his kindness. When the news of Rupa's absconding from home reached him, he reprimanded her strongly and advised her to control her wild emotions. Remembering how dear Rupa was to his deceased wife Sarada, he became tender in his behaviour with the girl. Driving her away from their home wasn't something which his heart accepted, at least not at the moment.

Kadambari drew Rupa closer to her and replied affectionately: "Didn't you understand, you stupid girl? It means, the men who are devoid of any talent or attribute, men who are unable to purchase even their own clothes wrap their grandfathers' shawls around their *gamchhas* to hide their real status, and they are the ones who vent out their wrath on others, born out of their envy.

Some of the women present there frowned their foreheads upon hearing this. They were well aware that they didn't have the money to afford the expensive silk sarees that Swarna and Kadambari picked for themselves. The wives were proud of their husbands' earnings; hence it was evident that they would spend their husbands' money generously. But what about the married daughters of Jorasanko? Well, their husbands were all *ghar jamais*, living in their in-law's house with their wives, and as a matter-of-fact, they were not as solvent as their wives' brothers. Saratkumari and Soudamini were stuck indoors all through the year, so they managed to get inexpensive traditional saris like *Begum bahar, Bager hat, Farash danga* etc. from the Jorasanko family fund. The open courtyard glittered with the spark and splendour coming from the multicoloured fibres of saris in all hues and textures.

Swarna's husband Janakinath was extremely well-off economically, and besides, he would never have to carry the stigma of being a *ghar jamai*, living with his in-laws in the same house. On the contrary, he lived a good life, filling Debendranath Thakur's daughter, his wife with earthly pleasures, comfort and an abundance of wealth.

Kadambari picked up a mauve-coloured exquisite Baluchari silk sari and said to Swarna, her sister-in-law: "This is my special gift for you for the auspicious occasion of the publication of your first novel! You have to wear this sari on the day of the book release program."

Ecstatic, Swarna came up to Kadambari, her dearest *Notun Bouthan* and gave her a tight hug. In just a couple of days, her first novel 'Deepnirvan' would be released officially, and her sister-in-law's excitement regarding the special event moved her profoundly, making her emotional.

Swarna loved dressing up with exquisite attires and accessories. Some days back, when she went to attend a women's party, invited by Ms. Croyd, all women present there looked at her in awe and admiration. She was dressed in a black silk sari with a thick white border bought from Bombay, a fashionable jacket with frills and laces, and a beautifully designed *saat lahari* pearl necklace, with seven distinct layers. The woman poet Kamini Roy who was present at the party was mesmerized by Swarna's gorgeous presence, and remarked that she was the divine Goddess Saraswati, descending on earth from heaven. Swarna, on her part, had decided to befriend Kamini and make her a '*soi*', a cherished female friend.

Though many women she knew were present at the women's party, Swarna was sad not to find Girindramohini there. Swarna admired her since quite a while, hence she had thought she would befriend her at the party. They were pen pals till now, and the letters they exchanged increased her urge to meet the woman in person, but unfortunately, the women in their family weren't allowed to step outside their homes.

Swarna detested the idea of women being cooped up inside their homes, and strongly wished to take part in a protest movement to make them come out of the closed confines of their domestic cages. She was determined to develop a sense of kinship among women, a precious 'female bonding' to ignite the flame of the swadeshi movement in their hearts. With this spirit, she had befriended so many women authors in the recent times! Saratkumari from Lahore was her 'bihangini soi', or bird buddy, and Girindramohini was her 'friend of union', though they weren't united yet. Swarna kept on sending letters to her in her intense, ardent emotion of friendship. Some of these letters written to Giri were almost akin to love letters in their literary and poetic expressions.

"With the pristine moments of *viraha* (separation), love is entwined

When the eyes don't see you, the heart floats amid the sea of desire.

In the pangs of separation, eyes wide awake, our emotions intensified,

Our eyes locked with each other, in bouts of laughter."

Giri also became restless to see her pen pal as these letters arrived, but she was trapped in her cage, being the bride of an orthodox family. Discreetly, she had started her writing endeavours, but when her husband came to know of it, he didn't object to it. If her wife took good care of her domestic duties and then wrote at the end of the day, he had nothing against it, he remarked. Many women in those times were writing for journals like 'Bharati',

'Bamabodhini'. Giri's husband encouraged her to submit her writings to those journals. It was quite honourable for an educated man to have an educated wife, and getting published in these journals was a mark of being educated and emancipated. But the woman of the house stepping outside was considered a blasphemy to Dutta *Moshai*, Giri's husband. Swarna had invited her on the occasion of her release of 'Deepnirvan', her first novel, but Grindramohini had to disappoint her this time too. The book was released in a breezy evening in the winter month of 'Poush', and just after its release, it created quite a buzz in the domain of Bengali books. Strangely enough, the name of the author was not mentioned in the book. It was widely rumoured that the author was a woman of the illustrious Thakurbari. In fact, before this, stories written by women had seen the light of the day, but none of them were as refined and beautifully penned as this novel.

In the magazine titled 'Sadharani' (The Ordinary Woman), there was a review which praised the novelist, albeit with a doubtful tone and voice:

"It has been heard that it is the work of a woman from an elite, aristocratic family, which is a matter of great happiness. A woman with so much education, empathy and creativity in her compositions, with such unique style of writing is rarely seen not only in Bengal, but in other civilized parts of our nation as well."

But why wasn't her name published in the book? Why was it published anonymously? Jyoti had it in mind to judge the reaction of the readers, and then surprise them all by publishing the name of the author along with the book. The outcome was quite amusing. During those times, it was beyond the imagination of people that women could write so eloquently and masterfully, hence, even those who were apparently close to Swarna were stupefied. Satyendranath, upon receiving the book, wrote in a letter to his brother Jyoti: "Can the magnificent splendour of 'Jyoti' remain hidden for long?"

The readers took quite some time to realize that the novel, quite a masterpiece of literature, was written by Swarnakumari. However, the year 1876 shone bright in the history of women's writing not only for 'Deepnirvan', but also for two other notable literary works penned by women. On one hand, the female nawab of the district of Kumilla, Faizunnesa Chowdhurani had penned a long, narrative love-poem titled 'Roopjalal'. It was really difficult for the regressive Muslim society of those days to accept the contents of such an outrageous book, but then the book was penned by the powerful monarch, and it was dangerous to invoke her wrath by opposing her.

On the other hand, yet another book penned by an elderly woman named Rash Sundari Debi belonging to a traditional Bengali family, was published under her own name. The autobiography of the woman titled 'My Life' was yet another milestone in the history of women's writings. In her composition, the inner quarters of an orthodox Hindu Bengali household came out with such bold eloquence that shook the core of the women readers. The life depicted in the book was vastly different than the enlightened life enjoyed by the women of the Thakurbari. Getting this explosive autobiography from Malini, the book seller woman and flipping through its pages, Swarna was awed and astonished at every paragraph, which was a new revelation. The autobiography recounted Rash Sundari's domestic life in vivid, poignant language.

'One fine morning, when Rash Sundari had gone to the other room after making her own children sit at the kitchen to have their breakfast, her husband's horse came to the open courtyard to have his own share of meal with paddy growing in abundance there. It was a daily chore for the horse to have his meal from the heaps of paddy lying there, but Rash Sundari felt very shy to even have a glimpse of the horse from a distance. Being a woman, she was accustomed to the purdah ritual; she toiled day and night and finished her piles of housework with her veil extended till her chest. Speaking with others in the household, even with her widowed sisters-in-law was intimidating to her, and being the docile bride, it was quite natural to have such feelings. The horse, with his strong masculinity, was only a representative of her husband, so she felt shy to come out in front of the animal. Upon noticing the horse, she went away to the other room, and was stuck there for quite some time. Her children started calling her impatiently in the kitchen, and after a while, some of them started to cry and wail. The horse too, went on chewing the grass, not willing to go away from the scene.

Rash Sundari thought to herself: "How would I go out in front my husband's horse? It will be shameful indeed, if the horse catches a glimpse of me!"

Her elder son came up to her and said: "Why are you afraid of our horse Joyhari, mother? He won't harm you in any way!"

Upon hearing her son's words, she started reprimanding herself silently. "Shame on me! All my children are thinking I am afraid of the horse, but honestly, I am running away from the animal out of shame, stigma… Won't they think I have gone mad, if they get to know this?

Nobody is admonishing me for this, but why do I fear living on my own terms, even inside my own home?" She thought.

Rash Sundari had sworn to herself that she wouldn't remain shy in front of their family horse ever again. With her son's hand in hers, she came back to her kitchen, her own private paradise. She spent the whole day in the kitchen, cooking for thirty people every day. There were as many as eight servants and maids, but they were all in the outhouse. There was none in the inner quarters where she lived. She didn't talk or interact with the servants and maids previously, but of late she had noticed that they weren't working sincerely without having instructions from her.

After the end of the day's toil, she started studying silently, discreetly, lest the family members got to know of it. Getting caught in the act of studying was a big stigma for a bride, and would invite censure. She had managed to hide the pages of the holy text 'Chaitanya Bhagavat' in a secret nook of the kitchen and slowly learnt to read its contents. She had also started to write down some unsaid words from her own life experiences. Today, like the other days, she wrote a couple of lines, reminiscing the precious memories of her life.

"These days, I remember often, those old days,

I remember the caged bird, the fish trapped in the net, those were the days."

Rash Sundari was married off at the tender age of twelve with Sitanath Sarkar of Ramdiya village, in the district of Faridpur, Bangladesh. The innocent child was playing indulgently with her dolls in her parental home when she heard that she would have to go away and live with rank strangers after her marriage.

She saw two people chatting with each other at the river bank. One among the two spotted the girl there and remarked, pointing a finger towards her: "This girl looks so pretty! The man who will marry her and take her home must be really fortunate!"

The other replied: "Ah well, so many people have come to take her home, but her mother is quite adamant; she won't give her child to anybody."

The seed of fear of going away to a stranger's home, away from the comfort zone of her mother's presence was sown in young Rashu's mind that very day. All around her, when child marriages were prevalent in the name of the tradition of *Gauri daan* (a ritual in which very young girls of eight-nine years were married off), the girl enjoyed the comfort and indulgence of her mother's warm lap, sans any worries. She was living her life like a baby goat, having no knowledge of herself being a sacrificial creature, one who would be slaughtered soon. The girls of her age, her playmates teased her, mocked her for being her mother's pet, and she cried profusely, anguished by their mockery. Till then, she had not known most of the rules of the domestic world, just because her mother wanted her to stay away from the murky truths of that world. To save her from the playmates bullying her, her playing became a forbidden act.

Those were the times when education for girls and women were not considered a possibility in Rashu's village. But a school for teaching Bengali to young boys was set up in her house. Every morning, Rashu's elder brothers would dress her up in a black *ghagra*, wrap a dupatta around the attire and make her sit like a doll in their makeshift *pathshaala* (school), where a *memsahib* used to come and teach them. The intelligent young girl had picked up some letters from that surrounding, while watching her brothers learn the language.

Even as she sat quietly at the *pathshaala*, the news of her magnificent beauty spread like wildfire. As young Rashu pondered on the words the village folks would say to her in praise of her beauty, she wrote these lines discreetly:

"I was blessed with a fair skin; my features, my structure, perfect it seemed to all,

My hands and feet were flawless, I was the most cherished golden doll."

The innocent young girl ran away from the river banks on that fateful day and hugged her mother tight. "Ma, if anybody wants to take me away from you, would you give me away?" She asked.

"Goodness! Why would I ever give you away? Who said such things to you?" Her mother asked, wiping the tears from her eyes.

Rashu had gauged from the tears she saw in her mother's eyes that she would have to go to a stranger's house very soon, she couldn't avoid it any longer. Her initial reaction was that of fear; overwhelmed by fear, she stopped bathing, eating, doing her daily chores. Later, however, when her family members mentioned her marriage, there were traces of joy in her heart at the thought of getting new saris, jewelry, when loud music reverberated from all parts of their house during her marriage day. But when her husband took her away from her parents' home in a palanquin, Rashu could no longer hold her tears. Weeping copious amounts of tears, she felt like a sacrificial goat, ready to be slaughtered any moment.

That was the day when the affection and tender care of her mother was obliterated from Rashu's life permanently. She said to her God silently on that day: "My condition is like that bird trapped in a cage whom its owners had kept there to derive entertainment of some kind. As for myself, I am trapped in this cage for a lifetime; there's no escape for me in my whole life."

For the first six-seven years in her in-law's house, Rashu was raised by her mother-in-law, who took very good care of her. The woman took little Rashu in her arms from the palanquin, and thereafter, Rashu didn't have to do any housework in her presence. Rashu found new playmates in her new neighbourhood, and played with them the whole day. She also loved creating dolls with clay, whenever she found some time for it. One day, she created a snake with clay, coloured it and left it beneath the big *palanka* (bed) in one of their bedrooms. After some time, when the folks in the house noticed it, there was quite an uproar as they mistook it for a real snake. Finally, when Rashu came to the room and broke the clay figure with a stick, they realized their mistake and started giggling loud. Rashu felt extremely shy and awkward at the turn of events, and had sworn never to create clay dolls any more.

In those olden times, rupees and coins weren't in vogue yet, and things were bought with *kori* (small shell, used as equivalent to money). Rashu, the young girl started exploring the *kori* to create new decorative items for the house. She created little chandeliers, garlands hung around mirrors, lotus flowers with those small shells, and stuck them at various nooks and corners of the house. The mother-in-law indulged the young bride's creative endeavours with a smiling face. But those moments of joy were temporary, transient. As fate would have it, Rashu's mother-in-law lost her eyesight and became bedridden, struck with a severe form of typhoid, and the responsibility of the entire household fell upon Rashu's young shoulders.

Rashu recollected the memories of those trying times and wrote her personal account in a palm leaf: "Gradually, by the grace of God, I could accomplish all this housework quite easily, I could prepare lunch and dinner for all family members myself, and after all housework was done, I had the opportunity to sit and relax. In those days, women of the household couldn't study or learn anything other than housework, so they had a bit of leisure time in the afternoon, after all domestic responsibilities were done. But they had to stand politely in front of the master of the house during the whole leisure time. It was as if being born as women, we knew the existence of no other work, apart from housework."

Rashu had followed all these rules to the book, with no aberrations whatsoever. Many days went by when she had no time to have her own meals after her back-breaking domestic work. Early in the morning, she would feed her husband with a full meal, and then start cooking lunch for the whole big family. After feeding all her eight children, putting them to sleep, offering her daily prayer to the gods, she would sit down to have her own meal. Some days when her children woke up early from her afternoon nap, she couldn't eat at all. When her husband, the master of the house would be at home, she would have to stand in front of him in obeisance, covering her face with the veil all the way till her neck. The master, on his part, never felt the need to ask about the wellbeing of his own wife. However, he was a good man otherwise.

As soon as he would enter the room, he would order his wife: "Where are you? Are you listening? Bring some water and wash my feet!"

Rashu would run out of nowhere like a robot and start serving him with all her dedication. Covering her face in a veil all the way till her bosom, she could only see the feet of her husband somehow. She washed the feet slowly, diligently, as her daily ritual.

After his morning meal, her husband Sitanath would sometimes sit down with a book. Sometimes, when he discussed studies with the children, Rashu listened with eager, attentive ears. She was very keen to read the holy text 'Chaitanya Bhagawat', but she didn't recognize the book among the huge pile of books in the house.

There was a sudden transformation that happened in Rash Sundari's life, like a magical phenomenon. This happened when Rashu met Malini, the book seller woman at the river bank close to her home. Gradually, with time, Rashu befriended her and started learning to solve math problems. She bought Vidyasagar's 'Barnaparichay' from Malini and learnt the letters of the Bengali alphabet from the book. Nobody knew how Malini, a teenager girl at that time, had fueled the fire of learning in Rashu's heart. But today, when the humble scribblings of Rashu that she documented in palm leaves finally got published as a book, Malini was thrilled, ecstatic. She ran to Swarnakumari to show her the very first copy of the book.

All along, Swarna had thought that she had to struggle a lot to establish her name as a writer, but once she got to read this book and know of Rash Sundari's life, her faith in her own struggles started wavering. She bowed her head in reverence to this middle-aged woman trapped in her domestic cage, realizing the risks and challenges she took to carve her own path.

The very next week, when Malini came again, Swarna gave her the honour of a discoverer of the exemplary talent, Rash Sundari. In their literary nook in the third floor, Swarna, Malini and Kadambari had a gracious gathering along with scrumptious snacks—puffed rice, cauliflower fritters and the new issue of 'Bangadarshan,' the literary mag.

"Did you read the new issue, Swarna didi?" Malini queried, curious. "Bankim Babu has done such a fabulous job for us readers with this magazine...so many fantastic new stories to read!" She exclaimed in joy.

Swarna came down from the *palanka* and brought out a copy of the magazine from her writing desk. "Look here! You know, I wait with bated breath always, to check when their new issue will come out! I can't sleep without reading his 'Bish Briksha' (The Poison Tree) every month." Swarna seemed excited.

Kadambari, who was attaching a garland of 'bel' flowers in her hair, looked at Swarna and replied: "You know, I really love the heroine Kunda Nandini of 'Bish Briksha'! I feel so restless to read about her agony, the anguish she has to go through in her journey...will nobody ever love her truly?"

Swarna was excited to get a new direction in their enlightening conversation. "You know, the conflict between the two women, Kunda Nandini and Suryamukhi is what makes the plot so interesting and memorable! And also think about how bold the author Bankim Babu is! How openly is he portraying the feelings of love in a widow's life, I wonder if the squeamish Bengali readers can digest it!" She remarked, in jest.

Kadambari came closer to her sister-in-law Swarna and gave her a hug. "Well, you have been such an inspiration yourself, overcoming so many obstacles on your way, and that is no mean feat! There are so many learned souls amidst us who still don't attach any value whatsoever to women's writings, but we know how you have toiled hard to attain the impossible task!" She cheered for Swarna.

"I know that you, my family members love and cherish my writings. But do you know, the outsiders think it is actually Jyoti dada who writes in my name?" Swarna replied.

"Ah, how absurd is that! Now you see how people can stretch their attribute of imagination!" Kadambari burst out into peals of laughter.

Swarna asked Malini: "Listen, Malini, can you see how such conspiracies and detrimental plans against women are hindering their growth?" She seemed tremendously annoyed. "Just imagine, my dear 'shoi' (writer buddy) Girindra Mohini has never been able to attend a literary meet in her life! We have exchanged so many letters, so many writings of each other, we've waited so eagerly to meet each other in person, yet she isn't allowed to come out of her house. Such is the abominable way in which a woman is treated! Can we ever get to see Rash Sundari's face too, now that her book is published?"

In the meanwhile, Swarna's youngest daughter, the angelic child Urmila barged in the room, in the midst of this womanly camaraderie. Kadambari lifted the child in her arms and filled her with love. Little Urmila, on her part, was overjoyed to receive such tender love and hugged her aunt tenderly. But Swarna, the mother of the child was not that indulgent towards her. This literary gathering was happening after such a long hiatus, and she wasn't willing to waste her time and the creative output of the long-awaited meet by catering to the whims of her children.

She called out for Urmila's maid. "Please take Urmila away from here. How did she even come to this room? Were you sleeping at this while?" She queried, impatient and angry.

The maid was visibly shy and embarrassed. "It's not my fault, *Ma Than* (Mistress)," she confessed. "I made her sit and wait while I had gone to urinate...and look, she escaped from there!"

Swarna was infuriated to listen to the uncouth use of language by her maid. "Go away, I say! Don't irritate me again...go downstairs with the baby immediately!" She ordered.

Kadambari couldn't keep silent any further, she intervened. "Go away, and let me look into the matter. Urmila will go nowhere; she'll stay with me!" She ordered the maid. Turning to Swarna, she said: "The little baby is such a darling, she won't create any problem for us! Why drive her away unnecessarily?"

"But you pamper the kids a bit too much, I say! Both you and *Mejo Bouthan* are the same about this." Swarna was adamant about her stance. "I want them to grow up just like we did in our childhood, in the air and surroundings of this house. I can't waste my precious time and my creative pursuits for their demands!"

Kadambari replied with moist eyes: "*Thakurjhi*, you

don't know how blessed you are to be the mother of such cherubic babies...you got them even without asking for them, that is why you can be so indifferent about them. And look at me, I don't have any child to fill my lap with joy! I will never have the heart to discuss anything about literature if I drive little Urmila away from this room."

Malini, the book seller woman came closer to Kadambari and rubbed her back as a gesture of solidarity towards her. Swarna said to Kadambari: "*Bouthan*, don't you know Urmila is your daughter? If she were mine, could I have told her to go away from the room?

Swarna and Kadambari hugged each other tight in an unbridled sense of sisterhood. In that joyous, emotional moment, the three women had built a unique sphere of protection around little Urmila.

Chapter 10

Annabai Nalini

In an eager summer evening of 1877, a pregnant Gyanada Nandini with her three children in tow, stepped in a ship for her first journey overseas, a ship that would take them to London. In this sojourn, Satyen couldn't be with them as a fellow traveler, but he arranged for a trusted companion to be with Gyanada—a British couple whom he knew well. He made a plan so that Gyanada could travel to Liverpool, accompanied by the couple. Gyanada also had a Gujrati and a Muslim servant along with her to take care of her daily chores. Satyen, for that matter, was extremely reliant on the intelligence of his wife; he knew Gyanada would manage things extremely well.

Their family friend, Mrs. Pandurang and their daughters had come to see off Gyanada at the sea port of Bombay. Anna, their elder daughter had lived in England for quite some time, but was extremely keen to explore the richness of Indian art and literature. Initially, Gyanada was a bit hesitant to travel overseas all by herself, but Anna had wiped away her apprehensions in only a few days' time. Gyanada, on the other hand, was deeply inspired by Anna Tarkhare's vivid description of the opulent lifestyle of London, her enthusiasm and the new brilliance that she derived from her stay in London. In her journey to attain emancipation as a woman, she was deeply indebted to this family and its women, and it seemed her debt had increased manifold in these few days.

Prasanna Thakur's son Gyanendramohan, who had been converted to Christianity and was living in London, became the local guardian to Gyanada and her children. Satyen encouraged the idea that Gyanada should go and live with him in England in order to learn the manners and the culture of the British. Most importantly, his goal was to train Suren, Bibi and Chobi and make them adept in the manners and way of life of the British. Next time when Satyen would travel to London, he had planned to seek the permission of *Babamoshai*, their father and take Rabi along with him to make him study there and be a barrister.

Gyanada was a bold, feisty woman. No Bengali woman in those days, with three children in tow would have dared to cross the 'Kaala paani' (the black seas) without a male partner as their companion. The other women of the Jorasanko Thakurbari shivered, their hands and feet froze, witnessing her grit and sheer courage. Still, the very first day when she embarked on the ship, the feisty Gyanada felt a tinge of pain when she stood by the deck of the ship at dusk.

The sunset was just about to begin. The image of her own motherland was about to diminish from her eyes gradually. The memory of Rammohan and Dwarakanath never returning to their motherland after going abroad was fresh in everyone's mind, hence that act of crossing that fateful 'Kaala Pani' terrified every Bengali. Just as the ship was leaving the jetty, and the figures of her husband

Satyen and the Pandurang women, waving their hands at her from the port became smaller and smaller, Gyanada's heart started palpitating. She was moving far, far away from her own country, and she didn't know if she would ever be able to return to her roots.

The journey across the sea was charming and ecstatic, in spite of these fears that overwhelmed her. After a while, she started enjoying the experience to the hilt, along with her children. The Muslim servant who accompanied her was very caring and attentive to her needs; he would return from the shores of England as soon as the ship would reach Liverpool. Another servant, a Gujrati man named Rama would stay with Gyanada and the children in England. Satyen had arranged for all of this meticulously.

As night descended, the blue waters of the sea turned dark, and the ship dressed up in a riot of colours. Charming men and women roamed around the deck of the ship, dressed in beautiful attires. Suren and Bibi, Gyanada's children were dressed up in charming attires too; they played around the deck with unperturbed mirth and gaiety. Little Chobi, the youngest child of Gyanada was in the lap of Rama, their servant. Upon seeing the cherubic child, the *memsahibs* were squeezing his cheeks every now and then. As the evening turned darker, everyone ventured towards the dining room.

Gyanada dressed herself exquisitely, despite her palpitating heart. She shed off her old sari and draped a deep blue *bandhni* or *bandhej* sari she had bought from Gujrat, the vestiges of intricate artwork done by the young woman artisans from India. The saris were used as white, blank canvases by them, and subtle threads were woven into the body of the saris bit by bit, and then, they were dipped into deep, bright colours. Thus, when the saris gained their full colour, they were dried and made ready for wearing. The borders of the saris were woven with separate threads, with separate colours. Once the threads with different colours were untied from the dried sari, magic unfolded—revealing dazzling, white stars over the red, green, blue colors spread throughout the body of the sari. During Gyanada's stay in Gujrat, she had visited various villages and collected these gems from the heart of those villages. Today, she had draped a blue *bandhni* sari with grey border, and sophistication was oozing out of her every pore. She happened to be the only Indian woman in the dining room, hence all eyes roved around her, followed her moves. She was seated at one of the corner tables along with her children Suren and Bibi, and with the British couple, her partners in this journey. They relished the flavour of all the food items served, with forks and spoons, chatting lightly and absorbing the delightful music by Mozart playing in the room. Gyanada noticed the off-shoulder gowns of a couple of British women, which seemed a bit too revealing to her. Their cleavages seemed to peep out provocatively, disregarding the loose warning of their attires. The men, needless to say, looked at the scene, bewitched by the seductive charm of these women. Gyanada felt a bit embarrassed to witness it all.

Gyanada took some red wine at the request of Mrs. Mary Phillip, her companion in this journey. Though she did indulge in some social drinking before when she attended a few parties with her husband, she felt a bit awkward to do so now, in the company of strangers. Though she was exposed to the act of social drinking once in a while, due to the nature of her husband Satyen's job, she had felt an air of anti-drinking in the Jorasanko Thakurbari, influenced by the Brahmo religion. In the *Sanjeebani Sabha*, a meeting spearheaded by Jyoti, her brother-in-law, there was a strong movement against any kind of alcohol. The intellectuals of this group shivered to even think of the neo-Babus of Kolkata, immersed in a sea of alcohol, accompanied by the *baijis*, the nauch girls and their seductive charm. God knows who among them would witness Deben Thakur's daughter-in-law drinking wine among strangers in a ship and report to the newspapers! Though wine was not an alcoholic drink, so to speak, yet Gyanada wanted to be cautious, when in public. In fact, *Babamoshai* had agreed to her going abroad after a lot of coaxing and persistent effort, she didn't want to ignite his anger for any reason whatsoever.

After dinner, the British men and women started to perform 'ball dance' together as couples on the deck of the ship, accompanied by rhythmic music. Gyanada felt awkward when a white sahib started to pull her hands, almost forcing her to dance with him. This was nothing new to her though; during her stay in Bombay and Ahmedabad, she had to participate in such dance moves in the company of McGregor. However, this time it was a stranger, and there was no question of dancing with a stranger. Hence, she turned down the offer with a gentle smile. Suren and Bibi, her children were dancing together as partners. Gyanada was enjoying the precocious moves of Bibi, much beyond her age. She sipped a bit of wine that night and indulged in the dance, the music and the festive spirit around her. The very next morning, however, she experienced fever and vertigo and also vomited a number of times. Satyen had warned her of the symptoms of sea-sickness, but she never imagined that it would happen to her so early on. The servants accompanying her were of great help in her sickness.

Gyanada's exploits in the sea did not go well with the 'Babu circle' in Kolkata. They unanimously contented that in his desperate bid to establish women's freedom, the esteemed civilian Satyen Babu was overtly pampering his wife, and eventually paving the path of nemesis for all other women of Bengal. What would happen to the domestic domain if all these women wanted to cross the ocean and venture overseas like Gyanada, neglecting their family responsibilities?

There was a clear criticism in 'Samachar Chandrika' regarding her act. "The wife of Satyen Babu, the Civil and Session Judge of Ahmedabad has reached Liverpool with her young son and daughter. The objective of this trip is to raise and educate her children in England, the foreign soil...What else are we supposed to see?"

The same year, Debendranath Thakur went to China with his son-in-law Sarada Prasad in winter. Jyoti and Kadambari went to their farm-house in Serampore at the banks of the river Ganges for change of air in the monsoon, and Rabi accompanied the couple as usual. After a long time, outside the four walls of the Jorasanko mansion, in close proximity to Mother Nature and the Ganges and in the company of his *Notun Bouthan*, Rabi's days were spent in idyllic pleasure, the pages of his notebook 'Malati Punthi' were filled with his poems all over again. Roaming the river in a boat, he wrote his new verse titled 'Music of Childhood'. The pristine raindrops of the new monsoon season ushered in, with torrents of joy in Rabi's adolescent heart. The shadows of the clouds hovering over the streams of water brought along a deep, intrinsic desire to love someone. But whom? Who would be the object of Rabi's desire, for whom he would compose one love poem after the other? Whenever he closed his eyes to concentrate, an enchantingly beautiful face appeared before him, the face of his Hecate *Thakrun*. What a blasphemy! He thought, spelling danger.

At the magical moment of dawn, Rabi woke up from sleep, and sat near the river Ganges. There were tears in his eyes, flowing like the raindrops that he saw all around the place, in his voice, the lines of Vidyapati, the poet, came alive.

"E bhara badar, maha bhadar, shunya mandir more..." (In the fullness of the monsoon season, the temple of my heart is barren, empty...)

The fishermen rowed their boats in front of his eyes. Rabi absorbed it all—their vague movements, the hurried preparations of cooking in the garden at the back of the house. His *Notun Bouthan* would be cooking at the garden today for an impromptu picnic that had been arranged. "Rabi, Rabi!" He was summoned from somewhere in the garden. Perhaps he was being called for having breakfast. Rabi's heart was filled with unbridled emotions, but he reprimanded himself quickly. He knew he wasn't doing the right thing, and such unbridled emotions would embarrass him a lot, especially in the presence of *Notun Bouthan* and his Joyti dada. Rabi couldn't stand it if they made a joke out of his present feelings. In fact, there was no better weapon than music in hiding his emotions which threatened to spill out. Rabi started humming the tunes of a melody composed by Vidyapati and sat in the garden.

Under the Bakul tree, a hearth made of bricks was burning. The utensils, masalas and condiments, vegetables for cooking were scattered all around. The maids were in terrible haste, arranging for the cooking, cutting the vegetables, grinding the turmeric into a fine paste in the *shil nora*, the ubiquitous pair of griding stones. Kadambari seemed to be the busiest person around, seated in a stool, supervising the whole affair.

Fruits and desserts for breakfast were arranged in a table along with a chair made of cane, placed just beside the stool where Kadambari was seated. Jyoti was seated in another chair like a majestic king, dressed in lose-fitted satin pajamas, a long sky-blue coat, embellished with fine Lucknow Chikan embroidery, and a dupatta finely pleated on his shoulders. Jyoti was quite a famed personality for his quintessential charm and his handsome features. In his student life, when he used to sit at the stairs of Presidency college, waiting for his vehicle to arrive, he attracted quite a crowd, all of whom wanted to catch a glimpse of him. Rasaraj Amritlal, who was a few years junior to him narrated his version of the story, explaining how he himself, a student of Hindu School would stand transfixed and ogle at Jyoti's features, as sharp and exquisite as a Greek sculpture. In Rabi's eyes too, his Jyoti dada was the ideal one in handsomeness, with his excellence in music and literature.

"Are you going to Kolkata, Jyoti dada? Why so early in the morning?" Rabi asked, curious.

Jyoti didn't answer his younger brother and sipped grape juice casually, nonchalant. "What were you singing, Rabi? Sing it again, a bit louder please." He requested Rabi. "The tune sounded familiar, and also a bit unfamiliar. Is it by Vidyapati?" He asked.

Rabi sat on a chair and replied: "The lines are of Vidyapati, but the tune is improvised by me in a new way. Hence, you can't recognize it fully." Rabi started humming the song again.

It was raining outside, and the canopy over their heads made for a marvelous sight. Vidyapati's romantic, pensive verse added to the beauty of the cloudy day. Jyotirindra sang along with Rabi and Kadambari listened to the rendition mesmerized, with closed eyes.

Rabi wasn't keen on tasting the grape juice, he stretched his eager hands to pick up the coffee cup instead, suiting his disposition perfectly amid such a rainy day. His hair was drenched in the rain, and his attire was wet too. In his eyes, there was a glint of his impending doom.

"Are you crazy? Have some food first!" Kadambari scolded him in her characteristic way.

"But I don't wish to eat anything, *Bouthan*!" Rabi replied. Looking into his eyes, Kadambari could sense the premonition of the strong gust of Nor'wester winds. She was noticing the unusual restlessness brewing within Rabi for quite some days now. Her bosom palpitated with unknown anxiety for the boy. What had happened to him? Would she be able to control his emotions?

She tried to joke with Rabi, not letting him know her innermost thoughts. "Well, you didn't sing that well either, Rabi. Perhaps because it's a rainy day, your Jyoti dada loved your rendition more."

Rabi failed to understand why Kadambari was never fully satisfied with whatever he did. She seemed to overlook any talent he truly had, any art form that he tried. He wanted to fight with his *Notun Bouthan* regarding her attitude. "You are jealous of my talents whenever Jyoti dada says anything good about me. That explains why you never praise anything I do."

Jyoti laughed, listening to this conversation. "Ah, you

both flight with each other so childishly! Rabi, sing another song for me, will you? I started the day while listening to you singing, let's see how the rehearsal goes today!" He said.

"Well, the drama is done now, everyone is praising it so much...Why do you still need to go to these rehearsals?" Kadambari pouted her lips like a demanding child. "Such a rainy day demands khichri, fried fish and music, isn't it? Do you really have to leave us?"

"No, I really have to go now, they will be waiting for me. But I will return early, so you can keep the khichri and music for the night; meanwhile, just enjoy singing and poetry with Rabi."

"Who will wait for you, may I ask? Is that Binodini?" Kadambari asked, in a rather nagging tone. She looked at Jyoti with her sharp, piercing eyes.

"Ah, you are such a suspicious woman!" Jyoti replied, annoyed, and stood up. "Well, I'll have to catch the nine-o-clock steamer, so I'll better leave now. Rabi, take care of your *Bouthan* meanwhile." He said while leaving.

As Jyoti left, Kadambari sat with a grim, sulking face. Rabi looked at her face, her demeanour and thought to himself: This woman who sits in front of me and feeds me, fights with me, pines for her husband is my very familiar *Notun Bouthan*. And the woman who has crept in my very being, making my life miserable is nobody's wife, nobody's sister-in-law. That mysterious woman is Hecate Thakrun. She is the Beatrice of my poetry.

Rabi tried to attract the attention of the sulking Kadambari. "O my Beatrice, when the golden rays of your Jyoti have sunken, why don't you give some thought to this new, rising sun in front of you?"

"I don't appreciate your jokes all the time, Rabi!" Kadambari retaliated. "Can't you see, your *Notun Dada* is getting so immensely attracted to the theater actresses he is working with? See how he left me alone, in such a romantic rainy day! Why, we could have well stayed in Calcutta then! Why did he have to take me here?"

Rabi replied: "*Bouthan*, you know, the banks of this river seem to be the most suited to your pangs of separation that you feel for your husband now! Though he has left you, you're not alone. You have the company of the river, your garden, your fawn, your beloved Rupkumari, and look at me, seated beneath your feet like the poor *chataka* bird, in the faint hope of receiving your merciful attention!"

"O my, so are you comparing yourself with your Jyoti Dada?" Kadambari looked at Rabi, her eyes burning in an unexplained sarcasm. "I don't see any special beauty or talent in you, not yet. You are just a seventeen-year-old child in my eyes."

Kadambari's words bruised the new, blooming masculinity in Rabi. A glint of tears was visible in the corner of his eyes. 'I know Jyoti dada occupies a treasured part of my heart, but you are dearer to me! Can you hurt me so cruelly, just because I keep begging for your affection and love, Hecate *Thakrun*?' He complained.

"Now, now, don't cry like a baby again! And don't irritate me when I'm angry." Kadambari moved away to her room. Dejected by this gesture, Rabi sat all alone. To whom would he explain the agony of his broken heart? Rabi was still an uninitiated teenager in Kadambari's eyes, while Kadambari herself was almost his age. And ironically, she didn't feel the need to know how the teenager Rabi had ripened, in body, mind and spirit. Why would she even care about him, when Jyoti, her husband had occupied her entire heart as her man, her Lord? The agonized Rabi entered a few lines in his notebook, in the form of a soliloquy.

"My beloved *sakhi*, I thought I would gain your affection if I would cry,

But in crying, I provoked your ire.

I beg mercy at your feet, *sakhi*, forgive me please...

Or else, how would I quench my inner fire?"

On other days, when Kadambari would be in a pleasant mood, it would give birth to a dreamy environment around Rabi. On those nights drenched with the numinous moonlight, the three of them would sit together by the river. It seemed as if the *apsaras* from heaven descended on the earth to listen to this poetic, musical soiree. And Kadambari, on her part, roamed around like a moon fairy, surrounded by her husband and brother-in-law. Some days, Akshay Chandra, the poet came along with his wife from Calcutta. His wife, Sarat Kumari had a namesake in the Jorasanko Thakurbari. Since she has just landed from Lahore, Rabi referred to her as 'Lahorinee' (The woman from Lahore) in jest."

One day, Rabi was listening to the narratives of the very young English poet Chatterton. Chatterton was famous, rather quite notorious for mimicking the poetic voices of ancient poets, who died by committing suicide at the tender age of sixteen and became quite a phenomenon. By listening to his life story, Rabi was inspired to write in the poetic voices of the famous poets Vidyapati and Chandidas.

As Rabi sat in the garden, a fountain of his verses

erupted in full elan. To his friends, he said, he had retrieved the poems of a very ancient poet whose name was Bhanusingha. The friends were only too excited to know of this poet, and remarked that such beautiful verse was never produced by even Vidyapati or Chandidas. Of course, they had to gulp their words when they got to know the true identity of the poet begetting those verses.

At that time, Jyoti was composing his new play titled 'Asrumati' (The Woman in Tears). He loved the first verse of Bhanusingha so much that he decided to add that verse to the play during the first stage show. The song was *"Gahana kusuma kunja majhe/Mridula madhura banshi baaje/Bisari traas lokalaaj sajani aao, aao lo..."* (In the dense flower orchard/ The sweet symphony of Shyam's flute carries her away. My friend, come, drowning all fears, all shame, all inhibitions, / Come along, and unite with Him.)

In the beautiful orchard of Moram *sahib*, in some lonely afternoons, Rabi and Kadambari would savour the sweet and sour tamarind pickle and chit-chat idly, their indolent bodies swaying in the swing. Kadambari was dressed very elegantly that day, wearing an attractive blue sari along with a fashionable, multicoloured lace jacket. Rabi, however, didn't like these jackets that women wore, hence he picked up a fight with her sister-in-law.

"Is this really a jacket, or a cover stitched by the local tailor Umesh?" He enquired. "Don't you have any discretion? Oh, how these tailors make nonsensible stuff, stitching together old, worn-out silk cloth pieces, and you women adorn yourselves with them, lovingly naming them as 'jackets'! It would have been far more befitting if you would wear the old-fashioned black and white *Dhakai* sari!" He added, taking the fight one notch ahead.

"Ah, what do you even know about fashion? You're just a boy!" Kadambari was quick to retaliate. "Do you know, I created all these designs and then sent it to the tailor? See this embroidery in the border of this jacket, it is created by me!"

"Hmm, what's so special about that embroidery work? There's no hard effort in creating these designs in jackets. If you can make an embroidery design for me just as you made one for Jyoti dada's coat, then I'll understand it's value!" Rabi replied.

"Ah, what a demand, I say!" Kadambari spread out an embroidery frame in her hand, flaunting it proudly. "See what I am sewing now! A mat, a cherished gift!"

"What is it, after all?" Rabi was curious, while scribbling in his notebook of poems that lay indolently in his lap.

Kadambari flashed a Monalisa smile, and answered coyly: "This is my gift for the esteemed poet Bihari Lal Babu...I have chosen four lines from a stanza of his poem and embroidering those lines, weaving them in this precious mat."

Rabi's face looked glum at the mention of Bihari Lal. Kadambari looked at him and said, as if providing him some solace: "One day, when you'll be able to write verses like Bihari Lal, you will deserve such a gift, I promise you!"

Rabi concentrated on his notebook and his pursuit of writing poetry, pretending he wasn't listening to Kadambari. When Jyoti came to the garden, he saw Kadambari swaying in a swing attached to the Bakul tree, while Rabi was lying on a mat in a turtle-like position, just beneath her feet, and writing a new poem.

"One day, I remember, I would sing whatever I could

Sakhi, you would love all songs I rendered.

You would listen to them quietly, and the river flowed along,

The full moon poured itself, to its light, we remained tethered.

Those days, like a joyous dream, passed away,

For this lifetime, my accursed destiny.

The songs of my soul, the laments of my innermost being

Don't touch you anymore, such is fate's treachery.

Still, my dear *Sakhi*, to you only, I bequeath my songs,

To you, I bequeath everything I possess.

I give it to you all, along with my heart, take it in your hands,

It's the loving gift of my broken heart, no more, no less."

While writing the lines, Rabi had it in mind that he would make it his dedication poem in his forthcoming book. 'I would have to read out the poem to Jyoti dada right now!' He thought. And the cruel, heartless woman who was swinging in the garden would be the subject of this heartfelt dedication. Would the fire of his heart be quenched still? Rabi pondered quietly.

Amid such a silent tug of war within Rabi's heart, his elder brother Satyen had made all arrangements of going away to London. Gyanada, meanwhile, had settled down along with her children in the coastal city of Brighton, very close to London. Satyen had planned to take Rabi there in only a few months' time. It had been necessary to take the restless boy along with him, the boy who detested the regular student life in school. He believed the change of environment in England would do him good.

Before embarking overseas, Rabi was ordered to stay at Satyen's workplace Shahibaag and also at Bombay, with the Pandurag family, so that he could familiarize himself with British manners. The Pandurang family was a wonderful amalgamation of the east and the west, and mixing with them would also pave the path for women to be enlightened about Western lifestyles. This was Satyen's decision, and Rabi had to abide by it all.

Rabi felt awkward and lost, as if he has been uprooted from one soil to the other without any forewarning. He didn't know how he would introduce himself to others publicly. He didn't have the habit of speaking in English too, which was a prerequisite. Anna, however, amazed Rabi with her unparalleled spontaneity, with which she could mix with strangers. The sixteen-year-old Anna had brought with her oodles of sophistication and the polish of education that she derived from London. She received Rabi, her fellow poet and friend with an exceptional, heartfelt warmth and esteem, something which Rabi hadn't experienced before.

Rabi hadn't seen any girl like Anna in his life before. The Bengali girls he knew were always stiff, awkward among men. Even the enlightened women of the Jorasanko Thakurbari never talked to men outside of their home so easily. Rabi was initially a bit hesitant around the very smart, restless, beautiful Anna. Gradually, however, his hesitation subsided. He had only one talent to boast of in the face of Anna's intelligent presence, and that was his poetry writing skill. He thought it would be a good weapon to use to combat her presence. It was Anna's daily chore to teach Rabi the various lessons of English literature, but he, instead, ended up reading his Bengali poems to her on most days. Anna, on her part, snuggled up to Rabi and tried to understand the meaning, the nuances of Rabi's verses. Rabi's heart palpitated to have such a young, beautiful girl breathing so close to him for the very first time, a girl who was not part of his own family, his own kith and kin. The intoxicating smell of the girl's persona wafted in the air along with the perfume she used, and messed up Rabi's restraint.

One day, Anna said to Rabi: "You have to promise me you'll never grow a beard. Don't spoil your handsome face with a beard, I warn you!"

Rabi shivered with excitement to listen to such effusive praise about his handsomeness. Until now, all his days were spent listening to *Notun Bouthan*'s insults, and that solidified the idea of his own plainness in his mind. But now, he was being attracted to Anna, her words glorifying his persona. He replied: "Why Anna, is growing a beard so terrible?"

"A beard isn't bad!" Anna almost rolled on the floor, laughing. "But if you have a beard, the girls will never allow you to kiss them! Let not a beard cover the peripheries of your face."

Rabi noticed Anna's beautiful face, brightened with humour; in her eyes, he saw the hint of an inexplicable mystery. Why did she even make that statement about kissing? What did she mean by that? What would he do now? Rabi felt bewildered, overwhelmed with thoughts.

Anna wanted to know, one again: "Did you ever kiss a girl in your life? How would you write poetry if you never learn how to kiss a girl or a woman, Rabi? Oh, why are you blushing? Come on, young man, are men supposed to blush?"

Rabi, terribly embarrassed at Anna's extreme frankness, wanted to go back and concentrate on his notebook of poems.

But Anna was persistent in her pleas, she wanted to listen to the romantic songs of Rabi. She held his hands and said: My beloved poet, your love songs pull me from my death-bed! How mesmerizing they are!"

Rabi remembered how Kadambari, his *Notun Bouthan* belittled his love songs and saddened him. In fact, Jyoti dada was the only support he had, and Rabi continued to sing and compose songs only due to his motivation.

"Anna, did you ever listen to my Jyoti dada's songs?" He asked.

Anna replied: "Oh yes, Jyoti Thakur, I know, has been a fabulous singer himself. But when you sing, there are goosebumps all over my body!"

Excited and overwhelmed, Rabi started to speak now. "Anna, you are the most beautiful young woman I've ever seen. Your body, your mind and spirit, your language, everything about you is exquisitely beautiful. You have made my music beautiful, Anna!"

"Would you care to give me a new name, beloved poet? Anna sat in front of Rabi and made the gesture of an *anjali* with both her palms. She pleaded again: "Tell me, you won't call me by the name which everyone else calls me.

Give me a name from any of your verses, or any of your songs!"

Rabi whispered with profound emotions: "I will, I surely will. But I won't do that today. Tomorrow at the break of dawn, when you will be asleep still, I will come near your window and wake you up with your new name!"

Anna went to sleep with exuberant joy in her heart, while sleep eluded Rabi's eyes. Ironically, the woman who occupied Rabi's heart even when he was miles away from her, didn't care about his fervent soul. And now, what would Rabi do with this young woman and her anxious, fervent soul? What shall he name her? How shall he wake him up? He pondered.

Rabi had chosen the name 'Nalini' for Anna. He composed a song with that name for the entire night, sleep-deprived and brimming with passion. Even before the sun woke up with its penetrating rays, he rose from his bed and came to the garden. In his hands, he held a bunch of sweet-smelling *bakul* flowers that he picked up before. And now as he came near Anna's bed chamber, he threw the bunch of flowers at the window and started singing:

"Wake up, Nalini, open your eyes!

Didn't the spell of slumber break yet?"

Anna too, on her part, waited for this song to be sung to her at dawn, hence she couldn't get any sleep. She stretched out her hand to Rabi at the window, and her delicate, flower-like fingers got entwined with Rabi's trembling hand.

Meanwhile, the one-month tenure of Rabi's stay was finishing fast; time seemed to fly. Rabi sang his enchanting songs to Anna, and read out the verses published in 'Bharati', and Anna drank the elixir of poetry, bewitched. Rabi sensed that something was happening to him, something magical, yet he couldn't take the initiative to express it to Anna.

Anna learnt more Bengali amid Rabi's presence, even more than the knowledge of English that Rabi received in her presence. She could read the contents of 'Bharati' now. Rabi decided he would gift all the published issues of the journal to her before leaving.

Rabi felt homesick from time to time, and the memory of 'home' brought to his mind the beautiful face of Kadambari. He could sense that everything back at home was as he had seen it. The banks of the river Ganges were still the same, the bird chirped in the same way still, Bihari Lal, the poet would take the betel leaves dressed by *Notun Bouthan* and chew on them with the same pleasure. It was only his own absence which made it different. Rabi wished he had wings, so that he could fly there and see what was happening.

Anna shut Rabi's eyes with her hands, approaching him from behind. Curious, she asked: "What thoughts occupy your mind always, dear poet?"

Rabi's heart palpitated. "What mischief is this girl up to now? She must be hatching something in her mind!" He wondered. Rabi regarded Anna with much love and esteem, yet he was afraid of her at times. Annabai seemed to him like a messenger of his near and dear ones, flying from distant, unfamiliar quarters, landing in his own familiar life, extending the boundaries of her heart to him gradually, by and by. To Rabi, the love, affection and tenderness coming from young women were like God's choicest 'prasad' offerings, showered on him. A 'favour' of the highest order. The love of these young women made flowers bloom in his heart. Even when the flowers withered, their scent lingered in his heart. Nalini was coming to Rabi everyday now, without any invitation. But one day might come, he thought, when she wouldn't respond, even after calling for her. Still, Rabi feared to respond to her call of love. He was scared, lest he would drown in that kind of love.

Still waiting for Rabi's reply, Anna snuggled close to him and sat on the cot nearby. She pulled Rabi's hand and said, in jest: "Rabi, please pull my hand, let's see who among us wins in a tug of war!"

Rabi didn't understand why she had to play this game at all. Just a few seconds into the game, Anna lost and surrendered herself to Rabi's lap. Then she wrapped her hands around Rabi's arms and tried to control herself. Her lips were now closest to Rabi's, yet couldn't he come forward and kiss her? "Such an idiot! He has no sense of romance in him!" She thought, disappointed. So many boys had roamed around Anna, in the hope of receiving an iota of her love and affection, and look at this young, adolescent poet! Anna's bewitching beauty seem to have no esteem in his eyes! Didn't he know that in her desperate bid to be the queen of Rabi's heart, Anna had snubbed so many suitors? Anna became impatient in her quest to win over Rabi; the young poet was turning down her love when she was offering it on her own. Rabi's impatient soul, on the other hand, carried the imprints of another mysterious, beautiful woman.

One day, the desperate Anna said to Rabi: "You know what happens when a boy steals a girl's gloves when she falls asleep?" She was dressed in a white laced gown in English design, looking as pure and demure as an angel. Yet, in her face, mischief gleamed as she spoke.

Rabi was utterly confused, wondering what the girl said. Why was she talking about gloves amid the sultry heat of the Bengali month of *Bhadra*? Astonished, he asked: "What happened if he would steal the gloves? I guess the thief would get a good beating in the hands of the girl's father, once he is caught!"

"No, stupid!" Anna stroked Rabi's cheek with her fingers and whispered in his ears: "That boy attains the right to wake up the girl and kiss her!" Anna's provocative words shook up Rabi, his ears seemed burning hot.

In which of the scriptures was this weird law written, and then, why was Anna pulling him into this whirlpool of emotions? He wondered. In order to divert her attention, Rabi replied: "Do you know this story by Goethe? In Europe, when men are defeated by women in the game of cards, there is this punishment with a kiss. In fact, Goethe also played this game, but he gifted women with poetry instead of kisses. Tell me, don't you think a poet's own creation, his poetry is more attractive as a gift, compared to a kiss?"

Anna didn't seem to like Rabi's anecdote one bit. She was steadfast and firm in letting Rabi know of her rejection of Rabi's narrative. "One cannot possibly write a poem without experiencing a kiss. But even if poetry perishes, the kiss will linger on." She said, and quickly fell asleep in Rabi's bed.

Rabi looked at the slumbering Anna with awe and wonder. The pair of gloves which she wore before was now lying just next to her. Rabi was bewildered, he didn't know what to do. Was Anna hinting at something? He doubted. However, his feeling of reluctance and hesitation did not subside. He extended his hands to pick up the pair of gloves, but then, immediately folded his hands and turned away. He wouldn't be able to kiss Anna, by any means. The face of his beloved sister-in-law Kadambari crept up in his memory at that instant, like an inevitable brushstroke of destiny.

Rabi left the sleeping fairy in his bed and came away from the room, silently, surreptitiously. Instead of a kiss, these lines of a new poem hovered around his consciousness.

"I've heard her name, I've heard her name so many times,

Nalini, Nalini, Nalini, Nalini, the name sweetly chimes."

****

Finally, in the year 1878, on the 20th of September, Rabi embarked on the ship to England with his elder brother Satyen, leaving behind the coastal boundaries of India and the tumultuous storm of Anna's pain and anguish. His prime work in the ship was to observe the scene around and write about it. Sometimes, those outpourings took the form of poetry, sometimes they took the form of letters. He wrote the longest letter to his *Notun Bouthan*, something that he took seven days to compose entirely.

"We embarked on the steamer from the city of Pune on the 20th of September. When the ship started its journey at 5 pm in the evening, we all were standing at its roof. Slowly, gradually, the last coastline of India, our motherland, dissolved in front of our eyes. Unable to bear the chaos around me at that moment, I went back to sleep in my own cabin. I don't find it necessary to hide this—my mind was being overpowered by a feeling of lifelessness, weariness, melancholy…Anyway, leave it, I don't have the leisure to write about such an account full of pathos, nor do I intend to do it; and, even if I write such an account, I can say that either your eyes will not be moist with feelings of sympathy, or you won't have the patience to read it all.

This being said, I bow down to the feet of the mighty ocean. I myself know how I've spent those dreadful six days—from the 20th to the 26th. You might know a bit about sea fever, but I'm sure you don't know how the pain of it is. I had fallen a victim of that disease, and if I write a detailed account regarding it, I'm sure even a stone will weep. Six days, you know, I didn't come out from my bed. The room in which I stationed myself was extremely dark, small, with windows bolted from all sides, lest the sea water enters inside the room. I was barely 'living' for those six days, my sick, weary body devoid of the sun, devoid of the air outside. In the first evening, a fellow traveller forcefully pulled me out of my bed and took me to the dining table. When I tried to stand up on my feet, it felt like every atom inside my brain was fighting tooth and nails with each other. My eyesight was not working, my feet weren't working, my whole body started wobbling as I tried to walk. With staggering footsteps, I went and sat on a bench nearby. My co-travellers saw my condition and carried me somehow to the deck of the ship. I supported my body at one of the rails and noticed the pitch-dark night, the sky shrouded with dark clouds. The wind was blowing in our opposite direction. I also noticed with awe and wonder how the ship, a lonely entity was cutting through the boundless sea in the dark, exuding fire from both sides; whichever way I was looking at, it was overwhelmingly dark, with the sea swelling, raving at every direction...It was indeed a sombre sight.

... After I got better and started venturing out of my room, I noticed the co-travellers in the ship and they, in turn, noticed me. As is my inherent nature, I am quite scared of the females, or the 'ladies'. One would have so many possibilities of falling into danger while getting close to them, that if pundit Chanakya would have been alive, he would have advised to stay ten thousand hands away from them. On one hand, in the kingdom of my mind, there was the possibility of myriad terrible accidents, on the other hand there was this constant fear of saying the wrong words unintentionally, and as a consequence, our impatient lady would be flabbergasted in terrible hatred and shame, unable to tolerate a slight aberration from her known manners and etiquette. I stayed away from all the ladies in the ship, lest I got puzzled, bewildered in the dense forest of their gowns, lest I would have to cut meat for them during our meal times, lest I would end up cutting my own finger while cutting chicken in their presence. There was no dearth of ladies in our ship, but the gentlemen were consistent in their complaint that none of these ladies were either young or beautiful in appearance.

Every day, during meals, B—used to sit right beside me. B—was a Eurasian person. But he had learnt to whistle like the English folks, and had also learnt to stand while stretching his legs, with his both hands tucked under his pockets. B—used to look at me with a strong sense of pity. One day, he came to me and asked in a sombre voice: "Young man, are you going to Oxford? Oxford University is a great institution!"

Another day, I was reading the book 'Proverbs and Their Lessons' by Trench *sahib*, when he came and took the book from my hands. While whistling in his characteristic style, he flipped through a couple of pages of the book and remarked: "Indeed, it's a very good book to read."

It took us five days to travel from Eden to Suez. The ones who travel to England through the Brindisi path have to get off from the ship and take the train from Suez to Alexandria, a port where another steamer ship waits for them. They have to embark on the ship to cross the Mediterranean Sea, and then they reach Italy. We being overland travellers had to deport at Suez.

Three of us Bengalis and one Englishman, our fellow passenger rented an Arabian boat. If you would have seen the face of the boatman, you would have understood how the divine contours of a human can transform to that of a beast. With his pitch-black skin, his eyes resembling a ferocious tiger, his small forehead and plump lips, the appearance of his face was very frightening. We tried negotiating with other boatmen, but their prices were very high. This boatman, however, agreed to take us with a much lesser price. Mr. B—was much reluctant to travel on that boat. He said: 'You must not trust the Arabians—they can easily cut your throat with a knife!' To justify his point, he recounted a couple of extremely terrifying anecdotes establishing their penchant for anarchism. But anyways, we embarked on that boat. The boatmen here spoke in broken English, they could understand a bit of the English language. We travelled on the boat for quite a while without any fight or scuffle. Our fellow traveller, the Englishman had to get off at the Suez post office for some important work. The boatman didn't agree to the idea initially, arguing that the post office was far away and it would take a long time to reach there, but soon, his objection was dispelled. After going a bit further, he asked again: "Do you need to go to the post office? It's impossible to reach there within an hour or two!"

The rough-natured Englishman among us got furious and shouted: 'Your grandmother!' At this, our boatman got angry and retaliated: 'What? mother? mother? What mother? Don't say mother!'

At this point, we had thought he had thrown the Englishman in the water, and he asked again: 'What did you say?'

The Englishman now replied stubbornly again: 'Your grandmother!'

At this, the boatman became furious and started exhibiting his anger. Seeing that the matter was going beyond control, the Englishman became a bit lenient now and replied: 'You don't seem to understand what I say!' Which meant he was hell bent in proving that calling out 'grandmother' was not spelling an abusive word.

The boatman abandoned his usage of English now, and shouted in his mother tongue, in a reprimanding voice: '*Bus...chup* (Enough...silent)!'

The *sahib* was shell-shocked at this treatment, and remained silent. After travelling a bit further, he asked again: 'How far is the destination still?'

The boatman shouted in his rough, wrathful voice, in broken English: 'Two shilling give, ask what distance?'

Listening to the boatman's words, we got the idea that one cannot ask such a question in the kingdom of Suez with a rent of just two shillings.

Meanwhile, as our boatman was reprimanding us constantly, the other boatmen were feeling extremely amused to witness the scene. They looked into each other's eyes and started smiling. They could hardly control their laughter, seeing the bad temper of our boatman. On one hand, he was scolding and shouting at us, on the other hand, they were united in their chorus of laughter and jeering, and the three of us, upon knowing that we could not take any more revenge on the boatman, joined them in the laughter riot.

…When we reached the port of Alexandria, we noticed that a steamer named 'Mongolia' was waiting for us there. We were now climbing the bosom of the Mediterranean Sea. I started shivering in cold. I returned to the ship and bathed meticulously, the dirt and soot was entering my very bones. After bathing, I went to take a tour of the city of Alexandria. A boat had been rented to escort us from the ship to the adjacent land. If you look at the boatmen here, you'll see the second version of Sir William Jones in all of them. Moreover, they can speak satisfactorily in multiple languages, including Greek, Italian, French, English.

We reached Italy in four-five more days, at 1 or 2 am, the wee hours of the night. We left the comfort of our warm beds, gathered our belongings and went to the roof of the ship. It was a full moon light, and the cold was severe. I didn't have too many layers of warm clothes, so the cold was seeping through my body. We experienced the silent, calm city in front of our eyes, the doors and windows of all the houses bolted, as if in deep slumber. After a while, we got the hint of some chaos among us passengers regarding the train timings. Some argued that the train would be there, some argued that it wouldn't be there. We were bewildered, confused, didn't know what to do with our belongings. We had no clue if we would remain in our ship or venture out of it. Just then, an Italian officer came to us and started counting the number of passengers, we couldn't think why he did that. It was rumoured inside the ship that there was a connection between this calculation of our heads and us boarding the train. However, after a while, we got to know that we couldn't board the train at all that night. We also got to know that we couldn't board the train before 3 o'clock in the afternoon on the following day. All the passengers got annoyed, frustrated, and put up in a hotel at Brindisi for the night.

As for myself, I had set my feet on the European soil for the very first time. Before travelling to a new country, I envision its uniqueness in such a way that it doesn't seem new to me upon my arrival. And so, when I confessed that Europe didn't seem so new to me after all, everyone around me looked at me, surprised.

Upon reaching the city of Paris, we were sent to a Turkish bath station. First, we were seated in a very warm room; some of us started sweating profusely while staying in the room for long. I, however, didn't have a seat, hence I was sent to a warmer room. This room seemed hot, fiery, and I could hardly keep my eyes open there, they were stinging in pain. I could barely stay in the room for a few minutes; when I came out of the room, I started sweating heavily. They took me to another place and made me lie down, after that. A huge, gigantic man came to me and started massaging my whole body. His body was bare; I had never seen such a fine muscular physique before in life. I chanted a Sanskrit mantra silently, awed by his larger-than-life appearance. I thought to myself—there was absolutely no need for such a huge canon to deal with a minuscule mosquito. He scrutinized me minutely and then remarked that my body had grown quite tall. If I would put on some more muscles and fat on both the sides, I would be a handsome young man. He massaged my whole body incessantly for half-an-hour. It seemed as if all the dirt I had accumulated on my body since my birth had diminished. When the massaging was done, I was taken to another room and then given a bath with hot water, soap and my whole body was scrubbed off with a sponge. After this whole process of cleansing my body, I was taken to yet another room, and they started pouring hot water on me with a big water gun. Suddenly, they stopped pouring the hot water and poured ice-cold water on me instead. After this crazy randomness of being washed with hot water and cold water in turns, I went to a water machine of some sort, with water squirting out from above and below it, water gushing from all sides that pierced my body like darts. Staying for a while amid such an icy, cold whirlpool, the blood of my bosom had frozen; I had to leave the war-zone, breathless, panting. As I came out and saw a pond-like water body, someone asked if I could swim. I didn't end up swimming, but my fellow traveller did. When he was swimming, I heard them saying: "See how strangely these Indian boys swim, just like dogs, don't they?" His bathing was complete now. I noticed that having a Turkish bath and getting your body washed by a *dhopa* (washerman) was more or less the same thing."

Upon reading Rabi's letter full of juvenile emotions, Kadambari laughed to her heart's content silently.

Chapter 11

Basanta Bilap / The Mourning of Spring

Jyotirindranath was reading from a Sanskrit drama at the literary soiree happening at the verandah of the third floor of the Jorasanko mansion. While reading the vibrant description of the *vasanta utsav* (spring festival) of the yore, he was mesmerized, imagining its sheer beauty; it seemed as if it was the festival of Holi of the human hearts. At that moment, he said to everybody present: "See, why can't we open our hearts more and play with the colours of *abir* uninhibitedly, like the old times? Can't we try to revive the festival of colours in our own homely fashion?"

Kadambari joined in the enthusiasm of her husband: "Why not? We can do *vasanta utsav* in our own courtyard! Or else we can have it in the courtyard of the mansion next door, 'Baithak khana bari', can't we?" She chimed in.

Swarna replied: "Then let's share this idea with Guno Dada...all us siblings and cousins from both the houses can have a fun-filled spring festival then!" She sounded ecstatic.

Gunendranath, on his part, was extremely enthusiastic about all festivals and cultural events. Earlier too, he had been involved in the arrangements of the Hindu mela (fair) and also the production of 'naba natok' (new dramas) by managing a group of cousins from both the houses. Meanwhile, things turned sour between both the mansions as Debendranath Thakur filed a lawsuit against his widowed sister-in-law Tripura Sundari regarding the inheritance of the 'Baithak Khana bari'. Tripura Sundari, the childless widow had intended to adopt her sister-in-law Jogomaya's younger son Gunendranath. In that case, Gunen would naturally inherit a significant chunk of Dwarakanath's property. To quell this fear and anxiety, Debendranath filed a lawsuit at the Supreme Court with a ubiquitous claim—a widow has no right to adopt a child. The case went in his favour, and as a result, he gained a huge part of his younger brother Nagen's property. Gunen, on his part, was deprived, and Tripura Sundari was anguished and heartbroken. However, Gunendra tried not to pay heed to such negative feelings and with heartfelt emotions, plunged himself in the joy of festivities with his cousins, like all previous years.

Though the two mansions were split regarding the ideologies of religion, the children of both the families were united in their selfless bond of love. The Hindu relatives of House no. 5 wouldn't attend the Brahmo marriage functions of House no. 6, and on the other hand, the members of House no. 6 wouldn't attend the marriage functions of House no. 5. However, there were theatrical performances and musical soirees on the occasion of those marriage functions, and the members of both the houses would unanimously indulge in them. Gunen was the one who was the most enthused and active in arranging these events. He, along with his elder cousin Jyoti had the 'Jorasanko Natyashala', a theatre academy inspired by Gopal Urey's *jatra* (rustic theatre) performance. The shows of their 'naba natok' (new dramas) and the music and dance performances of the *vasanta utsav* or spring festivities happened inside those premises. Gunen was truly unparalleled in involving everyone with his magnanimous community spirit, immersing himself in the festivities. Owing to his radiant spirit, one fine spring evening, the garden of the 'Baithak khana bari' was decked up in vibrant lights and Holi colours, transforming into 'Nandankanan', heaven's own garden of delight. The festivities increased manifold with the playing of Holi along with water guns.

Close friends of the Thakurbari were also invited at the festival. Amid such august company, the ecstatic duo Akshay and his wife Sarat Kumari were sprinkling colours over each other. Kadambari was decked up as a princess of the yore. With a traditional bun wrapped with a garland of bel flowers, her hair covered with a georgette veil, she looked stunning, ethereal. In her hands and neck, she wore a bangle and a necklace made of *madhabi* flowers; her ear was adorned with earrings made of the same flowers. Upon seeing her, the mesmerized Jyoti stretched out his welcoming hands and said: "Hail, *Madhavika,* the beautiful woman adorned with flowers!"

Kadambari sprinkled powdered colours of *abir* over Jyoti's white kurta and replied: "Oh handsome youth tormented with *abir*, come, let us welcome the onset of spring!"

Everybody present at the scene were witnessing this beautiful romantic play enacted by the majestic Jyotirindra and his gorgeous wife Kadambari, bewitched. It seemed as if the duo had created a magical web of love in their garden, way beyond the mundane spheres. Just a while after this, the scene was replaced by another one. Just like multiple scenes of a play unfolding one after the other, snippets of conversations, dialogues, gestures and images coloured the spring orchard.

At one point, Bihari Lal approached Kadambari with powdered colour in his folded fist. With his fingers, he sprinkled powdered colours in red, green, pink, like raindrops in Kadambari's head, her whole body. In youthful vigour, Kadambari too circled around him, getting herself drenched in the rain of these colours.

While circling around Bihari Lal, suddenly, her eyes fell on Rupa. She noticed that a *gora sahib* was sprinkling the colours of *abir* on her indiscriminately and she was rolling on the floor, laughing, unabashed. She had heard that this *gora sahib* and Rupa were in a very intimate relationship of late. Kadambari was pissed off, seeing such shameless public display of intimacy that Rupa indulged in.

Rupa pulled the *sahib*'s hand now, and came close to Kadambari. "See, *Notun Bouthan*, Harry *sahib* has seen a fairy in you, he's calling you 'Angel'! I want you to meet him, so I dragged him here."

Kadambari dragged Rupa by her hand and pulled her far away from the scene. "Will you never be sensible, Rupa? See, how shamelessly you are dragging that *firangi sahib's* hands, don't you know you shouldn't touch stranger men? And do I ever talk to strangers, for that matter?" She burst out.

Rupa almost broke into tears. "And what about you playing with colours with Bihari Babu? Harry *sahib* is no stranger, but a friend of Jyoti dada, and he is the one who invited us, how does it matter if I hold his hand?"

Kadambari, shocked to notice Rupa's courage, retaliated: "Listen, Rupa, I have never touched Bihari Babu's hands while talking to him, and even if the daughters and brides of our Thakurbari are educated, enlightened beings, we never talk to men who are strangers, because we think it taints our honour as women. As for me, I only talk to a very chosen few, those men are good-natured, talented, and very close friends of my husband. How dare you compare my situation to yours?"

Rupa remained steadfast in her own logic. "If you think of that, then Harry *sahib* is my friend. His real name is Harry Shephard. I call him by that name, and you know, I love chatting and spending time with him. He is so gifted, he narrates such different, fascinating tales. I don't like being stuck around the women in the inner quarters at all times. It is so dull, boring and devoid of excitement!"

"How did you even get to meet him?" Kadambari enquired in an angry tone. She looked divine in her angry face. She could gauge that Harry *sahib* was ogling at her shamelessly, and the others were looking at her too, with curious eyes. She felt a terrible anger on Rupa.

Rupkumari replied: "Well, I met him at one of the assemblies of your erudite friends. I like him a lot. Please don't be angry on me, *Notun Bouthan*, I beg of you!" She pleaded.

"See what I do to you!" The furious Kadambari tried to catch Rupa's hands. At this very moment, her gold bangle, *madhavikankan* dropped to the ground. It created enough distraction for Rupa to escape the clutches of Kadambari and run away.

Harry sat far away under the shade of a tall tree. Rupa

came and sat beside him, and, in pseudo-anger, said: "I don't like the things happening with me...I don't like them one bit! All they want is to chain me, all the time. Don't do this, don't do that, don't go there, don't mix with that man, and so on...Can't I have a will of my own?"

Harry placed a hand on her shoulder and said: "I can gauge your restlessness, Rupa. You know, there was a time when the women of our country were chained too, but now things have changed so much. Now the women of our country have taken to the streets in wake of the suffrage movement, demanding voting rights for all women. The European women have gained freedom after much struggle."

"But how free are they?" Rupa asked, curious. "Can they travel alone in a ship? Can they venture overseas? Can they go anywhere they want to? I also crave to see the world, to roam around everywhere indiscriminately." She stated, fervently.

Harry replied: "You know, even the men of our country are now seriously thinking about equal rights of genders. And the women are extremely enthusiastic about it."

Rupa started playing with a bunch of her *abir*-smeared hairs, and asked: "The women of your country are real fighters, as much as I gathered from you...then, hasn't any of them been a writer, documenting her struggles?"

"No...no...the truth is, we, the men folk wouldn't have felt the necessity of women's liberation ever, if the women wouldn't have told us about it." Harry looked at Rupa's curious face and added further: "You know, a century before, a woman named Mary Wollstonecraft had written an extremely radical book about the rights of women, and questioned: why would women always have to live as a doll of men's desires? Women would of course, love their men as their true companions, but why would they accept their reprimanding orders? Needless to say, she had to face much torture in the hands of the gatekeepers of society, because of these questions addressed in her book. But now, the suffragists have welcomed her, cheered for her book."

"What...what did you say?" Rupa, evidently, didn't understand the new word 'suffragists.'

Harry smiled and shook her chin a bit. "Suffragists are women who take to the streets to fight for their freedom to vote. Did you get it?"

"I wish we could also join them in the streets and fight for our own rights." Rupa said. "I must tell this all to Swarna didi. If she agrees, both of us can join the league of the suffragists."

"Will you come with me?" Harry asked Rupa in a deep, sombre voice, looking intently at her eyes. "Let us go somewhere, far, far away, where nobody will impose any restrictions on us, on our whereabouts. Would you care to accompany me?"

Excited by this proposal, Rupa pressed Harry's hand tightly. "Oh, I wish to go with you so badly, you know! But everybody will get to know and protest against it! Besides, I can't go without letting *Notun Bouthan* know of it."

Harry flashed a naughty smile and said: "Well, then you cannot be a free woman ever in your life. See, the big world outside is beckoning you, and you're stuck in this insignificant threshold of your home."

"No...no, I have to be free! I can't afford to spend my whole life, stuck in this threshold!" There was a tinge of faith in Rupa's voice that had come back now.

Harry laughed, and replied: "But you can't do it."

Rupa was angry at his comment. "Why can't I do it, tell me? Tell me, what do I have to do to prove it!" She said.

"Can you kiss me right now?" Harry said, as a mysterious smile danced in his lips.

The innocent Rupa trembled to hear such a proposal, and asked: "But...what does it have to do with me attaining freedom?"

"In our country, no man or woman gains adulthood unless he or she is involved in dating. And, kissing is a principal part of dating." Harry said. "If you don't kiss me, how would I understand whether you love me or not? If I have to elope with you from the threshold of this house, I'll have to ensure that you pass this exam first."

"Go...go away!" Rupa said, blushing like the sky at the break of dawn. Harry cupped Rupa's face with both his hands, and both their lips bent towards each other, just about to be locked. Just then, somebody called out Rupa's name, and suddenly, she stood up, evading the touch of Harry. The kiss remained incomplete.

Sarala was calling Rupa for her music lessons. Meanwhile, Jyoti Thakur had started singing in his open, mellifluous voice, and the girls, Pratibha, Sarala had joined in the chorus, abandoning the festival of colours. Gunendra, drenched in colours, sat with them, playing the Tabla, adding new life to the musical soiree.

Swarna was playing with colours, but more than

anything else, she was observing the scene, its beauty and its nuances. It seemed as if the festival of colours of the yesteryears had emerged again in the garden of the Jorasanko mansion. As she was witness to this beautiful scene, a plan of a musical drama unfolded in her brain.

Within a few days, Swarna was able to finish writing the musical drama titled 'Vasanta Utsav' (The Spring Festival). The ecstatic Jyoti started preparations for staging the drama with all the young members of the house. The Jorasanko mansion was filled with the undulations of music and melodies yet again, and Jyoti was instrumental in this reunion. The rehearsals continued, and everyone was humming the tunes of the songs merrily. Sarala, the child was humming the song penned by her mother: "In the night, I stare at the sky, blinded by clouds, with no moon, no stars,/ My heart is surrounded by the impenetrable dark..."

Kadambari was the one who sang this song in 'Vasanta Utsav'. In her big, surreal eyes, her long, flowing tresses, this tragic song overwhelmed everybody with a divine, unearthly melody.

Rupa had a lovely voice too, Jyoti called her to join in and contribute her voice in the chorus. But Kadambari noticed that during the rehearsals, Harry *sahib* was a regular face, seated amid a group of close friends. He had a particular interest in the music created by Bengalis. He had roamed among the *Baul* singers, the folk, rustic singers in the rural areas and learnt their own music, but now he seemed to have much fun, enjoying the distinct musical flavour of the Thakurbari. Kadambari, however, got annoyed to see him whispering in Rupa's ears, and chatting with her every now and then. How would she tame this wild, shameless girl! She wondered. The women of Jorasanko, her own clan would pounce on her, accuse her if they noticed the slightest aberration on Rupa's part. As for Gyanadanandini, through her letters, she was well aware of everything happening from the faraway England. Her scrutinizing acts went on unperturbed, even from the distance.

One day, Swarna took Rupa along with her to visit Anette Akroyd. Anette had been staying in Kolkata for some time, and had taken an instrumental role in educating the girls here. Her inspiration and role model was Mary Carpenter, who had come to India a couple of times before her, and started the initiative of a Girls' School with the assistance of the Brahmo Samaj. Anette discussed various issues like this with the Brahmo Samaj members, who happened to be her friends, and this time too, she summoned them for a discussion.

Anette had some problems with the ideologies of Keshab Sen, the head of Brahmo Samaj, which had happened two years back when Keshab had a bitter argument with Anette regarding the education of girls and women. Many of the so-called liberal Brahmas of those times frowned upon the idea of the education and empowerment of women.

During her stay in Europe, Anette had befriended another Brahmo member Manmohan Ghosh. Perhaps her friendship with Manmohan and his wife had developed rapidly because of the couple's proclivity for English etiquettes and manners. It was in England that Anette had come to know of the Brahmo Samaj's initiatives in the education of women. In fact, while getting introduced to Keshab Sen, Anette had the strong impression of him being a champion for the cause of women's freedom and emancipation. But upon arriving in Calcutta, it dawned upon her that it was not possible for her to be on the same page with him on the question of women's education. Keshab, who was actually quite orthodox in his views, believed that the act of thrusting the knowledge of math and sciences in the brains of women in the name of education was absolutely unnecessary. It would only turn them as *memsahibs* with no real utility at all. He believed that women needn't be exposed to any such education that detached them from their households. Hence, he arranged for the study of literature and the arts only in the Girls' Schools.

Anette Akroyd couldn't accept this act of Keshab Sen at all. She called a meeting at Manmohan Ghosh's residence and appealed to the members present there: "Do you really support the cause of women's education? If yes, then kindly protest against this gross injustice perpetrated by Keshab Sen!"

Shibnath Shastri, who was present there, spoke out. He opined that Keshab Chandra was acting like a true orthodox. These were the times when women would be progressing, he said. 'Our girls can do the same things that girls in Europe are capable of doing.' He added further.

In the meeting, liberal men like Manmohan Ghosh, Dwarakanath Ganguli concurred with the idea of teaching science to the girls and women, thus being on the same page with Ms. Akroyd.

Anette had also called Swarnakumari to the meeting. She looked at Swarna and said: "It's not acceptable that only the males will decide things for us. Can you voice your opinion in the matter, Swarna?"

Swarna had come to the meetings organized by Anette quite a number of times previously, but those were literary meetings with mostly women as participants. The meetings were hosted in Manmohan Ghosh's house, as Anette stayed there as a guest. His wife helped her immensely in organizing and hosting those gatherings.

Swarna replied to Anette: "You know, *Babamoshai* used to give us lessons in science since our childhood. Whenever he is at home, he still shows the stars in the sky, teaches lessons in science. Hence, my heart is in both science and in literature and arts. I think women like us should be given lessons in math and sciences. Unless they become scientifically inclined, the blind prejudices won't diminish from their minds."

Anette hugged Swarna tightly and said ecstatically: "Keshab Babu should come and see what the Bengali women are saying!"

Harry *sahib* was also seated among the invited guests, a sincere accomplice of Anette in all her initiatives. Once Rupa came and sat beside him, the guests looked at her with frowns in their foreheads. Swarna noticed this and called her: "Come and sit beside me, Rupa!"

Harry looked at Swarna and said: "You emphasize on giving education to Bengali women, don't you? You aim to teach them science, but then, you don't allow them to mix with men. Why is this discrepancy in your attitude?"

The guests were visibly embarrassed and irritated to face such a question. Shibnath replied: "Well, we aim to give them Western education while retaining their Indian-Bengali identity. They can be well-educated even without mixing with stranger men, Harry!"

Harry argued: "But how will the horizons of their minds expand if both men and women won't mix with each other freely?"

Anette replied in support of Harry: "You know, the women in our country mix with men freely and indiscriminately, so they have been able to demand for equal rights for themselves. By the way, Swarna, you are a progressive woman by all means. Why do you still wear a veil when you are outside? What's the need for it?"

Swarnakumari had worn a veil over her head, made with a separate piece of cloth, and on top of that, she had worn a small cap. She felt annoyed at Anette's question. "It's a culture of our country which I choose to respect, Anette; besides, there's no correlation between rejecting the veil and the progress of women. Remember, the women of our country are venturing outside after eons and ages, they are harshly criticized upon the slightest aberration! Hence, we need to be careful about mixing with men in our circles!" She replied.

Harry, on the other hand, felt annoyed because Rupa was forcefully taken away from his side a few minutes back. He remarked: "I have had this impression that the women of Thakurbari are very progressive and emancipated, but then I've also learnt that they don't talk to men outside their mansion, which means that you have still retained the 'purdah' ritual. Are we men such monsters?"

Swarna, furious at Harry's words, looked at him with a reddened, flustered face. She looked at Rupa with fiery eyes and replied: "If you ask me, I strongly believe that our emancipation will be attained, not through revolt, but through acceptance. If we choose to hurt the society with our sudden, abrupt rejection of the purdah, our liberation will not fall from the heavens."

Amid such controversial discussions, the anguished Brahmo members present in the meeting decided to establish a new school for girls with the assistance and support of Anette Akroyd. With their hard work and perseverance, the Hindu Mahila Vidyalaya, a school for girls was formed, with the aim to teach them arts and the sciences. Anette took the responsibility of running the school, and she maintained her responsibility with elan for a long time. After she got married, the school was rechristened as 'Banga Mahila Vidyalaya' and later, it got merged with the esteemed Bethune College, another premiere institution for girls. But around this same time, there had been a rift between Keshab Chandra and the progressive, liberal Brahmo members, on account of their ideological differences.

There was yet another issue which caused mayhem and chaos within the Brahmo Samaj, and Keshab Chandra was at the core of it. The Brahmo men had created a movement, appealing to the British Raj to raise the minimum age of girls to get married, and a law had been passed to that effect, as a result of the movement. Ironically, however, around the same time, the fourteen-year-old daughter of Keshab Chandra, Suneeti, fell in love with Maharaja Deependra Narayan, the monarch of Coochbehar. Once Keshab Chandra, her father accepted the alliance, it wreaked havoc within the members of the Brahmo Samaj. Keshab Chandra's image took a massive beating in the eyes of the Brahmo youth, who hadn't expected such hypocrisy and double standards from their leader. In order to save his face somehow, Keshab argued that the couple would get married, but not live together yet as man and wife, till they attained a mature age. Deependra Narayan would venture overseas just after the wedding rituals, and Suneeti would continue living in her paternal home. But the fire of revolt couldn't be diminished with this argument. As Suneeti's own insistence, the minor girl was married off by her father, and Brahmo Samaj was divided into two separate groups.

The women of the Thakurbari were pretty excited about the story of this wedding, a hot topic that rejuvenated their spirits. The members of Thakurbari had a long-standing association with the family of Keshab Sen, since Keshab's father had disowned him after accepting the Brahmo religion. Keshab had decided to leave his father's home then, due to their differences. He had idolized Maharshi Deben Thakur, and during those difficult days, he became Keshab's benefactor and provider. For some days, Keshab took shelter in the Thakurbari along with his wife. Jyoti, Rabi, Swarnakumari were young boys and girls at that time, so they became closer to his young wife. Today, though they didn't cohabit in the same house anymore, their strong connection remained. And though there were rifts and conflicts between Deben Thakur and Keshab, for which their paths were separated, their mutual interests in each other weren't diminished.

Swarna said to Kadambari in her chamber in the third floor: "*Bouthan*, do you know what mayhem is going on with Suneeti's wedding? Everyone is getting angry with Keshab dada, but Suneeti is actually the one to blame for the mess!"

Kadambari was seated on her bed, reclining on a pillow. While working meticulously on a *zari* embroidery work over a velvet cloth, she lifted her eyes and replied: "*Thakurjhi*, I must say, I admire Suneeti's courage! See how unabashedly she refused the suitor that her father liked, and fell in love with the prince of Coochbehar! Moreover, she made her father too accept the union…"

Swarna replied: "Can you imagine? To keep up with

his daughter's demands, the father has been subject to such harassment among his own tribe, his old friends! No Bengali girl has been so fortunate ever before, to receive such unconditioned love from her father. Think about us, did we get the pleasure of marrying a man according to our wishes? Suneeti is the first one to make it happen, hats off!"

"I will marry a man according to my wishes, too!" Rupa chirped in. She was somewhere nearby, listening to the juicy conversation. Swarna and Kadambari didn't notice her all this while, as Rupa was seated at their back.

Startled to listen to Rupa's shameless wish, Kadambari scolded her: "You have been such a precocious girl, I tell you, Rupa!"

"But just now you both were praising Suneeti for her exceptional courage and her love marriage, weren't you? Why am I the one to blame if I wish to do the same?" Rupa pouted her lips like a child, in rage and anguish.

"Do you have a father like Suneeti who dotes on you? No, on the contrary, people will blame me if you commit a single mistake. Because of your deeds, I feel terrorized all the time, listening to their caustic comments. Do you wish to put me in more danger, Rupa?" Kadambari replied.

Rupa replied, tucking her face like a pampered child in Kadambari's lap: "I don't like this hackneyed, monotonous life here, *Notun Bouthan*! I wish to be freed from all ties, I want to fly as a free bird and explore this big, wide world."

Swarna was annoyed to hear such words from Rupa. "Don't you think everyone wants that, Rupa? Everyone dreams about that, but in reality, it cannot be accomplished. You're talking like a child, when will you grow up and use your senses?" She said.

Rupa was adamant. "If you want it intensely, you can accomplish your dreams. It's only that your desires aren't that strong. Come, let the three of us venture together to explore the mountains, the seas. Just the three of us!" She replied.

Kadambari laughed at Rupa's proposition. It was too good to be true. Rupa started pulling the piece of cloth she was sewing, and asked: "Whom are you sewing for? May I ask, how much more embroidery work will you do for Jyoti dada? The more exquisite clothes and shoes you'll make for him, the more that will entice the actresses on stage. Then you'll be the one crying in pain!"

The environment turned sombre within seconds, at this discussion. Swarna scolded Rupa, looking at Kadambari's sullen face. "*Notun Bouthan* has indulged you so much that you've lost your mind, Rupa! See how you hurt her with your bitter words! Will you never learn to use your brains?"

Kadambari raised her hands, gesturing Swarna to stop. "She didn't say anything wrong, *Thakurjhi*!" She replied. "She just uttered a bitter truth, something which you know already, but never say it pronouncedly. Honestly, these days I cry silently, for there is a bevy of *apsaras* and *kinnaris*, beautiful, other-worldly women surrounding your *Notun dada* at all times. But this embroidery work isn't for him. I'm making a new embroidered shoe for Rabi; since he left for the foreign shores, I'm fondly remembering him."

Swarna replied: "Okay, but you're being angry with *Notun dada* for no reason, and that sounds unjustified to me. Imagine how his handsomeness and intellect mesmerizes even the wealthy, sophisticated ladies, then why won't the lowly, public women on stage not fall madly in love with him? And why is he to blame for that? Would he stop producing his plays for such a flimsy reason?"

"Why? No... I'm not even suggesting that. But is it necessary to make those prostitutes act in his plays? For all these days, the plays have been staged without their presence, so why are they indispensable now?" Kadambari argued.

"Now, now, you're talking like the members of those conservative groups, *Bouthan*!" Swarna replied. "You know, when the great bard Michael Madhusudan Dutta had initiated the role-playing of women for the first time ever in his play titled 'Sharmistha' in Bengal Theatre, there was a lot of criticism and censure among the public, which spread like wildfire. Even Vidyasagar *Moshai*, one of the main organizers of Bengal Theatre, couldn't support this whole affair of women being convinced to act on stage, hence, he withdrew himself from the theatre as a mark of protest. There is still debate and controversy amid the gentlemen in society regarding the matter, but at the same time, women are continuing to act on stage. They have already proved that they can act, so, on what grounds can we belittle women on stage?"

Kadambari didn't seem to buy this logic. She argued further: "I am condemning it because these days, public women, prostitutes are being hired to act on stage, to prove the point that women can act. And this whole affair is corrupting the character, the moral fabric of our men. Don't we need to think about that, *Thakurjhi*?"

"Why, just because you fear your own man will spoil his character, his moral fabric, those fallen women of our society wouldn't get any opportunity to salvage their lives? Do you know, in performing arts in theatre, there is a huge possibility of these women attaining salvation of their souls? And don't you think, when we ourselves act in plays in our own homes, even then our characters can be spoilt?"

"Well, I don't think I can ever win in any argument with you!" Kadambari replied. "But honestly, I feel afraid, I don't like the idea…can't I share that feeling with you, *Thakurjhi*?" Kadambari sounded hurt, anguished, not getting her desired support from Swarna.

Swarna wanted to divert Kadambari's attention elsewhere, and said: "You know, when I was at *Mej dada*'s place in Bombay, I had the good fortune of watching the Marathi production of Shakespeare's 'Hamlet' and 'Othello', and I must say the acting was quite remarkable. It had a strong oriental flavour, with Othello carrying his Marathi look and demeanour, and Desdemona wearing a nose-ring that suited her perfectly well. But in this play, men played the women's' roles, and that surprised me. The Marathi women are quite liberal, progressive, compared to our own Bengali women, but the fact that Bengali theatre became the pioneers in bringing our women on stage gives me much delight."

Kadambari settled herself now, and said: "Anyway, share with me your new writing, read it out to me."

Rupa reclined her body on Kadambari's and listened to the incessant chatter of the women. The small world of their joys, their pain, anguish reverberated, filling up the tiny literary assembly in the inner quarters of the Thakurbari.

Chapter 12

Gyanadanandini's Stay in England

Gyanada spent the first Christmas evening in the city of Brighton with much pleasure. The near and dear ones of her family weren't with her this time. But still, she was happy that those long days of sickness and the trauma of losing her babies at birth were over. She sipped a glass of wine after a long, long time, and smiled. The small Christmas party was arranged by her in her rented apartment to express her thanks and gratitude to Dr. Joseph Lister, the wonderful human who treated her in her illness and saved her life. Among the guests, she had also invited her neighbour, Mrs. Donkins, and Gyanendra Thakur, her relative who was a resident of England, along with his daughters. In her expatriate life in England, these handful of people seemed to her like her own kith and kin.

There was an entire row of small houses by the sea in a secluded island, and the community was named Medina Villa. Gyanada was living with her children in one of those houses. Though the houses were named as villas, they were small-sized, with a couple of trees in the front yard. The rooms were small, compared to the average size of rooms in her homeland, with a low-lying roof, and the windows had to be closed all the time for the dreadful winter breeze. There was no room for any air, but because the windows were made of glass, there was no obstruction for sunlight. Gyanada, with her fine sense of artistry, had decorated the small rooms in an absolutely charming western fashion.

However, all these chores of decorating the rooms were just a façade that she had to maintain, to sustain her social position, and also to keep herself busy, and uplift her mind. Beyond the façade, she wasn't doing good at all. With three children in tow, and pregnant all over again in an alien land, she was a totally exhausted, troubled soul. Sometimes, she felt terrible anger on her husband Satyen, why did he have to send her to an exile in this way? Sometimes, she cried all alone, why did she have to come so far away, listening to her husband's plan? Satyen was a thoughtful, but impractical man, with zero knowledge about domestic life. He had no idea whatsoever that his wife was grappling with so many challenges in the faraway land. The only support she received was from her servant Rama, and also from a couple of her immediate neighbours, the *memsahibs*.

Before settling down in Brighton, she had to move houses for a couple of times. Upon arriving in the foreign land, she had first taken refuge at the home of Prasanna Thakur's disowned son Gyanendra. Gyanendra, on his part, had turned into a Christian and married Rev. Krishna Bandyopadhyay's daughter, which explains why his father severed all ties with him. Since then, he had been living in England, expanding his family there. Gyanendra, upon noticing Gyanadanandini descending from the ship with her children, was startled. 'What did Satyen do to his wife?' He thought, amazed.

After a few days, he arranged for a different house which Gyanada had rented for stay. The two young daughters of Gyanendra, Satu and Bala came to visit her often, and strolled the entire neighbourhood with her. Gyanada also waited eagerly for their visit.

Gyanada didn't have to take the trouble of cooking in her rented home since she made a contract with her landlady about supplying food to her family on a daily basis. However, she kept herself occupied with the studies of her children, and then, their health started to deteriorate with frequent illnesses. Also, in a few days' time, the harsh winters came, making her days more difficult.

Gyanada was excited and exhilarated like a child, witnessing her first snow in England from the window. She looked at the men and women in the streets, rubbing the snow in their bodies gleefully. She came out in the streets to join them in their adventure, dressed only in her silk saree. Her landlady had forbidden her to go outside in the terrible cold, but she didn't listen, and started picking up the pieces of frozen ice in childlike enthusiasm. That night, she started having high fever and body pain. Her body temperature accelerated rapidly, and her hands became red, swollen. Rama, the servant brought a doctor to treat her, but her condition didn't improve much. She kept groaning in pain in her bed, with the severe bruise in her hands.

Soon after this, her neighbour Mrs. Donkins came to visit her, listening to her children crying for the condition of their ailing mother. Seeing Gyanada in such a miserable plight, the woman asked: "What made you come to this alien land alone, with your children?"

Gyanada replied in a strained voice: "My husband sent us here because he wanted us to learn British etiquette and manners. We want our children to study in good schools in this country."

"Oh, but how can you manage all alone in an alien land like this? Besides, you cannot converse in English well. Look at you, how you ventured out in the snow without any warm clothes? Poor lady!" Mrs. Donkins empathized with Gyanada.

Mrs. Donkins felt a strong sense of pity for her. How will this Indian lady save her children if she doesn't know how to save herself? She wondered, and tried to salvage Gyanada's life. If the elderly woman wouldn't come to Gyanada's rescue at that time, who knows if she would be able to survive at all? Mrs. Donkins had brought along the brilliant Dr. Joseph Lister to treat Gyanada. At that time. Dr. Lister was an acclaimed name in England for his pathbreaking discovery of antiseptic medicine. Dr. Lister was extremely shocked to observe Gyanada's condition. The wound from the frostbite was turning into a septic wound. The patient was suffering from high fever, and was mumbling incoherently in her sleep. Incidentally, around the same time, Dr. Lister had discovered the phenomenal healing medicine, the antiseptic in the components of phenol or carbolic acid. He watched the bruises of Gyanada intently, meticulously. Discovering her as a patient, he found the opportunity to explore and experiment on his own medicines.

Gyanada, on her part, was startled to receive the touch of a man, a stranger even in her acute state of delirium. Yes, he was a doctor, but he was a man all the same, her senses told her. Gradually, she started liking the good-looking, middle-aged doctor. From her limited experience back in India, in the Thakurbari, she didn't see British doctors attending female patients, unless disasters happened to any of the women. Dr. Lister's treatment proved effective for her; she was recovering bit by bit. She was totally alone during her illness, with no dear and near one beside her, other than her children. If she would write a letter to Satyen, her husband, it wouldn't reach him before a month's time. In despair, tears rolled down her cheeks, and drenched her face.

"Brave lady, why are you crying?" Dr. Lister asked. "You know how courageous you are, living alone in a faraway land with your children? I haven't seen such exemplary courage in any British woman I know! You will be cured, mark my words!"

Dr. Lister appeared like an angel from heaven, in Gyanada's eyes. Overwhelmed with strong emotions, she did something which she never dreamt of doing before. "Save me...save me, please! You're my angel!" She pleaded, squeezing the hand of Lister.

"Oh no, I'm just a doctor! Please thank Mrs. Donkins instead, for bringing me here!" He replied, smiling.

Gyanada looked at Mrs. Donkins now, and replied: "True! If she hadn't been here, I would have surely died in this faraway land, long back!"

"No, Ganada..no! Don't ever speak about dying! If an Indian woman dies without proper treatment upon arriving in Brighton, we have to cover our faces in shame. You know, we British women live by helping each other in our difficult times. You are really fortunate that Dr. Lister arrived just in time!" Mrs. Donkins said, massaging Gyanada's head.

Gyanada was mumbling still: "Angel, angel...please save me!"

"Mrs. Tagore, your frost bite has turned into an infected wound, which explains why the other doctors couldn't cure you. And you know, my research involves the study of the different procedures through which one can disinfect wounds in humans. This is why no other doctor can prescribe the medicines which I am giving you. You are really lucky in that regard!" Dr. Lister said.

Mrs. Donkins said to him: "Doctor, you have experimented on her at your own will, but these drugs haven't been approved in this country yet. You can't gain permission from any British woman to experiment with these drugs, not so easily. Aren't there any risks involved with these?"

Dr. Lister was annoyed at Mrs. Donkins' remark. "Well, if you don't have trust on me, I will be leaving right away. But let me tell you, you have absolutely no idea how many patients I treat with this procedure every day. This discovery of mine regarding antiseptics is not only approved, but much discussed in the country. Do you know how I have dramatically decreased the death rate of patients with amputation by using carbolic acid in their wound dressings? Also, do you know, my pathbreaking discovery of a mouthwash has been named Listerine after myself? Not only that, the bacteria has also been named Listeria after me! If you don't trust me as a doctor, I'll write a couple of routine drugs for Mrs. Tagore, see if you can save her life with them! But you have no right to insult me. I'm leaving!"

Gyanada was scared to see the angry face of Dr. Lister. She lifted her feeble body and sat up with some effort, and grabbed his hands tight. "Don't leave me, angel! I won't live if you go away…Would you forsake this frail foreigner woman and go away? I'll take any medicine you will give me; I'll do exactly as you say. But please don't desert me!" She pleaded earnestly.

"I didn't mean to insult you, please don't misunderstand me, Doctor!" Mrs. Dunkins said promptly. "I'm afraid if something bad happens to Ganada, her family members in India will blame me for it. But I really trust you, hence I brought you here!"

At this, Dr. Lister became a bit tender. His Indian patient lay back on the bed, trying hard to manage the stress of her sudden excitement. She muttered to herself: "Don't leave, please don't leave me, angel!"

He looked at the frail body of the beautiful, ethereal Indian woman in the bed and experienced a strange feeling of empathy for her. It felt as if a princess from some distant land was summoning him to wake her up with the touch of a silver wand. Lister came close to her and stroked her cheek softly. "My Indian princess, I will not leave till I cure your illness completely. I'll come and see you every morning." He assured her.

Gyanada pressed Dr. Lister's fingers to her cheek and closed her eyes with a sense of relief. She drifted off to the realm of sleep in no time.

Gyanendra's daughters had written a letter to Satyendra, letting him know of the severe illness of his wife. They all were annoyed on him as poor Gyanada had to bear the onslaught of his stubborn indiscretion. Mrs. Donkins was the most opinionated about this issue. "Ganada, don't mind, but let me tell you, men are irresponsible anyway. And I can see that your husband is the epitome of irresponsible behaviour!" She said, unabashed.

Gyanada herself was anguished due to her husband's actions, but she didn't like the open criticism of her husband in Mrs. Donkins' words. She replied, rather promptly: "No, no, Mrs. Dunkins, my husband is a very caring person. He sent me alone to this alien land so that I become independent, self-reliant. Do you know how much of opposition we both had to face among our relatives and family because of this decision?"

"Let it be!" Mrs. Donkins replied. "The men always take women for granted, and do not consider them as humans! Do you know how our women are fighting for their suffrage rights since 1840, and still we haven't been able to accomplish the rights? Is the country run only by the men? If we women don't supply them food on time, if we don't sent them to office properly dressed and well-maintained, if we don't concentrate on home management effectively, won't their lives be jeopardized? And still, they won't grant us the basic rights of a citizen?"

Gyanada smiled and replied: "But remember, in our country, there are no suffrage rights for even men. We never get the opportunity to elect the British rulers who run our nation. Since you are born in a free country, you can think of these things."

Mrs. Donkins was excited to continue the discussion further. "You know, among the various politics existing in our world, the man-woman politics is the oldest. A couple of years ago, John Stuart Mill's book titled 'The Subjection of Women' had created quite an uproar in our entire nation! Earlier, the society had chosen to ignore women's voices, but once a man chose to fight for the rights of women with his sharp logic, the men themselves were in a false position. The women, on the other hand, were inspired, motivated like never before. I will give you the book, please read it." She said.

"But why would I read it? In the face of terrible opposition, my husband wants to see the manifestation of the emancipation of women in our society through me. You don't know how hard it is in the society that we are a part of! In our tribe, there is simply no politics between men and women!" Gyanada replied.

Mrs. Donkins seemed a bit irritated at Gyanada's response. "You don't understand my words, Ganada! It's not a question of the freedom of only you or me…the day when all women, irrespective of societies or nations will gain their voting rights, when they will be honoured as absolute humans within their families, considered equal to men, we can say that emancipation of woman has truly happened. Since you are already fighting for women's right to freedom, you have to read this book by Mill, your husband too has to read it!" She said.

The very next day, when Dr. Lister came to visit Gyanada, his patient, he seemed happy with her recovery. "You truly look like a princess today! You are almost cured now!" He remarked.

"Are you speaking the truth, Doctor? Will I really be cured?" Gyanada asked, eagerly. She was waiting for Dr. Lister to come and see her.

"No, no, you won't be cured if you call me 'Doctor'! You didn't call me 'Angel' today, did you?" Dr. Lister joked, light-heartedly.

The medicines had worked in her body, but more than the medicines, the magic of Dr. Lister's presence had worked wonders for her. Gyanada was recovering rapidly.

One night, however, her labour pains started suddenly. It wasn't time for the baby yet, but she writhed in pain, and her water broke. Rama, her servant called her neighbour Mrs. Donkins promptly. But Mrs. Donkins couldn't arrange for a doctor in the middle of the night, and came up with a midwife instead, who happened to live close by.

Gyanada's baby, however, couldn't be saved. Due to the mother's illness, the baby was sick, premature. Just after birth, it died in its mother's lap. That day, when Gyanada cried profusely due to the loss of her baby, nobody other than Mrs. Donkins was by her side. Those were the days when danger struck the household, and accidents happened, one after the other. A few days after, her youngest son, Chobi went to the seaside with the servant Rama. The little boy had played for a long time in the beach, in the scorching sunlight, and came up with high fever. For two days, he suffered with the fever and then succumbed to it, not giving much scope for any treatment. With the sudden loss of both her children, Gyanada was stoned in grief and trauma. She remained cooped in her room all day, silent and friendless, in deep despair.

The day Dr. Lister came to see her, Gyanada broke into tears in front of him. Seeing their mother cry so helplessly, little Bibi and Suren went and hugged her tight. Lister took Bibi in his arms and said to her: "Sweetie pie, why don't you sing a song? Tell us what song you have been taught in school; it will uplift your mother's spirits."

Indeed, Bibi's melodious voice wafted in the air around the room, bringing in the spirit of jubilance. Dr. Lister started dancing to the tunes of the song, holding little Bibi's hands. After a while, he stopped dancing and sat beside Gyanada. "Indian princess, it's really a pity that your baby couldn't be saved. You will be surprised to know, in England, the death-rate of newborn babies is in fact very high, especially the ones born in the hands of surgeons. Compared to that, the babies born in the hands of midwives have a higher rate of survival." He remarked.

Gyanada was astonished to know this fact. "But most of the midwives don't know anything about modern science! I was thinking the whole time that my baby would have been saved if the doctors had been there. It died only because of the midwife."

Joseph Lister replied: "No, Princess, I'm sure you're not aware, the surgeons mostly don't have the practice of washing their hands regularly. Often, they apply medicine on the wounds of the patients in the hospitals and then, without washing their hands, go out to deliver babies of women, which results in unwanted infections. On the contrary, midwives have the habit of washing their hands continuously, so child mortality in their hands is apparently lower. In your case, I strongly feel the midwife was not responsible for the baby's death. Unfortunately, the baby couldn't manage the stress and pain of your prolonged illness. Let us pray for his peaceful after-life!"

After a momentary pause of silence, Dr. Lister extended a beautiful coloured gift pack to Gyanada and said to her: "Princess, I've brought for you some wine and chocolates, let's celebrate your good health! Do you know, drinking wine is very good for your health!"

That evening, Gyanada's bruised, bleeding heart seemed to search for a home in another heart for a few moments, and found one. The two glasses filled with blood-red wine kissed each other in the air above. In December, Gyanada arranged for a big party during Christmas with

Dr. Lister, perhaps in her quest to search for a semblance of that tender, painful evening.

****

After a few months' time, Satyen arrived along with Rabi, changing ships for two-three times, making transit stops at Alexandria, Paris and London before reaching Brighton. Just as he reached Medina Villa, he knocked on the door with the expectation of seeing a beloved face after a long, long time, but the British landlady opened the door, to his disappointment. But once Rabi and Satyen entered the house, there were moments of fun waiting for them. Gyanada was waiting with her children, decked up in nice clothes. Bibi and Suren were already going to school now, and the memories of Calcutta were fading from their minds, by and by. Since a few days they were being told, 'Papa is coming, papa is coming!'

Little Bibi had the impression that her papa would be a *sahib* with a coat and hat, like the other papas of her friends in school. But upon seeing Satyen, her idea and vision of her papa was shattered. As Satyen stretched his hands to catch the little fairy and take her in his arms, she ran away. The child started crying, hiding herself at one corner of the door: 'That's not my papa! He is not white!'

At this moment, Satyen understood the hard way that western education was not necessarily good. The subdued racism of this country had made its way through the chambers of the innocent little girls' heart. He would have to drive away this sinister darkness from his daughter's mind. It took a long time for him to befriend his daughter once again.

"Has my foreigner wife changed too? Will she make love to her black husband?" He asked her in jest, looking at Gyanada. She was preparing the dinner with meticulous care. Wouldn't she have to astonish her husband, showing him how much she had imbibed the British manners and etiquette?

"Well, you didn't care much when you sent me here alone, why are you mocking me now? I would have died, I didn't only because Dr. Lister didn't let me. Do you have any idea how many *sahibs* are after me, dying to elope with me?" Gyanada gave her husband a sardonic look and said to him.

"Whosoever wants to elope with you, tell me about it! Is that Dr. Lister?" Satyen was quite amused.

"Ah, don't talk as if he has no other work to do!" Gyanada replied, blushing. Of course, Satyen didn't notice the flustered cheeks of his wife then.

"Hats off to you, *Mejo Bouthan*!" Rabi looked around the whole house and remarked, "Such a huge difference compared to our Jorasanko house swarming with so many people, servants! Such a lonely villa this is, and you are managing everything alone! Only you can do it. If you would have left me alone here, I would have ran away long back. Why did you have to undergo such pain?"

"Well, I have this huge responsibility to teach British manners to my children, don't I? Besides, your *Mejdada* taught me the manners of the British *memsahibs*, he doesn't like the domesticated Bengali brides tucked inside the quiet confines of the house. How would I learn all these things if I wouldn't live alone here in this country?"

"Hmm...let me see what are the things you've learnt!" Satyen said, placing a hand on his wife's shoulder. "Remember, I've lived alone all this while, sending you away with the children in this faraway land! Won't I have to compensate for all the pain I myself took, living on my own?"

"My landlady is a very nice woman…she taught me so much!" Gyanada replied. "There mustn't be an iota of dust in this house, I leant how to keep the space spik and span. But you know, we can't use water to clean anything, like we do in India, instead, the mistress of the house carries a napkin in her pocket, and she has to wipe off the table, chairs, the furniture of the house and also the dishes and plates in the kitchen with the napkin. And then, she has to put it back in her pocket with all that dirt. She has advised me, the basic mantra to maintain cleanliness in the house is to tuck the napkin inside the pocket of your coat at all times. You can stroll around the whole house with that, and whenever you see any dirt or dust anywhere, you can just use the napkin and clean it off."

Rabi laughed out loud at this. "*Mejo Bouthan*, are you serving us English dinner with the plates cleaned up with that all-purpose napkin?"

"Are you crazy?" Gyanada laughed too. "I employ Rama, our servant to clean everything with warm water. I don't think anything cleans well without using water!"

"What did you learn then, *Bouthan*? Cleaning everything without the use of water is a magic every British-born believes in! Sorry to say, you've remained that Bengali bride at heart after all!" Rabi replied in jest.

Satyen remarked: "You know, Rabi, when the *sahibs* catch cold, they wipe their noses in those napkins, they spit out in those napkins, and then they tuck it in their pockets, for using it the next time.

"What a shame!" Rabi's body trembled with disgust. "Why don't they use the 'pik daan', the pot for dispensing waste? In that way, they don't have to spoil their pockets."

Gyanada laughed, shaking her head. "No, no, Rabi, that is a nasty object in their eyes! They won't keep such pots anywhere within their sight...the napkins tucked in their pockets aren't visible, after all. In this country, they give first priority to things pleasing the eyes. You know, they don't even rinse their faces with water after eating their meals, as the scene of water dripping from their mouths looks bad to them. Even the dresses they wear during their mourning period must look good!"

"Well, looking at it all, *Mejo Bouthan*, I can understand that there might be beauty in these British people's houses, but no real cleanliness!" Rabi replied, while starting to have his food in the dinner table. "Did we have to come overseas to learn these manners?"

"No, Rabi! I must say, there are plenty of great virtues that the British are naturally endowed with, and we have come here to imbibe them!" Satyen retaliated. "If we can combine our own virtues with theirs, it will result in our complete enhancement...But Gyanada, I must say I'm enjoying your English dinner quite a lot!" He added, looking at his wife lovingly.

"Yes, it's quite good, with so little salt and so little spice or flavour! *Bouthan*, I beg of you, don't forget the authentic dishes with your signature style while cooking these bland mashed potato soups and breads." Rabi remarked with a tinge of sarcasm in his voice.

"Well, I've only cooked the roasted chicken, all the other dishes are from the landlady's kitchen." Gyanada replied, amused. "Listen, Rabi, don't be afraid, I'm not cooking these western dishes anyway! It's the responsibility of the landlady to supply our daily meals. We will have our daily dose of authentic English breakfast, lunch and dinner, all thanks to her!"

Startled at this revelation, Rabi said: "Good Lord! In that case, I'll have to run away very soon, *Bouthan*!"

"What do you mean, Rabi?" Satyen admonished his younger brother. "Just look around you, how many Bengali youths like you are grateful to have the company of such British landladies! They are literally going crazy, thanking their good fortune of being so close to these living, breathing *memsahibs* with hats, coats and gowns!"

"Well, I've seen enough of such youths while travelling in the ship, *Mejdada*!" Rabi smiled and added: "You know, *Bouthan*, there were quite a number of these anglicized Bengali origin youths, and all of them were so amusing! They were referring to all British servants of the ship as 'sir', instead of bossing on them. During disembarking the ship, when the British guards came for help, these youths melted with gratitude and love, grateful to offer them one shilling each in exchange of their *salaam* (gesture of greeting). Also, I've heard from one of my co-travellers the story of meeting his landlady for the very first time, and it was quite an experience! On the very first day, he was quite puzzled to enter the room which he rented—a room with carpet strewn all over the floor, with framed pictures on the walls, with expensive flower vases and a piano. He wondered how he would manage to live in such an exotic place. He had no idea then, that all houses in England looked like that, and his habitual Indian home with a flat wooden bed and a mat was obsolete in this country. Moreover, to his utter surprise, when the British landlady came to greet him 'Good Morning', he felt overwhelmed with emotions.

Gyanada almost rolled over the floor, laughing, listening to this amusing account. "Then, did he befriend the landlady? You know, landladies are indispensable here, you have to offer your life to these women in this country!" She remarked.

Rabi laughed at this, and replied: "Ah yes, eventually this fellow grew so close to the landlady that he could now flirt with her daughter to his heart's content!"

That evening, the dinner table reverberated with the unanimous laughter and sweet warmth of the chatter of them all. From the very next day, life in Brighton started in its characteristic pace and rhythm. Rabi woke up around 8.30 in the morning every day, and then took a long, relaxing shower, drenching his whole body in cold water. He hated sponging his body in warm water, which was a common habit of the English people. It was not for him, he felt. At 9 o'clock, the landlady sent in the breakfast every day. After having English breakfast with toast, omlette, milk and porridge, he would get busy with his work and studies, and then, play with his nephew and niece Suren and Bibi for quite some time, till lunch arrived at 1.30 in the afternoon. The days in England was much shorter, with morning starting not before 9 o'clock, and within 4 o'clock, the daylight started diminishing. The days here seemed to Rabi like the 10 am to 5 pm officegoer *Babus*. The nights, on the other hand, seemed to arrive in style in a horse carriage, and left slowly, walking away, reluctantly. Early in the evening, tea arrived along with cake and cookies, and dinner would be served at 8 o'clock, which was quite a lavish affair.

The sea coast of Brighton was quite a treat to the eyes. Winter had not yet extended its vicious fangs in the month of October, hence often in the mornings after breakfast, they would come to the beach and enjoy the scene around. They witnessed the beautiful spectacle of the beach, the sahibs and memsahibs strolling around the sea with their children, having immense pleasure in the outing. Even the ailing and elderly men and women came, seated on wheelchairs pulled by their family members. Rabi would be astonished to see the women at the beach with their tempting clothes and get-up. 'How easy-going and unpretentious are these women at the beach!' He wondered, thinking about the dear woman he had left at home, thousands of miles away. 'Ah, only if my *Notun Bouthan* could roam around the beach with such free spirit, such wild abandon!' He sighed.

Gyanada couldn't keep pace with the constantly running, vivacious Suren and Bibi. The more their servant Rama ran after the children, the more they jumped on their uncle Rabi's body. Rabi started picking oysters from the seashore along with the children. He noticed the young women dressed in minimal clothes, either sitting or lying beneath the shade of vibrant coloured umbrellas, and the Italian beggars playing their organs in front of them, asking for coins.

Amused to watch the scene, Rabi remarked: "*Bouthan*, can you tell me why these beggar men are loitering around the women only?"

Gyanada replied: "Well, it seems they are just beggars of beauty, they don't care much about the money. And why do we blame them, even you are ogling at them every now and then, Rabi *Thakurpo*!"

"Bouthan, I cannot say that your kohl-laden Indian

eyes aren't attracted to those *gora sahibs* with swimsuits!" Rabi remarked, rather mischievously.

"Shame! What are you talking about, Rabi? My eyes sting, watching that so-called 'beauty'!" Gyanada struck back, as if in vengeance. "When will these people understand that the beauty of being well-clothed is much pleasing than nakedness? You must acknowledge that Indian tastes are much more refined, sophisticated!"

Rabi laughed at this remark. "Then, I must say you are becoming more of a Bengali woman in this country. Why, you had been sent to England to learn British culture, and look at you, each day, you're becoming a stern hater of the English culture! You know, I had imagined to meet the fashionable Mrs. Tagore with gown and hat, and you, on the contrary, are basking in the sunlight at the beach with your Bengali Baluchari silk sari?"

Gyanada smiled sweetly and replied: "Well, this suits me well…can't you see everyone staring at my beauty every now and then? I can proudly say that the flag of my country is strewn all over my body!"

These days, the Tagore's were frequently invited to evening parties and dinner parties with ball dance. In fact, their invitation to an evening party initiated them to free mixing with the English society. Besides, Gyanada was alone with her children till now, but with her husband joining her, their English neighbours started coming over, and thus, invitations starting pouring in.

One day at the evening party at Dr. Marlow's residence, quite a huge number of men and women had gathered. Upon entering the house, they greeted the host and the hostess with generous words, and then, the introduction and chitchat among the guests continued. Because of the scarcity of space in the living room, there was shortage of chairs for all guests. The women were seated in the couches, while the men were mostly chatting while standing. The hosts and the old, familiar guests started chatting with first-time guests in the party by indulging in weather-talk, then moving to other topics.

Dressing and fashion were of utmost importance in such evening parties. The men would have to wear milk-white shirts on these occasions, paired with black waistcoats completely open at the front, with the collars of their white shirts peeking from the waistcoats, and white neckties adorning their necks. Their tailcoats seemed the most fashionable accessories, extended till their waists. Although Rabi and Satyen wore those tailcoats in the characteristic English style, Gyanada chose to wear a sari to the occasion. The British women, ecstatic to see her draped in an exotic Baluchari silk sari and pashmina shawl, started asking her questions. Mrs. Marlow, the hostess exclaimed in joy and excitement that Gyanada's sari, with its meticulously arranged pleats, looked more graceful than the stitched English gowns.

That very moment, there was a tinge of excitement in Gyanada's heart as she noticed Dr. Lister approaching her from a distance. She looked at her husband with questions in her eyes, as Lister invited her to dance with him.

Satyen promptly said: "Go with Dr. Lister, Gyanada... He's calling you to be his dance partner! It is an honour!"

The dancing couple, Gyanada and Dr. Lister looked very nice together. Did this scene create a dent in Satyen's heart? While looking at them dancing together in sync, he thought to himself—he would not cow down, he wouldn't ever be defeated. Let his dear Gyanada mix with as many men in the world, after all of that, if he remains the same attractive man in her eyes, it will be the victory of his manhood.

"When did you come to Brighton?" Gyanada asked Dr. Lister. He was practicing medicine and also working as a professor at Edinburgh, Scotland, and came to Brighton occasionally, like the way he was at Brighton during Gyanada's illness.

Lister said to Gyanada: "Indian princess, you know, I have treated so many patients in this country, but the happiness I experienced while treating you and curing you is truly special, it is unparalleled!"

"Then why aren't you staying back in Brighton?" Gyanada demanded like a little girl. "If you do, I'll get to see you whenever I fall sick! My whole body, mind and spirit get refreshed as soon as I see you!"

"Is that ever possible, Princess? Just like your own life is tethered to a particular rhythm of life, my life is too!" Lister smiled widely and replied: "I have my wife Agnes back in Scotland, my work, my patients to tend to. My work there has given me the honour and recognition I have today. How can I leave all of that and come here? Would you be able to leave your husband, your country and settle anywhere else? And why would you do that, after all?"

"Do you love your wife very much?" Gyanada asked, curious.

Lister replied: "Agnes is a true companion in all the work I do. She is the mistress of my house, the assistant of my lab."

"Is she also a doctor, like you?" Gyanada asked, filled with awe and wonder. She didn't see a good number of female doctors in England till then.

"Well, she's a student of medical sciences, and she is the daughter of my guru, my mentor. You know, Agnes is fluent in French, and has even translated Louis Pasteur's Theory, that has been an eye-opening text which opened my eyes to the subject of infection from germs!" He replied.

"Bravo!" Gyanada exclaimed, jubilant to know this. "You're such an ideal pair! I wonder when such a husband and wife will ever be made in my own country....I'm not sure if we are going to cross paths again, but I will always remember you fondly!"

"I also pray that whether we meet again or not, and wherever my princess is, may she remain hale and hearty always. I pray that no amount of sorrow wipes the smile on her face." Dr. Lister said, in a deep, affectionate voice.

At that moment, a beautiful British woman came to meet and greet Rabi, and all the eyes in the room roamed around both of them. In this country, beauty was worshipped with much pomp and grandeur. Shameless flatterers roamed around beautiful women, dying to cater to their orders.

Just after this, a musical siesta started. The master of the house requested an elegantly dressed woman to play the piano and she obliged him immediately. As she sat playing, the rings in all ten fingers of her hands sparkled in their brilliant light, in sync with the piano reed. It seemed as if she had adorned her fingers with the rings just so that she could showcase them while playing the piano. After a little while, Rabi spelled danger when the mistress of the house requested him to sing a song. He knew it very well that these people wouldn't value the richness of an Indian song, hence it didn't make any sense to sing a song in front of them. But then, there were repeated requests coming from the guests, and he couldn't avoid it.

However, as he started singing, he gradually noticed the smiles of mockery playing in the corners of the lips of both the British men and women. Some the women couldn't suppress their laughter any longer and giggled while stooping to pick up their handkerchiefs. Some others hid their faces at the backs of their female friends and laughed away. The ones who were successful at suppressing their laughter seemed to send telegraph messages to each other through their eyes. Rabi felt his blood freeze at the sight of the woman who happened to play the piano. The insolence and disregard in her eyes infuriated him. When he saw Mili's face contorted in a smile, he felt like dying in embarrassment and shame. He had never felt so let down in his entire life when he sang a song. He finished the song in a haste, and sat with a flustered face.

There was a faint flicker of appreciation in the room, but Rabi didn't find it convincing at all after the bouts of shameless laughter. The environment in the room seemed sickening to him. When Mili came close to him and asked him the meaning of the song he sang, he started to explain the meaning of it by translating: "Don't talk about love…"

At this, one of the guests at the party remarked: "Do you even have the freedom to love anyone in your country?"

Gyanada could no longer tolerate such humiliation of her dear brother-in-law Rabi at the hands of the people at the party. She dragged the hands of Rabi and took him to the dining room so that they could have dinner and leave right away. She noticed that the guests weren't approaching the dining room together, that would disrupt the mood of the party.

Gyanada whispered in Rabi's ears: "You know, these people laugh about everything that is outside their own limited periphery. They are the uneducated ones! I pity them for not understanding the beauty of your song, the core value of it! You sang wonderfully today, Rabi!"

There were teardrops glistening in Rabi's eyes. He said, "They belong to the king's race, don't they? They dare to belittle and mock other civilizations because they have the scepter of the king! But *Mejo Bouthan*, you see, I have thought of something. I will learn their music, and with their music only, I will give back my answer to their insult and humiliation!"

Gyanada replied: "So true, Rabi! These women who were laughing a while ago after listening to your song are really blunt and ignorant! Just like in our country, where the girls are taught housekeeping and get prepared for domestic lives without education, these women here are polished and decorated to get sold off in the marriage market. They are exposed to as much education as is needed to get them married. If a woman learns a bit of music and piano, a bit of embroidery work, a bit of dance and French language, she is ready for the marriage market."

Rabi laughed and replied: "This means our own women are Indian dolls, and these English women are foreign dolls, that's the only difference! Both women of the east and the west are ready to get themselves sold in the shop of marriage? What did you come to learn then, in this faraway land across the seas, *Bouthan*?

"At least I learnt this much by coming here...If I hadn't come here at all, I would keep thinking how educated, how emancipated these English women are!" Gyanada said.

"Yes, you're right, *Bouthan*." Rabi said. "I have also noticed that the men seem to reign over the women, and the women are subservient to their husbands at the Homefront. The men command their wives, they strive hard to harness the wives' minds according to their own whims, and they assume it is their God-given right. But let me tell you, I like the ordinary middle-class women much better than the fashionable women of the rich families. They have to work really hard at home and outside the home. They are endowed with clear brains, though they aren't highly educated. They are aware of many issues, since they aren't bound inside the four walls. They are capable enough to express their clear opinions on any subject when they are among friends and relatives.

Gyanada took two plates of desserts in her hands and spoke while handing one of them to Rabi. "If you ask me, I like their familial relationship, and the way they express it. At the end of the day, when the man returns home, all of them gather around the fireplace and chat openly, sing songs and make themselves merry. So beautiful, isn't it?"

Rabi replied, while putting the caramel pudding in his mouth with a silver spoon: "The man-woman relationship is uninhibited in this country, nobody ever tries to hide it, so it can spread its wings so effortlessly. Just like a man wants to change his formal office wear and sit at home relaxed, relieved, in the same way, he craves to wear off the mask of his formal behaviour and talk freely with his near and dear ones. Why would he have to whisper in the ear of his wife, lest other family members listen to their conversation from the next room? Why would hell break loose if somebody hears the voice, or the laughter of the wife? You know, this is the reason why Bengalis who return to their native lands discover with regret that they have no home in their motherland, their true homes are in England, the faraway land. In the familial structure in this country, you'll find a tinge of free, jubilant spirit, a source of true happiness among all the family members gathering around the fireplace after a long, tiring day."

"Yes, you are right, Rabi!" Satyen joined them now in their conversation. "In this country, they attach a great significance to the free, uninhibited mixing between man and woman, both within the family and beyond the family. This is why the women here, in spite of their limited freedom, can uphold the ecstasy of their spirits. They can admonish their husbands in front of others, and in the same breath, they can kiss their husbands in front of everyone without any hesitation."

Rabi and Gyanada had finished having dinner, so Satyen could come to the dining room. It would be inappropriate if all the guests would come to have the dinner together, all at once, hence such an arrangement. However, Satyen's presence added the much-needed charm to their familial conversation.

Life in Brighton for Rabi and his family was full of such vibrant evening tea parties, dinner parties, balls, dance parties and lawn assemblies. It was totally a different life, so much different from Calcutta, where the madness of creating poems and songs filled their lives. Here, on the other hand, there was this meticulous effort to become the main attraction of the party. Rabi felt dejected, disheartened to even think of the situation at times.

On lazy afternoons, the British people had the ritual of visiting each other's houses and chitchatting. Rabi had noticed that the women of rich families had a natural skill in chatting and socializing; when the guests were large in number, the mistress of the house was adept at distributing the elixir of her smile and words with all the guests equally. One couldn't chat with a particular guest more than others; it would offend them immensely.

Rabi had accompanied Gyanada in some of these visits. He noticed that the women would start speaking about something while looking at the face of somebody, and then, smiled, looking at all others present. Right then, they would start another topic, addressing someone else, and while speaking on that topic, their eyes would roam on everybody else.

One day, Mrs. Johnson, the queen bee of a gathering addressed another woman and said to her: "Lovely morning, isn't it?" Even before the woman could respond to the question, she looked at another woman and threw a fresh, new topic to her. "Have you heard Madame Neilson singing at the musical soiree yesterday? It was exquisite!"

The other women started adding a plethora of adjectives, with full enthusiasm. Some said: "charming!" while the others said: "superb!" The last one who was the only one left to comment, exclaimed: "isn't it?"

Rabi whispered in Gyanada's ears: *"Bouthan*, see, aren't their words rolled towards all the guests like cards played in a card-party? And you see, the words are roaming so swiftly and so skillfully, it is quite clear that they have a good number of cards in their hands!"

Gyanada roved her eyes and replied: "It might as

well be a repartee of words…or brandishing a club early in the morning."

Mrs. Donkins came close to Gyanada now, wishing to chat with her at length. She asked, rather curious, "Mrs. Tagore, are there any social visits in your homeland where men and women both are present? What do you talk about on such occasions?"

"Yes, we have such visits in our house in Jorasanko. But generally speaking, it's not as common among aristocratic Hindu families…our women don't come out in front of the public still." Gyanada replied.

"How horrible is that! I must say then, that women in your homeland are living like sub-human creatures behind the curtains! This should be changed!" Mrs. Donkins reacted rather harshly.

"Well, do I look like a sub-human creature to you? Can you come alone with your children to a faraway land, crossing the oceans, like I did? How many women of your country can do this?" Gyanada retaliated.

Donkins had understood the folly of her statement. She held Gyanada tight and said: "Oh Ganada, my darling, don't take it personally! You know, you're an exception, I've seldom seen such a courageous woman like you. I adore you!"

A few days after this incident, Satyen, Gayanada and Rabi went to London with the children. After roaming around exotic locations like Trentbridge Welsch, Devonshire and so on, Rabi started living with a family as their guest. After his tiring, exhaustive travels, he remembered his dear *Notun Bouthan* while going off to sleep every night. He wrote letters to her almost every day. He could never finish a letter in a single day; he wrote and erased a lot of his words. But every single night, he wrote a letter to her.

"Before I arrived in England, I had fostered a foolish hope that the two handfuls of lands in this small island are replete with the oratorial skills of Gladstone, the erudite explanation of the Vedas of Max Müller, the scientific theories of Tindal, the deep philosophies of Thomas Carlyle and Benet. Fortunately, I have been deeply disappointed that my anticipations have proven false. The women here are deeply involved in fashion and dressing up, the men are busy with their work, and their domestic lives revolve around these in the usual manner, only a lot of noise is heard around political issues.

The women in their conversations ask cliched questions like "have you seen that dance recital?" or "how did you like that concert?" or "there's a new actor in the theatre", or "tomorrow there will be the show of a new band", etc. The men, on their turn, ask, "what do you think about the Afghan war?" or just state that the Londoners had adored Marquis of Lorne, or just plainly remark that today is a fine day, while yesterday was quite miserable.

In this country, women play the piano, sing songs, enjoy the warmth of the fireplace, read novels while snuggling in the sofa, chitchat with visitors and also flirt with youths, necessarily or unnecessarily. The spinsters, on the other hand, live their lives with worthy and meaningful causes. Their voices are heard in all groups and assemblies, including temperance meetings, working men's society and so on. They don't have to go to office like their male counterparts, nor do they have to raise children like the married females. Many of them, due to their advancing ages, cannot attend ball parties and dance or flirt with men over there. Hence, they have all the time to devote in worthier pursuits, and that has its benefits in society.

There are liquor shops in every corner of the cities. Whenever I am out in the streets, I can spot shops selling shoes, meat, toys for children, but bookstores are very rare. Once, we had to buy a book of poems, but since I couldn't spot any bookstore within my familiar periphery, I had to order that book through a toy seller. Before this, I had the idea that in this country, book shops are as necessary as butcher shops. But I was wrong.

.... Once you're in England, the first thing you'll notice is the busy lifestyle of its people. When you walk down the streets, it is quite amusing to notice the people walking by, swiftly, with umbrellas tucked under their arms. They never care to notice the other humans walking on the same street with them; their faces are filled with unexplained anxiety, they strive hard to capture 'time', to make sure that 'time' cannot escape their clutches. The city of London is surrounded by railways on all sides. The trains keep arriving at the stations every five minutes. When I travel from London to Brighton, I notice the trains running from all directions, in a maddening speed. Even the trains look like the people on the streets of London, running to and fro with immensely anxious, busy demeanour. Imagine, the country is so tiny, if I venture a few steps, I fear I can land into the sea! I don't understand why this country needs so many trains. Once, while travelling to London, we had accidentally missed a train, but we didn't have to return home. Just half an hour later, another train arrived and we boarded that."

In her chamber in the third floor of the Jorasanko mansion, Kadambari was lying down on her bed all alone, with her dark, open tresses. There were letters, scraps of paper and betel box scattered on the bed. She picked up the letter to read it for some time, and then left it on the bed, and got lost in her thoughts. Some of the letters were written from London, some from Devonshire.

Rabi had written: "Gradually, slowly, I have been acquainted with a couple of people here, and I am about to develop a friendship with them. An amusing thing is— some people here assume I am rather foolish. One day, I had been out on the streets with the brother of Dr. ---. There were a few photographs in front of a shop, he took me closer to them and started explaining what photographs are. He started explaining to me that those images were created with a machine of some sort, and not hand-drawn by humans. People then started gathering around me. We went in front of a store selling clocks, and with the notion that a clock is a strange object, they tried to arouse prejudice in my mind. At an evening party, Ms. --- asked me whether I had ever heard the sound of a piano. You know, many people of this country can perhaps draw a map of heaven, but don't have any idea whatsoever about India, our homeland. They can never imagine the existence of any other country that is vastly different than their own England, let alone India."

In another letter written by Rabi, there was a fascinating description of a fancy ball party, which reminded Kadambari of the fairytale of Cinderella.

"We had been to a fancy ball that day, it was such a fascinating assembly of men and women dressed up in fashionable attire, and all of them danced so elegantly. It was a huge hall, lit up with bright gas lights, and the band music mesmerized all of us...there were six hundred to seven hundred beautiful women and handsome men in the party, truly an august company. The men and the women formed micro-groups among themselves, held each other's hands and circled around each other, dancing with wild abandon. There were almost seventy or eighty of such dancing couples, standing so close to each other that one could easily fall over the other's shoulder! In one room, there was an epic fight over bottles of champagne; there were also meat and various other kinds of alcohol, and a huge crowd flocked to that room. Moreover, there were some women who kept on dancing for two-three hours at a stretch, their feet were moving at a wild pace without stopping for a moment.

One *memsahib* was dressed up as a snow-queen with white attire, white accessories and pearl ornaments, and it all glittered in the ethereal light. Another woman was dressed up in a traditional Muslim attire, with a red flowery dress, a silk gown on top of the dress, and also an elegant cap-like head-cover, which suited her looks perfectly. Yet another woman was dressed in our traditional Indian way, the sari and the *kachuli* covering her bosom was her only ornament, and the shawl she draped on top of that added to her beauty. In this attire, she looked much better than wearing the typical western attire. Oh yes, some other woman was dressed up as an English maid-servant. You know, I was dressed up in my traditional Zamindari attire of Bengal! I wore a satin dress with intricate 'zari' work on the border, and also 'zari' work in my satin 'pagdi' (head-gear)..."

The letter ended on a detailed, enthused note.

Chapter 13

Malini, the Book-Seller Woman

Anna felt sad, dejected after Rabi left for England. She was disoriented and didn't feel like doing anything at all. Fearing his beloved daughter's attitude, Atmaram Pandurang brought his daughter to Calcutta along with him. For some time, they had put up at his friend Manmohan Ghosh's house. Within a few days' time, they visited the Jorasanko mansion to see Maharshi Debendranath and his family. While Pandurang, sat at the main living room with Deben Thakur, Anna, his daughter went to the inner quarters to visit the women of the family.

Anna was unparalleled in her natural ability to make everyone her own, within no time. In the third floor at Kadambari's bed chamber, Anna hugged Kadambari's neck tightly and reclined in her bed, chatting with her endlessly. 'Which is Rabi's room?' 'What does he do in his room all day?' The never-ending queries of her impatient mind drove Kadambari crazy.

Kadambari lifted Anna's pink chin with her nimble, flower-like fingers and said: "Anna, you're dead, aren't you? It seems Rabi has plundered everything from you!"

Anna blushed in shame, and looked away. "Ah, only you, *Notun Bouthan*, are his muse and inspiration. You have damaged his head, I tell you! I envy you a lot for that!"

"Ah, you cannot digress from the truth with these words!" Kadambari seemed adamant, hiding her own discomfort. "Tell me the truth now, please! You love Rabi, don't you?"

Anna almost buried her face in Kadambari's bosom out of shame and embarrassment. "I've never seen a poet so closely before! It's almost impossible not to love such a poet like him!"

Kadambari saw the semblance of a new Rabi through Anna's lens; a different Rabi who was no more a teenager worshipper of his *Bouthan*. Far from her eyes, he had metamorphosed into a man considered attractive to women, and Kadambari had no inkling of it. It stung like a secret pain somewhere deep within, the young boy who was like her own pet, tied to the 'anchal' of her sari was now venturing in other, newer pastures. Kadambari became a bit pensive, noticing the trembling shadow of her own Rabi in the pupil of another woman. But then, did Kadambari's own shadow darken the eyes of somebody else?

Pandurang, on his part, had gauged the condition of his daughter's mind quite well, and hence, he had brought her to Calcutta. Anna appeared pensive and unmindful from the very moment Rabi had left for the foreign shores. Rabi seemed to have stolen her heart while he was about to go. As a matter-of-fact, there was no dearth of suitors for Anna, but her restless soul didn't look at any of them. After a casual conversation with Deben Thakur, Pandurang enquired whether he was thinking about his son Rabi's marriage. Though as a good host, Debendranath did everything to please Pandurang, his esteemed guest, he couldn't agree to the gentleman's proposal of Rabi's marriage. 'Rabi has gone abroad to study. Let him finish his studies first, and let him start working. Then I'll give it a thought.' He said somehow. Besides, he could make out what this Marathi fellow had in mind for Rabi, but unfortunately, he couldn't ever agree to it. First, the girl was not a Bengali, and secondly, she was five-six years older than Rabi. This was probably a norm within the Gujrati and Marathi community, but within Bengalis, it wasn't considered normal. Deben Thakur talked about other things, sidelining the topic of Rabi's marriage intentionally. Pandurang was an intelligent man, and he quickly understood that there was little to no possibility of his daughter's marriage in this family. He left the Jorasanko mansion with his daughter in a depressed, dejected state.

Did Anna leave behind her depression for Kadambari to get possessed with it now? In her private chamber on the third floor, she rolled impatiently, sometimes on her bed, sometimes on the floor. Her days and nights seemed too long, almost never-ending. The literary and musical soirees didn't take place on the terrace any more. After Rabi's departure from Jorasanko, Akshay and Bihari Lal didn't come any more. And whom would they come to anyway? Jyoti was so engrossed in his drama productions, he had absolutely no time to come back home. And even when he was home, he would be immersed in writing his new plays. 'Asrumati' (The Teary-eyed Woman), his new play was being staged in a grand way, and Jyoti was omnipresent at the rehearsal of the play. He had taken upon himself the responsibility of mentoring and grooming the heroine. This pained his wife Kadambari immensely.

Jyoti was also suffering from a different kind of pain.

Binodini, the diva had left Bengal Theatre, so she was not available to play the role of the heroine in 'Asrumati'. Sukumari and Banabiharini, the other actresses were no match to the feisty Binodini, no matter how much he tried to groom them. Still enamoured by the very powerful young actress Binodini, he ran to see her performance at the National Theatre. Binodini was quite a rage with her histrionics on stage. As Kundanandini in the play 'Bishbriksha', as Kanchan in the play 'Sadhaba-r Ekadashi', as Britannia in the play 'Palasheer juddhe', she was a phenomenal actress. Moreover, in the play 'Meghnad Badh Kavya', she performed in as many as seven roles, creating a sensation in the theatrical world. Under the able guidance of her mentor Girish Ghosh and with her own exemplary dedication to theatre, Binodini was blazing in the stage with her inner fire, towering over the other heroines of her times. Jyoti repeatedly insisted her to play the heroine in his play 'Asrumati', but she turned him down every time. It was impossible for her to return to Bengal theatre, abandoning her mentor Girish Ghosh, she stated categorically. Was she in love with Girish Ghosh, then? Jyoti felt a tinge of envy deep within his heart.

Rupa sat close to Kadambari, and together, they read Rabi's letters from the foreign shores, and also the reviews of the plays published in newspapers and magazines. One day, while reading out the elaborate descriptions of the magnificent beauty and talent of Binodini, Kadambari suddenly noticed that Rupa wasn't actually listening to any of it, but looking at her with wide, gaping eyes.

Kadambari put down the magazine and said, while reclining on the pillow: "Rupa, what are you ogling at? Tell me?"

"I am looking at you!" Rupa replied, unapologetically. "And I am in awe of your ethereal beauty, your flawless physical structure...your presence seems to dazzle the eyes like a sudden awakening of light! Why does Jyoti dada play truant with you, then?"

"As if you don't know...he is now enamoured by the beauty of Binodini, Sukumari, Banabiharini and all! Where does he have the time to look at me? It's just you who flatters me too much, praising my beauty overtly...If I were truly beautiful, would I have to rot here in this room all alone?" Kadambari retaliated.

"No...no...why do I have to tell lies about your beauty unnecessarily, *Notun Bouthan*?" Rupa replied, angry and hurt. "If your husband jumps like an insect in the blazing fire, that doesn't negate or falsify the pure diamond of your own beauty and essence!"

"Why does he abandon me and run to them, in that case? Have those actresses, those prostitutes been more accomplished in their beauty, tastes, education than me? Do they read Bihari Lal's poetry the way I do?" Kadambari said, anguished.

"*Bouthan*, listen...the actresses of the stage deck themselves up in front of everyone, exhibiting their beauty, but I really don't believe they are more beautiful than you." Rupa said in a bold, convincing voice.

At this, Kadambari stood in front of the mirror. She dropped her clothes on the floor and started looking at her own body meticulously, scrutinizingly. At that moment, she felt that Rupa was speaking the truth. For some moments, she felt as if she was besotted by the youthful charm and exuberance of her own beauty. But how did Binodini look?

Kadambari was dying to find out. She asked Rupa rather impatiently:

"I kept telling your *Notun Dada* to take me to the theatre, but we never dared to go because *Babamoshai* didn't like the idea. Let us both go together secretly one day and see how Binodini looks!"

"You'll go there? Are we really going there?" Rupa seemed to jump in excitement at the very alluring proposal of tasting the forbidden.

"Hmm…you better go there with Malini first!" Kadambari sounded hesitant now. "If they ever get to know I've been there, they might drive me out of the house! Don't you know, they insult me and taunt me all the time for being a barren woman? Moreover, now that they think my husband doesn't love me or pay that much attention to me, they are being even more aggressive to me. I so much wish to go, but I'm afraid, you know!"

Rupa hugged Kadambari tight and said: "No, *Bouthan*, it won't happen. Let's go together…I'll arrange for everything secretly, there's no way anybody can find out."

"What will you arrange for, let me ask? Whatever can you do alone?" Kadambari enquired, as if desperate to search for a beacon of hope. "But beware, don't drag Harry *sahib* into this!"

"No, *Bouthan*, remember, you just spoke of Malini, the book-seller woman? Let me call her now, she will arrange for it all. Let the three of us go to the theatre and watch it all first-hand!"

"Ah, leave it, it's just a futile hope of something impossible…" Kadambari was scared, and tried to change the subject out of fear. But Malini appeared on the scene just shortly after. Listening to it all, she said: "You know, *Notun Bouthan*, I can narrate to you the lines of the story that will be written about you in future. If you want to listen to it, I can oblige you."

"What do you mean by that anyway? Are you consuming opium and writing stories these days, Malini?"

"Why will I have to write? Perhaps one of your near and dear ones will pen such a story. When I close my eyes and meditate, the letters and words of that story glitter in the dark and come alive in my consciousness. Listen… please listen to some of it."

Malini started narrating the story.

"The beauty of Giribala was like sudden ray of light, like a sudden wonder, like consciousness awakened after slumber. Childless and married into a rich, aristocratic household, Giribala had enough leisure to indulge in her solitude, as she strived to store her rich, exquisite beauty within herself. However, after an extent, she was incapable of containing it within herself any longer. She had a husband, but she had no control on him, whatsoever. In her transitioning from girlhood to womanhood, her beauty had bloomed fully, but somehow it had evaded the sight of her own husband.

However, when she was a child, she was fortunate to receive her husband's love…But now Gopinath seemed to have been a slave to the beauty of Labanga, a theatre actress. She had the ability of pretending to faint on stage effectively. When she wailed in her unnatural nasal voice, breathing heavily, almost panting on the stage and called out for her 'Prananath' (Lord of her heart) in a slanted, infant-like pronunciation, her audience consisting of well-dressed men in dhoti and waist-coats welcomed her with their ecstatic comments. 'Excellent, excellent!' They would cheer her on from their seats."

Kadambari, listening to the narration reluctantly till now, stopped her with admonishing words. "Ah, such a nonsensical story you are narrating, Malini! Does your *Notun dada* wear such commonplace clothes, after all? And is my name Giribala? Why are you telling me this fictitious tale of Giribala-Gopinath-Labanga?"

"Couldn't you make out, *Notun Bouthan*, that it's your own story? Couldn't you see, it's all based on the facts of your own life?" Malini said.

"But you made things up, and embellished it with false words." Kadambari was furious. "I trusted you so much, Malini, how could you weave such a scandalous tale about my life? It seems my pain and anguish have been a fodder for your own entertainment! Such a shame!"

Malini apologized, bowing down at Kadambari's feet. "Believe me, *Notun Bouthan*, I didn't imagine all this in my mind! Strange, unexplained things happen once I close my eyes, unwritten words dance in front of my eyes, and I can read them all. When I sat in front of you today, these lines started crowding my head instantly. I haven't written this story myself, believe me.

Kadambari implored Malini to go away from her sight. She couldn't tolerate her at the moment. "Go away, please, Malini...it's all so weird, eerie, whatever is happening to you!"

"Rupa, please read to me the letters of Rabi once again, please." She ordered Rupa.

"But how many times would you listen to them, *Notun Bouthan*? I've memorized the letters by heart now, after so many times of reading them out!" Rupa replied, rather amused.

"Still, read them out to me...I love listening to them again and again. Read the letter where he writes about the quarrel between Mr. and Mrs. Baker, it will be fun!"

Rupa reclined her body in the *takia* (pillow) placed on the bed and started reading again:

"For some days I was living with my mentor's family. What a strange family it was! Mr. B—was a middle-class gentleman, well versed in Latin and Greek. He happens to be childless, hence I lived with him, his wife, his maidservant—just the four of us were together in the house. The master of the house was middle-aged, a dark, sombre man who used to fuss over everything all day and night from the room where he lived. The room was downstairs, close to the kitchen, absolutely dark with a little window and a door that remained bolted at all times. Sunlight couldn't enter the room easily, moreover, the only window in the room was covered with a curtain to block it. The walls of the room were covered with old, brittle, queer-looking Greek and Latin books of all shapes and sizes, filled with dust and dirt. One would feel suffocated the moment he would enter the room. This was his study, where he spent his entire day reading books and teaching his students, with a sullen, annoyed face.

His annoyance was centered on simple everyday affairs. For instance, if it would take some time to tie his tight boots, he would get angry on the boots. While going out, if the pocket of his shirt would get stuck to the nails, with a frown in his brows, he would move his lips in immense anger. And the most amusing fact was that-the more finicky he became, the more reason he found to exhibit his finicky behaviour. He would stumble upon things at every turn, the drawers of the chest in his room wouldn't open after constant pulling, and even if they opened, he wouldn't find the object he was searching there. Some days when I would enter his studio in the morning, I would notice him sitting at a corner and sulking unnecessarily, with no other soul in sight. But all said and done, Mr. B—was a good man. He was finicky, but not truly angry; he would be irritable and fussy, but never really quarrel with anyone. And seldom would he express his anger to humans, but his dog named Tiny would be the one on whom he directed all his wrath and annoyance. The dog would get scolded by him at his tiniest efforts of moving, and kicked by him all day and night. I've seldom seen this man smiling. His clothes were almost always shabby and unkempt. He was queer in every way, and one would have to accept him like that. I can say with certainty that this man was a priest before; every Sunday at the church, he would make people visualize the terrors of inferno. But now he had so many students to teach that some nights, he would end up not having his dinner. On some days, he would get up from the bed and remain busy with studies and work till 11 pm. Under such circumstances, it is not unnatural for anybody to turn irritated and fussy, after all.

His wife, the mistress of the house, was a fine lady, not angry or arrogant at all. Perhaps she was good-looking in her youth, but now she looked older than her age. She wore glasses, and dressed quite plainly, without any grandeur. She cooked all the dishes herself and did all chores without any household help. With no children in the house, there was not much housework anyway. She looked after me with great care. Within a few days' time, I had gauged that there wasn't much love existing between the husband and wife. It was not that they quarreled a lot, though. There was an unusual silence with which their domestic life went on, each single day. Mrs B--, for that matter, never went to her husband's studio to call him; the only time they both met every day was in the dinner table, and then also, they had those meals silently, without much of a word exchanged between themselves. Most of the times, they spoke with me while having their daily meals, but never spoke among themselves. One day, I did hear them speak a bit, though.

Mr. B—said to Mrs. B—in a hushed tone: "Some potatoes..." (he didn't add the customary 'please', or it wasn't audible enough)

Mrs. B—replied: "I wish you were a little more polite."

Mr. B—said: "I did say: 'please'.

Mrs. B—replied: "I did not hear it!"

Mr B—said again: "But it was no fault of mine!"

Until this point, the two of them spoke, and then they became silent again, and imagine how embarrassed I started feeling among them.

One day, I was a little late to join them for dinner. When I reached, I saw Mrs. B—scolding Mr. B—for taking a few extra potatoes with his meat. Upon seeing me, Mrs. B—stopped scolding him, and Mr. B—, on his part, became bold enough to take his own sweet revenge on his wife, and took too many potatoes in his plate. Mrs. B—gave a helpless glance at her husband, piercing through his soul. Both the parties never addressed each other as 'dear, darling', even by mistake, nor did they call each other by their Christian names. They just referred to each other as Mr. B—and Mrs. B—. To give you an idea of how they talked among themselves, one day, Mrs. B—was conversing with me. As soon as Mr. B—entered the scene, both of them went quiet. Another day, Mrs. B—was playing the piano in my presence, and just as Mr. B—arrived, he remarked: "When are you going to stop?" Mrs. B—replied: "I thought you had gone out!" The piano stopped playing. From that day onwards, when I wanted to listen to the piano from Mrs. B--, she would say: "I will play when that horrid man won't be at home." I would be much embarrassed to hear this.

In spite of their apparent incompatibility, their domestic life went on smoothly. The Mrs. cooked and ran the house, and her husband worked and earned money. The two of them didn't really quarrel, but there were hot exchanges of words among them occasionally; and then also, they talked so softly that the words didn't reach their next-door neighbours. Anyway, I stayed with them for a few days and with a lot of embarrassment, I left their abode and am now at peace."

Finally, Rupa and Malini made Kadambari a party to their plan. Since the drama 'Sarojini' was staged, Kadambari was dying to see Nati Binodini in person. Her curiosity knew no bounds. One evening, Rupa and Kadambari ventured outside the Jorasanko mansion to have the taste of an adventure at the National Theatre. Dressed in traditional *dhonekhali* saris, covering their heads in veils, they set out with palpitating hearts, experiencing the secret excitement of a blasphemous act. In a parallel literary universe, the same events had unfolded.

"At last, one evening, Giribala went out of the house secretly with her maid Sudho (Sudhamoyee) to see a theatre show. Her heart was full of excitement for the forbidden act. There were numerous light undulations in her heart, and in the rhythm and pace of those undulations, the world outside, with its people, its splendour and music, the beautiful scenes embellishing its stage seemed all the more magnificent in her eyes.... That day, the drama 'Manbhanjan' was being staged. Radha, Krishna's consort was swimming in a sea of anguish, and Krishna was getting lost in that boundless sea of her soul. He begged and pleaded and cried to her so many times, yet she would not budge.

Giribala's heart heaved with pride, just as Radha's heart. In Krishna's betrayal, she transformed herself as Radha and started feeling the incredible glory of her own being. Nobody had ever pleaded to her in this way before; she was a discarded, neglected wife, but now, in the intoxicating beauty of this moment, she felt that she had the power to make her man cry for her....

Finally, the drama ended; and the gas lights on the stage became dim. The audience was about to go away, but Giribala sat at the stage, mesmerized, transfixed. She seemed to have forgotten that she had to return to her home.... From that day, she started going to the theatre almost every week."

Like Giribala, Kadambari didn't go to see theatre shows every week, but after that incident, she went to the National Theatre secretly a couple of times with her daring accomplices, in search of an adventure. And indeed, nobody in the Thakurbari mansion came to know of the act. They were busy with the show of the new play 'Asrumati'. It became quite a sensation since the first show, and the women of the household deserved to see it for once. There were arrangements made to stage the play in the premises of the mansion. It did satiate their thirst for the play, but needless to say, they couldn't enjoy the full ambience and the authentic environment of the theatre. Hence, on September 23rd, 1879, at the behest of Gunen Thakur, the Bengal Theatre was booked for a show, exclusively for the members of Thakurbari. Though some like Kadambari and Rupa might have seen theatre shows secretly, this was the first time that the women of an aristocratic household stepped inside the theatre hall formally, with much grandeur. The hall was decorated with carpet, reclining chairs and other furniture brought from the Thakurbari. Also, flower garlands, hookah and 'chik', special curtains for girls were arranged for. The members of the Thakurbari mansion number 5 and 6 went to see the theater with much eagerness and enthusiasm. Kadambari joined them too.

That day, Sukumari played the heroine. While the other women watched the show with awe and wonder, Kadambari was restless, unmindful all the time. She had witnessed Binodini's incredible beauty and grace at the National Theatre before, and since then, was immersed in a complex feeling, a heady concoction of envy and melancholy. She was the one who had to listen to the effusive praise of Binodini from her husband's mouth most of the times.

Meanwhile, Anna Tarkhare had returned to Bombay, her home with a broken heart. With the strong sensitivity and anguish she harboured in her heart regarding Rabi, she couldn't write letters to him. However, she wrote a couple of letters to his sister-in-law Kadambari, letting her know about her life. Nalini, the name given by Rabi to her was now her constant companion. She wrote in journals, literary magazines using her pen name, Annabai Nalini.

Gradually, Anna had come to realize that Rabi would remain elusive to her. In a letter to Kadambari, she let her know that she had a new man in her life. The two of them had met in Dublin, and had fallen in love at the first sight. The man, Mr. Littledale was then the Vice-Principal of Baroda college. Then, in a fine wintry evening in the month of November, Anna was married to the young Scottish professor Harold Littledale.

"Anna might have taken the right decision!" Kadambari remarked, while keeping away the card she was playing with. She was playing the card game with Swarnakumari and Rupa, seated on a mat spread over the bed in her room.

"Why are you saying this? How can you measure right and wrong in this way, *Notun Bouthan*?" Swarna couldn't help asking. "Why would she be wrong if her marriage had happened with Rabi?"

"Well, *Babamoshai* didn't agree to the alliance, and besides, we don't know if Rabi himself wanted to marry her. If he was in love with her, he could have told her. But… you know, I was thinking, the men of this house can easily forget their wives for the enticing beauty of other women, isn't it? In that case, her English husband is a much better choice!"

"Ah, you're speaking like this out of deep anguish!" Swarna couldn't agree with the cause of Kadambari's resentment and anger that she felt towards Jyoti. She believed wholeheartedly that the men of their house possessed strong, firm characters. The sensitivity of the men of Jorasanko was unmatched in the whole of the nation.

Rupa burst out in anger now. "Swarna didi, you

aren't aware of everything happening these days!" She said. "Everyday, *Notun Bouthan* waits for *Notun dada*, dressing herself with such grace, and when he comes to her, he takes money from the chest, changes his clothes, wears *attar* (perfume) all over his body and leaves within a while, it seems he doesn't have any time to look at his wife, not even for a few seconds.

"Do you know what happened yesterday, *Thakurjhi*?" Kadambari's eyes started getting moist. "I stopped him from going out, and said to him: 'I won't let you go today… Please spend today evening with me!'

He replied, resisting me: "Leave me, *Bou*, I really have to go."

I embraced him tightly and said: "Let me see how you can go now!"

"Don't be so childish and stubborn!" He replied, annoyed.

"I will be stubborn!" I said.

At this, he released himself from my hands with cruel, brutal force. While he pulled himself away, I fell down on the floor. But even then, he didn't stop. He went away, unfazed by my vulnerable condition. Is this the same husband I had, who went with me at the Maidan riding a horse, ignoring the apathetic, censuring words of people? Is he the same man who read out poetry to me, sang songs to me with so much love nestled in his heart? I can't seem to recognize the same man today."

Malini, the book-seller woman was there at the door with her basket full of books, and asked: "Should I, or shouldn't I enter your room today, *Notun Bouthan*?"

Kadambari looked at Malini with wistful eyes like the clouded sky. "Malini, come inside, I was thinking of you for some time. What happened to your Giribala? I didn't get to hear after that day."

"Well, that day, you got angry with me and drove me away." Malini spoke in an anguished voice.

"Let that be, please let me know today, Malini!" Kadambari said, curious. "Since that day, I think quite often, what happened to Giribala."

Malini started to narrate. "It was 10 o'clock at night. The other members of the family had finished their dinner and went away to sleep. At that moment, Gopinath arrived, smelling of *attar*, swaying his dupatta (scarf) in the wind. Upon seeing him, Sudho, the maid bit her tongue in embarrassment and pulled her veil to cover her face entirely, and ran away with bated breath.

My day has arrived, finally! Giribala thought to herself. She didn't lift her eyes and look at him. Like Radha, Lord Krishna's consort, she sat, steadfast in her stubborn pain and anger. However, she noticed that the scene remained the same. With a non-musical, dry voice, her husband Gopinath said: "Give me the keys!" Giribala went up to him, giving up her resolve to remain frozen in anguish. She grabbed her husband's hand and said: "I'll give you the keys. But first, please come to our room."

Gopinath replied, stubborn and angry: "I can't delay much...Give me the keys quickly."

Giribala watched all this violence, insult and injury, as she stood, stoned, gripping the doors with all her might. After all his failed attempts, Gopinath came up to her again, and burst out in a mad rage: "Give me the keys at once, you will see what I will do to you otherwise."

Giribala remained quiet, stoic in her resolve, not opening her mouth to answer. Gopinath gripped her tightly and snatched away all her precious ornaments, the choker from her neck, the armlet from her arm, the ring from her finger. In a gesture of uncontrolled triumph of his manhood, he kicked her and went away."

Listening until this part, Kadambari started crying like a child. "Stop, please stop, Malini, I can't tolerate the pain of Giribala anymore!"

Rupa tried to console Kadambari, giving her a warm, tight hug. Kadambari too leaned on her shoulders to seek her utmost shelter and comfort.

Swarna said: "I don't understand anything, Malini… How strange is it that you are weaving this cock-and-bull story and *Notun Bouthan* is crying so much upon hearing it! And, to think of it, it's not a cheap roadside story, but one embedded with a fine language and vivid description! Who is the writer of this story?"

"I don't know, Swarna didi!" Malini confessed with all honesty. Whenever I'm in front of *Notun Bouthan* nowadays, the lines of this story start crowding in my head!"

"What? How strange!" Swarna exclaimed, astonished. "How are you able to narrate all of this so effortlessly, closing your eyes? Tell me more of it, now!"

"Listen… it's all unfolding in front of my eyes like a graphic picture!" Malini stood up, excited, and started explaining. "Gopinath is creating a ruckus in the theatre, shouting the name of Labanga in the presence of all the audience, throwing flower bouquets on the stage insolently. Utterly helpless, the owners of the theatre hall are expelling him from the hall. And this act fuels his anger; Gopinath rides a boat along with Labanga and elopes, to teach the people of the theatre group a lesson.

"Oh my! What a mess!" Rupa says, brimming with excitement. "What happened next, Malini didi? I can't keep my patience!"

"Rupa, keep quiet, will you?" Swarna said, annoyed. "And Malini, narrate the story in a literary voice, not in this way."

Malini started narrating again. "The theatre people were now in troubled waters. After their futile wait for Labanga, they got hold of a new actress for the role of Manorama, the female protagonist, and made her practice the part. This delayed the show of the drama for quite some time, but that wasn't a major loss. The theatre hall started filling with audience very promptly. Hundreds of people returned from the doors every single day, and the newspapers were full of words of praise for the drama.

All this praise reached the ears of Gopinath in the faraway land, and he couldn't keep away anymore. He came to see the acting of the new girl, a queer mixture of resentment and curiosity playing in his mind.

Gopinath was a quiet observer until Manorama was posing as the subservient wife, her face veiled, hidden from the world around. But the moment she, draped in a blood-red sari and an abundance of ornaments, unveiled her beautiful face, her entire being erupted in waves of her beauty, her inexplicable feeling of pride and haughtiness.

When she threw her sharp, sarcastic glance at the audience and especially at Gopinath like the flash of a sudden lightning. Shocked and fuming in rage at the sudden turn of events in the stage, Gopinath stood up and started to scream: 'Giribala, Giribala!' His screams mingled with the sound of the claps and the overwhelming appreciation of the audience that echoed in the stage. While he ran and attempted to jump over the stage, the musicians caught him.

The audience, annoyed by this sudden disruption and chaos, shouted: 'Drive him away! Get the rascal out!'

However, he continued with his wild, broken screams and threatened to kill Giribala. Finally, the police arrived and took him away, forcefully. The huge crowd present at the theatre applauded the unforgettable histrionics of Giribala, only her husband Gopinath was not allowed to see her."

Swarnakumari started clapping as soon as Malini finished narrating the story. "Such a fine use of language, such refined sense of humour in the story, I'm amazed! Please tell me, Malini, where did you read this story? From which source did you memorize it?" She demanded to know.

"Giribala won, after all! She won, didn't she? Can a woman take revenge in this way? How awe-inspiring!" Kadambari said, as if still in a state of delirium.

"What fun! If you want, you too can take revenge thus, *Bouthan*!" Rupa clapped and remarked.

"Keep quiet, Rupa! What rubbish are you uttering?" Reprimanding Rupa for her garrulous nature, Kadambari stood in front of the mirror rather unmindfully. She seemed to search for something, an unnamed attribute in her reflection in the mirror.

Swarna asked again, impatiently: "Tell me whose writing this is, Malini! Why talk in riddles? Are there any more stories by the same writer? In fact, where did you find this one?"

"Honestly, didi, I don't know!" Malini admitted. "Strange, unexplained things possess my mind from time to time, I told you…I think these stories haven't yet been written, but maybe the process of writing these is going on somewhere! I can foresee the story and its title, 'Manbhanjan', but there is a blank space in the name of the writer…My head is reeling, didi! Let me take your leave now!" Malini went away.

Soon after this theatrical episode, a tragic accident took place inside the Jorasanko mansion. It was a wintry afternoon, and Kadambari was sleeping with baby Urmila on her bed after lunch. She didn't know when she had fallen fast asleep, and little Urmila got off the *palanka* bed and went to the crooked stairs leading to the terrace playfully. When the child attempted to come down the stairs, she fell down accidentally at the bottom of the stairs. Kadambari woke from sleep, at the sudden, piercing shriek of the child, and ran to her rescue. However, by then, brain concussion had happened to the child, and she stumbled on Urmila's still, lifeless body.

Kadambari took Urmila's body in her arms and fainted right away. When the maids of the house went to give the news of the tragic death to the child's mother Swarna, working at her writing table with a meditative trance, she too fainted due to the sudden shock and trauma of the news.

A dark shadow of gloom overwhelmed the entire mansion. The children of the house were forcefully kept inside their own rooms; Swarna's children were moved to Satish Pundit's quarter inside the mansion, so that they couldn't see the brutal, unforgiving face of death. 'Urmila has gone away for a vacation.' They were told when they enquired where she was.

The women of the house, the kith and kin of little Urmila had gathered around her lifeless body. Soudamini was immensely worried. Janakinath, the deceased child's father was staying abroad. How would Swarna, her mother deal with the terrible agony of the loss of the child under such circumstances? She looked at Kadambari weeping silently in a corner and remarked: "The maids are paid so highly in the house, and the children are taken care of by them quite well…If you can't pay enough attention to the little girl, why do you pretend to be so loving and caring to her?"

Soudamini's sarcastic words pierced like a dart through Kadambari's already bruised heart. "Isn't Urmila my child too?" She revolted. "Could you utter such cruel words because I didn't carry her for nine months in my own womb?"

"Whatever it might be, *Notun Bou*, you ought to be more careful surely! How could you fall asleep, leaving a child unattended near the open stairs? Couldn't you call any of the maids?"

Kadambari wept more profusely at this allegation and came close to Swarna who was weeping too. She asked, shaking her shoulders: "Are you too thinking that I am the one to blame, *Thakurjhi*? Tell me the truth, please, I need to know what exactly you're thinking!"

Swarna didn't reply, she kept on crying. Soudamini said to Kadambari in an annoyed voice: "Let her cry, don't disturb her anymore. There's nothing more traumatic to a mother than the unnatural death of her child."

Kadambari was shocked and astonished at Soudamini's sharp, apathetic words. In fact, she too had lost her only darling child, why was nobody trying to feel her agony? How cruel, unsympathetic these women seemed to her!

'And why is Swarna silent after all? Is she too blaming me?' Kadambari thought.

Someone seemed to call her from behind. "Would you be able to fall asleep thus, if she was your own offspring? Remember the old adage: 'An aunt's love can never be stronger than a mother's love!'

Alas, why didn't she die before listening to such words? Her life seemed meaningless to her at the moment. Swarna's silence seemed to her the most shocking phenomenon of all. The childless Kadambari flopped down on the floor and wept uncontrollably, in terrible humiliation.

All of a sudden, Rupa ran into the room and took Kadambari's drooping head in her arms. She hugged Kadambari, and lifted her body, trying to take the helpless woman in her own bed chamber. While going away with Kadambari, she looked at the women in the room and shouted: "Are you all human beings? Can't you see how *Notun Bouthan* is under the terrible shock of her dear Urmila's death? On top of that, you are throwing darts on her with your caustic words? Shame on you!"

The women gathered in the room were stoned in shock

to witness the daring, unabashed attitude of Rupa. The teary-eyed Kadambari was leaning on the girl's shoulders and walking towards her own room. The flowing *anchal* of her sari dragged through the entire expanse of the long verandah as she walked, like an ever-flowing, melancholy river.

Chapter 14

Lucy and Binodini

Rabi had been brought to England for academic purposes, and especially to study for the ICS exams, so that he could be a barrister. However, in the comfort of home away from home, in the affectionate, caring presence of his *Mejo Bouthan* Gyanadanandini, though his long verse titled 'Bhagna Hridoy' (Broken Heart) kept expanding and flourishing, his studies were not going on well, as Satyen, his elder brother observed. Soon enough, he was sent away to London at the initiative of Taraknath Palit, a friend of Satyen. For the initial few days, Rabi had to practice living alone in a rented house in front of Regent Park. In those days, when people came to meet him occasionally, Rabi felt like retaining them forcefully, not letting them go away. He felt claustrophobic, utterly miserable amid the damn cold, couped inside the silent, isolated house.

Satyen came to visit him from time to time. Some days, Rabi, Satyen and Tarak joined the assembly of the Indian Association in the city. Some other days, they would attend the summer assembly of the British parliament to witness the structure and foundation of the British democracy. But Rabi was rather disappointed by visiting the assembly for a few days in a row. At home, he shared his displeasure with Satyen and Tarak. "The mountain peaks of the parliament, the incredibly huge building, the wide, open halls had filled me with awe and wonder, but when I went inside, my reverence for it was diminished. Whatever lofty ideas about the British democratic system and the intelligence of the British I had fostered in my mind were all crushed to the ground; they disappointed me to no end." He remarked.

Satyen himself was displeased with the situation. "It never occurred in my worst nightmare that the English people can shout in the parliament like savages!" He said.

Rabi added: "And you know, they don't allow anybody to talk…it's unimaginable how they try to prevent the speaker from expressing his opinions! On one hand, some people clap, while the others make hissing sounds… they are terribly intemperate!"

Tarak attempted to lighten up the mood of both Rabi and Satyen. "Ah, you don't understand, this is the actual face of politics; nobody would give others a chance to speak, nobody would leave an inch of land without waging a war!"

"Hmm, what about the big talks about politeness and courtesy and etiquette, then? Isn't it all a big farce, an act of hypocrisy?" Rabi uttered, furious. "Had you seen the Irish member speaking about the Indian Press Act the other day? Nobody seemed to listen to his words with any amount of attention. But to think of it, they are literally thriving on the tax money of the Indian people! Why won't there be any representatives from India, then?"

Rabi was fuming in anger, Tarak was afraid he could soon talk like a rebel, a traitor to the British government. He remarked jokingly: "You better finish your studies and be a barrister soon, Rabi! Then you can initiate your argument about these issues officially!"

Rabi added: "But yes, I must admit, it's not that I learnt absolutely nothing in these sessions. I had been overwhelmed by the superb oratorial skills of Gladstone! As soon as he entered the stage, the entire hall went silent. As soon as the other members roaming outside heard his voice, they started to sit to listen to his speech. Soon, the benches on both sides started getting filled with people. Like a true source of light, the speech of Gladstone emanated with all its splendour. He was gifted with a fierce voice, but he never shouted; he spoke with full conviction always, which came from deep within his soul. On the other hand, my attraction for the marginalized Irish members is increasing by the day, just like the way I am completely steeped in the beauty of Irish melodies!"

That day, they had been to Tarak Palit's home. Suddenly, Bala came and started pulling Rabi to the piano.

Satu started remarking from behind: "Enough of your political discussions, now sing one of your Irish melodies, Rabi! You know, my English girlfriends are praising your singing voice a lot!"

"That's better!" Tarak said, sipping scotch from a glass. "Let's listen to Rabi's song...If the English girlfriends of Bala and Satu are praising his singing voice, there must be something in him!"

As soon as Rabi finished singing, Bala remarked: "You know, this tenor in Rabi's voice has mesmerized the English girls! Moreover, they have effusive words of praise for your face, your appearance, Rabi!"

Satu said: "Rabi cannot look at the girls directly, out of shame. Come on, Rabi, flirting a bit in social settings and in parties is quite a norm here, why can't you come to terms with that? And to think that the girls like you so much, isn't that fascinating?"

Rabi replied with a shy smile: "Well, my eyes are still trapped to the black doe-eyes of a Bengali woman, and I couldn't free myself from them. The blue-eyed English *memsahibs* seem to me like pussy cats!"

Within a few days' time, Rabi was involved in a sweet friendship with such two blue-eyed beauties whom he had referred to as 'pussy cats.' For a few days that he had stayed with the Barker family, he was distressed with their familial quarrels and took shelter with the family of Lucy Scott. This British family in England became like his own kith and kin. Mrs. Scott, especially, showed a distinct fondness towards Rabi deprived of motherly love, and forged a strong, unforgettable bond of affection with him.

In a letter, Rabi wrote to Kadambari again: 'I stay with the K—family now. Mr. K—himself, his wife, his four daughters and two sons, three maids and myself, along with Taby, their dog constitute of the family now. Mr. K— is a doctor with white hairs and a milk-white beard. He has quite a bold, yet pleasing personality. His graceful features reflect his magnanimous nature, and it's not a surprise that he cares for me with all his heart. If I don't wear warm clothes during the winter, he scolds me; if he thinks I haven't had enough food during my daily meals, he keeps pestering me to have more food till I eat enough, according to his wish. You know, in England, people get scared of coughing; so in case I would cough even twice in a single day, he would forcefully stop my bathing. He keeps giving me numerous medicines, and pours warm water on my feet every night before sleeping, then only does he leave me for the day.'

When Lucy and Jessy came to Rabi to give him warm water therapy, they started indulging in a bit of mischief. Rabi's hesitation started to melt away, seeing their juvenile restlessness. He himself joined in the fun and mischief along with the two sisters.

Lucy laughed and said to Rabi: "You know, Rabi, when we heard that we are having an Indian guest in our house, we were frightened and ran away to our aunt's house!"

"Why, am I a ghost or a demon?" Rabi asked, amused by Lucy's revelation.

Jessy said: "No, no…We thought an uncivilized wretched human was coming, the one with big nails, and a nasty smell!"

Lucy giggled and added: "And you know, I thought you would have tattoos all over your body, and wear heavy jewellery in your nose and ears."

"Ah well, then you had thought of a red Indian, didn't you?" Rabi asked, doubly amazed to listen to the sisters. "Wait, one day, I'll dress up just like them and scare you both! You'll have to run away to your aunt's house again!"

"Ah, you'll scare us? Let's see who can scare whom!" Lucy said. "See how idly you're sleeping and taking the warm water massage in your feet! You'll scare us, of all people, really?"

Rabi replied: "Well, you had absconded out of fear, didn't you? What do you think of me now?"

"I won't say…You get the meaning yourself." Lucy said in a naughty voice.

That night, Rabi had beautiful dreams in his sleep, and woke up at the spell of dawn. He came to the living room right after waking up and sat on the sofa. He didn't know how the early morning in this house started every day. Everyone was sleeping, and there was a peaceful quiet all around.

After a while, the elder daughter came downstairs and doused the fire in the fireplace. "Good morning, Rabi. Did you sleep all right?"

This was the usual norm of starting conversations in this country. Rabi replied to her: "Good Morning."

The girl went to the kitchen with brisk steps and instructed the cook regarding the breakfast in a few words. When she returned to the living room, she added a few pieces of coal in the fireplace and then seated herself in the sofa. Just then, there was a heavy noise of human footsteps in the stairs. Mr. Scott descended downstairs, shivering in the cold. He went close to the fireplace to warm up his freezing hands, and while doing that, said 'Good Morning' to Rabi. Then he picked up the newspaper and sat at the dinner table. While he read out a couple of news articles to Rabi, he started sipping coffee at the table. Lucy and Jessy came to him and started their day with an affectionate peck on their dear father's cheek.

Mr. Scott said: "Lucy and Jessy, you'll be fined today yet again! You woke up after me today…Give me your fine of four *annas*!"

"Ok, ok, I'll give you, Papa! I'll give you surely!" Lucy assured, hanging around her Papa's neck. Jessy too hugged her Papa affectionately.

Mr. Scott took Rabi as his witness and said: "Rabi,

these girls aren't keeping their promise. We had decided that if they wake up before me, I'll give them five quarters as their prize, and if I wake up before them, they will give me four annas as their fine. In all these days, they have incurred a lot of debt...tell me, is it an act of politeness to evade such debt of honour?"

At the end of all these discussions, Mrs. Scott joined them for breakfast. The breakfast was done by 9.30 in the morning, and after a bit of laughing, joking and merrymaking, she instructed the girls to hurry up and start working on the household chores. Aunty Scott wore gloves in both her hands and toiled hard along with the maids of the house, scrubbing the whole house clean, from the first floor to the fourth floor. She went to the kitchen and cleared all the bills of the vendors—the vegetable man, meat man, bread man et al. She was adept at all of it—discussing household finance with her husband, supervising the work in the kitchen and so on. Her elder daughter tagged along with her, wherever she roamed. The younger daughter Jessy had a separate task at hand—as soon as the maids went away after cleaning the rooms, she would take a duster and start cleaning the remaining dust from the drawing room. At the same time, her elder sister Lucy sat with her sewing work. She had a particular fascination for fixing pillow covers, socks, and also for writing letters. Lucy was also fond of singing, in fact, she was the only singer and instrumentalist in the entire family. Rabi accompanied her to several musical soirees these days, brimming with enthusiasm.

It was Lucy's wish to start a new adventurous game in the house, a game called 'planchet', and it started soon enough. Often in the evenings, a table was laid for the game. Some of them gathered around the table, seated in chairs, and placed their hands over a teapoy. The teapoy started roaming around the whole room in a mad frenzy. There was a point when anything, any object that they touched, would start moving, stirring up. One day, when they had attempted to take Mr. Scott's hat for the game, Aunty Scott ran out of nowhere and moved the hat away; she would never allow any demonic touch to taint any of her husband's belongings.

It was during those days that Rabi had been enrolled at the University College in London to study English language and literature. Tarak Palit's son Loken became his classmate in the institution. In spite of their age difference, the friendship between the thirteen-year-old Loken and the eighteen-year-old Rabi blossomed quickly. When Rabi struggled with the etymology of Bengali words while trying to teach Bengali to Lucy, Loken became his assistant in the mission.

Rabi was having a feeling deep within that not only Lucy, but her sister Jessy too was much attentive towards him. He felt some sort of mystery unfolding between the trees in the orchard, in the south-facing room close to the terrace, in the delicate fingers playing the piano, softly touching the planchet. He didn't understand it all.

At the break after their English class, Rabi discussed this issue with his friend Loken. He said, Lucy seemed to say something to him, but he didn't understand what that was. Even Jessy did mysterious things to him, hiding them all from her elder sister.

"Why don't you understand, the sisters have fallen in love with you!" Loken said to Rabi.

"What can I say? I don't have the moral courage to believe such a thing! What should I do now?" Rabi asked, hesitant and shy.

Loken was a smart, matured young boy. He replied: "Go ahead and love them back, flirt with them...what else? The girls are ardent admirers of your singing voice, your melodies, they are mesmerised by your handsome appearance!"

Rabi lacked the courage to do anything about it, though. Time and again, he remembered the mysterious black doe-eyes watching him from a corner of his faraway home, in his motherland. The young Rabi felt lost in the tug of war between the black eyes and the blue eyes.

The news of Rabi's intense friendship and intimacy with the two Scott sisters gradually blossomed and reached the ears of Debendranath Thakur in India. Moreover, the fact that Rabi was enamoured by the free, emancipated spirits of the English girls was published in 'Bharati,' in the series titled 'Letters of an Expatriate in Europe.' Enough of furor was created as a result of those letters penned by Rabi.

Maharshi Debendranath ordered his son Rabi to return to his motherland without further delay. Rabi was agonized by the irony of his fate. Just after his wayward travels in England, when he was getting attracted to the teaching of his mentor Mr. Morli and his English classes, he was being summoned to return to India.

While he was bidding adieu to the Scott family, Mrs. Scott cried, holding Rabi's hand. In Rabi's heart too, there was a riot of emotions. In his sacred, private notebook 'Malati punthir khata,' Rabi scribbled haphazardly and wrote down the following lines documenting his pain:

'The days passed by, /Nobody knew in those two days

What revolution had been born within a pained heart!

Those two days/ Had returned the stream of waves for me forever...

The footprints of those two days/ Would remain forever etched in the heads of a hundred years

All the tears I have shed in these two days/ All the laughter I have laughed in these two days

All those tears and smiles will amalgamate, and be engraved in my heart, forever.'

Suppressing all his personal agony, jeopardizing all his efforts to be a barrister or an ICS, bruising the hearts of the two blue-eyed beauties, Rabi returned to India in the spring of 1880. At the same time, Satyen and Gyanada too returned home along with their children and Rabi, after their travails in France along the way.

In the new face of Calcutta, amid the newly established 'Babu culture', Binodini was a wondrous miracle, a newly born star. The daughter of a prostitute named Punti had transformed her whole persona, as if by virtue of some extraordinary magic. In the depth of her classical style of singing, in the glittering splendour of her beauty and her histrionics, the stage would be illuminated night after night. The aristocratic Babus of the city fell over her feet, mesmerized by her unparallel beauty. After the shows were over, some of them would visit her with thick bundles of money, some would come with flowers, some gifted her diamond necklaces. Some others, with their truant hands, would try touching her thighs on the pretext of offering her a 'pranaam'. Binodini, on her part, didn't pay attention to everybody, though. Only selected Babus would receive her favour. A young man from a wealthy family was her lover recently, however, his family members were busy arranging for his wedding.

But Girish Chandra was above everybody else; Bindoni looked up to him as her God. Girish Babu had been arranging lavish soirees at Binodini's home these days. Stalwarts of theatre like Amritlal Basu, Amritlal Mitra frequented these soirees. Some days, Girish would recite Keats' poems in these parties, some other days he would read out parts of Shakespeare's plays. Some days, there were discussions of poetry, while some other days, they talked about the actresses of England. Girish would often refer to the extraordinary performance of Mrs. Sidens in the role of Lady Macbeth. Like the *chataka* bird, Binodini absorbed the essence of all these discussions. There was no dearth of effort on her part to mould herself according to her mentor Girish Babu's wish.

Suddenly, one day Jyotirindra arrived, with his embroidered satin dupatta flying in the air, the fragrance of foreign perfume wafting in the air around him.

Girish said to Binodini: "Whom have you dragged here, Binod? Jyoti Thakur is here in this shabby neighbourhood in the abode of a *nati* (whore)! People will blame me for this blasphemy!"

"Why, Girish Babu, if you can come here, why would it be unfair if I too come and visit?" Jyoti asked. "The playwright has to come to the actress one day."

"Jyoti, listen, you are the son of an aristocratic family. If you come here frequently, our society won't accept it, people will talk negatively about you!" Girish Babu insisted. "If you ask about myself, that is a different story. I am intoxicated the whole day…I'm obsessed with theatre and do whatever I wish, carried by my whims. Nobody would say anything about me, and even if anybody does, I don't care much."

"I want to read out my new play to you." Jyoti said. "Binodini cannot act in it if I don't seek your permission for it."

The diamond nose-stud of Binodini glittered in the room, announcing her presence. All this while, she was listening in silence, now she spoke up. "I can't act in any other theatre, apart from National Theatre. 'Sarojini' was the last theatre show I was in. Jyoti Thakur Babu, how can I take part in your drama in my present condition, tell me?"

Jyoti's heart seemed to have stopped for that moment; the earth seemed to sway in front of him. Sarojini! Ah, what a cruel, heartless woman you are! The maddening smell of *attar* from Binodini's body that had swept him off his feet, seemed to choke his breath now. He felt claustrophobic.

Girish said to Jyoti in a wooden voice, mixed with a tinge of sarcasm: "Ah, I see, this is the real cause of your visit! Reading out your new play to me is only an excuse, you actually wanted to see Binodini!"

Some others present in the room remarked: "But tell us, whosoever doesn't want to see Binodini? Why would Jyoti Thakur be blamed alone?"

Jyoti felt a bit insulted by the snide remarks of these insignificant folks, but in all honesty, there was no denying the fact that he had run to Binodini's house, attracted like a magnet to her ineffable charm and beauty. Her smile, her magical aura, the inviting call of her nose-stud made him crazy in love with her. No housewife would ever be able to offer him such a frenzied feeling of passion, not even his beloved wife Kadambari.

Jyoti replied to Girish in an annoyed voice: "Look, Girish Babu, how am I to blame? Binodini is such a powerful actress; if I intend to make her act as the heroine of my play, why would it matter to you?"

One of Girish Babu's young, garrulous disciples remarked: "Every evening, Jyoti Thakur comes to National Theatre to see Binodini! Every evening, without fail!"

"What does that prove?" Jyoti became furious.

"Ah, why get angry? Come, sit down and cool your head a bit!" Binodini pleaded, holding Jyoti's hand.

"Sarojini, tell me, why do I have to stumble over so many rocks while coming to you?" Jyoti asked, looking at her eyes wistfully.

"Why? That's not even my real name!" Binodini replied in a shy voice. "I've played so many roles in my life...whenever I play a role, a character, she surrounds me like a playmate at all times, I don't remember the other roles at that time!"

Jyoti said: "You will remain my Sarojini to me till eternity...You will remain that until you play the role of the heroine in my new play! Remember your incredibly fiery avatar in the scene where the song *'Jwal, jwal chita'* (Burn, pyre, burn) was being sung? I can never forget that role you played, the beauty you exhibited in that scene!"

Binodini replied humbly: "There was immense craze among the audience regarding 'Sarojini', but Thakur, such a thing has happened even before this! When our entire crew of Great National was touring all over India, performing the play 'Neel Darpan', we witnessed something unimaginable...When that scene was enacted where the *sahib* was tormenting Khetramani, the heroine, she started crying, pleading to save her religion: "Oh *sahib*, you're my father, and myself, your daughter. Leave me, please leave me!" Just then, Torap, the main protagonist of the play came and pounced upon the *sahib*, strangling his neck, punching his body, slapping his face. Suddenly, there was an uproar amid the white audience of the show. The *gora sahibs* among the audience opened their swords and jumped on to the stage! There were shouts, chaos and mayhem everywhere in the vicinity!"

"I know, Binod!" Jyoti said. "When I watched you act in that role, I had decided to offer you the role of Sarojini! And you know, 'Sarojini' was even a greater sensation among the audience!" He looked at the others present in the room and said: "Didn't you all see, due to the tremendous popularity of 'Sarojini', the play has spread all across the villages in the form of *jatra*, with a massive impact in the public minds?"

This remark of Jyoti bruised the ego of Girish Babu. He replied: "I can understand you can't seem to forget her role in 'Sarojini', then what about the seven characters she played with equal elan in 'Meghnadbadh Kavya'? What about Kundanandini, the tragic heroine of 'Bish Briksha'? You know, when Bankim Babu had seen her acting in the play 'Mrinalini', he had remarked: 'I had created the visual image of the character of Manorama, but I never hoped I would get to see the living, breathing Manorama! In Binodini playing the role, it is as if I am seeing the lively manifestation of the woman Manorama!"

One disciple of Girish remarked: "What about Kanchan in the play 'Sadhabaa-r Ekadashi'?"

Another remarked: "What about Britannia in 'Palashee-r Juddho'?

Amritlal Basu said: "It is indeed a remarkable role that Binodini had played in the play 'Sarojini', but when our Girish plays the role of the hero and she plays the heroine, pitted against him, that sets the stage on fire, really. Their chemistry is unmatched by anything else."

Jyoti felt dejected and sad by such a comment. This was indeed Girish's own kingdom. If Binodini couldn't be freed from the clutches of Girish Babu, it would be impossible to make her do the role he wanted for her.

Jyoti came to Binodini, his muse time and again. Binodini too would be happy to see him, and read out the poems she scribbled from time to time. There were waves, undulations of happiness all over her body when Jyoti Thakur praised her effusively. When Jyoti came to her, she converted her poetry to songs, infusing tunes and melodies to her lines, and started singing those songs.

"I don't want, I don't want your love that you weigh and measure

It is as huge as the Sindhu River; how can you quench my thirst in a few drops of the treasure?

My love doesn't have impurities, my love is pure gold,

Why squash all my hopes when such pure love is bought and sold?"

Jyoti's heart was full of fervent emotions when he heard Binodini singing such a song. "Whom did you compose the song on, Sarojini? Who is the one who bruised your heart in such a way? Please tell me! Don't you know, I come to you over and over again to hold all your pain, all your agony in my bosom?"

Binodini smiled mysteriously and started singing another song.

Jyoti would read out the plays he wrote to Binodini, and also sing to her the songs he had composed; in those moments, Binodini would become a mesmerised listener. But whatever Jyoti did, he felt like he couldn't reach the deep, dark, silent corners of Binodini's heart. Why were those corners so unreachable? Who was seated there? Was it Girish, or someone else? He wondered. His impeccably handsome features and appearance, his incredible talents seemed useless to himself, and he deemed them all a big failure. With a broken heart, he returned from Binodini's abode time and again. From Binodini, he returned to his wife Kadambari. But even in returning thus, happiness eluded him. Kadambari, his wife repeatedly accused him, as if he was a criminal. She cried and wailed restlessly, complaining of an imagined love affair between Binodini and her husband that she had woven in her own mind.

One fine day, Jyoti sailed along with Kadambari in his steamer; Akshay and a couple of other friends joined them. They were in a musical mood that day, with Jyoti composing his music, giving tunes to songs and Akshay creating his lyrics to the tunes. The friends clapped along, humming the tunes. Kadambari was the queen bee in the musical soiree. Jyoti was looking at her the whole time while creating his music, while Akshay was writing down his lyrics with Kadambari as his muse. The birds in the sky, the water of the fertile river seemed to indulge in the festivities surrounding her ethereal presence, and she was feeling joyous. It was a musical siesta after a long hiatus, like the cherished memory of last spring, like the many evenings she spent at their terrace of the third floor, fragrant with the essence of the buds of *bel* flowers. Today, she felt she was the three-headed witch Hecate yet again.

Over their heads, the black sky emerged, and a storm followed, and then, the raindrops started pouring. Kadambari's sari was getting drenched like the sail of a boat, but they didn't seem to care. Kadambari, the Hecate of their dreams covered her head with the end of her dark blue sari, while the two men went on composing songs, as if in a never-ending spell. Jyoti and Akshay, in their euphoric state, devoid of worldly consciousness, composed love songs one after the other, their themes centered on the lives of Indra, Sachi and so many other gods and goddesses. When they reached Chandannagar, the two friends settled down with all these songs, modified them, refined them a bit more, and thus, the musical play titled 'Manmayee' was born.

Once the play was fully prepared, Jyoti became restless all over again. "This play needs to be staged as soon as possible!" He demanded. Amid the preparations of the musical play to be staged at the Jorasanko premises, Rabi, Satyen and Gyanada returned home. Rabi's soul danced in ecstasy as the old, familiar waves of music, dance and festivities were revived in his ancestral home. While humming the tunes of the songs of 'Manmayee', Rabi composed a new song of his own.

While listening to Rabi sing, Kadambari remarked in jest: "Rabi, look how you've changed, your voice is sounding a bit like a foreigner!"

"Ah, did I return to my homeland to listen to such a comment, *Bouthan*?" Rabi joked. "In England, I couldn't sleep at night, thinking of you...You know how many cupid's arrows thrown at me by the English girls I had to reject, so that I could return to you? And now that I'm here with you, you are behaving like I'm an outsider?"

Kadambari pouted her lips and replied: "Rabi, don't you dare to lie! You didn't even remember me a bit while you were in England. Only you know how many girls you did kill in your love, but I've myself seen Anna, the poor girl shed tears for you in this house!"

Rabi held Kadambari's hands and his entire body twirled and swirled in the gesture of a dance. He hummed a song: *"Aay tobe shohochori"* (Come with me, my dear friend) ...

Jyoti was ecstatic. "Sounds like a beautiful song! Is it your new composition, Rabi? We can add it in our play, then!" He said.

Swarnakumari remarked: "Rabi, I think *Notun Bouthan* didn't say anything wrong, your singing voice has indeed changed quite a bit! It sounds a bit western now, and quite appealing too!"

Akshay said: "His voice has transformed due to the intense western influence; moreover, Rabi has crossed his adolescence now, and this change of voice is quite natural! There's a tinge of Irish melodies in his voice now, isn't it?"

From his head to toe, Rabi shivered in an inexplicable feeling of ecstasy, listening to Akshay's remark. Once, he was an ardent admirer of the poems replete with Irish melodies in the voice of Akshay; he listened to Akshay recite them, hours on end. The adolescent Rabi used to wonder when he would go to England and learn all those tunes, and then sing them in front of Akshay. He had learnt most of them by heart, but he didn't like all of them. Some of those tunes were sweet, melodious, tragic in their essence. But he had realized that the semblance of the fantasy of his boyhood regarding those ancient melodies was somewhat lost when he was in England, trying to explore them. In England, he had learnt various other tunes too. Wasn't it just a few days back that he was occupied in a musical game with Lucy? And now, the broken music of the piano played in his bruised, tormented heart. Rabi went near the window and stood there for a while, attempting to hide his tears.

Gyanada was the more pragmatic one. "Let us first rehearse the various roles of 'Manmayee' among ourselves ... Then we can decide our individual roles accordingly!" She commented.

Satyen added: "Then let us start rehearsing the acting before I go to Surat and join work there. So many days, we were living away from this musical environment... but now I want to return to work with the flavour of music, melodies and acting!"

In the room where they sat, they decided their roles; Jyoti would play the role of Indra, the King God, and Rabi, the role of Madan, the God of love.

"Who would play the role of Sachi?" Kadambari asked, in all eagerness.

It seemed that the resentment towards Kadambari that Gyanada had fostered in her heart had decreased a bit due to her stay in England for a long time. The young woman looked somewhat frail to Gyanada, with the dark clouds of monsoon accumulating under her eyes.

"Well, you can dress up as Sachi, *Notun Bou*!" Gyanada suggested. "You will look good together as a pair, once you are decked up properly!"

"Don't we look good together otherwise?" Kadambari replied instantly. She seemed to have got the hint of her sister-in-law's hidden sarcasm. "What do I have to do to look good with him?"

"Ah, I'm sure *Mejo Bouthan* didn't mean it like that!" Jyoti was quick to cover up. "Don't start with your old squabble among yourselves, *Notun Bou*, I beg of you!"

Kadambari, with her anguished heart, went close to Rabi and stood by the window. Rabi held her hand with his own hand, and whispered the lines of a poem he had composed in her ears.

"Perhaps you don't know, my goddess, with invisible ties

You have made my heart return to the routine path.

I've ventured far and near, but the attraction for you remained unwavering,

With the power of your love, I could never sway from your path."

In the Bengali month of Baishakh, the play 'Manmayee' was staged within the Thakurbari premises in a majestic way. Kadambari acted with all her dedication in the role of the female protagonist Sachi; her own pent-up anguish and tears were mingled with the tears of Sachi.

The play was quite a sensation among the audience, and they had been awed, mesmerised by Kadambari's amazing histrionics on stage. When all others were showering their eloquent words of praise for the play, she dragged her husband Jyoti to a far-off corner and asked him, while fumbling with the gold button of his robe. "Is Binodini, your muse a better actress than me?"

"Uff, you have gone out of your mind, *Notun Bou*!" Jyoti moved away from her in a sudden jerk. Binodini was the name of an unattainable fire, and he wished to forget the memory of the fire with all his might. Why was this woman hell bent on igniting the fire yet again?

'Manmayee', the female protagonist of the play had been appeased by the love of her life, but the woman who played the role stood in a corner, transfixed, teary-eyed, unable to cherish her success on the day she deserved it the most.

Chapter 15

Sreemati (Mistress of my Heart)

Kadambari, despite being Rabi's muse, was restless to attain her husband Jyoti's affection. Jyoti, on the other hand, was mad after Binodini. It was a rather complex chemistry of love. Jyoti wondered at times, was Binodini the femme fatale of his life? In her inevitable attraction, he was jeopardizing everything in his own life. *Notun Bou*, his beloved wife was not so dear to him anymore, but then, even Binodini remained unreachable to him. And how would he save Kadambari who was destroying herself bit by bit everyday?

Kadambari, on the other hand, kept thinking how Jyoti was plunging into the fatal fire like an obsessed insect, how she could possibly move him away from the burning embers of that woman, Binodini. How would she save herself too, she wondered.

Rabi, on his part, understood both Jyoti and Kadambari. To his Jyoti dada, Binodini was both the goddess and the muse now; he was mad for this woman ever since his play 'Sarojini' was staged. But in Rabi's young, blossoming heart, *Notun Bouthan* was his muse. Like the splendour of the moonlit night, like the fragrance of *kanakchampa* flowers, she lingered in his imagination, drowning in a pool of tears, an emblem of pathos forever. Drowned in the thoughts of this beloved woman, he kept on composing one poem after another. The long poem 'Broken Heart' composed by Rabi was almost complete now; the first part was penned before Rabi embarked on his journey to England.

They moved away, far away from Binodini, the femme fatale. Rabi, Jyoti and Kadambari went away to Shantiniketan. In the land of green pastures, the lives of the two handsome, extraordinary young men centered around Kadambari, creating two different cyclonic undulations in both their hearts.

One day, Kadambari picked up a handful of *bakul* flowers from the garden, and said in a childish voice, while toying with the flowers: "Just like these flowers will wither away soon, so will I; and lie in a corner of your room like a dead garland of flowers."

In Rabi's ears, these words echoed like the tragic music of the three-headed Hecate. His new poem sprung up from the feeling of pathos embedded in Kadambari's words.

Jyoti, on the other hand, spelled danger. "Oh no, why did Kadambari have to start this all over again? He had moved away from the madness of Calcutta, from 'Natyaranga', from his plays so that his wife's mental sickness would be gradually healed. Wouldn't she be in a better mental state here as well?

"*Notun Bou*, aren't you finding any pleasure amid this grand, magnanimous environment of Shantiniketan?" He asked.

"You call me *Notun Bou* (new bride), but honestly, I

am no longer new to you. I'm old, very old now…There are so many new people in your life, aren't they?" Kadambari's anguish and pain didn't seem to diminish.

Rabi was startled at the words. Somebody seemed to whisper in the winds: "Go away, go away from here, the old, the forsaken!" Who was that? Who?

"No, no, Goddess Hecate! Don't you really understand whom I intend to dedicate this book to, at whose lotus feet I would like to offer it?" Rabi said in a mysterious poetic gesture. "My broken heart, I offer at your feet, / Let the stream of blood from my bruised heart colour your feet, my goddess…"

But whose lotus feet are they? Kadambari was intrigued, though she understood partly.

"They belong to the woman whose shadow never left me even when I ran away to England…It is she whose shadow chases me from behind, no matter where I go!" Rabi said.

"Now, now, see how that woman will pounce upon you and break your shoulders like a witch!" Kadambari replied, giggling loud. Her laughter was showered on Rabi's entire being like the fragrant jasmine flowers.

In a barely audible voice, Rabi whispered: "In the dark kingdom of the heart, the goddess resides…"

Rabi's long poem 'Broken Heart' was first published in 'Bharati', then later it was republished as an independent book of poems in June, 1881. Since then, there were many speculations centered on 'Srimati He' (Oh Mistress Mine), which was none other than Kadambari. Once, Kadambari played the role of Hemangini in the play 'Aleek Babu', and her dear ones called her Hecate, the witch. Was she the mistress, then, referred by Rabi?

Upon seeing the book 'Broken Heart' for the first time, Gyanada too remarked: "Did you have to dedicate the poems to Kadambari, of all people, Rabi? I had known all along that poets dedicate their poems to the women of their dreams in such language!"

Rabi felt a bit hurt; he liked everything about his *Mejo Bouthan*, only he didn't understand why she couldn't stand Kadambari, his *Notun Bouthan*. There was an invisible rivalry between both these women. However, he replied: "How did you know whom I dedicated the book to? We poets cannot come out with all our secrets, then we would land in danger. But I cannot deny the fact that *Notun Bouthan* is the muse of many of my verses. To me, she is more an idea than a woman in flesh and blood."

Gyanada was visibly irritated. "I really don't know what special you have seen in that woman! I had thought you would give up fancying her once you travelled to England and met the many beautiful, accomplished women there. But I see that childishness is still very much a trait you have kept alive in you!" She remarked.

Gyanada had initiated many new rules in her own quarters after returning from England. Her children wore dresses which were clearly inspired by English design. On their birthdays, they celebrated by cutting cakes, following the British manners. Suren was now enrolled in St. Xavier's and Bibi was Studying in Loretto. Every evening, they went for a stroll nearby, along with their servant Rama, which was quite a matter of envy to the other children. The children of the Thakurbari had never received this kind of attention. On the other hand, Suren and Bibi roamed around freely, lavishly, soaked in the regal love and affection of their mother Gyanada.

Gyanada had made it a rule that every day, one child of the household would go for a stroll along with Suren and Bibi and get some fresh air from outside. Each child waited with bated breath to know when his or her turn would come for the adventure.

Sarala, the child was quite close in her age to Bibi and Suren. Her mother, however, didn't have the time or inclination to raise her like Gyanada raised her children. Hence, the child's days passed by in the most humdrum of ways, in the care of her maids and amid the strict reprimanding measures of her *Gurumoshai* or family tutor. One day, when her turn came to go for a stroll along with Bibi and Suren, and she was on the verge of going out, all decked up, the strict *Gurumoshai* prevented her from going out and gave her a good scolding. Bibi and Suren went out in front of her eyes, moist and swollen with tears. Her much-cherished dream of exploring the world outside vanished into thin air.

Among the girls, Bibi, Sarala and Pratibha had very melodious, musical voices. With full enthusiasm, Rabi was making the children of the house join in the musical events of Jorasanko. The preparations for the annual winter festival *Maghotsav* started in full swing, with the fragrance of eastern and western music wafting in the air with all their jubilance. Earlier, Satyen, Dwijen or Jyoti were at the helm of affairs for this festival. But now, Rabi had taken the responsibility of the music for the festival. He was writing new songs in the genre of Brahma sangeet, he was borrowing the original tunes from the *bandish* of the ustads and breaking them up to compose new tunes for the songs. Every year, just before the annual *Maghotsav*, it was a ritual to get a new book of songs published; but this year, Rabi picked up quite a number of proof copies of the books from the Adi Brahmo Samaj press and distributed the songs beforehand, so that the singers could do their *riyaaz* (practice) well. In the songs composed by Rabi, the various different tunes and a multitude of emotions provided happiness beyond measure. Even the children's hearts were full of joy emanating from the songs.

Jyoti couldn't help commenting: "In the songs we composed, there was the sombre depth of the Upanishads. But in Rabi's creation, the Brahma sangeet received its closure!"

In fact, during that phase, when Jyoti was experimenting with both eastern and western music, recreating the pieces of the Indian ustads in the piano and churning their tunes with his own musical persona, Rabi was his closest accomplice in that mission. Rabi didn't use these experiments in the Brahma sangeet he created, but when the dance drama 'Balmiki Pratibha' was written and enacted on stage to celebrate the arrival of erudite guests in the Thakurbari, it brough forth a true revolution of music, illuminating the whole space. More than an opera, in Rabi's words, it was a musical drama in its truest sense. Rabi himself in the role of Balmiki, the saint, put on an extraordinary performance, but it was the young girl Pratibha, Hemen's daughter who mesmerized everyone, playing the role of Saraswati, the goddess of learning. Rabi's exceptional abilities in singing and music composition as well as acting were revealed to the world outside Jorasanko for the first time with this show. Bankim Chandra, the literary doyenne of those days was ecstatic to see the wonderful talent of the youngest son of Debendranath Thakur.

The days were passing by in the joys of creativity. But Satyen and Gyanada were still concerned about Rabi's future. Gyanada wanted Rabi to go to England once again. He needed to explore the greater universe and be a part of it, rather than just spending his days looking at Kadambari's face. Why wouldn't Rabi go back to England and finish his studies which he had left midway? Satyen too wanted Rabi to do that. Taraknath Palit requested Maharshi Debendranath the same, 'Let Rabi go to England and finish his degree so that he can become a barrister.'

Rabi, on his part, wished the same. None of his dear and near ones, his friends and relatives were happy that he returned to India without completing his studies. Just when he had started to immerse himself in his studies, his father beckoned him to India. He sought his father's permission to venture overseas and finish the unfinished task. Finally, Debendranath gave him the much-needed permission, on a single condition. Rabi would have to write him a letter every month from England without fail. But despite all preparations, Rabi could not go, and Kadambari was the cause behind it.

Jyoti, besides pursuing his music, started visiting Binodini all over again, upon returning to Kolkata. After crying silently over this for some time, Kadambari summoned Malini, the book-seller woman.

Malini flopped down on the floor, keeping the bundle of her books there. "*Notun Bouthan*, there is a strange smell in your room, whenever I come here, I feel so sad and melancholic!"

Kadambari was restless. She came to the point right away. "Malini, come, let us plan to see a theatre show one of these days! I've heard Binodini is acting in the new drama directed by Girish Ghosh!"

"Really, *Bouthan*? Do you really want to go?" Malini suddenly became cautious. "Be careful though, what if somebody sees you venturing outside? Remember, *Mejo Bouthan* is in the house now, and she pries around everybody all the time!"

"I don't care if she sees me going." Kadambari sounded desperate. "Just arrange for your tickets…it will be just like the last time, you, me, and Rupa."

Rupa, brimming with excitement at that moment, said: "*Notun Bouthan*, let us ask Rabi dada to join us secretly! It will be great fun!"

'Not a bad idea at all!' Kadambari thought to herself. 'But what if Rabi doesn't agree to it? But then, there is no way he would disagree…He runs after me, follows me always like the mesmerised baby deer of Shakuntala!'

Kadambari was standing in front of the mirror, adding a garland of bel flowers to her newly made bun. Sounding a bit unmindful, she said: "I can tell him to go, but people will recognize Rabi in that case, and then they will speculate, who is the veiled woman accompanying him!"

"Let them speculate!" Rupa didn't seem to care. "Your face will be covered, nobody will be able to see it, isn't it?"

But Kadambari couldn't be as daring as Rupa. "No, no! We can't take that risk! He will be terribly embarrassed if he gets caught. And people will doubt me, above all!" She said.

Finally, when Kadambari did venture out to see the theatre show, it spelled her doom. After all the praise she had received for her acting in the play 'Manmayee', she harboured the thought that her expertise in acting was in no way lesser than a professional stage actress. Her own acting, shaped by her education and aesthetic tastes can let her spread her wings much beyond the elevated stature those prostitutes, public women can accomplish with their performances. But that day, in the theatre show, Binodini startled her with amazement beyond her imagination. Her free, effortless movement on the stage seemed like that of a majestic queen. Her illuminating presence amid the frequent claps of the audience was felt with her perfectly groomed beauty and elegance, her controlled voice modulation, which flourished under the tutelage of Girish Ghosh. Somehow, Kadambari felt that if she were there on stage like Binodini, she could have awed the audience in the same way. If that would happen ever, what would Jyotirindra do, seeing the beloved actress floating amid waves of the 'encore' sound of the masses? Would he love it, or would he be envious, wrathful at her success?

At the very next moment, her joyous dreams, her fantasies withered. Her body, covered under the simple, unceremonious *dhanekhali* sari seemed insignificant to herself. Just then, she noticed her husband Jyoti. He was sitting at the front row, and till then, she couldn't see him from behind. Just when he stood up and started throwing a flower garland at Binodini on stage, giving her a standing ovation, a sense of sordid darkness and gloom overpowered her whole being. Her numb body leaned on Rupa's shoulders. After a while, when she started feeling a bit better, Rupa and Malini took her back to Jorasanko.

Upon returning home, Kadambari took out the globules of opium, long hidden inside a silver container in her bed chamber and consumed all of them at once. At night, when Rabi entered the room to make her listen to a new song he had composed, he discovered his *Notun Bouthan* lying on the floor like a broken vine, with white frothy foams coming out from both corners of her lips.

For the next three days, the people of the Thakurbari gave up all their other works and responsibilities in a desperate bid to cure Kadambari. Rabi was especially devastated due to the sudden onslaught of this incident. He simply didn't have the heart to go away to England, leaving her at God's mercy at the end of a dangerous mountain ditch.

As Kadambari regained her senses, Jyoti took her along with him to the mountains in the far west. Inside her empty, abandoned room in the third floor, Rabi started writing the verse 'Suicide of the Star' in his notebook, churning all the agony of his heart he felt for his *Notun Bouthan*.

He wrote a letter to her: "I so much wished that you would say: 'I just saw such a beautiful valley over there, with a quaint little waterfall flowing. As soon as I saw the beautiful scene, I thought, if Bhanu would have been here, he would have really enjoyed it!'"

'Broken Heart', the long verse of Rabi was quite a sensation among the readers; the youth started to revere and look upon Rabi as the reincarnation of Shelley, the English poet in Bengal. His big, flowing hair, his sense of dressing, everything regarding him became a fashion statement that the youth idolized and tried to imitate.

The messenger from Tripura came all the way to Jorasanko, bearing news that the king of Tripura, His Majesty Birchandra Manikya had appreciated the poem very much. But Priyanath Sen, one of Rabi's friends didn't seem to like the poem at all. Bihari Lal, the eminent poet, of course, liked it a lot. Rabi would frequently visit Bihari Lal these days. He would witness without fail how every day, Bihari would sit on the embroidered rug on the floor and write his verses, and while writing, he would call Rabi and express his pleasure in meeting him. Both the poets, the senior one and the junior one indulged in exchanges, arguments regarding the rhythm of poetry.

Once Kadambari returned, there were preparations going on inside the Thakurbari regarding their new play 'Vasanta Utsav' (Spring Festival). Kadambari would play the lead role of the play, the heroine Leela. Jyoti would play the hero. The female monk who was kind enough to reunite Leela with her lover would be played by Swarnakumari. Rabi played the antagonist, fighting a lot in the play, twirling and swirling with his sword.

During the show, Kadambari sang a tragic song in the raga *Bagesri*:

"In the moonless, starless night sky shrouded with dark clouds, / My heart is covered with an impenetrable dark…"

In her long, open tresses flowing all the way till her back, in her dark pool of melancholic eyes, the imagined beauty of the sad, mourning Leela was enlivened in the viewers' minds.

Meanwhile, though Rabi, Jyoti and Swarnakumari tried to keep her in happy spirits always, the other women in the inner quarters didn't seem to leave an opportunity to belittle, insult Kadambari. Their sarcastic remarks started pouring as soon as she joined them in cutting the vegetables.

Some said: "*Notun Bou*, why all this drama? We all go through some amount of pain, don't we? But we didn't have to swallow poison for that!"

"And if you had to have poison, why did you take such little amount? See, you had to return amid us, after all! And for nothing, the men of the house had to bear so much pain for your sake! Haven't you heard the rumours spreading outside, regarding Jyoti Thakur? How can you show your face after maligning your husband so much?"

How toxic their tongues are! Kadambari thought to herself, and her face turned dark. Indeed, it would have been better if she had died then, why did Rabi have to save her life? Tears of her ashen pain started pouring from her eyes.

Gyanada too expressed her resentment upon Kadambari. Such humiliation faced by the people of the mansion due to this woman was unacceptable to her. "What use is your crying now, *Notun Bou*? You have brought shame upon yourself, and also on others! Do you know how much money was spent to cover up this act of yours? Besides, I can't look at the face of *Notun*, did he deserve such an outcome after loving you so much?"

Rupa couldn't remain quiet any longer. "*Mejo Bouthan*, nobody understands her pain, not even you! Whosoever attempts suicide out of will, and not guided by circumstances? Please give her some time to get healed, to manage her trauma!"

Gyanada was annoyed at Rupa's audacity. "Shut up,

Rupa, don't interfere in all our matters! *Notun Bou*, I tell you, we all face so many storms in our daily life, but taking up those challenges is what life is all about! You can't imagine how I passed my days in England with my frail, ailing body, with my sick children…Swallowing opium to commit suicide is an act of cowardice! You are burning yourself in your agony, and *Notun* is also burning in it. I knew from the beginning; you can't do it. Women like you will never be able to tie back men like him! I knew it!"

"Women like me? What do you mean, *Mejdi*?" Kadambari asked, with her agonized face, her tear-filled eyes. "Would you be able to tolerate it the way I did with a smiling face, seeing my husband running towards the prostitute, just like an insect runs to catch the fire?"

"It is nothing but your false suspicion, *Notun Bou*! All those women are awed by Jyoti's handsome features and his talents, but he never neglected any of your wants! Even today, he goes out with you for a 'change,' he stages dramas, with you as the heroine."

"All of that is an eyewash!" Kadambari said in a low voice. "He doesn't love me anymore. I can't recognize my life partner any longer."

Soudamini was at the helm of affairs within the inner quarters. She sat on a low stool and spat out beetle juice in a silver container and then remarked: "Listen, child, give me a sweet *paan* (betel leaf) to chew on!"

Kadambari looked at her curiously at this sudden proposal of offering her the *paan*. Soudamini picked up a betel leaf and offered it to Kadambari and said: "See, you must remember that men always love to venture outside, go to other women, but if you continue with your suspicious attitude, Jyoti will never step foot inside the house. Live your life with him maintaining a cool head and with some diplomacy, and your crisis will be over."

Some woman remarked from the back, hiding her face: "Just imagine the tantrums that this barren woman throws! Can't you see that your husband is moving away from you because you are childless? If only you were capable of producing a son, I bet your husband would return to you!"

"Who just said that?" Rupa was furious. "What venom are you spewing, hiding behind us? Look at you, ungrateful woman! You utter vile words at the ones who are feeding you, giving you shelter in this house!"

"Oh God! I see that our *Notun Bou* has fostered a venomous child snake!" Some other woman uttered from behind Rupa. Among the innumerable women who were sheltered inside the illustrious Thakurbari, many joined in this soiree, on the pretext of cutting vegetables. The acerbic, jeering remarks and comments came from those women.

An elderly widow told Kadambari on her face: "*Notun Bou*, please don't mind dear, you are somewhat ominous! The child Urmila was with you only; she fell from the stairs and still you didn't wake up from sleep! Also, you couldn't bear a child of your own yet, after so many years...when you are clearly the one to blame, you should keep quiet. All this while, you were doing good, having fun with your musical siestas; why this drama all of a sudden, consuming poison?"

Kadambari's head started reeling at this sudden wave of shock. She started losing her consciousness, thinking of Urmila and her tragic death. Gyanada came forward and somehow made her sit down, and then instructed Rupa to take Kadambari to her own bed chamber. While Rupa escorted her there, Kadambari, like a mad woman, leaned over her shoulders and started humming the lines of a song from the play 'Manmayee':

"Dear, my dear, why, why did this useless life not perish? / Bring me some more poison, I cannot take the pain any longer…"

After this incident, Kadambari didn't wish to stay on in the Jorasanko mansion any more, she accompanied her husband Jyoti and Rabi to their farm house in Chandannagar at the banks of the river Ganges. Some years back, when they had arrived here, they had discovered this little haven of their dreams in the arms of the mighty river, far away from the chaos and mayhem of the Thakurbari.

A canoe boat would be moored to the river bank. When Akshay, their poet friend came along, they sailed in the boat till the middle of the river and held their musical soiree there. The days passed by lazily, indulging in the illusion of a musical world. Most evenings were spent sitting on the grassland close to the banks and singing. Some evenings extended till the dark night, yet Kadambari refused to move away from the river banks. Jyoti had come closer to her now that they were staying together in such an idyllic setting, but he would travel to Kolkata every now and then.

A few days later, they moved to the bungalow of Moram *sahib*. It was a new, elegant-looking bungalow by the side of river Ganges, fortunately. The soothing air emanating from the river seemed to bless the anguished heart of Kadambari with its loving, affectionate touch. Rabi remained cautious not to let any mundane pain cloud her psyche, her consciousness. In Jyoti's absence, he filled Kadambari's leisure time with laughter, music and poetry.

From there, they again moved to another house, this time they rented a house in Suder Street, Calcutta. From 1881 to 1882, the trio spent a whole lot of time outside the peripheries of Jorasanko. Most of all, Kadambari had opposed the idea of returning to the house. Far away from the insults and oppression of the women of Thakurbari, far away from the infinite loneliness of her bedroom in the third floor, she was settled well in the new house at Suder street. While Jyoti wasn't present there always, Rabi was there to give her company. When Rabi would sit and work at his writing table, she would bring him fruit juice. Sometimes, both of them would spend their evenings chatting indulgently, looking at the sky at dusk from the parapet of the terrace.

Some days, Malini came to them with her bouquet of delectable stories. When she saw Malini these days, Kadambari craved to listen to those magical stories, just as she did earlier. It seemed her addiction for those stories had enlivened in her once more. But now, Malini seemed a changed woman. Magic didn't unfold in front of her eyes any more, not in the way it used to.

"Let me show you some new books I have, just like I used to do before! See this book for once, I showed it to Swarna didi the other day and she loved it!" She said.

Kadambari was not much impressed. She would know about such new books from Rabi and Jyoti whenever she wanted; she was not stuck within the inner quarters of Jorasanko any longer. She had other ways to procure books too. When she met Malini, her heart palpitated; she wondered what new, mysterious stories she would narrate, which would follow her like as a lingering shadow, reminding her of the hidden secrets of her own life, and stand in front of her like her own reflection in the mirror!

"Tell me, Malini!" She pleaded every day. "Tell me that strange, mysterious story which hasn't been printed, or published anywhere yet, but which has been inscribed in an unknown ether wave!"

One day, Malini came in with a few barks of the birch tree, in which words were inscribed in handwriting. Her face was lit up in enthusiasm as she said: "Today I will fill you with awe and wonder, *Notun Bouthan*!" With a strange, inexplicable humour embedded in her lips, she started reading out from the pages of the new 'book.'

Rabi didn't compose any song for quite some time now, but now, in his feverish, intoxicated state, he started writing a song. The first two lines came up effortlessly, but when he thought of the third line, he seemed to forget the first line. And when he somehow found the first line, the third line sunk into oblivion.

He was startled, feeling the touch of somebody's warm hands on his forehead. When he turned around, he saw Kadambari standing close to where his head was placed in the bed. With her disheveled hair, her moist eyes, her traditional yellow *taant* sari, she looked ethereal, otherworldly. They kept staring at each other's eyes intently for a while.

He had gone to Kadambari to ask for her forgiveness, but she had been indifferent and answered in sharp, rough words, quite uncharacteristic of her. Rabi had gauged that her anger hadn't diminished fully. Right after this, Kadambari was bed-ridden with her illness, and the two maids, Mano's Mother and Nistarini *dashi* would sit in her room and watch over her. Rabi had gone to see her every morning and evening, yet they hadn't talked much. Jyoti has gone to Shilaidaha for the work of his zamindari estate, hence there were two employees from Jorasanko who stayed on in the house.

"*Notun Bouthan!*" Rabi uttered in an inaudible voice.

Kadambari: Rabi, you are so sick, why didn't you let me know?

Rabi: Even you have high fever, why did you have to come upstairs to me?

Kadambari: Fever is nothing significant for us women. I am letting Sarkar *Moshai* know of your illness, he will bring in Nilu doctor for your treatment. The fever seems quite high, and you haven't got the *jalpatti* (cold water pads) in your forehead yet!

Rabi resisted. "Why such fuss over it? No need to call the doctor…It's just a mild fever that lasted a day, it will be cured on its own!"

"Don't utter a word more…just lie down quietly! I am coming again shortly." Kadambari said, and vanished.

She returned after some time, with a silver bowl filled with cold water and a piece of clean cloth to use as a cold pad for Rabi. Then she sat beside him in the bed and started applying the cold pad on his forehead.

"This is not fair, *Bouthan*…You were supposed to be lying down in the bed now. Why didn't you take the cold pad yourself?" Rabi asked.

"Well, you have the burden of so many complex thoughts on this head of yours. It will harm you if you keep it hot! Our heads, on the other hand, have no value at all." Kadambari replied.

Rabi said: "Every human being thinks, isn't it? But I don't have any hint of what you think these days, what is going on in your mind!"

"Where is the time for you to know that?" Kadambari replied, laughing.

"Yes, I have erred, I admit that! I had been led astray for a while, but is that a mistake which cannot even be forgiven?" Rabi asked.

"There's no question of forgiving, Rabi!" Kadambari said. "Would you always remain inside the house for my sake? Don't I have the ability to understand that?"

Rabi replied: "You know what, *Notun Bouthan*, from this ordeal, I have gained a new realization, a new understanding! In all these months when I have wandered to other places, been close to other people, I realized that I feel the best when I am close to you!"

After two days, Rabi's fever subsided, and Kadambari's fever was gone the next day. The next Sunday, both of them fell ill with fever all over again. Doctor Nilmadhab, their family physician prescribed medicine for both of them. The fever struck them, off and on. Gradually, both of their bodies tolerated this intermittent fever.

When the fever went away temporarily, Rabi started writing again, and Kadambari, on her part, started to clean up the house. After dusk, the two sat face to face with each other and started chatting or singing. Rabi would read out his poem, freshly penned. Kadambari inevitably was the first reader or audience of every composition of Rabi.

One day, while climbing the stairs, the sound of a reading struck Rabi's ears. Who was it reading? He wondered. It didn't seem like Kadambari's voice. With all his curiosity, Rabi swished past the verandah and entered the room of his *Bouthan*.

Just as Rabi entered the room, Malini became cautious and kept away her pile of books, attempting to go away from the scene. Before that could happen, Rabi enquired: "What book were you reading, Malini? I just heard you uttering my name!"

The sudden arrival of Rabi in the room seemed to have shaken Malini from her awed, almost intoxicated state. 'If Rabi Babu hears all this, he will surely think I've gone mad!' She thought to herself.

Malini wanted to put away the book in her bag, but Rabi snatched it from her with an electrifying speed and now it was in his hands. In front of the curious, astonished gaze of all three in the room, the pages of the 'bhurjapatra', the bark of the birch tree turned into shards and vanished into thin air.

Chapter 16

Binodini

Gyanada was gradually feeling stifled, suffocated within the monotonous environment of the Thakurbari. For some days, she decided to settle down with her two children in the mountains of Shimla. She had started to strongly believe that drifting away from Jorasanko would do her good, and also benefit her children. Bibi and Suren were admitted to a school in Shimla, but their actual education happened within the confines of their home, under the tutelage of their mother.

Gyanada read out all classic works of poetry and literature to the children. Her favorite poems included 'Sensitive Point' and 'The Cloud' by Shelley, 'May Queen' and 'The Brook' by Tennyson. She also read the contemporary writings of the poets and writers published in their home journal 'Bharati'. Among the daily chores of Suren and Bibi, they also loved to scribble letters in their raw, wayward handwriting to their cousins of the same age. Thus, avoiding the routine rules and instructions of grammar, they started to cherish their education, touched by the essence of life and the enthusiasm of literature.

Another favourite poem of Gyanada was poet Thomas

Moore's 'Lalla Rukh'. Moore's poems, due to the Irish melodies which were essentially a part of their structure, were read by the members of the Thakurbari in abundance. Satyen had sent the fairy tales of the Grimm brothers and Hans Anderson; and Suren and Bibi fought with each other at all times to get a chance to read the books. Thus, the inheritance of literary tastes of the elders started spreading in the consciousness of the two young children in faraway Shimla.

However, after some time, Gyanada thought it would be wiser and more convenient for her to come back to the plain lands of Calcutta, rather than spending her whole life with the children all by herself in Shimla. Of course, staying in the Thakurbari wasn't an option for her; hence she rented a house and started her domestic life in the neighbourhood of Birjitalao in the Bhowanipur area. It was a grand, spacious two-storied house, with a big hall in the centre of the house as the living area in pure western style, four rooms surrounding the living area, and one more room above the garage. Gyanada found the house very comfortable for living with her children. Living in England for a considerable amount of time had altered her habits forever. The children, Suren and Bibi couldn't eat their daily meals without sitting at their dining table with mats and napkins in western fashion. The traditional environment of the Thakurbari was utterly inconvenient to them. Besides, the stifling surroundings of the inner quarters of women, replete with women's domestic politics seemed intolerable to Gyanada now. She would never want her children to grow up in such a negative environment.

Gyanada's house became the new den for Rabi and Jyoti's *adda* (chitchat) and cultural soirees. From the literary meets of 'Bharati' to the musical evenings, playing newly composed songs on the piano, everything happened here. Their friends including Akshay, Priyanath, Biharilal gathered here, as well as Swarnakumari and her husband Janakinath. Janakinath had been to England for studies, leaving his wife Swarna in her paternal home, but he returned to India, following the tragic death of their child Urmila. Sometimes, Soudamini and Barnakumari too came here to indulge in chitchat. The only person who never visited was *Notun Bou* Kadambari, who was staying in Suder Street now. She was, in fact, never invited to Gyanada's house. Gyanada herself wanted to be the centre of attraction in such gatherings, hence she didn't want to invite her competitor to ruin the fun. She was rather enthused to inspire the poets and composers Jyoti and Rabi to create plays and musical collages, dance dramas, and it was obvious that they both would discuss literature and poetry with her. In fact, she took it all for granted. Didn't she build herself for this purpose, bit by bit, from the scratch?

She thought of Swarna, her sister-in-law. The fact that Swarna could read out her poems in broad daylight in literary meetings along with her brothers, or that Kadambari could sail on a canoe boat with Jyoti's friends and mesmerise them with her singing was all due to her! Who else but herself paved that path to freedom for them, she thought to herself! Would they have seen the face of light if she hadn't stepped out, breaking the dark, patriarchal threshold of the Thakurbari? They would have remained within the threshold, trapped within the four walls of Jorasanko and spent their lives in the same monotonous routine of the household.

And yes, Kadambari was the only person to whom she

had been defeated a number of times. How could Gyanada forget the shameless conduct of Jyoti, Rabi, Akshay, Biharilal with *Notun Bou* in their literary gathering at the terrace in spite of her own towering presence? And now, look at Jyoti—his heart and soul are away from home, she thought. No surprise at all—she said to herself. She always had this strong belief that a creative, talented soul like Jyoti would never be content with such a wife. Moreover, Kadambari had turned into an extremely nagging wife these days, crying and complaining at all times. How long would Jyoti tolerate her?

After their musical evenings, Jyoti often didn't feel like returning to his own house, hence he stayed on in Gyanada's place. Gyanada too, loved to tend to her dear brother-in-law, with all her love, affection and care. She felt a strong connection with him, a bond which was still strong, years after his marriage. Jyoti bought expensive furniture and decorated his new house in Suder Street with them, and Kadambari's distinct touch embellished the house further. However, Jyoti felt a sense of monotony usurping him in the house. Amid all the extravagance of music and poetry, amid all luxuries of life, their conjugal life felt suffocated due to the dearth of a new life force.

Jyoti felt a whiff of fresh air in the liberated, affectionate environment of Gyanada's house, he felt his spirits enlivened amid such surroundings. Not only his *Mejo Bouthan*, but her children surrounded him with tender love. If only he could gift his wife Kadambari with a baby! Alas, that was not meant to be! Jyoti blamed himself for that, and decided not to return home, in sheer frustration.

Rabi warned him, "*Notun Bouthan* will be very angry, Jyoti dada…I won't be able to manage her anger!"

"I will return tomorrow and take care of her. You better return to Suder Street and keep a watch on her for the night, Rabi." Jyoti ordered him.

"Why can't she stay alone for just one night? Is that such a big deal?" Gyanada remarked, while laying down the dining table. "Let me send the driver and give her the news…Rabi, you too stay here for the night!" She added.

Bibi came close to Rabi and started pulling his hand. "Please don't go tonight, Rabi *Ka*, let us all sing together, like the way we used to do in England." She implored.

Rabi was now in a strange dilemma, looking at the little girl's tender face, hungry for love and affection. But then, he instantly remembered the face of his lonely, dismayed *Notun Bouthan* and proceeded towards the house in Suder Street.

The next morning, when Jyoti woke up from sleep, he instinctively remembered not his wife's face, but that of Binodini, the actress. At the start of the day, his meditation was centered on his muse, the lady of his dreams, and since Kadambari couldn't enter that dream world, his love that was hibernating since long, was rejuvenated once again. He decided that the visit was long overdue; so he would go to Binodini's abode and see her before returning home.

The breakfast table started ringing in Gyanada's dining area, in pure British fashion, which meant that food was ready at the dining table. Gyanada was not appreciative of all that the English folks did in their daily lives, but she imbibed their qualities and attributes that she personally liked or admired. She thought much highly about their well-mannered domestic life, the rules surrounding that life, including the manners of sitting at the dining table together for the daily meals. In the Bengali households, it was a norm to arrange for the meal of the masters of the house first, according to their time and convenience, followed by the meals of the boys and girls, the young members of the house. Finally, the women of the house would have their meals when everybody else had finished eating. Gyanada felt it was a wastage of time, and also, the women toiled unnecessarily in the process. If everybody in the household had their meals together, the women could clean the table much earlier and devote their time and energy to other fruitful pursuits, like reading, or other favourable hobbies. Moreover, it was such a bliss to sit and eat the meals together, she thought. The free, uninhibited mixing that was inherent in the close personal talks, the laughter and cheer among the family members, was the real elixir of a familial relationship in her eyes.

When Jyoti came to the dining table, he noticed that Bibi, Suren and Gyanada were already seated there. But they hadn't started eating yet; they were all waiting for him. The menu for the breakfast was purely Bengali, though. When he looked at the smoking hot fish kachoris, a staple favourite of the Thakurbari, he could gauge his irresistible hunger. Along with the tempting kachoris, the fruit juice with ice chips and the *mohan bhog* (dessert) garnished with cashew nuts and raisins in the porcelain bowl beckoned him.

"Would you return home now, Jyoti? Why, you have just come, haven't you? Stay here and relax for a couple more days!" Gyanada insisted.

Jyoti laughed at the suggestion. "What are you saying, *Mejo Bouthan*? I come to your house almost every day! Don't I have any work to do during the daytime?"

"Well, come back after your job is over, then. You know, we are having Hilsa fish in the menu for lunch!" It seemed as if Gyanada was luring a young boy with scrumptious dreams of food.

Jyoti laughed at this offer. "And what about my anguished wife, she will probably go and lock herself up in a room out of anger and frustration! Will you feel amused if she does that? Why are you still so angry with that poor woman?"

"Ah, why do you think I care?" Gyanada was furious. "Is she a member of my family that I will get angry on her?"

"And what about me? What sin did I commit, that you want to detain me in your prison, my Goddess?" Jyoti asked, in jest.

"As if you don't know...I want to hold you back because I am so fond of you! Your *Mej da* is so far away from home always, do I like to carry on with this home only with Suren and Bibi? Once you're here, there is a wave of joy that bounces back in all of us! Even Bibi and Suren get so happy to have you, don't you understand that?" Gyanada said in a childish, demanding voice.

"Well, I promise I'll come back either tomorrow or day after, *Bouthan*...but do grant me leave for today!" Jyoti placed a hand over Gyanada's hand and pleaded.

"Which kingdom are you going to conquer now, let me ask?" Gyanada was curious. "I'm sure you aren't going back home so soon!"

"I need to go and meet Binodini; I want to make her a heroine in my forthcoming play." Jyoti replied, turning away his face.

Gyanada looked at Jyoti with her sharp, piercing glance. She held him by his chin and directed his face towards her. "Can you speak the truth, *Notun Thakurpo*, is Kadambari's suspicion true? Have you truly fallen for Binodini?"

Jyoti moved away from Gyanada and stood by the window. "How would I make you understand, *Mejo Bouthan*? Don't you know how sometimes, the heroine becomes a muse, an inspiration to the playwright? It sounds really gross when you perceive inspiration as mundane love! Don't belittle this relation and pull it to the ground in this way, I beg of you!"

Gyanada was afraid, lest Jyoti thought about her the way he imagined Kadambari to think, regarding the presence of Binodini in his life. No, she couldn't be as crude in her thoughts as Kadambari, hence she rectified herself quickly. "No, don't worry, *Thakurpo*...If Binodini happens to be the inspiration behind your creative works, I won't judge her by blatant standards of love. And also, I won't detain you any longer. Go to your muse right away!"

When Jyoti reached Binodini's place, the environment there seemed gloomy and sullen to him. In Binodini's face, he noticed a shadow of oncoming doom. Girish Babu was tearing the hairs on his head, and Amritlal was sitting quietly in a corner with a glum face.

Binodini was blessed with a rich lover and admirer of her art, and recently he had got married secretly. Jyoti knew that she was in deep agony due to this reason. However, it was most unlikely that everybody in the room was depressed for the same reason. What else had happened? He wondered.

Jyoti looked around at everybody's face and enquired: "What happened, Binodini? Has anyone fallen sick?"

Binodini replied in a moist, tear-laden voice: "No, Jyoti Babu! It seems my dreams will remain elusive forever. You know, I've been driven away from National Theatre. Girish Babu wants to form a new theatre group now, but that will be a failed pursuit too, due to dearth of money!"

"Then Girish Babu will be a part of other theatre initiatives, now that he is leaving National! That is such great news!" Jyoti seemed ecstatic.

Girish said: "Listen, Thakur Babu…No gentleman in his right senses can stay in National Theatre anymore! The owner is insulting everybody at the slightest pretext. Since Binodini had been to Banaras for a holiday, he deducted money from her monthly wages. Hence, she left National out of sheer anger. Even I have severed my ties with National and want to do my plays with a new company. You are a wealthy, prosperous man with such great influence! Please see what can be done under such circumstances."

"Tell me what I can do!" Jyoti replied, eagerly. He was prepared to go to any extent, just to wipe away the tears from Binodini's eyes.

"Money, lot of money is needed to make things happen. Can you bring us money? Theatre is not a passion or a hobby for me, my daily bread and my life depends on it."

Jyoti cursed himself silently, blamed himself in severe words. How would he afford to give Girish Babu tons of money? At the most, he could try to collect some amount of money somehow. *Babamoshai*, his father wouldn't allow squandering so much money on theatre, and presently, his financial condition was not that sound. However, looking at Binodini's distraught face, he became desperate, and uttered: "Well, I can give some amount of money, and I can also collect some more. You must not sit idly with no hopes at all!"

Binodini came closer to Jyoti and held his hand. "Is it true that something can be done? If you can really build our new theatre company, I swear I'll be your slave forever!" She said, brimming with emotions.

Jyoti's whole body shivered in an unnamed rhapsody. For all these days, Binodini hadn't let him come this close to her. Now, when she herself came to him, he wished he could immortalize this moment of togetherness.

But at that very moment, a young man entered the room, with the smell of foreign liquor all over his body. With an exquisite coat, with a long gold chain dangling in his neck, with expensive diamond rings in his fingers, he looked regal indeed. As he entered, he took his cues from the conversation between Jyoti and Binodini and remarked: "Binodini, would you care to be a slave of another great man now, leaving me alone?"

Binodini became stiff and awkward the moment she noticed him. She quickly moved away and said: "Gurmukh Babu, please have a seat. Don't wobble so much!"

Girish Babu came forward to greet Gurmukh a bit more politely. The son of a wealthy father that he was, he might be of help in their theatrical pursuits. He covered up for Binodini and said: "Ah, don't speak like that with him, Binod! He seems to have a fondness for theatre, so treat him well, I say."

As for Girish himself, he did not want to be a part of National Theatre anymore. The owner Pratap Chandra usually listened to him, though he neglected the other artists. The artists, though anguished with such discrimination and injustice meted out, listened to Girish Babu and kept working. However, of late, Pratap started neglecting Girish too, overlooking the fact that National Theatre had thrived and attained commercial success for all these years due to Girish and Binodini. Girish, under such circumstances, was dying to turn around and start afresh. He had founded a new theatre group named 'Kolkata Star Company.' Stalwart actors including Amritlal Mitra, Nilmadhab Chakraborty, Aghornath Pathak and actresses including Binodini, Khetramani, Kadambini, Gangamoni had joined his group. Their old play titled 'Sita Haran' (Sita's Abduction) was being staged under this new banner, but since they could not secure a definite stage yet, it was performed all over the city. Girish was certain that it wouldn't work like this forever, so he was desperate to form a full-fledged stage for these plays. Hence, it had been imperative to get hold of a wealthy 'Babu,' a true connoisseur of theatre. With his cunning manipulation, Girish wanted to use Binodini as the bait to secure that 'Babu.'

As Binodini came closer to Gurmukh, he said: "No, Girish Babu, you're wrong! I don't love theatre; I only love Binodini. Come, Binodini, come to my bosom!" He pulled her by the hand and ordered, shamelessly.

Annoyed, irritated at this gesture, Binodini released her hand. The trivial mention of the word 'theatre' irked her immensely. Since the past few days, this young boy who had just grown a beard and turned into an adult had started to flirt around her, demanding her attraction. However, Binodini didn't attach any importance to him as her heart was still full of love for her ex-lover.

Girish was annoyed too. "In that case, you can leave now, Gurmukh. We are having some serious discussion with theatre, you see!" He said.

Jyoti couldn't tolerate the audacity of the fellow, who seemed to be a drunkard. He stood up and said: "Will you go on your own, or will I have to drag you away from here?"

"Ah, whom do I see? Is this Jyotirindra of the famous Thakurbari? The moon has suddenly arrived, piercing the darkness!" Gurmukh remarked, laughing defiantly, irritating every soul in the room. "So, were you selling yourself off to this gentleman, Binod? Is this the serious discussion that was being mentioned just now?"

"Listen, Gurmukh Babu!" Binodini said, loud and clear. "You are surely mistaken. We have left National Theatre, and want to form a new theatre group. We need money to form and sustain our initiative. Hence, we were having this meeting on how to collect that money for our cause. I was telling Jyoti Thakur, if he can form our theatre group and fund it, I would be his slave forever."

"How much money do you want?" Gurmukh appeared valourous all of a sudden. He could buy everything in the world which could possibly be bought with money. He proclaimed, rather ecstatically: "Binodini, I swear, I will give you the full amount that you'll need to form your theatre company."

Jyoti felt as if a dart had pierced through his heart just then. But then, he realized his helplessness; he couldn't promise to pay the lumpsum amount the way Gurmukh had promised to.

"Will you be able to? But Gurmukh Babu, you don't

know how much money we need! It is indeed a huge sum." Binodini replied in a honeyed voice now.

"Well, I will donate as much money as it takes, just for your sake, beautiful woman!" Gurmukh proclaimed with pride. "I don't care much about theatre; but I'll give the money anyway, to fulfil your desire!"

Girish chimed in now. "But Gurmukh, will you give away so much money out of nothing? Won't you demand a share of the theatre company? Of course, we will give you that, even if you don't ask for it! If you can really contribute to this cause, your name will be immortalized in the history of Bengali theatre!"

"Huh, life is short, who cares about share? And who cares about immortality? I only care about Binodini; I want her!" Gurmukh replied, laughing out loud.

"Why are you talking in this way?" Jyoti interrupted him. "Is this a fish market? Are you saving our theatre with your money or buying Binodini with it?"

"Now, now, finally you speak my mind, Jyoti Babu!" Gurmukh jumped in excitement. "Both theatre and Binodini are same in my eyes! This is nothing else but a transaction in the marketplace of beauty and youth!"

"Shame on him, Binodini! How are you still putting up with him? Why aren't you pushing him by the neck, and driving him away from here?" Jyoti replied, furious.

"Ah, Jyoti Babu, try to understand…If he really gives us money as promised, and we can form our new theatre company with it, we are okay to accept any condition that he asks for. Let us discuss freely, don't spread violence unnecessarily!" Girish tried to refrain Jyoti.

"But...but this man is insulting Binodini repeatedly!" Jyoti's heart swelled in anger and dismay.

"What kind of insult?" Gurmukh seemed astonished, and added. "I will do everything for Binodini, as I said. I will even name the theatre company after her! Binod, won't you love me after all this?"

Binodini smiled softly and came closer to Gurmukh. "Are you speaking the truth? Will the theatre company be named after me? Nobody has ever said this to me before!" The promise of Gurmukh seemed like a balm to heal her bruises.

She placed her own hand over Jyoti's hand to soothe his angry soul, and said to him: "See, Jyoti Thakur, he has made such a wonderful proposal; don't be angry on him anymore! You know, I don't feel insulted so easily these days."

Girish wasn't happy with such a proposal, obviously. He couldn't accept the fact that the theatre of his dreams will be named after Binodini. Won't the public condemn the act? One could make a prostitute act in plays, but naming a theatre company after her was outrageous!

He camouflaged the discussion regarding the name and replied: "We can think about the name of the theatre company later; let it happen first. If Gurmukh Babu really contributes money for this theatre, he will do it for your sake, Binod. But remember, theatre is always greater than yourself, or any actress, for that matter!"

"No, Girish Babu! I will name the theatre company after Binodini...I will also write the share in her name. I don't want any share for myself, I only want to have Binodini." Gurmukh said.

Amritlal chimed in at this moment. "You have a good proposal. However, it's not a norm to name a theatre company after living actors or actresses. And you also have to think that if you name it after Binod, the heads of our society will start boycotting our theatre. Why create such a hustle unnecessarily? All of us present here know that you want to dedicate it to Binodini, isn't that enough?"

Gurmukh wanted to know Binodini's opinion. "My beautiful lady, I can give you fifty thousand rupees right now, you decide whether you want to keep the money for yourself, or listen to these people and invest the whole amount on your theatre!"

"I don't have any greed for money, Gurmukh Babu," Binodini said. "If you want to contribute the money, do it for our theatre…if Girish Babu writes a share in my name from that amount, I will happily receive that."

"This girl has really surprised me!" Girish exclaimed, laughing heartily. "She seems to have no interest in money, she is only keen to do theatre, and sacrifice her life for it! Jyoti Thakur, have you seen any other actress like her?"

Jyoti left Binodini's abode, deeply annoyed and frustrated. Binodini couldn't detain him even after she ran after him, calling his name several times.

Gurmukh bought Binodini with the amount of money he had promised, and Girish finalized the deal with him. Binodini, however, was a bit reluctant to agree to the terms and conditions of Gurmukh. It was still okay to give him company once in a while, but her heart did not agree to be his kept woman. On one hand, there was the star-studded sky of the stage beckoning her to be a fairy of that sky; on the other hand, her fellow artists of the stage pestering her for a dark, murky life. The more she strived to elevate her being, her life, leaving behind her dark past of a prostitute, the more everyone forced her to be drowned in the muck.

The members of the Calcutta Star Company pleaded to her earnestly. Finally, Girish summoned her and said: "There is no other option, Binod...You love theatre, don't you? You have to sacrifice yourself to the cause of theatre."

The earnest request of Girish was like the final order for Binodini. And since the theatre was formed in her name, Binodini sacrificed herself to the desires of Gurmukh. A plot was bought in Beadon Street shortly after, and the rehearsals started in a rented house near it. For quite some time, Binodini was hopeful that to honour her, the theatre would be named B-Theatre, if not Binodini Theatre. Gurmukh had promised her that, professing his love for her. But Girish Babu and Amritlal didn't agree to it till the end. Binodini got to know that the name had been registered as 'Star Theatre.' The cause for which she sold herself seemed utterly futile when the theatre didn't carry an iota of her own name. The mammoth betrayal broke her soul. She noticed that during the rehearsals, the behaviour of everybody around her had changed drastically. Nobody seemed to treat her with any respect. Even Girish Babu seemed to avoid her, out of his sense of guilt. Tears of anguish and humiliation gushed out of Binodini's eyes. She stopped going to the rehearsals and for days, lay down in her bed in her dark, gloomy room.

This frustrated Gurmukh to no ends. Did he splurge all this money to treat a pain-stricken woman? Where was the lively spirited Binodini, where did all her glamour vanish? He met Girish one day and blurted out in anger. By then, Girish had understood the injustice meted out to Binodini. He had already rejected the idea of giving a share of the theatre to her. But in spite of everything, he couldn't exclude her completely. On one hand, Gurmukh was getting angry, on the other hand, the audience were still in love with her performance.

Girish managed to convince Binodini to return to the theatre. In fact, Binodini was feeling suffocated and literally dying to return to it. She adjusted to all deprivation she was subjected to. Upon returning home, she wrote in her own diary: "I returned to work because I loved theatre, but I couldn't forget the bruise, the agony of being deceived."

On July 21, 1883, Star Theatre was inaugurated with the play 'Daksha Jagya' written by Girish Ghosh himself. Binodini's acting in the role of Sati seemed to surpass all her previous roles in her entire acting career. During the first show, the gate of the theatre hall couldn't be closed due to the pressure of the audience; countless people had to return from the gate.

Binodini, on her part, was engrossed in a new game of love with Gurmukh, her new companion with whom she shared her joys and woes. But then, one day, Binodini's old lover came back to reclaim her.

"Why did you have to go to that scoundrel Gurmukh? Is it only for money? In that case, I can give you ten thousand more than what he has given you." He said defiantly.

Binodini was enraged. "You didn't care for anything when you left me! You can leave your money with you! I have earned loads of money all my life, but money could never buy me...The money that you are offering me will come to me again!" She said.

Furious at Binodini's words, the old lover opened his sword and came to attack her with it. There was a mayhem everywhere in the room. If there was even an iota of love in Binodini's heart for this man, it was diminished with this incident. Gurmukh took her away from Calcutta to protect her from the evil clutches of the man. With their departure, a new episode of rumours and scandals about them unfolded.

One day, upon returning to Kolkata, Gurmukh said to Binodini: "Binod, I am so overwhelmed with the pressure of my family members these days! I think I have no option left but to go back home and live with them…My heart and soul doesn't agree to leave you and go back home, what do I do, tell me?"

Binodini's eyes were moist with tears. She lifted her eyes like un unfathomable ocean and replied in a teary voice: "I left everything at your overwhelming demand! I left my old lover, I even turned away Jyoti Thakur whom I respected so much, and now you are leaving me amid this deep mess?"

There was an inexplicable tug of war between desire and pain that was reflected in the face of nineteen-year-old Gurmukh. It seemed that the two opposing emotions were playing with his whole being like sunshine and rain. He belonged to a very wealthy Marwari family; it was quite natural that after witnessing his arbitrary, despotic ways for quite some time, his family members and relatives were trying to control him now. Initially, they were not able to separate him from Binodini. However, his mother threatened to commit suicide, and that made him change his mind.

"I don't want to go away from you, Binod, but I have to go, for the sake of my mother." Gurmukh tucked his head in her lap and assured: "But I promise I won't leave you in deep mess, I'll arrange something for you before I leave."

"But once you leave me and go away, which sort of arrangement can make me happy? And what is the use for it?" Binodini replied, anxious, worried. "Besides, things were different before you started to live with me…but now, the relation between the people of the theatre group and myself has changed so much! The fact is that, you founded this theatre group for my sake, and now, too many people are dictating the group. I am totally unnecessary now!"

"No, no, Binod, I wouldn't let that happen!" Gurmukh said in a firm voice. "You have given me immense happiness in all these days and I also know how important a role you have played in forming the Star Theatre. Let me transfer all my shares of the theatre in your name. You will be the very deserving partner and shareholder of Star!"

But this was not meant to be. Girish Ghosh and his accomplices prevented this from happening with all their might. After all, Binodini was a whore, and nobody agreed to work under her. Girish, after his failed attempts to convince Binodini to work under such circumstances, went to her mother with the request to intervene. They would be in grave danger if Binodini remained stubborn in her decision not to act for them. In fact, Star Theatre would stop functioning.

Finally, the four of Girish's accomplices—Amritlal Basu, Dasucharan Niyogi, Hariprasad Basu and Amritlal Mitra bought Star Theatre with a paltry amount of eleven thousand rupees. Binodini was deprived once again. She felt despicable and lost. Her old lover had left her, as did Gurmukh. The betrayal of her mentor Girish Babu and the cold, indifferent behaviour of her fellow actors saddened her. She didn't have any dearth of admirers among her audience, but as soon as the light on the stage went off, they too vanished into thin air. She didn't have any real human she could turn to, for love and support.

Under such circumstances, the only shoulder that Binodini found solace and comfort in was that of Jyoti Thakur.

Chapter 17

Mrinalini

When Rabi's second attempt to study in England failed, Debendranath Thakur was determined to marry him off quickly. After Kadambari's sickness, when she had recovered a bit, Rabi had even boarded a ship to England with his nephew Satya. But the more the ship drifted away from the main land, the more homesick Satya started feeling, deep within. He had been married for a couple of years by now. Remembering the tender, loving face of his wife, his heart ached with indescribable pain. They had barely reached Madras when he decided that he wouldn't proceed with this trip any more. 'I'm having acute diarrhea, a terrible dysentery'—he announced, and decided to go back to Kolkata from there.

Rabi, on the other hand, was acquainted with a gentleman named Ashutosh Chowdhury. Rabi was not willing to go back to Calcutta, but when both Rabi and Ashu were unable to convince Satya and make the trip, Rabi had no other choice than to disembark the ship with Satya, along with his belongings.

But just disembarking from the ship was not enough, Rabi needed to prepare an explanation for this decision too. With a lot of fear and anxiety in his mind, he wrote a telegram to his father from Madras. Deben instructed both the offenders to come to Mussourie without further delay and meet him. Rabi made a trip to Surat from Madras, stayed with Satyen for a day and then reached Mussourie.

Debendranath was living in the mountains for quite some time now. He had quite an eventful journey from Darjeeling to Calcutta, and from Calcutta to Haridwar, a long, long way which he travelled in a boat. Then, he had been to Mussourie via Dehra Doon, where he had sheltered himself for quite a while. Of late, he had been suffering from various ailments, like piles and an infection in his foot, for which he came down to Dehra Doon for treatment and then, went back to Mussouri again. Dr. Maclaren, the surgeon in Dehra Doon was his medical advisor. In Mussourie, he had visitors from time to time. His sons and sons-in-law visited him sometimes. Jyoti had recently stayed a month with him. Besides, Satish, Barnakumari's husband came to visit him after he had returned from Scotland with his coveted degree. Ecstatic at the success of his son-in-law, Debendranath had gifted a cheque of twelve thousand rupees in the name of his daughter and son-in-law, so that they could build their own home. He had also gifted some money to Swarnakumari, his other daughter.

Debendranath didn't scold Rabi and Satya much; contrary to Rabi's fear. In fact, he was doubtful since the beginning whether Satya would be able to make it to England at all. He turned to Rabi and said: "If being a barrister is not in your destiny, you should get married now and be a family man!"

Rabi lowered his head and sat down, quiet, wordless. He didn't wish to marry an illiterate girl according to his father's wish, not at all. After spending some quality time with his father in the mountains, he returned home.

Upon Rabi's return, preparations had been started to search for a suitable bride for his marriage. However, the old tradition of the maids searching for potential brides was discarded this time. Rabi's elder sisters-in-law decided they would themselves venture out and choose a bride for him. This marked a new phase in the history of Thakurbari. Gyanada intended to be entrusted with this responsibility, and once she found a suitable bride, she was determined to groom the girl herself and then send her to convent school with her own daughter, Bibi. Kadambari, on the other hand, didn't rely much on convent education. It was her strong wish to teach Rabi's wife lessons in poetry and literature.

Meanwhile, there was a marriage proposal for Rabi that came from a very rich zamindar family in Madras. The prospective bride, the zamindar's daughter was the inheritor of seven lakh rupees. Rabi went to see the bride-to-be, accompanied by Jyoti, Gyanada and Kadambari. When they stepped inside the zamindar's house, two young girls came to them and started chatting uninhibitedly. The more beautiful, smart girl among the two attracted the attention of everyone. She seemed to have an avid interest in music too, apparent in her conversations. The other girl, silent, reticent, sat quietly, away from all attention like a bundle wrapped with expensive clothes. When the master of the house, the zamindar entered the room, he pointed his finger at the smart, beautiful girl among the two and introduced her: "Here is my wife!" Then, pointing towards the quiet, almost immobile girl, he said: "Here is my daughter!"

The guests looked at each other, surprised, shocked, yet trying to maintain their decorum of politeness. As soon as they came back home, they burst out, laughing to their heart's content.

"Ah, poor Rabi had fallen in love with the wife of the zamindar!" Kadambari almost rolled on the floor, laughing. Gyanada joined in the riot of laughter and added: "See, this tells us that we shouldn't take any more risk and go to Jessore, to look for Rabi's Mrinalini…"

Jyoti laughed and replied: "Yes…I'm sure that some girl is observing a strict penance in Jessore; she knows Rabi will rescue her from there!"

Jyoti, Rabi, Gyanada and Kadambari set out together for Jessore in the hot, sultry summer month of *Jaishtha*, accompanied by Rupa, Bibi, Suren, the servants and maids and the Brahmin cooks of Jorasanko. Upon reaching Jessore, they took shelter in Gyanada's brothers' house. Almost every day, they would venture out to the adjacent villages--Changutia, Dakshindihi and so on, in palanquins or in boats, to see the prospective brides. But there seemed to be a dearth of brides in Jessore this time; Rabi's sisters-in-law didn't feel any of them were up to the mark.

Soon enough, the rains poured in to bring some relief from the unbearably hot, sultry month of *Jaishtha*, and the village roads became muddy, slippery. The women usually travelled in a palanquin, and Rabi usually walked with the other men in the neighbourhood, if the distance was short. Since the people of aristocratic gentry of the Thakurbari never walked on such muddy streets, the fear of falling down overpowered them at every turn.

Soon, one day, this fear turned true when the groom himself slipped and fell down while walking on the muddy road of Dakshindihi village, in his quest to see a prospective bride. Rabi, decked up in a fancy gown embellished with *chikan* embroidery work of Lucknow, in a shawl with exquisite *dhakai* design, was now bespattered with mud and dirt. And the pair of shoes made of carpet, which his *Notun Bouthan* had designed for him was nowhere in sight. Strangely enough, a young girl emerged out of nowhere and laughed out loud at Rabi's tragic predicament. Embarrassed beyond explanation, Rabi remembered the words: "From where did that sweet, high-pitched sound of laughter emerge in its full vigour and rhapsody, with its liquid, lyrical waves, startling the birds perched on the *Ashwatha* trees nearby?"

As the men were busy pulling Rabi up from the muddy road, his sisters-in-law peeped from the palanquin behind, trying to gauge the situation. Some of them even tried to look for the source of the ringing laughter. Meanwhile, poor Rabi found out a young girl seated on a pile of bricks, breaking out in wild laughter. Some acquaintance of the girl ran after her and brought her to them.

It was soon discovered that the man who ran to catch the girl was an employee of the estate of Thakurbari, Beni Roy *Mahashay*, and the young girl was his daughter Bhabatarini. He had come to his ancestral village to meet his family for a short vacation. While he was pleasantly surprised and overwhelmed to see his employers in his village roads, he was equally embarrassed and ashamed of his daughter's uncouth, impolite behaviour. He kept apologizing and insisting that Rabi and Jyoti visit his house, especially Rabi, who needed to change his clothes right away. Though he didn't have the capacity to provide expensive attire befitting his *chhoto Babu*'s status, he could certainly give him a clean dhoti and a shawl to wear.

Rabi pondered on the suggestion and deemed it a good decision. How long would Rabi stand in such a despicable mud-smeared condition? And honestly, he couldn't go to see the girl they were supposed to see today under such circumstances! With no other option in sight, the full team reached the house of Beni Roy and received their warm hospitality. Once the women of Jorasanko came to know of the actions of Beni Roy's young daughter in full details, Gyanada and Kadambari broke into peals of laughter. Bhabatarini, of course, was brought to them now, decked up in a sari and looking entirely different.

"I like the girl, not bad at all!" Kadambari commented, reclining on a pillow, once they returned to their relative's house from Beni Roy's place. "You might say she isn't beautiful enough, but she is innocent and bubbly, spirited in her demeanour. She will be a good match for Rabi, I believe."

Jyoti said in an easy banter: "How do you solve all these strange mysteries of matchmaking? Do you really think Rabi won't get a more beautiful girl as his bride?"

Gyanada was hesitant. "We need to see a few more girls and then take the final decision. Besides, Bhabatarini doesn't know singing; she is uneducated too."

Kadambari couldn't agree. "We can teach her everything!" She said, with confidence. "Which bride of Thakurbari didn't come uninitiated, young? Our education began at the school of Jorasanko and ended here, isn't it?"

"But why did you like this girl so much, after seeing so many others? What did you find in her that attracted you so much? Is it because she made Rabi feel miserable?" Jyoti was curious to know.

Kadambari had her own logic, and she made it clear now. "Didn't you see, this girl isn't as rustic as the other girls! She didn't sit, awkward and shy in a corner, rather, she can talk without inhibitions. We can educate her and groom her according to our desire."

"Actually, Kadambari doesn't want a beautiful bride for Rabi!" Gyanada laughed and threw a sarcastic comment. "She is afraid, lest Rabi would forget her *Notun Bouthan* once his beautiful bride ensnares his heart!"

Gyanada had thrown a dart with her words, piercing Kadambari's heart. How crooked and twisted her thoughts were, Kadambari thought. She too had to reply in her defense: "What are you talking about, *Mejdi*? I would never think of Rabi's wife as my competitor! In fact, I would love her, cherish her so much! May she never have to go through the life experiences which I have had to tolerate!"

The sting of Kadambari's words were felt by Gyanada now. "Listen, *Notun Bou*, you have no idea what I myself have done, what I had to tolerate! You will never be able to tolerate them, not in seven births!" She said.

Rabi remained quiet all this while, but he couldn't take it any longer. "I beg of you both, don't start with all this again! If you go on like this, I'll cancel this whole idea of my marriage! Rather, I'm thinking of writing a fresh new story about this expedition of seeing the prospective brides." He remarked.

Kadambari replied, laughing: "Listen, Rabi, don't forget to write the story about the groom-to-be, slipping in the mud and falling miserably!"

Jyoti added: "And also about the girl and her ringing

laughter while seeing him falling down! Don't omit that, I say."

Then he kept a hand on Kadambari's back and said to her: "Listen, *Notun Bou*, it's great that you liked this girl for Rabi. But if *Mejo Bouthan* finds peace in seeing a couple more girls, why would you object at all? We also need to know Rabi's opinion, don't we?"

Rabi wished to lighten the clouds of misunderstanding shrouding them and said: "No, *Bouthan*, I'm being really impatient now! Let them be illiterate, let them not know singing, I don't care about any of it! Tomorrow, first thing in the morning, hang myself to the neck of any girl that you can see in town. Besides, don't you know, the pundits have forbidden the society to educate women folk? Once a housewife starts reading novels and drama, her domestic duties are totally forgotten!"

Kadambari pulled Rabi's hair and replied: "Wait, let me show you the outcome of worshipping your pundit!"

There was a magazine in Rabi's hand. He moved away, laughing, and said to Jyoti: "See, Jyoti Dada, how that shy child bride of yours has changed after being educated, see how quarrelsome she has been! Bhudeb Mukhopadhyay, the author is right in his opinion, isn't he? Let me read out what he writes: 'The men have turned into *sahibs* after having their English education, and the women are turning into *bibis*, even without learning English…their homes remain messy, untidy, the quality of their daily meals deteriorate, their health declines…'"

"Huh! How ridiculous!" Kadambari said, enraged. "One doesn't understand what cleanliness and hygiene mean, if he/she remains uneducated. If only I would have

Bhudeb Babu in front of me, I would have explained this to him!"

Gyanada chimed in at this point, laughing loud. "You know, because of people like Bhudeb Babu, the emancipation of women in this country is still unattainable. These people need to be forced to travel to England and see for themselves—how vain and wrong their notions regarding educated women and domestic duties are. I would rather say we ought to take lessons in neat domestic lives from British women! Rabi, can't you reply to these false writings with the power of your pen?"

Jyoti laughed and said: "*Mejo Bouthan*, you're asking Rabi, but don't you know that Rabi had written that article in 'Bharati' which carried effusive praise of the British women he happened to meet, and our *Babamoshai* was so scared, reading that article? Don't you remember how scared he became, thinking that Rabi would marry a *memsahib*, and strictly ordered him to return home right away, leaving his studies in the midway? And now, you are telling Rabi to write a reply to Bhudeb Babu?"

Rabi laughed too, and replied: "Why do I have to write a reply, when there are so many women among you, the reincarnations of Goddess Saraswati, who can write as a mark of protest? What do you think about the writings of our own 'Lahorini' which are published in 'Bharati' recently?"

Kadambari replied: "But you know, she had to undergo a lot of criticism and censure from her in-laws' for her articles! Ironically enough, she has been voicing the truth all along! Why on earth would men determine what clothes women would wear?"

Gyanada looked at Kadambari and asked: "*Notun Bou*, just think about it...How would Rabi, who had been so fascinated by the smart, emancipated British women seem to grow a liking for the village belle Bhabatarini? And if he marries her, would he want to design her dresses too?"

"But then, why did you yourself come to travel in this village area, *Mejo Bouthan*?" Rabi said, in order to save Kadambari. "You could have just gone ahead and searched for a *memsahib* for me!"

"Well, then just say that you liked Bhabatarini a lot!" Gyanada said with a sullen face. "If both of you like her so much, why do I still bother about finding a bride for you? Isn't it like the old proverb: To be abused by them we do good?"

Jyoti added: "Or else, you can say: "Though the groom himself is careless about his own marriage, the neighbours are moving mountains for him!" *Mejo Bouthan,* you better start applying *maida* and cream on the girl Bhabatarini's skin, just the way Mother used to apply on the skins of all of you as child brides!"

Rabi gauged that Gyanada was angry, by looking at her face. In the tug of war between two sisters-in-law, he had taken the side of Kadambari. He quickly sat beneath Gyanada's feet and tried to appease her. "Goddess mine, if you remain angry, this humble human offspring will never marry at all! I don't care about marrying this mischievous village belle at all! Let us cancel this plan of my wedding and leave the sultry village roads of Jessore. Let us return to the mesmerizing Brighton villa shrouded by clouds instead."

One fine day, Rabi and Jyoti met Harry *sahib* in the

streets of a village in Jessore. With his disheveled hair, he looked sad and lost. A teenage boy with the same disheveled look was accompanying him. Harry said that the boy was a warrior, engaged in the freedom movement of India. Harry himself was actively involved with this Swadeshi group. Together, they wanted the support and assistance of the villagers to materialize their mission.

When Rabi and Jyoti brought along Harry to their relative's house where they were staying, Rupa ran out of nowhere, in her ecstasy to meet her dear Harry Sahib. Rupa's heart was filled with pride to know the fact that Harry had joined hands with the Swadeshi boys to attain *swaraj* (freedom) of the motherland. But she couldn't speak to him in the open, in front of everybody. And since they were living in a rural area now, speaking to men was even more forbidden there. Rupa had to go inside the house after merely exchanging a couple of words, for the fear of being severely reprimanded by Kadambari.

However, Rupa came to the 'baithak khana', the living area outside once more, on the pretext of offering tea and snacks. Just as she came, Harry tucked a small piece of paper in one of her hands. Rupa went away with it to the edge of the pond, her heart palpitating in anxiety and excitement. As she opened the piece of paper, she saw its contents. Harry had asked her to meet him at the backside of the haunted temple in the neighbourhood in the afternoon the very next day! A tinge of rebellion swayed Rupa's heart at that very moment.

Rupa and Harry *sahib*'s clandestine love affair went on for all the days that the Thakur family stayed in their relative's house in Jessore. Their volatile days of love were replete with their dreams of revolution. Harry brought out a copy of the holy Gita from his bag, wrapped in a red cover. Seated on the brittle stairs of the haunted temple, both placed their hands on the Gita and promised to remain beside each other, unfazed by their rough, uncertain future.

Meanwhile, scrutinizing all prospective brides in the whole district of Jessore, Gyanada couldn't find anyone better than Bhabatarini. With no other option in sight, they left Jessore with the final decision of getting Rabi married to Beni Roy's daughter. Rupa left her beloved Harry *sahib* amid tears of separation.

Upon reaching Jorasanko, Rabi was in a dilemma about his own marriage yet again. When Debendranath knew about it through Jyoti, he summoned Rabi to Mussourie to have a heart-to-heart talk with him. In this trip, Bibi and Suren accompanied Rabi in a second-class train compartment. His journey became an exciting, exhilarating one, filled with childlike adventure with the incessant chatter, endless singing, and mischief of these two dear young ones. No servant or maid accompanied them in this trip. Hence, Bibi and Suren had to share some regular chores among themselves. Sometimes, after the meals, Bibi had to go to the toilet to wash the dishes, and sometimes, Suren had to run to buy food from the vendors. They were really cherishing their freedom through these necessary, inevitable lessons of life.

Maharshi Debendranath scolded Rabi for the dilemma in his mind regarding his marriage. 'You cannot while away your time like this...It's high time you settle down and have a domestic life! From now on, you have to be attentive about familial matters, and also learn to take the responsibilities of the zamindari estate. Rabi's objections weren't taken into consideration at all after this. In the official notebook of the Thakurbari, 'the accounts of Rabi Babu's marriage' were documented. A messenger was sent to Jessore at Beni Roy's house for the 'paka kotha' or final words about the wedding, along with diamond ornaments and a doll as a token of blessing for the would-be-bride.

During those days, the city of Calcutta was turbulent with Sir Surendranath Banerjee, the nationalist leader, his two-month-old prison sentence and his subsequent release from prison. Following his release, he was felicitated at Free Church College in Nimtala. The students and the youth, in their zeal and their patriotic fervour, adored the presence of Surendranath as their ubiquitous leader. Rabi sang a couple of new songs for Surendranath in a public assembly. However, in his writings published during that time, there was no mention of this incident, and this made the skeptics critical of him. Among his own family members, his elder sister Swarnakumari enquired: "Rabi, don't you think you should have written a piece in protest of Surendranath's arrest by the British?"

Rabi seemed annoyed. "*Naw didi*, why do you have to assume that your thoughts will always align with mine? I already wrote songs for him, didn't I? Why do I have to write a fresh piece of protest for him yet again? I don't like exaggeration in anything, so to speak!" He said.

Janakinath, the strict nationalist was extremely enthusiastic in these matters. He asked: "Why, Rabi, what did you see as an exaggeration?"

Rabi replied with a smile: "Well, what do you think about your young girl Sarala and her friends and their newfound zeal of patriotism? They are tying black bands in their hands and going to school every day as a protest against the arrest of Suren Banerjee, isn't that outlandish?

How much of politics do these young children understand, tell me? Of late, I've learnt that they have two gurus— Kamini Roy and Abala Basu in Bethun School, who study in higher classes. Sarala and her gang of friends blindly follow their teachings and emulate them without knowing anything. This creates unnecessary excitement in young minds, but can never give birth to true patriotism."

Swarna, his sister, was a bit offended. "Rabi, I can't agree with you here. I didn't know of Sarala's recent actions, but now that I know, I truly feel proud of her!"

"But I cannot accept such strange and outlandish behaviour, however you may try to justify it! Nationalism among the students and the youth today has been just a fad, instead of being a strong, inherent feeling! And you know, the Bengali newspapers have made this a huge political issue and started bashing the British in a tasteless way, which is again intolerable to me. Have they forgotten the decency of language in their reproachful reporting?" Rabi asked.

Both Swarna and her husband Janakinath were immersed in the pursuits of nationalism and theosophy, apart from their daily work. The husband and the wife seemed to be enthusiastic about these two apparently disconnected subjects. Janaki, on one hand, was actively involved in the politics of the National Congress, while on the other hand, he was cultivating the studies of the after-life and the supernatural as a member of the Theosophical Society.

Swarna was recently elected the President of the Women's Theosophical Society. Everyone gathered at her home in Kashiabagan now; the women whose husbands were active Theosophists were members of this society. Thus, Swarna had befriended many women belonging to the aristocratic households of Calcutta. The two founders of the Theosophical Society, Madame Blatavosky and Cl. Alcott were also regular visitors at her home. They both initiated the women into this society, and the women regarded them with the highest esteem and reverence, just after the Gods.

One day when Rabi went there, he saw that they were all seated at the hall. Cl. Alcott rushed to the bedroom adjacent to the hall, while speaking something important. After a couple of minutes, he came back and said that the great soul, Mahatma Kuthomi had emerged in that room. He had summoned Alcott to listen to his message, and left after that.

The ladies present in the hall trembled in unexplained joy and astonishment. Swarna seemed to be illuminated in a divine splendour. Her residence had been sanctified by the pure, divine aura of the supernatural arrival of Mahatma Kuthomi. Her elder daughter Hiranmoyee had already been initiated into the society, now the very young girl Sarala too insisted on being initiated, inspired by the celestial aura of the environment that had been created in their house. Rabi himself was into the studies of spirituality and after-life, and had a deep interest in planchet and connecting with souls. But with his recent exposure to the Theosophical Society in Swarna's house, the environment seemed fake and hypocritical to him. How did his dear *Naw didi* Swarnakumari get involved in all this, he wondered. Rabi felt his world drifting apart from his sister's, gradually. They were now poles apart in their thoughts, their mental worlds. Rabi flew away from Kashiabagan silently, discreetly.

After a few days, there was a new madness and

excitement at the Thakurbari, as the preparations for a trip to Karwar began. At the *Baithak Khana* (living areas) of both Kashiabagan and Jorasanko, the tailors started to sew clothes of various designs. Kadambari and Swarnakumari had ordered for jackets with attractive new designs. A big gang of the Thakurbari had decided to go for a trip to Karwar. The travelers included the gang of Suder Street, comprising of Jyoti, Rabi and Kadambari, Swarna and her husband Janakinath from Kashiabagan, Soudamini and Pratibha of Jorasanko Thakurbari. This wonderful coastal city surrounded by the mountains in the state of Karnataka was now the workplace of Satyendranath.

In Rabi's heart and soul, there was a subdued pressure of his upcoming wedding day. Would he be able to adjust to his new married life? While strolling around the beach with Kadambari, Rabi expressed his deepest anxiety to her. "That unknown young girl would come out of nowhere and change my life! What would I even speak about to that shy, timid village girl, *Notun Bouthan*?"

The waves of the ocean crashed at his feet with an intense noise and commotion. He felt as if they wanted to assure Rabi that all would be well.

It was the first tryst of Kadambari with the ocean, and she felt happy, content from within. She patted Rabi's cheek and replied: "Ah, would I have to teach you now, what you would talk to your wife about? She is the same age as Sarala and Indira. Don't you speak to both of them endlessly? Why would you have difficulty in speaking to your wife, then?"

"No, *Bouthan*, you don't understand, before I can talk to her, I will have to groom her, teach her some lessons of life, isn't it? Will I have the time for all that? Besides, Bibi,

Sarala are the girls of our own Thakurbari, they have been raised in our own familiar environment. Can we really compare Bibi and Sarala to that village girl?"

Kadambari replied: "Well, that is quite natural! And you know, the grooming lessons in the bedroom are the most romantic ones! Myself, as a young girl would wait the entire day for the most cherished apprenticeship of that 'school'; I would wait eagerly for your *Notun dada* to teach me 'Meghdoot' written by the great poet Kalidasa, I would wait for him the whole day to teach me piano lessons…"

Suddenly, the memory of an intimate scene between Jyoti *dada* and *Notun Bouthan* that Rabi had witnessed years back flashed in his mind, and it seemed as if a wave of current flowed through his heart. He looked at Kadambari with eager eyes and said: "In those days, both of you thought I was just an insignificant young boy; I really felt envious of you! Promise me that you won't move away from me once my wife comes to our house, *Notun Bouthan*?

They had come a long way while strolling along the beach, and there, the thin, emaciated river Kalanadi had merged with the ocean along the rough mountainous coastline. Just behind them, they could hear the mellifluous singing voices of Bibi and Pratibha, and the melodious chitchat of Swarna-Soudamini and Gyanada. Kadambari started playing with the sand, sitting by the beach. Rabi sat beside her and started scribbling on the sand bed. Kadambari lifted her face to read what Rabi had scribbled, and found these two words engraved on the sand bed: 'Hecate Thakrun.'

With a gloomy face, she said: "From now on, you'll forget Hecate, since some other lady is coming to your life!"

Rabi was shocked at this statement. "What are you

saying, *Notun Bouthan*? I cancelled my England trip just for your sake; I don't stay at *Mejo Bouthan*'s house even after her strong and continuous insistence, just for you! I have dedicated so many of my verses to your beautiful eyes." He took Kadambari's hands off from the sand and pressed with his own hands.

Bibi and Pratibha rushed to them and hugged their dear ones, Rabi and Kadambari. The gang of the elders who were walking behind them, reached near them. All of them sat in a big circle on the sand, and started a new session of chitchatting.

Gyanada noticed Rabi's special attention towards Kadambari. What do they talk about all day, Gyanada wondered. Kadambari seemed to usurp Rabi with her magnetic spell. Rabi's Hecate Thakrun was chewing on his young head. "Why do you always get separated from us, Rabi?" She enquired. "Don't you like speaking to us at all?"

"Why such an unjust allegation, *Mejo Bouthan*? Both *Notun Bouthan* and me have a good speed of walking, are you angry because of that?" Rabi said.

Gyanada wasn't the one to give in so easily. "Don't try to cover the truth by camouflaging it, Rabi! Actually, Kadambari doesn't want you to be with me; you don't stay in my house because you fear her crying in despair! Remember how much we chatted together while we were in Brighton?"

Soudamini, Rabi's eldest sister, who was presently the mistress of the Jorasanko Thakurbari, wanted to adjust with everybody and mediate their differences. She stopped Gyanada gently: "Ah, *Mejo Bou*!"

Kadambari couldn't take the allegations against her

silently. "Did you see, *Thakurjhi*, how *Mejdi* is accusing me? This was the reason why I was walking alone, distanced from all of you! There is no peace in my house anyway, wouldn't I get any peace here, in close proximity to the ocean?"

Swarnakumari was the most calm and indifferent soul, in spite of remaining with the rest of them. Without looking away from the sea, she remarked: "Why are you talking about such trivial issues even while standing in front of the huge, magnanimous sea?"

Kadambari detested everything around her at that moment. She turned her back to everybody and started walking briskly along the seashore. Bibi and Pratibha tried to follow her with their light footsteps. The rest of them — Rabi, Gyanada, Swarnakumari and Soudamini started to follow them and return to the bungalow. Along their way, the ocean roared on with her rebellious spirit, like a mark of protest against their petty squabbles.

Satyen was a judge now, and his bungalow, made with pure Burma teakwood, looked like a magnificent palace. The sea and its waves greeted the members of the bungalow every day with a gesture of salaam at their feet. In the solitary evenings, Jyotirindra sat in a pensive mood, amid the lone sound of the water bodies. The magical ocean and its proud stance of not surrendering reminded him of the defiant face of Binodini. Her beautiful face and her eyes, her full breasts, her waist floated in the canvas of his memories and kindled the fire of passion in his whole being. The devil Gurmukh's paws had ravaged her inexplicably attractive body. But had he found a place in her heart and soul too? This magnificent seashore, this star-studded night seemed meaningless, insignificant to Jyoti. He wished to run away to Binodini at this very instant. The irresistible essence of her body seemed to hit his nose from across the miles and miles of their distance, piercing the salty sea winds, and made him crazy for her. When Gyanada returned with the rest of the family, she noticed him sitting silently, with his face lowered to the ground. Rabi and Gyanada sat near him, surrounding him on both sides.

Gyanada, a bit worried to see him like this, placed her hand on his shoulder fondly, and asked: "What happened to you, *Notun Thakurpo*? What makes you sad? Why didn't you come along with us?"

Jyoti silently leaned over his *Mejo Bouthan*'s shoulders. Just as the waves of the ocean arrived at the Bungalow and gently stroked its stairs, with her nimble fingers, Gyanada stroked Jyoti's forehead with her tender love and care.

Suddenly, Rabi pointed his fingers at Gyanada and started singing, breaking the silence around. "Oh Nandarani, please leave my beloved Shyam..."

Soon after he sang the song for a couple of times, Rabi's nieces started singing along with him. They possessed the exceptional quality to pick up new songs and memorize their tunes. The sweet, ringing voices of Bibi and Pratibha mingled with the cherubic voice of Rabi and transformed the anxious evening to a pleasant and lovely one.

A few days after this, there was news from Jorasanko that the arrangements for Rabi's wedding were finalized. Towards the end of the Bengali month of *Karthik*, Rabi, Jyoti and Kadambari traveled from Karwar to Bombay in a ship, and then took the train to Kolkata. For a strange reason, Gyanada didn't attend Rabi's wedding. Soudamini too stayed on in Karwar.

By now, Rabi knew for sure that he had to marry, come

what may, but still the anxieties regarding his marriage overpowered his mind. He wrote a rather humorous letter to his friends Priyanath Sen and Nagendranath Gupta, inviting them for the marriage ceremony.

"On Sunday, the 24th of the Bengali month of *Agrahayan*, in a very auspicious moment, my closest relative Mr. Rabindranath Tagore is about to get married. For this occasion, you are cordially invited to be present in the evening at Debendranath Tagore's residence at 6, Jorasanko, to witness the wedding ceremony and oblige myself and my family members.

Yours sincerely,

Rabindranath Tagore."

The 'gaye holud' ritual of Rabi's wedding was done without much grandeur. Thereafter, Rabi had to go to house number 5 of Jorasanko where his *Mejo Kakima* had arranged for a lavish spread as part of his 'ayeeburo bhat' ritual, his last meal as a bachelor. Jogmaya, Rabi's *Mejo Kakima* (one of his paternal aunts) herself hailed from Jessore; moreover, Bhabatarini was a distant cousin of hers. She was very happy with this alliance.

The three nephews of Rabi—Aban, Gagan and Samar were excited to have their dear Rabi Ka coming to their house and peeped to get a glimpse of him. When Rabi arrived to have his lunch, decked in a gorgeous embroidered shawl in green, his nephew Aban felt as if the Badshah of Delhi had stepped inside their house. There was a meticulous arrangement of various dishes decorated together, and Rabi was made to sit on a beautifully designed 'piri' (stool) to taste them all. All his sisters, sisters-in-law, aunts surrounded him and hurled their insistent queries at him.

"Rabi, did you like your new bride?"

"Rabi, how do you feel about your new bride?"

Rabi had his lunch with his head lowered all the time, so that he could avoid answering these queries. However, he pondered about the same question in his mind. True, how would his new bride be?

The marriage ceremony of Rabi was held in a rather ordinary way, without much grandeur. Rabi walked from one room to the other to take part in the marriage rituals, he roamed around the verandah to the west and then came back to the inner quarters. The marriage happened inside the Jorasanko Thakurbari, where the bride and her family had to come and stay, as per the rules of the Thakurbari.

There was no extravagant arrangement in the wedding. Apart from the immediate family and his in-laws' family, only a few of Rabi's friends and peers attended the ceremony. As for Rabi's marriage attire, he wore an heirloom shawl from Banaras, which all the men in his family have worn as part of the groom's marriage dressing. Rabi came to the marriage altar and stood on the 'piri' (low stool), while an elderly woman, his relative, dressed in a Banarasi sari with a black border greeted him as part of the marriage ritual.

The bride was brought to the inner quarters and made to circle around the groom for seven times. Thereafter, the bride and groom proceeded to the outhouse, where the 'sampradaan' rituals would take place. The women of the house weren't allowed to stay for the 'sampradaan', only the children were witness to the ritual.

After the rituals were over, when Rabi went to the

'bashor' for the post-marriage celebrations, he started to indulge in jokes and pranks to hide his nervous disposition. The women of the house had arranged for a game of 'bharkulo' (a ritualistic game with earthen pots and winnowing fan) and surrounded the bride and the groom to participate in the game. Just as the game started, Rabi turned all the earthen pots upside down and jeopardized the game. His restless mind seemed to wander elsewhere. There was quite an uproar among the women in the room after this sudden act of Rabi.

His *Chhoto Kakima* (aunt) Tripura Sundari couldn't help asking: "What did you do, Rabi? What kind of game are you playing? Why did you turn all the earthen pots upside down?"

Rabi looked all around him and was unable to spot his dearest *Notun Bouthan* anywhere in the room. He replied, restless: "What shall I do, tell me, *Chhoto Kakima*! Can't you see, everything here is helter-skelter, everything in my life is disrupted…Hence, I ransacked the earthen pots with my own hands."

But where was *Notun Bouthan*? It was her dearest Rabi's wedding, and she was nowhere around! Rabi thought of going away from the wedding scene, searching for her, but in the very next moment, he looked at the veiled face of the child bride and thought: 'How innocent this little girl is! She has done nothing wrong to deserve this!' The women of the house, including his *Chhoto Kakima* insisted Rabi to sing for the auspicious occasion. Rabi looked at his new bride with his eyes full of mischief and hummed a song written by his *Naw Didi*, Swarnakumari.

"O my beautiful woman, / Who is that embodiment of lightning?

Her face is beaming with the splendor of the full moon!

Alas, my eyes can't look elsewhere, looking at her wondrous beauty,

Is she an Apsara or Goddess? I don't know who is more beautiful than her!"

The poor bride, the dusky, petite village belle felt awkward and ashamed at this, and pulled her veil a bit more, to cover her face entirely. She had no idea whom she was married to, and which place she was sent to by her parents. Rabi sang a couple more songs, but still the assembly seemed bland, devoid of charm. Where did his Jyoti Dada and *Notun Bouthan* vanish? Even his *Mejdada* Satyendra and *Mejo Bouthan* Gyanada weren't there, and he couldn't understand the reason of their absence. There was the joy of creation in every pore, every curve and crease of the Thakurbari mansion, but ironically, during his wedding, none of that joy resonated.

Instead of the much-deserving joy, there were waves of a gloomy news that dampened the spirits of the house further. Saradaprasad, the eldest son-in-law of Debendranath had gone to Shilaidaha to look after the zamindari estate there, and he died there suddenly. Soudamini, his wife was still in Karwar at that time; Jyoti sent a telegram to her with news of her husband's grave illness. After a couple of days, Satyen and Gyanada reached with Soudamini at the grief-stricken Thakurbari.

The child bride of Rabi was introduced to the members of her new family amid this overwhelming situation of grief and mourning. Keeping in sync with her husband's name, she was rechristened in her in-laws' house as Mrinalini.

Chapter 18

Suicide of the Star

Just after Rabi's marriage, there was a great upheaval within the Thakurbari.

Due to her husband's death, Soudamini became indifferent towards her domestic life. Upon receiving such news, Debendranath visited Jorasanko, coming home from the mountains of the north. After blessing the new bride and groom Rabi and Mrinalini with four precious pieces of 'mohor', he entrusted on Rabi the responsibility to look after the zamindari estate. He also ordered Rabi to send him a mandatory report about the estate every week. For a few days, Debendranath roamed around the river Ganges in a boat, and then, he took shelter in a farmhouse in Chinsura, in the Hoogly district of Bengal.

Maharshi Debendranath had instructed Rabi in a letter: "Please send *Chhoto Bouma* to Loretto House for proper English education. I am quite pleased with the separate arrangement that has been made for her education, segregating her from all other girls in her class. Please use fifteen rupees from the *Sarkari* (office of Jorasanko) which will be needed for her school clothes and the monthly fees for her school."

Meanwhile, Gyanada had made all arrangements to take Mrinalini away from the Jorasanko mansion and to educate her at her own home. To teach her separate classes in isolation in Loretto House, there was an additional seven rupees expense. There was a great need and urgency to groom her as a wife befitting the stature of Rabi, and as a step in that direction, she was enrolled in music school too.

Rabi, however, was a bit indifferent to all this. He couldn't figure out what to do with this child bride who ushered in suddenly, amid the natural flow and rhythm of his life. For all these days, his life was divided between Suder Street where he stayed with his *Notun Bouthan*, and Birjitalao, where he had the company of his *Mejo Bouthan*. Compared to the addictive life in both these houses to which he was attached, the uneventful life of Jorasanko seemed too complacent to his tastes. Presently, in the Jorasanko house, there was neither the fire and zeal of Jyoti dada's creative life, nor the refined literary and artistic environment nurtured by his *Mejo Bouthan* Gyanadanandini. Rabi felt utterly suffocated in the terrible isolation of the room in the third floor. Mrinalini came here as a migratory bird sometimes, but mostly she was at *Mejo Bouthan*'s house. Moreover, his friends seemed to discard him for the fear of disrupting his honeymoon phase. Restless and impatient, Rabi had to write a letter to his dear friend Priyanath Sen: "Is there any chance that the honeymoon stage will be over at all? However, there are certainly phases where the 'moon' itself can increase or decrease in size...also there is the 'poornima', the full moon and the 'amavasya', the no moon stage. Therefore, I request you to barge in suddenly, without bothering about the significance of our honeymoon."

Rabi was restless as he couldn't be party to all the fun at Suder Street or Birjitalao now, leaving his new bride. But now he was relieved that Gyanada, his *Mejo Bouthan* had taken away Mrinalini and the child bride was in her company. Hence, he could be at Gyanada's house in Birjitalao almost every evening, and sometimes, stayed there for the entire night. Gyanada was doing all of this for Mrinalini's education apparently, but she was fulfilling her deepest desire in the process. She was glad to have accomplished the task of severing ties between Rabi and Kadambari. Gyanada envisioned her as *Rahu*, the evil planet who was eclipsing Rabi, bit by bit.

Gyanada, while tying Mrinalini's long tresses into a neat bun, narrated the tale of her own bygone days when she was herself a new bride. "You know, once our Guru Thakur, the saint who was the guru of this entire family arrived. *Babamoshai*, our father-in-law had asked him about the process of *kanyadaan* (offering a daughter in marriage), and at what age, the act of *kanyadaan* was considered the most pious act. He had replied: offering the daughter in marriage at the tender age of seven, which was also referred to as *gauri daan*, was the most pious act. I was married off at the age of seven. The people of Thakurbari in Calcutta would send their maids to Jessore to search for brides, as the girls from Jessore were beautiful. The maids who were skilled to understand the tastes of their masters were sent along with dolls to look for young girls. One such maid went to my parents' house to see me."

"Then, when the maid liked me and finalized my marriage date, *Babamoshai* sent people from the Jorasanko office, maids and servants and also a palanquin to escort me all the way from Jessore to Calcutta." She added, with a sense of nostalgia.

The child bride replied quietly, in her rustic dialect of Jessore: "There were some beautiful toys, saris and jewellery sent from your house for me too! The village folk have never seen such beautiful things before!"

"Ah, don't speak in your Jessore dialect here, girl!" Gyanada warned the naïve Mrinalini. "And listen, my wedding ceremony didn't happen in the Jorasanko premises, as my mother-in-law was still living at that time." Gyanada added, and was immersed in more storytelling and nostalgia of those old days.

"After my marriage, there was a ritual called 'bashi biye', in which the elders of this house, both men and women came to take me away in a palanquin covered from all sides. When the palanquin stopped at the inner quarters of my in-laws' house, my mother-in-law came and picked me up in her arms. She was a very heavy woman, but since I was little and very thin, she could lift me up easily and then, she made me sit in a quiet corner, like a doll. My face was covered in a veil, all the way to my neck, and heavy ornaments were piercing through the skin of my feet. An elderly woman was sitting beside me, counting the money received as part of my dowry. I was crying the entire time!"

She flipped through a few more pages of her old days, immersed in the past: "When my father-in-law came to ask for the dowry money, I started crying more loudly. He asked me: 'Why are you crying, my child?' The people around me replied: 'She wants to go back to her father's house'. 'Tell her I'll send her there.' He replied. 'Look, how clever this girl is! She had to purposefully cry at the exact time when her father-in-law came to ask for the dowry money!' The people around me commented. Thereafter, for quite a few days, those people came to see me regularly and demanded strange things from me.

'Look upwards, Ma!' Some would say, while some other women would see my skin, opening my clothes. I was an extremely shy girl, just like you; I couldn't even talk properly to girls of my age back then."

"But who would tell that now, looking at you! You look like the Goddess Jagatdhatri reincarnate!" Mrinalini said, mustering enough courage to speak up.

"Ah, great! The girl is speaking up, finally!" Gyanada smiled brightly, in utter joy. "But you'll have to get rid of your Jessore accent!

Every evening, the musical soirees started all over again, as Akshay, the poet came along with Jyoti. Gyanada's residence in Birjitalao was filled with a classy concoction of eastern and western melodies played on the piano.

At night, after the exciting episodes of music were over, Rabi slept beside his child bride and at that unlikely hour, the lonely, melancholy face of *Notun Bouthan* haunted his senses. What was she possibly doing now? Had *Notun Dada* returned home? He wondered. It was quite possible that he hadn't returned by then, Rabi knew that his brother had started visiting Binodini yet again. How was the lonely woman spending the night then, all by herself?

Anxious and restless, Rabi left the bed and started loitering around the room. Mrinalini, the young girl asked: "What happened to you? Are you having difficulty in sleeping? Shall I massage your head?"

Rabi felt a tinge of pity, looking into the girl's face.

The naïve, innocent girl had no idea how difficult it was for her to enter the complex psychological world of the twenty-four-year-old Rabi.

Kadambari, however, was truly lonely these days. Rabi couldn't find the time to come and see her. Her husband Jyoti didn't return to her almost every night. When confronted about his whereabouts every night, he got angry and created a huge uproar. Deep within, Kadambari was intensely suspicious about the relation between Jyoti and Binodini...she doubted that he stayed at Binodini's place almost every night.

All night, she struggled to sleep, all day, she remained impatient, agonized. She peeped through the holes of the window in her room and gazed at the streets, the hawkers, the cart-pullers in the streets. She lost attraction in her habit of sewing; the colours in her own soul had faded. She had brought Rupa to her new house in Suder Street, she played cards with her sometimes. Sometimes, she also read out poetry along with her. Each and every small, minuscule sound startled her these days; she looked intently at the door, as if with an eager sense of waiting for someone special who would come back to her.

Meanwhile, Jyoti spent his lazy, indulgent evenings in the presence of Binodini. In Binodini's lap, he rested his head and chatted for hours. "You know, Binod, I have got my ship's hull from an auction recently. Now I will dress up the ship in a grand way and sail with you far, far away!"

"Well, can you buy a ship's hull from a marketplace? What use will it be to you?" Binodini asked in amazement, while massaging Jyoti's head.

"Don't you understand?" Jyoti sat up, in sheer

excitement, and explained to Binodini. "Rather than buying an entire ship, it is more prudent to buy its hull; then you can add an engine and compartments to it for the passengers, and thus create a fine ship in a more economical way! You know, I have a plan to start my own shipping business, competing with the British businessmen! You will see, Binod, how people will love my Swadeshi ship!"

"But aren't you the son of a great zamindar? Why will you get involved in the shipping business, then?" Binodini's amazement didn't cease to expire.

But Jyoti was brimming with a newfound zeal and excitement. He said: "What if I belong to the zamindar family? My grandfather Prince Dwarakanath had founded the 'Tagore Company'; he had created a huge business empire, being the owner of a ship named 'India'. He is still remembered as the first Bengali entrepreneur! Listen, if the Bengali gentlemen can work wonders with their pens, why can't they work wonders with their ships? Binod, you'll see, our shipping company will grow really big one day, and we'll earn loads of money! And I will invest that money in our theatre, I promise!"

He took Binodini in his arms and kissed her with a passionate fervour. "I will create a theatre in your name, my dearest Binodini Sarojini! I will leave none of your desires unfulfilled!"

This felt as a sweet balm in Binodini's bruised soul; she felt overjoyed. In gratitude and intense love, she merged her body, her being with the body, the passionate longings of Jyoti. In every pore of Jyoti's thirsty body, she ushered in as moist raindrops. In that euphoric moment of love, Jyoti immersed his face in the breasts of Binodini, which appeared as heavenly as wood-apple fruits.

After a few minutes, he lifted his reluctant face from her breasts and said: "You are as intoxicating as a forbidden fruit!"

"Why, I've heard you have an incredibly beautiful wife at home, Thakur! Didn't you receive physical pleasure from loving her?" Binodini asked in a rather ironic voice.

She saw a shadow of guilt looming over Jyoti's face. Truly, Jyoti was an offender in Kadambari's life. Pulled by Binodini's irresistible charm, he was betraying her day after day, night after night. And Binodini had hit him in that weak, vulnerable spot.

"Why, my handsome lover, you didn't answer me yet!" Binodini clung to Jyoti's neck and asked him again. She craved to listen to the effusive words of praise about her lovemaking prowess, cherished by men many times before.

Jyoti replied, quietly, in a melancholic voice. "She is the Goddess Lakshmi of my home. When I used to make love to her, it held a pure, divine joy, like lighting a lamp underneath the Tulsi plant. You, on the other hand, are the intoxicating alcohol, the madness behind my creations! Can there be any comparison between the two?"

"What do you mean?" Binodini asked in pseudo-anger. "Are you saying that she is a pure, divine woman and I am an impure, public woman? Why do you come to me, then?"

Binodini forcefully moved herself away from Jyoti. Jyoti went to her and entangled her body with both his hands. "Oh, my *manini*, my dearest angry woman, if you desert me, my writing will stop, my music will desert me. Do you want that?"

Thereafter, the playwright and the queen of the stage became immersed in a wild game of lovemaking yet again, like the primordial man and woman of the earth.

Kadambari writhed in the pain and emotional distress of her lonely, wasted youth, loitering from one room to the other. Her unparalleled beauty and grace didn't attract the attention and loving admiration of mesmerised men anymore. No Rabi followed her around like a pet deer-child, no Biharilal looked at her, spellbound, while reciting his poems. No Akshay Chowdhury burst open in melodious songs, looking intently at her eyes, no lovelorn husband trembled in passion, seeking her company in romance, no infant craved to taste the elixir of the milk in her bosom. What would she do now with all her youthful voluptuousness?

In the portico, the clock struck three in the afternoon. The chiming of the clock was a customary tradition of the Thakurbari and the tradition was kept intact in her Suder Street house. At Jorasanko, the women at this hour would sit down with their maids in the long verandah, and the maids would tie their hairs in fancy buns in various shapes and sizes. There was her own maid who came to Kadambari's house at Suder Street to tie her hair. She tied Kadambari's hair in a fancy bun today, embellishing it with flower buds made with expensive elephant teeth.

After dressing up fully, Kadambari said to Rupa: "Let's elope from the house and explore the world! There are so many things to see in the world outside!"

Rupa was overjoyed at the proposal. "Yes, let's go! But where shall we roam around? We don't know the streets well enough!" She said.

"What if we roam around one house to another with a bag full of books, like Malini? Won't that be great fun?" Kadambari asked.

"But nobody will identify you as a book-seller woman. Even if you wear a simple sari, how will you hide your beauty and your aristocratic presence?" Rupa replied.

"Okay, let us go to Girish Babu then!" Kadambari proclaimed, kindled by an intense desire. "I'll tell him, please groom me, prepare me as a greater actress than Binodini; I want to enthrall and amaze the audience, being on the stage, like the heroine of Malini's story!"

"And what about *Notun dada*? Won't he be furious and attempt to beat you, appearing on the stage?" Rupa burst out into peals of laughter.

"And the police will come and drive him away!" Kadambari too joined in the laughter riot. But after a few moments, she became cautious of the plan, and said: "But what after that? He will inevitably go to that wretched woman Binodini again and hide his face in her bosom! This plan won't work, I tell you…We will have to think of a different way, just wait and let me think!"

Rupa said now, with a newfound excitement: "Shall we go and join a Swadeshi group? Come, let's go to the Swadeshi's in Jessore…we shall serve our country then—"

"And also get to see your dearest Harry *sahib* again, isn't it?" Kadambari took Rupa's hair in her fist and shook it in pseudo-anger. "If you are so keen to go and meet your love in a clandestine *abhisaar*, why do you want to camouflage it with your intention to join the Swadeshi's, and why are you dragging me into all this?"

Rupa's eyes were filled with tears in a sudden burst of emotions. "I won't live without him, *Notun Bouthan*! But nobody in this house will accept this relation…Please save me, I beg of you!"

Kadambari was shocked and startled. "Rupa, what a mess you have created! Whom should I tell this? He is a vagabond Englishman with no house, no shelter of his own! Moreover, he has joined the Swadeshi folks now, and I'm sure the policemen are already after him! If you have to marry him, you'll have to elope from this house…but where will you both stay there? What will you both eat?"

Rupa giggled like child and said: "You know that old proverb: We will practice living a wild, vagabond life, with no settled place for eating or sleeping?"

"Ah, what a sight it will be, Rupa!" Kadambari laughed, rolling on the floor. "You and your dearest Harry *sahib* sleeping in the premise of a temple and people are crowding all over you, shouting: Encore, encore!"

"Ah, what are you saying, *Notun Bouthan*!" Rupa ran away, ashamed and embarrassed.

Startled at the sound of human footsteps near the door, Kadambari saw that Rabi was there. Her eyes became moist in a sudden burst of pain. Instantly, she looked away from him and asked: "Have you come to see if I am alive, Rabi?"

Rabi came near her and turned Kadambari's face towards him, holding her chin. With all his tender love, he wiped away the tears from those kohl-laden eyes with his fingers, and said: "Don't be angry with me, please! Every day I remain worried for you, every night, I remain sleepless, thinking about you. But I couldn't come for all these days…"

"How could you come at all?" Kadambari moved to a distance, pushing away Rabi's hand. "This is the time for you to play with dolls with your new bride! Why would you enjoy the company of your old *Bouthan* now?"

The words of Kadambari shook the very core of Rabi's heart with intense wave of emotions. Was this the same woman whom he reminisced every second of his life? Didn't he have to battle with his own self every fraction of a second to move away from the shadow of this woman who was a Goddess of his heart?

Rabi shrieked in unnamed agony: "If only I could tear apart my bosom and show you my ravaged heart!"

"Don't lie, Rabi!" Kadambari's anguish still lingered within her. "Even you are consoling me with lies like your brother, your *Notun dada*! Nobody loves me anymore!" The light green georgette sari was disheveled from her body and fell on the ground, in sheer indifference.

Rabi's head reeled to see the sudden uncovering of the electrifying beauty in front of him. His eyes seemed to burn, witnessing the unabashed insolence of her silken jacket. He wrapped his hands around her waist and sat on his knees on the ground. "My love is there...it is constant and undying...I have never loved anyone like I've loved you, *Bouthan*! If only I had the means, I could have wiped away all your pain!"

Kadambari too embraced her beloved deer-child, like Shakuntala of the epic Mahabharata. Both embraced each other in intense emotions and wept in an unspoken, indescribable pain.

Unable to spend time at home with Kadambari, Jyoti returned to Jorasanko with her. There were still plenty of people, especially women in the mansion; he felt that Kadambari could spend her time with them in petty domestic squabbles, in laughter and womanly chitchatting. Jyoti, on the other hand, would be able to spend his time with Binodini with the indulgence of love.

Also, he was very involved with his ship these days. He had designed the ship and decorated it with a hefty loan. Gyanada was entrusted with the beautification of the ship's rooms. He could have given that responsibility to Kadambari too, but he couldn't face her these days, due to his immense sense of guilt. Besides, Kadambari, in spite of her fine tastes, didn't have any idea about a ship's rooms or compartments. Gyanada had travelled inside both French and British ships; it was her sheer experience that had contributed to a wonderfully attractive decoration of the ship's interiors.

Jyoti had big plans to start the ferry services in the Khulna-Barishal route with his ship, competing with Flotilla, the British shipping company. 19th of April had been fixed as the day of inauguration of the ship. Jyoti was confirmed that his desi ship would be loved by the people of his own nation. The day of the ship's inauguration in the year 1884, he envisioned, would be inscribed in precious golden waters in the history of shipping business of the Bengalis. He didn't imagine that the day would turn into the darkest, the most doomed day of his life.

Preparations had started with all vigour and enthusiasm for 19th April. All the eminent people of the city were invited for the inauguration of the ship. The *borolaat* or viceroy was invited. Though Jyoti wasn't too fond of the British, he was certain that if the heavyweight *Sahibs* wouldn't attend the event, his ship wouldn't get the much-needed publicity. He also knew that the press would surely come, pulled by the curiosity to witness the shipping business of a Bengali man, but they would literally flock to the event to experience the reactions of the British folks to the phenomenon.

Gyanada, on her part, was busy arranging for the special attires that she and her children, Bibi and Suren would wear for the inauguration. The tailor she employed was working to make the clothes. She was a bit more concerned with the attire that Jyoti would choose to wear for the occasion. She was contemplating whether Jyoti would like to wear a suit, bought from one of the British shops, or he would dress in the regal Indian 'choga-chapkan-pagri', the traditional wear. Of course, Jyoti looked absolutely handsome in whatever he chose to wear. A Punjabi shawl-seller had come to Gyanada's place from Barrabazar area, along with various pieces of cloth with zari and other exquisite embroidery work. Gyanada chose two pieces of cloth from those for Jyoti and Rabi and ordered 'chapkans', the traditional long coats for both of them.

Far away from all this madness, Kadambari sat all alone, with her deep, dark tresses spread out like the monsoon clouds, with her silent, yet intense anguish centered around her husband Jyoti. Her husband didn't involve her in any of the activities of the ship's inauguration. He had involved *Mejo Bouthan* in all those duties and responsibilities, to whom Kadambari was an eyesore. He wasn't at home most of the times, she didn't even know where he spent all the nights these days. She had tolerated all of it, but had their love diminished so much that he would have to rip off her honour of being a companion in such a significant initiative? She wondered.

Jyoti had promised to her that he would surprise everybody by presenting her on the ship on the day of the inauguration. Whoever wants that kind of surprise? All she wanted was to be a participator in the activities surrounding the event. Why this indifference towards her, then? Wouldn't the sweet, dreamy nights with her husband never return to her life again?

However, in spite of everything, Kadambari was silently preparing for the day. She had called in Bishu, the weaver woman and had chosen an orange *Swarnachari* sari to wear for the occasion. Would only Jyoti surprise Kadambari that day? She would also surprise him with her beauty and elegance. She would dress up in the most magnificent look of her entire life, and defeat Gyanada with the unique splendour of her beauty. When she would appear on the deck of the ship, all eyes would be centered on her presence. Gyanada might be more privileged than her, but she knew she wouldn't be able to match Kadambari in beauty and sensitivity. All women in the inner quarters of the Thakurbari discussed this, discreetly. Perhaps, out of this anger, *Mejo Bou* Gyanada tried hard to snatch Jyoti away from her.

Jyoti, on the other hand, ardently wished to bring along Binodini to the ship's inauguration, but Binodini disagreed with him. Jyoti left his home in haste, wondering what he could do about the matter.

Kadambari was in her room, giving some clothes to the washerwoman for washing them. Just as she habitually put her hands into the pockets of one of Jyoti's shirts to remove some papers, she discovered a fragrant envelope and in awe and wonder, opened it. In one corner of the envelope, the word 'Sarojini' was inscribed in feminine letters, and in the middle, Jyoti's name was inscribed with much love and attention. Kadambari's heart palpitated in intense anticipation to read the contents of the letter. She sent the washerwoman away and opened the letter—

'My beloved,

The love and honour that I have received from you is the precious outcome of many of my dreams. I am writing this letter to let you know something which I couldn't utter in your presence. After your mischievous acts of the noon, you are sleeping in deep comfort, resting your head in my pillow, and at the same time, I am writing to you, sitting right beside you. There is a secret brewing between us; in my body, there is a tiny seed of yours that is growing, slowly, gradually. I was feeling sick and nauseous for some days, and also discovered that my menstruation has stopped this month. It felt the same way when I had been pregnant for the first time. I didn't know whether you would be happy to receive this news, hence I couldn't tell you. I wouldn't reveal the identity of my child's father to anyone, it is enough that both of us know. The world would know that the child is mine, and mine alone. I don't wish to lose you at any price whatsoever. Sending you hundreds of kisses and my love, please accept them.

Yours truly, one and only,

Sarojini.'

Kadambari sat down, thunderstruck. The words and phrases mentioned in the letter revolved in her head in all their vehemence—' mischievous acts of the noon', 'tiny seed', 'identity of my child's father'...Holding the letter in her hand, she fell down on the ground, losing her senses. After quite some time, Rupa came to her room and made her regain her consciousness.

For two long days, Kadambari sat transfixed, with the letter in her hand. Her worst fear had come true—Jyoti actually went to Binodini, betraying her faith. The seed of Jyoti was implanted in Binodini's womb—which meant that his manhood was not in vain. This meant that she was truly a barren woman. Everybody in the house mocked her as a barren, infertile woman—and they were right all along! In frustration, in a nameless stigma, she wished to die every moment...but wouldn't she meet Jyoti, her husband for one last time before that? No, she had to wait till the day of the inauguration, and then decide what step she would take.

She touched the saris, read all the letters and anxiously waited for the evening of 19th April. Rupa called the women of Jorasanko to come and see the traumatized Kadambari. Soudamini and Saratkumari came to see her a couple of times, but none of them could break her silence.

A day before the ship's inauguration, Gyanada came along with her children and took refuge in the ship to supervise the entire event herself. Jyoti was there already, for the past three days. Gyanada took on herself the mammoth task of serving exquisite continental and Mughlai cuisine for the guests. She was handling it all meticulously—laying the dining table, taking care of the décor of the ship's interiors. Rabi and Akshay were also frequent visitors—they were taking care of the musical party for the evening.

While on one hand, there were these overwhelming activities, on the other hand, there was an endless waiting. Kadambari pondered on how she would face Jyoti. Would she tell him about the letter, or would she remain mum? If she blamed Jyoti openly for his betrayal, he could also blame her for being a barren, incomplete woman! Would she be able to suppress such emotional distress and stand in front of him with a smiling face?

Meanwhile, there were last minute preparations going on inside the ship. Rabi, seated on the piano, was fumbling with its reeds. He asked: "Jyoti dada, shouldn't you go and bring *Notun Bouthan* now?"

"Yes, I will go…I will go a little later. Let the low tide subside a bit!" Jyoti sat on the piano now, and asked Rabi: "Why aren't you bringing your wife too?"

"I don't know about that, *Mejo Bouthan* must be knowing…" Rabi replied, a bit unmindfully. Jyoti went away to the other side of the ship as the servants summoned him.

Kadambari was anxiously strolling in and out of the house. She had already obtained some opium globules from Bishu, the weaver woman; she had kept them carefully inside a beautiful container made of elephant teeth. The salvation from all her agony, all her pain was within her reach now. But before she ended her life, she wanted to see what destiny had in store for her, for one last time. Just before the evening of 19th April, Hecate *Thakrun* was decked up, resplendent in the orange *swarnachari* sari. She would surely be a head-turner in the party; she anxiously waited to win the end game. She must strive to make his husband return to her heart from all the *dakini-joginis*, the witches, the enchantresses. What if she was a barren woman, she was still beautiful and attractive!

Jyoti, however, couldn't get the time to leave the ship yet. Just like always, she requested Rabi to bring along Kadambari. But Rabi was certain about her fiery rage at the moment. "No, Jyoti dada, you have to go yourself! I can't manage her today!" He said.

But as soon as Jyoti was about to leave, Gyanada, and then the captain of the ship called him back. He also had to stop as some guests reached before time.

****

Kadambari kept on waiting. The early evening turned into late evening, and then into night. She heard a voice enquiring from the terrace: "*Notun Bou*, didn't your husband come to take you along?"

One by one, she took off all her ornaments from her body, then gradually took off her sari and threw it on the floor. She lay down on her bed with her satin petticoat and her silken jacket. She could sense a few faces peeping from the window. They were mumbling something among themselves. In her delirium, Kadambari heard some voices saying 'Sarojini, the ship's name is Sarojini!' Ah, the insult, the betrayal, the shock of her life!

At the wee hours of night, she came down from the bed, opened the container carrying the opium globules and poured all the globules in her mouth. She drank copious amounts of water and then, wobbling like a drunk soul, she fell down on the floor and lay there indefinitely. In the morning, she was discovered in an almost dead state, and then, the excruciating struggle to save her life began. As she struggled in an ocean of pain; her twenty-five-year-old heavenly beauty seemed to gradually transform into a poisonous ivy vine.

Rabi sat beside Kadambari in her bed for two days continually, with a guilty heart. Jyoti moved around the house in a frenzied, alarmed state. He should have speculated beforehand that Kadambari would commit such a disastrous act. All official work of Jorasanko was shelved temporarily. Two famous, eminent doctors—Nilmadhab Haldar and Satish Chandra Mukherjee were appointed to treat Kadambari at home.

However, their heartfelt and best efforts went into vain. Kadambari died at the break of dawn on the fateful day of April 21st.

In her final journey, her companions included Rabi, Somendra, Deependra and Arunendra. Rabi was silent during the entire journey, and remained silent after returning home. In his twenty-four years of life, he hadn't seen death so closely, so intimately. The dearest person of his life went far away from him in a deep, silent anguish, with so many unfulfilled desires, with so many unspoken words between them. If only they all had been a little more attentive to her, this disaster might have been evaded. Also, because Jyoti dada had distanced himself from her, Rabi ought to have come closer to her, to protect her from further distress. This would be a permanent regret in his life.

At Maharshi Debendranath's order, all documents, pieces of paper from Kadambari's room, Binodini's letter, Kadambari's handwritten notes were burnt and destroyed forever. The newspapers were bribed with hefty amounts so that the news of her suicide wouldn't be published. Thus, the tragic death of the most beautiful, melancholic woman of Thakurbari remained shrouded forever in a veil of mystery.

In spite of her physical demise, nobody on earth could uproot the ill-fated Kadambari from Rabi's heart. Rabi had composed these lines after her first attempt of suicide in his long poem titled 'Suicide of the Star':

"If anyone had asked her, I know what she would have said.

All the time she was alive, I knew what burnt her from within."

In his traumatic, delirious state, he started to converse with his *Notun Bouthan* through his verses, one after the other.

Chapter 19

Bijayini

Rupa and Malini had come to Gyanada with a pall of gloom looming large on their entire beings. *Mejo Bouthan's* cold, indifferent attitude, however, amazed them both. Looking at her, it didn't feel that any mishap had happened in the family. Instead of crying after seeing them, she started to look for books inside Malini's bag. Mrinalini, the young girl was seated beside her and looking at the books too.

Mrinalini wasn't wearing a sari, she was dressed in a blue *nayansukh* gown. Gyanada was hell bent on transforming her from a village belle to a fashionable urban girl. With a curious demeanour, the teenager girl asked: "Malini didi, do you have the Second Book of Arithmetic? I just finished the First Book. And do you have the book 'Useful Knowledge?'"

Gyanada smiled and said to her: "No, silly girl, they don't have textbooks of Loretto House! I'll get them for you from College Street very soon…"

Rupa was Kadambari's accomplice in everything she

did. She couldn't tolerate this pronounced indifference of Gyanada anymore. She was well aware of the cold war brewing between Kadambari and Gyanada. But still, she said in an agonized voice: "*Mejo Bouthan*, I can't live in this house any longer! My heart feels empty whenever I stare at the room on the third floor!"

Gyanada remained mum and kept looking at the books of Malini. A servant girl entered the room with a tray full of snacks for Rupa and Malini, the guests. Mrinalini quickly extended the tray to them.

Malini looked once more at the silent Gyanada and remarked: "I wonder why *Notun Bouthan* committed such an act; it's a mystery to me!"

"I'm sure she got tremendously hurt from her near and dear ones!" Rupa added. "She had dressed up with so much love and care for the inauguration party…"

Gyanada interrupted Rupa midway and said: "*Notun Thakurpo* might have been unable to come and take her along to the party, would she have to swallow opium and take her life for such a petty reason?"

"Not everyone can be as strong as you, *Mejo Bouthan*!" Rupa said. "You have a complete domestic life with your children… moreover, you have taken away Jyoti dada and Rabi dada from her. How would you understand what pain she was suffering from?"

"Taken away from her? What do you mean, Rupa? Please think about the consequences of your words before you utter them! I don't like such baseless remarks!" Gyanada was visibly annoyed.

Mrinalini, the innocent young girl couldn't gauge

why the environment in the room suddenly turned gloomy. Looking at everybody's faces, her own face turned sullen and sad.

Rupa was forthright in her voice, in spite of Gyanada's rage. "I have felt her tremendous pain day after day, I've seen it all with my own eyes, as Jyoti dada stayed in your house almost every night."

Malini too spoke up now. "*Mejo Bouthan*, you are such an intelligent woman, how could you fail to understand the way she was decaying bit by bit as her husband drifted away from her? If you wished, you could have easily insisted Jyoti dada to go and reunite with her?"

Gyanada felt she was being cornered by these two women. "You both are misinterpreting the incident, I must say! The dangerous seed of suicide and self-destruction was embedded in Kadambari's own nature…And if you point fingers at me, I could never understand her! Suicide to me, means the ultimate form of defeat. I don't understand why a human would want to end his/her precious life! Is it right to blame *Notun Thakurpo* for this attitude of hers?"

"Anyway, *Mejo Bouthan*, let it be." Malini said. Did you read the poet Akshay Chowdhury's new poem 'Abhimanini Nirjharini' (The Melancholic Fountain)? Let me recite a few lines:

> "To please her, to appease her, I take much care
>
> I laugh and cry, to satisfy her heart's desire.
>
> Hiding my deepest core, I retain her honour.
>
> I chase after her, guided by my own blunders,
>
> But she never looks at me, why such lack of care?"

Gyanada's facial expressions changed while listening to the poem, her face became overcast with gloom. "This poem is clearly written about Kadambari!" She remarked impatiently. "This is gross injustice on the part of Akshay Babu…he doesn't know anything; he only threw random complaints against Jyoti to gain the appreciation of the readers.

"Well, being an outsider, the truth dawned upon him! Why didn't it dawn upon you, being a member of the family, *Mejo Bouthan*?" Rupa didn't leave the opportunity to speak out.

There was a twisted smile in Gyanada's lips after Rupa's comment. "You know, when I had come to this house as a new bride, it was a huge taboo to come out in the open, especially in front of strangers who were men. I feel amused to reminisce the memories of those days. Once, your *Mejdada* wished to introduce his friend Manomohan Ghosh to me. But I was not allowed to venture outside the Thakurbari, and no visitor was permitted to visit us women in the inner quarters. Hence, they both conspired a plan and came together inside the house discreetly in the wee hours of the night. When they both came to my room, my husband let him sit on the bed, inside the shield of the mosquito net, and lay down quietly on the bed. Both myself and his friend sat clumsily inside the mosquito net, me on one corner of the bed, with my veil intact, and he, on the other corner, clueless and lost. Both of us were too shy to utter a word! After a while, my husband stepped out of the bed along with him, their footsteps in sync with each other, and then he escorted his friend out of the house."

Everybody broke out in laughter, listening to Gyanada's story.

Taking a sip of fruit juice from a fancy looking cut-glass vessel, Gyanada said again: "Remember, just because I was the first one to break the glass ceiling, to have provided the courage to the women of this house, Kadambari received so many worshippers and admirers in her garden of paradise! Akshay Babu recited so many poems, sang so many songs in the musical soirees at the terrace, only to get Kadambari's attention, didn't he? The same person is now blaming Jyoti *Thakurpo*, in spite of being his friend...By the way, why aren't you having the snacks?" She passed on the tray of snacks and the glasses to them.

Malini took a bit of the *sandesh* (dessert) and said: "Well, you can discard Akshay Babu's poetic statement, but Biharilal Babu, in his poem 'Shadher Ashon' (The Cherished Seat), gives some descriptions which evaded your eye. Listen to this:

"The men have weird minds, they don't recognize you,

They wonder with what they will get your love—

With their heart, soul, their youthfulness?

Like animals, they crave everyday for new sources of love..."

"Like animals? Really? The poets sometimes have no control over their words and expressions!" Gyanada was annoyed.

Mrinalini uttered, restlessly, impatiently: "Let me ask, did *Notun Bouthan* receive much pain and torment from her husband, *Notun Thakur*? If not, then why did she have to swallow opium and kill herself in spite of a happy life?"

After a few seconds of silence, Gyanada muttered to herself: "*Notun Thakurpo* isn't the one to blame...I had warned from the very start, this marriage will be an unhappy one! She didn't have the power to tie back the bright star that he was, hence she had to end her own life."

Suddenly, Rupa stood up and shouted, pointing fingers at Gyanada. "You...you killed her, you and Jyoti dada killed her together! Bit by bit, she was dying from the poison of your envy, and then she swallowed opium to kill herself. Whom will I live with now? Who will give me shelter?" Kicking at the tray full of sweets and fruits in front of her, turning the glass full of fruit juice upside down, she ran away from the room, perhaps towards an unseen future.

Mrinalini shrunk in an indescribable fear. For a few moments, Gyanada stood transfixed, her tenderness withered for a while. Confused and lost, she thought to herself: "Did I really push Kadambari to the brink of her destruction and death?" She moved to her bed chamber slowly, with a glint of clouds and a shimmer of sunshine playing in her face intermittently.

With Kadambari's death, 'Bharati', the journal of Thakurbari died too. All the members seemed to lose interest in the publication of the journal. Kadambari had been instrumental in bringing together the brightest stars of Bengal's literary world for 'Bharati,' creating a bouquet out of their beautiful presence. But with her absence now, the bouquet was torn. Though Gyanada's house was the meeting place for 'Bharati' and its members of late, deep within, they all knew that it was a temporary affair. Kadambari's room on the third floor was the real address of 'Bharati.'

Rabi didn't wish to carry on his editorial work for 'Bharati' without his *Notun Bouthan*'s company. He became engrossed in the manuscripts of his new books of poetry. Four of his poetry books came in quick succession. He dedicated three of them—'Shoishob Sangeet' (Childhood Songs), 'Prakriti-r Pratishodh' (The Revenge of Nature) and 'Bhanusingher Padabali' (The Hymns of Bhanusingha) to Kadambari.

It was impossible for Jyoti to devote time or attention or his concentration to 'Bharati.' During the daytime, he would wander aimlessly in a confused, lost state, and during the nights, he stayed on either at his *Mejo Bouthan*'s house, or with Binodini. After a few days, an advertisement was published, announcing the closure of 'Bharati.'

But Swarnakumari couldn't accept the sudden and drastic news of the closure of their beloved journal. According to her own opinion, the value of literary work was much more than the value of personal loss. 'How terrible it is that the journal has to stop due to my brothers' indifference!' She thought. She came forward to take the responsibility of the journal on herself. Thus, a new chapter of 'Bharati' started, in the hands of the first woman editor of the times.

However much ravaged Jyoti was deep within, he maintained a normal, unperturbed demeanour in front of the outside world. He was engrossed in both his shipping business and his romantic partner, Binodini. There were enough rumours regarding his prime role in Kadambari's suicide, but his father Debendranath Thakur had shut the mouths of both the newspapers and the immediate family and friends of Jorasanko, ending the possibility of a scandal. Of course, Akshay and Biharilal didn't stop sharing their emotional outpourings in the form of their verses, and Rabi's elegies too reflected his deepest regrets. But such artistic acts of dissent created subtle undulations within the society and then vanished quickly. According to Rabi's own description: 'Jyoti remained as he was previously, resplendent as ever.'

Within a month of Kadambari's death, all arrangements for the ferry services of Khulna-Barishal route were ready. It was decided that on the auspicious day of 23rd May, Jyoti would set out with his ship from the bank of the river Ganges and travel all the way to Barishal, along with his regular companions, Rabi and Akshay. Gyanada was the main motivator behind this initiative. A couple of Jyoti's business initiatives had failed previously, but Gyanada had faith that his bright, enterprising brother-in-law would be successful this time.

With a deep turmoil brewing in his heart, Rabi had agreed to accompany his Jyoti dada. He knew *Notun Bouthan* had left her husband, being bruised by his truant nature, but that didn't diminish his love for his brother. Hiding his intense trauma and pain in a secret container in his heart, Rabi was trying hard to appear normal in his daily chores, maintaining a saner façade to the outer world. Akshay too felt intense anger towards Jyoti for Kadambari's death, but he couldn't leave his old friend. Their friendship was entwined with a strange bond of tender affection.

Nothing stopped for the deceased one. In the morning of 23rd May, they set out for their expedition towards the river banks of the Ganges. With teary eyes, the perfect backdrop was created for the sister-in-law to bid adieu to her brothers-in-law. But at the last moment, Gyanada, unable to trust the three young souls, accompanied them in their journey along with her children.

In the morning, all of them journeyed towards their destination, Koilaghat, via Chitpur road. They traveled the path, witnessing some strange, unique scenes—the chandelier shops and the stables of the horse carriages on both sides of the streets. The gaslights were on since the previous night, and the rays of the sun on top of those lights were glaring to the eyes. The empty trams and the garbage cars of the municipality trudged along the streets in a slow, monotonous pace. They also saw the sheekh kababs and rotis being made right by the meat hanging at the goat meat shops of Muslim owners. While some were seen dusting the streets, some others were reciting from the holy Quran beside the mosque.

When they reached Koilaghat, Rabi looked intently at the boats on the river banks. Don't they look like rows and rows of shoes of humungous giants, standing together? He wondered. The boatmen, upon seeing the group of aristocratic men and a woman, vied for their attention. 'Come to my boat, come to my boat, please!' All of them shouted together at once. Somehow, they rode on one of those boats and reached their next destination, the ship.

The transition from the boat to the ship was an adventurous act in its own right. The boatman, with his incredible skill and acumen, moored the boat to the body of the ship 'Sarojini', approaching from the middle of the river Ganges in its gushing force. Gyanada followed her sprightly children in boarding the ship. She climbed one stair after the other slowly, gracefully and stepped inside the ship. Rabi, Jyoti and Akshay followed her.

Thus, the first historic expedition of 'Sarojini' started in an adventurous spirit, with six curious co-passengers. The ship was running through the water bodies in a frenzied pace. Just as they sat with some chairs at the deck of the ship, their clothes were disheveled in the wind. Rabi's long shirt swelled in the mad gust of the wind; his scarf started flying in the sky. The long, open tresses of Gyanada started dancing like a vigorous snake over her head. Her *nayansukh* sari spread its wings in the mad wind. Bibi's frock, with its beautiful expanse, started roaming round and round like a ballerina, Jyoti's dupatta marched ahead of him like a flag, an emblem of his expedition. Just below them, above the numerous waves of the water bodies, the rays of the sun danced in a mirthful spirit.

Gyanada shut her eyes in intense emotions and said: "*Notun Thakurpo*, I can stay on this deck of yours my entire life! This whole journey in the bosom of river Ganges is unique and unparalleled!" She bent slightly backwards and reclined her head at the back of a chair. After a while, her eyes shut on their own, due to the soothing comfort of the swaying motion of the ship. Jyoti too felt incredibly relaxed after a long time, his agitated nerves were soothed by the beautiful wind blowing by the Ganges. He reclined his head on a chair adjacent to Gyanada and fell into a slumber, snoring lightly.

The small boats nearby were journeying swiftly with a couple of office goers towards one of their familiar river banks. Rabi looked at those boats and became pensive, wrapped in his private thoughts, while Bibi and Suren started pulling his hands continuously.

Just then, *Karta Babu*, the old man in charge of the ship came to them and announced: "Something very alarming has happened! After the ship has started to sail, we have discovered that the captain is absconding!"

"Oh God! What will happen now? How will the ship

sail without the captain?" Jyoti said, waking up from his slumber with a sudden jolt of anxiety.

Gyanada too felt disillusioned; her spell of intoxication was over. Was she going to fall into deep waters with her two children and three stupid, young co-travellers? "In such a situation, it is perhaps best to stop the journey right away and drop the anchor of the ship!" She instructed.

But Jyoti was adamant. "No need to do that...The other employees can operate the ship skillfully. They are no less efficient than the captain!" He said.

The old *Karta Babu* too agreed with Jyoti's opinion. "No need to stop the ship, they will be able to run the ship quite capably."

The ship, of course, stopped abruptly at a point, after an apparently smooth sailing. When they reached near the Shibpur Botanical Garden, the ship's heart stopped responding, the machine stopped functioning. It was discovered that one of the parts of the machine had opened and needed immediate repairing. Jyoti had to anchor the ship there for a couple of hours.

As Rabi glanced at the ethereal beauty of the river Ganges, he remembered his blissful days spent with his beloved *Notun Bouthan* at the banks of the river. The scenes, the visuals of those days flashed in front of his furtive eyes. The river Ganges of the present times merged with those priceless images of the past. Rabi wrote in his diary:

"I am sitting pensive, lost in thoughts, looking at the beauty of the banks of the river. Such unparalleled beauty of the river, starting from the southern part of Shantipur... The trees and shadowy huts on both sides that we pass through, endlessly, offer such soothing pleasure to the eyes!

Somewhere, the banks are filled with green grass, spilling over the lap of river Ganges, somewhere else, the water of the river gushes forward, enmeshed with the dense trees and creeper vines, their shadows swaying over the water continually. Some random sunrays shine resplendent over those shadows, and some others shine over the smooth, tender, trembling green leaves of the trees. One boat is moored to the bark of a tree, and it is sleeping peacefully under the comforting shadow, swayed by the melodious, incessant music of the water bodies. On one side of it, amid the dense canopy of trees, a brittle, crooked road embedded with footprints has descended till the start of the river body. The village belles walk through that path with earthen pots tucked in their waists to get water from the river, while the young boys have a lot of fun while falling over the mud, throwing water over each other, swimming in the shallow waters near the river bank. Looking at these ancient, brittle river banks, one can almost forget that they are man-made — like the trees nestled here, the banks seem to be the natural belongings of the river. The *Ashwatha* trees have sprouted from within its crevices, and grasses have emerged from the bricks of the stairs… Moss has accumulated on the skin of the river banks with years and years of the monsoon rains, and its colour has merged seamlessly with the luscious greenery all around. It is nothing but the marvel of Mother Nature, who seems to have added her own brushstrokes in the places where humans thought their job had ended. She has meticulously destroyed the proud, white shield of cleanliness and established unique sweetness in all its fragile, chaotic beauty. All the boys and girls, men and women of this village who come to the river bank have a special relation to it—either a grandchild, or a nephew, or mother or aunt. When their grandfathers and grandmothers were young boys and girls like them, they used to play in the stairs of the banks, in the monsoon season, they slipped and fell down, just as they do now. And that eminent blind singer Srinivas who sang with his violin every evening at the river bank, and the village people who gathered around him to listen to his music—does anybody remember those old days anymore?

There is such a special appeal even in the fragile beauty of the old, brittle temples on the shores of the river Ganges! They might not have any idols of Gods left inside them, but like an ancient saint, each of these dilapidated temples have been divine, pure, worthy of worshipping in their own right. In isolated spots where humans inhabit, we can see the boats of the fishermen anchored in rows. Some of them keep floating in the waters, some moored to the land, some are turned upside down for repairing—indeed a rich, diverse sight. In the same landscape, we can see the huts huddling close to one another, some with crooked fences, a herd of cows grazing outside the fences. On the other side, a couple of emaciated dogs are seen wandering along the shores of the river like jobless beings, along with a naked little boy standing in front of a vegetable field, with his fingers in his mouth. With curious, amazed eyes, he looks in the direction of our ship. With amazement and awe, I also take in yet another spectacle, where the young boys of the fishermen float rice vessels in the river and run with small nets tied with sticks to catch fresh prawns along the shore. In front of the shore, beneath the roots of the banyan tree, the soil has eroded with the incessant flow of the river for years, thereby creating a solitary shelter within the roots of the tree. An old woman lives there peacefully with a couple of her pots and pans for cooking and a sackcloth for resting her head.

On the other hand, there is the pastoral beauty of the land near the river where the forest of *kash* flowers is extended far beyond...During the autumn, where the flowers bloom, I can feel how, with every undulation of the wind, the water bodies dance in waves of rhapsody. And what can I write about the heaps and heaps of bricks lying at the banks of the river? They are a special treat to my eyes—whatever be the reason for it. Devoid of any trees or greenery around them, with all their haunted, desolate look, amid the infertile, rough terrain, the heaps of bricks look lost, forlorn, like wretched, unfortunate men. There...I can see the twelfth temple of Lord Shiva amid the rows of trees, and also listen to the alluring music of the *nahabat* (a musical orchestra) being played from a *nahabatkhana* near the ghat. Just beside that, the ferry ghat can be seen from a distance. At the southern end, the houses of the potters can be seen, with pumpkins hanging from the roofs of the houses. An elderly woman is spreading cow dung over the walls. The courtyards are clean, spik and span. In one corner I can spot bottle gourds sprouting from the trellis, and on the other, there is a Tulsi plant on an altar. In the quiet river body during the sunset, when the boat sails, the western shores of the river are filled with an ethereal beauty. One who has missed seeing this pure, blissful scene has never seen the true beauty and essence of Bengal. In the dim, golden light of the evening, the tall coconut trees, the peak of the temples, the lonely heads of the trees, the tinge of the evenings on the still water bodies become emblems of soothing comfort and peace, ending the chaos of this world.

Slowly, gradually, the light of the evening diminishes, lamps start lighting up here and there in the forest. Suddenly, a gust of wind blows from the south, the leaves keep trembling in the wind. The river keeps flowing in the dark, and its incessant waves echo on the shores with a musical sound. After a while, everything goes dark—nothing is visible, or audible anymore, except the crickets chirping, and fireflies blinking amid the impenetrable darkness. The night darkens further. Slowly, the moon of the *Krishna paksha* starts emerging in the night sky, over the pitch-dark head of the *Ashwatha* tree. It creates a beautiful contrast—the clusters of dark in the forest, and the beauty of the dim light of the moon shining above. In the mesmerizing play of light and darkness, the river breaks out in waves, one after another. A tinge of light falls over the faint landscape of the forest on the other side; in that light, nothing much is visible, yet it made the scene immensely alluring in its mystery.

All these visual images of the river Ganges emerging in my mind—are they only the culmination of this trip of mine in the steamer? No, they aren't. Perhaps they are an amalgamation of all the images of the river etched in my mind since long. They are all immensely pleasurable images. Today, I am immortalizing these scenes with my crystal tears. I don't think I will ever see such beauty ever in my life."

Meanwhile, the passengers of the ship had finished their lunch. As Gyanada reclined her head on the chair, there were haywire thoughts running all over her mind. Her beloved playmate since her childhood days, her brother-in-law Jyoti had come back to her again. Her children were fully immersed in playing and chatting with Rabi, just like their old days in Brighton. They have no obligation now, Kadambari no longer waited for them in her room. Didn't she crave for this moment? Who else would nurture the immense talents of Rabi and Jyoti? Kadambari had deprived her of this happiness for a long time, emerging in her cherished kingdom suddenly, out of nowhere. The inconsequential daughter of Shyam Ganguly had taken away the ground beneath her feet. But she is dead now; like a coward, she has accepted her defeat and ran away. Gyanada has won over her.

But did she want this victory at all? Had she really inflicted immense cruelty over Kadambari, detaining Jyoti in her house night after night? Were Rupa's words true, then? Could Gyanada have averted Kadambari's untimely death in any way? She kept thinking of all this, looking at the ceaseless flow of the river.

Meanwhile, the ship started sailing after the repairing work. After enjoying the river journey for a while, they had snacks and fruits at the deck of the ship around 3.30 in the afternoon.

"If *Mejo Bouthan* hadn't come with us, we would have surely been deprived of such scrumptious meal...we would have surely starved ourselves to death over here!" Rabi remarked.

Akshay was humming a sweet tune. He chewed on a juicy grape and said in a nostalgic tone: "I'm remembering her so much today!"

In Rabi's bosom, there was already a full reservoir of intense agony...Fueled by Akshay's words, it wanted to spill over like an uncontrollable flood. These days, Rabi took extreme care to hide his tears from the public eyes. Either he shielded his tears with the garb of laughter and fun, or he started singing out loud, just like he did now. *"Achhe dukkho, ache mrityu..."* (There is pain, there is the trauma of death)—he sang in a full-throated voice, hiding his face from his co-travelers.

"How strange, Rabi!" Akshay remarked, "Just a few days before her demise, you had composed this song for singing in a meeting at the Brahmo Samaj...Who had known then, that we would have to hide our own tears with this song!" Akshay joined Rabi in singing the song, replete with pathos of the philosophy of death. Bibi joined in too with her melodious voice, and it felt as if a fountain of melody flowed at the deck of the ship.

After a point, Jyoti too added his voice to the pathos and irresistible melody of the song, but soon, an uncontrollable bout of tears spilled over his eyes and choked his voice. Gyanada started feeling embarrassed to witness such a scene of unrestrained lament, initiated by the three young men. She felt as if Kadambari was present right there in flesh and blood. She wiped the tears from Jyoti's eyes with the *aanchal* of her sari, and massaged his head with her fingers to sooth his agonized soul.

Jyoti broke open in tears yet again. "Did she go away because of me, tell me? *Mejo Bouthan*, am I the one to blame?"

Gyanada tried hard to pacify him with her tender love. "No, *Notun Thakurpo*, you are not the one to blame...I know you loved her; the silly girl couldn't understand your love for her!"

Gyanada's unkind words bruised Rabi's heart like a sharp arrow. Akshay and he exchanged meaningful glances between each other, and grasped the nuances of each other's unspoken words. They stored their words in their hearts, and chose to remain silent. However, Jyoti knew the meaning of their silence, he was agonized by the fact he was guilty in the eyes of his old friend Akshay. As for Rabi, he was dying in his own agony for *Notun Bouthan*, but he couldn't bring himself to blame his dearest elder brother Jyoti dada.

"*Mejo Bouthan*, if the other people among us could think like you, we didn't have to worry about anything... Can't you see how silent Rabi and Akshay are about the matter? I know they think I am the one who is guilty!" Jyoti said, lifting his face from Gyanada's sari.

Gyanada looked at the two other men, and glanced at Rabi meaningfully, as if requesting him to speak up. With moist eyes, Rabi looked away from them and replied: "It is just not you, but I am also the one to be blamed!"

The ship seemed to sway in the waters, in sync with the swaying, turbulent minds of its passengers. Giant waves gushed in and pushed against the rib cage of the ship, and the ship in turn ran in a frenzied speed.

The old man, *Karta Babu* ran towards the driver of the ship, instructing him to stop the ship. The passengers summoned him from downstairs, 'Stop, stop the ship!"

With fearful eyes, they all saw that the ship was running towards an iron machine floating in the waters... or else, the machine itself was rushing towards the ship to push it with all its might. It pushed the ship forcefully, and the ship, with a tremendous loud jolt, stopped at once. The lives of the passengers were saved fortunately, but the ship couldn't sail anymore.

After a few hours, when the mayhem of the entire incident subsided, Rabi sat at the deck of the ship and started writing an account in his diary, adding a bit of his subtle humour to this terrible experience.

"There is surely a substantial difference between

true events and the narrative in a novel. We witnessed the same today—our ship didn't drown in the river, in spite of getting into collision with the iron machine! Nobody had to save us, the passengers with their chivalrous valour...like the contents of a novel, nobody had to die, drowning in the river in the first chapter, and emerging alive in the land in the sixteenth chapter. Undoubtedly, I am happy not to get drowned in the water, but writing this account isn't giving me much pleasure, honestly! I'm sure the readers will be immensely disappointed, but it's not my fault that I was not drowned; it is just the workings of our destiny."

The co-passengers of the ship were saved for that day, but they were deeply scared of their expedition. The anchor was cast there right away. The enthusiasm of the travellers had reduced substantially, blinking like the gas light of the fag end of the night. Rabi wrote again:

"Gradually, the enthusiasm of the passengers of the ship subsided; in the morning, while their faces were lit with pleasure, while the engine of their wild imagination had rushed forward in great force, in the evening, nothing remained the same. As the anchor was cast, our enthusiasm seemed to drown deep into the waters of the river. The only solace was that our bodies weren't drowned that deep. However, we suddenly became conscious of the fatal possibility of drowning. The deeper we thought about it, the thought of death and doom emerged stronger within us. Just then, the sun started to prepare for setting behind the horizon. Jyoti dada started loitering around the terrace of the ship, pondering whether the route to Barishal was short and easy, compared to the route that didn't lead to Barishal. I was seated on a fat bundle of ropes amid the crystallized dark, trying hard to kindle a light of my humour under such harsh circumstances, but the light blinked faintly, like matchsticks blinking during the monsoon season. When our ship Sarojini started resting in peace along with its passengers in the mucky, slippery shelter in the bosom of the river, I started to contemplate about the brief newspaper report placed in the 'sad accident' section of the news daily, depicting our nirvana, our ultimate salvation within a single paragraph, consisting of just four lines! I imagined how this piece of news would be gulped down by the reader uninhibitedly like a tiny globule of medicine with hot tea...Our friends might say about this writer: "Alas, what a great soul went away from our world! Such a man will not be born anymore!" They might remark about my revered sister-in-law: "Ah this woman was a human with all her virtues and vices, yet she filled the home with her presence..." and so on. At that moment, I witnessed the waves of smile on *Mejo Bouthan*'s face, breaking open from the tight pair of her lips."

In the star-studded night sky, the sound of the *namaz* reading of the shipmates echoed from the lower level, resounding along with the soothing southern winds. Amid the shipmates, a mad man started singing, swaying his head while playing a string instrument gleefully. As the night descended, all of the co-passengers of the ship lay down, resting their bodies in the open deck of the ship. The picnic-like environment comforted the soul—there was no inhibition regarding maintaining anybody's purdah or privacy, no boundaries of the stifling four walls of a home, no reprimanding attitude of the so-called society. But there was the gentle nearness of dear ones, the emotions of sadness, desire, repentance, love and affection.

Suren had been tired after playing sitar for a while,

and lay down. Bibi was asleep too, beside him. In the dark terrace, some were yawning lightly, while some others were snoring deeply. Sleep eluded Rabi's eyes, though. Where was that North Star hiding among the constellation of stars in the sky? He started searching. He was asleep for a while, but woke up at the dead of the night, hearing a strange sound. Slowly, he managed to open his eyes and decipher where he was, but then, he heard the faint moaning sound of a human, coming from somewhere near. After a while, as his eyes opened fully, he witnessed a strange scene. His Jyoti dada was crying like a child, resting his head on *Mejo Bouthan*'s lap in one corner of the deck. The familiar scene of the vine entwined with the body of the tree had perhaps changed tonight.

In the solitary night, Jyoti's faint, moaning cries resounded in the air: "Why did I immerse myself in the witch-like spell of Binodini, *Mejo Bouthan*? That is the reason why she left me in terrible pain!"

Gyanada seemed to kiss on Jyoti's forehead while wiping off his tears. Rabi reminisced an intimate emotional scene with Kadambari at that moment. Unbeknownst to Jyoti and Gyanada, the silent spectator of the solitary night fell asleep again. In his half-asleep state, he felt as if his *Notun Bouthan* touched his head, like the sudden gust of a wind. Right then, he did not know why his new bride Mrinalini's face appeared before his eyes. Rabi himself had left his child bride at home and came far away, would Mrinalini feel anguished and pained like *Notun Bouthan* and commit a disaster? Rabi was scared to think of it.

The ship stopped for the time being. Gyanada returned with Jyoti and her children to her Birjitalao home. As Rabi was also returning to Jorasanko, he thought about grooming Mrinalini according to his heart's desire. Now that he was married and committed to her, he couldn't leave her anywhere else. He would have to take her to Jorasanko and start living with her.

Rabi summoned the young Mrinalini to his room. A teenager girl appeared in the room, wearing a *Dhakai* sari with red border, the anklets on her feet creating a musical sound. Looking at her entering the room, Rabi thought to himself: 'Wow, look at her…she is no longer the little girl I knew! She is now the young, elegant Radha'! He extended his hands towards her and instructed: "Come closer!"

Mrinalini didn't come closer; she remained at a distance, lowering her face and rubbed the big finger of her foot against the floor. Rabi pulled her hand and made her sit close to his lap. "*Chhoto Bou*, won't you come close to me? See, I've returned home now…would you still remain at a distance from me? Should I leave again?" He enquired.

Mrinalini replied in a childish voice, with her stiffened shoulders: "Why did you have to go, leaving me all alone?"

"Are you angry on me for that?" Rabi hugged her tight and promised to her: "Okay, I won't repeat this act from now on… I will never leave you and go away!"

The woman selling utensils was passing by the very next alley, calling out her customers. The man selling bangles in the noon-time was also calling them habitually: "Do you want bangles, new toys?" On the other days, Mrinalini would come and sit with the bangle-seller along with the other women and girls of the house, and wear glass bangles in her hands.

But today was a different day; she was somewhat overwhelmed, as her husband had come back to her after so many days. She was afraid of her destiny. Just upon her arrival in her in-laws' family, the innocent young girl had experienced a dreadful episode of conjugal separation, that had haunted her like a nightmare. In her sheer desperation to hold her husband close to her, she uttered: "I tell you; I will also swallow opium if you leave me alone and roam around like *Notun Thakur*!"

Rabi trembled to hear her frightful words. "What did you say, *Chhoto Bou*? Never utter such awful words before me again! Remember?" He lifted her face close to him and said.

As Mrinalini remained silent, he softly touched her eyes, her face, her lips with his fingers and started singing a wistful love song.

"Slowly, softly, o beloved, come to my life,

Flashing that sweet smile of yours, love me with all your might."

After singing a few lines, Rabi wished to plant a tender, passionate kiss on her lips with the warmth of his own lips. Partly in shame and embarrassment, partly in her own anguish, she evaded that much-awaited kiss of her husband and ran away, separating her hands from Rabi's.

Rabi felt bruised too at this sudden departure of his wife from his room. 'What kind of a girl is she, who runs away even when summoned with so much love? Is she immature, silly, not knowing the sweet, alluring call of conjugal life still?' He wondered. Had he been waiting for this foolish young girl all this while, evading the inviting love of Anna Tarkhare, Lucy Scott, the delightful dream girls of England? He felt disappointed. He had penned innumerable love poems since his teenage years, but how long would he have to wait for an intense real love, a beautifully feminine lady-love in flesh and blood?

Rabi sat at his writing desk, all alone. When he closed his eyes, Kadambari's face appeared in his notebook. He wrote the following lines: "O you, whom the world has forgotten, but who is alive in my memories, I am writing these musings for you, lest you forget my voice, lest you cannot recognize my presence when perchance we meet, when our paths cross in our journey to eternity…Hence, I reminisce your thoughts every day, telling you these words of mine, aren't you listening?"

In the evening, there were voices in unison echoing in the alleys nearby, 'We want *bel* flowers! Where are the *bel* flowers?' The maids bought *bel* flowers in abundance and tied them in the hairs of the girls and the brides. Today, Soudamini, Neepamayee and the other women of Thakurbari had dressed up Mrinalini beautifully, like a newlywed bride. They tied her long tresses in a fancy 'bibiyana' bun, and wrapped a garland of *bel* flowers around it. Rabi had returned home after a long hiatus; Mrinalini would sleep with her husband tonight.

After dinner, Rabi lay on the bed with a melancholy spirit. The lamp in the room had extinguished with a sudden gust of southern wind. For some moments, he wondered if the soul of Kadambari had arrived in the room and put out the light! He slept on the bed silently. 'At that very moment, suddenly, a tender feminine arm with the musical sound of bangles, wrapped him in an irresistible bond of love, and a pair of female lips, like a calyx of a flower, approached to plant incessant kisses on his lips, replete with emotions, leaving no space for him to express his own amazement.'

This intense, emotionally drenched self-surrender of

his young wife Mrinalini filled Rabi's heart with inexplicable delight; his heart and soul trembled in pleasure. Just when he wrapped Mrinalini in a warm embrace, he felt Kadambari standing in front of him, like an enchantress, a faint apparition. Rabi whispered to her slowly: "Oh olden days, take your leave from here, for a new game has now begun..."

With a soft, captivating smile, waving her supple, flowery fingers at Rabi, Kadambari vanished into thin air, like a mirage. No trace of hers remained in the curves and creases of Jorasanko ever again.

Acknowledgements / References: Mentioned in the Original Bengali Novel:

Satyendranath's letters to Gyanadanandini, 8, 11, 12, 13, 14, 22, 51, 52, 75,

95, 'Puratani'

Surama and Sushila's conversation, 'Nari o Bamabodhini', pages-40-43

'Europe bashi-r Potro' (The Letters from Europe), 1, 7, 10

Sunil Gangyopadhyay, 'Prothom Alo' (First Light)

Rabindranath Tagore, 'Sarojini Prayaan' (The Death of Sarojini)

Abanindranath Tagore: 'Jorasanko-r Dhare'

Amit Mitra: Rangalaye Banga Noti, Annanda Publishers, 2004

Ekantar: Edited by Arup Acharya, Special issue on Swarnakumari Debi, 2008

Indira Debi Chowdhurani, Smriti sampoot

Kalyani Dutta, 'Khara Bori Thor', Thema, 2005

Kazi Albul Odud, 'Kobi Rabindranath'

Chitra Deb, 'Thakur barir Andarmahal', Annanda Publishers, 3rd edition, 2006

Gyanadanandini Debi, 'Puratani Katha'

Durba Deb, 'Atmakatha-r sthapatya', Shilchar

Neerad Chandra Chowdhury, 'Bangali Jeebone Ramani', Mitra & Ghosh Publishers, 1965

Prashanta Kumar Pal, 'Rabi Jeebani', 1st and 2nd volumes, Annanda Publishers, 5th edition, 2007

Rabindranath Tagore, 'Galpaguchchho'—'Manbhanjan', 'Samapti' (two stories)

Rabindranath Tagore, 'Jeeban smriti', 'Rabindra Rachanabali', West Bengal Government

Rabindranath Tagore, 'Birpurush'

Rabindranath Tagore, 'Europe Prabashi-r Diary'

Rash Sundari Debi, 'Amar Jeeban' (Autobiography)

Satyendranath Tagore, 'Amar Chhelebela o Bombai Probash'

Samir Sengupta, 'Rabindranath-er Atmiyo Swojon', Shishu Shahitya Sansad

Sarala Debi Chowdhurani, 'Jeeboner Jhora pata'

Sudhakanta Roychowdhury, 'Dwijendranath Tagore', Kolkata 1969

Sushil Ray, 'Jyotirindranath, Jiggyasha', Kolkata 1963

The Complete Novels of Swarnakumari, Volume 1, Dey's Publishing, 2009

Collected Works of Swarnakumari Debi

Hiranmoy Bandhyopadhyay, 'Thakurbari-r Katha', Biswa Bharati

AUTHOR'S BIO

Mallika Sengupta (1960–2011) was a Bengali poet, feminist, and reader of Sociology from Kolkata, and a celebrated literary figure whose «unapologetically political poetry» has been critically analyzed in India and abroad. She had been described in 'Poetry International' as "a proponent of an unapologetically political poetry and an important voice in contemporary Bengali literature". Her journey with poetry started in 1981 and since then she has published eleven books of poetry, two novels and several essays, and edited an anthology of women's poetry from Bengal. She had been the head of the department of sociology in a Kolkata college, and also served as the Poetry Editor of *Sananda*, the leading fortnightly magazine for women (edited by actor, filmmaker Aparna Sen). Sengupta has been the recipient of many prestigious awards, including the Sukanto Puraskar (1998) from the Government of West Bengal, India and a Junior Fellowship for Literature (1997 – 99) from the Department of Culture, Government of India. She also travelled to several poetry festivals, conferences and seminars in India, Sweden, Austria, USA and Bangladesh. Several English translations of her work have been anthologized and also published in various literary and academic journals.

Along with her husband, the noted poet Subodh Sarkar, she was the founder-editor of *Bhashanagar*, a culture magazine in Bengali. As an activist and academician, Sengupta has been actively involved with the cause of gender justice and other social issues throughout her lifetime. She also initiated *Aloprithivi* along with her fellow poet and artists, a forum committed to raising consciousness among marginalized women and children through poetry, music and drama. 'Kobir Bouthan' (Ananda Publishers, 2011) is one of her three published novels which received critical acclaim.

TRANSLATOR'S BIO

Lopamudra Banerjee is an author, poet, translator, editor with eight solo books and six anthologies in fiction, nonfiction and poetry. She lives in Texas, USA with her family, but she is originally from Kolkata, India. She has been a recipient of the Journey Awards (First Place category winner) for her memoir 'Thwarted Escape: An Immigrant's Wayward Journey' (Authorspress, 2016), the International Reuel Prize for Poetry  (2017) and International Reuel Prize for her English translation of Nobel Laureate Tagore's selected works of fiction (2016). Her poetry has also been published in renowned platforms including 'Life in Quarantine', the Digital Humanities Archive of Stanford University. She has been a Featured Poet at Rice University, Houston in November 2019. 'Bakul Katha: Tale of the Emancipated Woman', her English translation of Ashapurna Devi's award-winning Bengali novel 'Bakul Katha' has received Honorable Mention at London Book Festival. Her recent collection of poetry and monologues 'We Are What We Are: Primal Songs of Ethnicity, Gender & Identity' (Black Eagle Books, 2022) is a collaboration with Mexican-American poet and storyteller Priscilla Rice.

Black Eagle Books

www.blackeaglebooks.org
info@blackeaglebooks.org

Black Eagle Books, an independent publisher, was founded as a nonprofit organization in April, 2019. It is our mission to connect and engage the Indian diaspora and the world at large with the best of works of world literature published on a collaborative platform, with special emphasis on foregrounding Contemporary Classics and New Writing.

www.ingramcontent.com/pod-product-compliance
Lightning Source LLC
Chambersburg PA
CBHW020512080526
44583CB00013B/576